D1251013

Snow in May

Snow in May

An Anthology of Finnish Writing
1945–1972

Edited by

Richard Dauenhauer
and
Philip Binham

Rutherford • Madison • Teaneck
Fairleigh Dickinson University Press
London: Associated University Presses

© 1978 by Associated University Presses, Inc.

Associated University Presses, Inc.
Cranbury, New Jersey 08512

Associated University Presses
Magdalen House
136–148 Tooley Street
London SE1 2TT, England

Library of Congress Cataloging in Publication Data
Main entry under title:

Snow in May.

    Bibliography: p.
    1. Finnish literature—20th century—Translations into English. 2. English literature—Translations from Finnish. 3. Swedish literature—Finland—Translations into English. 4. English literature—Translations from Swedish. I. Dauenhauer, Richard. II. Binham, Philip.
PH401.E1S6   894'.541'08003   77-24549

ISBN 0-8386-1583-X

894.54108
S674

PRINTED IN THE UNITED STATES OF AMERICA

Contents

6

PHOTOGRAPHS

PROSE

DRAMA

Preface

The words with which I concluded my introduction to the Finnish issue of *The Literary Review* (Fall 1970) are still relevant and I would like to repeat them here as a preface to this book.

A final word about this Finnish issue of *The Literary Review*. I lament that my chief misery as guest editor was first of all in locating fellow readers and translators of modern Finnish literature, and, secondly, in knowing that because we work in great obscurity, I have failed to locate many persons who might have made valuable contributions to this issue.

I am grateful for the help and contributions of those whose work is included here, and I would like to emphasize that my fellow translators are in every sense fellow editors of this very cooperative and certainly esoteric venture: they are entitled to a full share of whatever professional glory may arise from it.

I would like to take the liberty, on behalf of all the contributors, of dedicating this first major collection of recent Finnish literature in English translation to all of the Finnish friends who have helped each of us—not only in the work which has gone into this project, but throughout the years of mutual interest in each other's countries and literatures. Naturally, I cannot list all the names. Let it suffice for me to say that this Finnish anthology is dedicated to all those whose friendship has meant so very much.

Now, happily, I can make one change: I can thank by name some friends and teachers who helped me along the way, especially Sumner Ives, Philip Booth, and Robert Harms. In Finland, thanks go to many scholars, critics, writers, publishers, and friends for their direct or indirect help: especially to Professor Esko Ervasti, who first "turned me on" to Finnish literature, to comparative literature in general, and to the works of Gottfried Benn in particular. I will never forget our first literary discussions—punctuated by the dripping of sweat—in his sauna one summer afternoon in 1963. His help and guidance in subsequent conversations and letters has been substantial.

Also in Finland, the aid of Professor Irma Rantavaara, Pekka Virtanen, Professor Kai Laitinen, *Parnasso* magazine, and the various publishers here represented, especially the staff at Otava, have all been greatly appreciated, not only on the original *Literary Review* project, but on the present anthology as well.

7

8

It is important here to note another change. Through a proofreading oversight, for which I accept full blame, the names of Soini Pirttila, Marjatta Utriainen, and Patricia Rosenbröijer were omitted as collaborators from the final printed version of Philip Booth's translations of Turtiainen. I wish to apologize to the cotranslators for the failure to credit them, and to Philip Booth for the embarrassment I know my oversight has caused him.

Turning now to publishers in this country, I wish to thank Mr. Thomas Yoseloff and the editorial staff of Associated University Presses (not to mention my coworkers on this book) for their understanding and patience over the delay in the delivery of the manuscript during a long period in which my time and energies were diverted to a series of academic emergencies here in Alaska. I note especially the help of Mr. George Magee in spotting and suggesting resolutions for various errors and inconsistencies in the manuscript.

Paul Foreman and Judy Hogan of Thorp Springs Press generously released Pekka Virtanen's Swedish translations, which they had already accepted for publication.

Most of my translations were done in Helsinki during the winter of 1966–67 on a Fulbright grant. Accordingly, I would like to express my thanks to that foundation both in the United States and in Finland, and especially to Sven-Erik Sjögren and his staff for helping to create an atmosphere conducive to pleasant and fruitful work. In this vein, likewise, I note with pleasure the fellowship of friends gained from that experience, especially Lloyd and Elsa Hackl, Andrejs and Barbara Plakans, Dave and Arlene Robinson, and Ralph Corkrum. Their pleasant hours of conversation are inseparable from this work. Sandy Dauenhauer, also, is more than inseparable from the fond memories of a year devoted to intense study, leisure reading, scholarly conversation, cross-country skiing, and bird watching.

In Helsinki, a very special word of gratitude goes to Kaarina Buure Hägglund, an old American Field Service friend, and to her husband Jyrki for their hospitality, friendship, and patience in checking texts. In Anchorage, thanks go to Mr. and Mrs. Floyd and Hazel Johnson and to Professor and Mrs. Carl-Erik and Margareta Måwe for their generous and timely help in checking translations of Finnish and Swedish, respectively.

This project has been underway, in one form or another, for over ten years; for her help in the final stages of the project, I happily credit my wife, Nora, who urged it to completion.

My deepest gratitude, however, is one I will never be able to express adequately—to Professor and Mrs. Seppo and Eeva-Liisa Ervasti, who opened their home, country, language, and culture to me first in Syracuse, New York, and then again in that memorable summer of 1963, which remains as one of the most profound experiences of my life. In 1966–67 they regularly spent many tedious hours checking and correcting my first drafts. Throughout our entire relationship, they have silently suffered through my various poetic moods.

When people ask me—as they often do—how I ever became interested in Finnish, I can only answer with these names, for they are truly the genesis of all that I have done. I can never thank or repay them enough. Whatever portions of this book are mine to dedicate, I dedicate them to Seppo and Eeva-Liisa Ervasti.

Richard Dauenhauer
Anchorage and Sitka

Iris Murdoch has said that translation is like opening your mouth and hearing someone else speak.

If this is true, then translators are like performing artists, and the art of translating is as demanding and satisfying as that of actors, musicians or singers.

Certainly, there is no better way to come to grips with an author, with his manner and his meanings, than by trying to translate him. The rhythms and tugging undercurrents of Mannerkorpi, Manner's arrows of association, a glimpse of "something beyond" in Hyry—all these are revealed to the translator, though he may despair of conveying such riches into another language.

As the translator chiefly responsible for the prose in this anthology, I am acutely aware that important writers of the period are not represented. Works by Rintala, Holappa, Joenpelto, Tapio, Vartio, and others of equal stature are all absent. Naturally, we could not attempt a definitive work; limited knowledge of the field and attraction to favorite authors have no doubt influenced our choice. But if this collection gives some indication of the versatile and dynamic quality of Finnish literature in the past twenty-five years, we shall, I believe, have achieved our purpose.

Editorial thanks are first due to the authors, the translators, and the essayists. The Finnish publishers have been helpful in providing photographs and information. Also, we acknowledge with gratitude grants from the Finnish Ministry of Education and the Finnish Ministry of Foreign Affairs. I wish to express my thanks for a personal grant from the Committee for Finnish Literature. And finally, on behalf of all concerned with *Snow in May,* a special word of appreciation to Richard Dauenhauer, who has from the start been the leading spirit in this venture, and who has given so much of his time and energy to the anthology.

Philip Binham
Helsinki

Acknowledgments

The editors wish to thank the following publishers for permission to quote from copyrighted works:

Robert Bly for permission to quote "Watering the Horse" from *Silence in the Snowy Fields* published by Wesleyan University Press, copyright © 1962 by Robert Bly.

Books Abroad (Norman, Okla.), for Paavo Haavikko's "The Greeks Populated Mycenae," translated by Richard Dauenhauer, vol. 42, no. 3 (Summer 1968): 385.

Doubleday & Co., Inc., for quotations from the book ZEN POEMS OF CHINA AND JAPAN: THE CRANE'S BILL, copyright © 1973 by Lucien Stryk, Takashi Ikemoto and Taigan Takayama. Reprinted by permission of Doubleday & Company, Inc.

Harper & Row, Publishers, Inc., for quotations from Gabriel Garcia Marquez, *One Hundred Years of Solitude,* translated by Gregory Rabassa.

Holt, Rinehart and Winston, for quotations from LION AMONG ROSES by David Bradley. Copyright © 1965 by David Bradley. Reprinted by permission of Holt, Rinehart and Winston, Publishers. And for permission to quote from "Reluctance" from *The Poetry of Robert Frost* edited by Edward Connery Lathem. Copyright 1934, © 1969 by Holt, Rinehart and Winston. Copyright © 1962 by Robert Frost. Reprinted by permission of Holt, Rinehart and Winston, Publishers.

Alfred A. Knopf, Inc., for quotations from Veijo Meri, *The Manila Rope,* translated by John McGahern and Annika Laaksi, 1967. And for quotations from Wallace Stevens, *The Collected Poems of Wallace Stevens,* 12th ed., 1972; Wallace Stevens, *Poems by Wallace Stevens,* ed. Samuel French Morse, 1959.

Limes Verlag Max Niedermayer, for quotations from Gottfried Benn, *Gesammelte Werke in vier Bänden,* Band 3 *Gedichte*; mit Genehmigung des Limes Verlags, Wiesbaden und München.

The Literary Review (Fairleigh Dickinson University), for all material first published in the Fall 1970 issue.

Michigan Academician (Michigan Academy of Sciences, Arts and Letters, Ann Arbor), for quotations from Jaakko Ahokas, "Finnish Drama and Culture" (Winter 1971).

11

New Directions Publishing Corporation, for quotations from William Carlos Williams, COLLECTED EARLIER POEMS. Copyright 1938 by New Directions Publishing Corporation. Reprinted by permission of New Directions Publishing Corporation.

Gary Snyder for permission to quote from *Myths & Texts* published by Totem Press in association with Corinth Books, copyright © 1960 by Gary Snyder.

Swallow Press (Chicago), for the excerpts translated and copyrighted by Anselm Hollo, which appeared in Pentti Saarikoski, *Helsinki* (1967).

Verlag Der Arche Peter Schifferli, for quotations from Gottfried Benn, *Statische Gedichte*, Copyright © 1948 by Verlags AG "Die Arche," Peter Schifferli, Zürich.

The editors wish to thank the following Scandinavian publishers and individuals for their support of this project:
Arvi Karisto
(Mrs.) Sirkka Kukkonen
Norwegian University Press
Otava
Books from Finland
The Publishers' Association of Finland
Holger Schildts
Werner Söderström
Tammi
Weilin and Göös

The editors also wish to thank for their support the following American publishers, who first published or accepted for publication some of the translations contained in this anthology:

Grossman and Cape Goliard (New York and Santa Fe, N. Mex.), for the Paavo Haavikko and Tuomas Anhava translations copyrighted by Anselm Hollo and published in *Paavo Haavikko: Selected Poems* (1968) and *Tuomas Anhava: In the Dark, Move Slowly* (1969).

Hyperion (Thorp Springs Press, Berkeley, Calif.), Paul Foreman and Judy Hogan, editors, for Pekka Virtanen's translations from the Swedish.

Quixote (Madison, Wis.), edited by Morris Edelson, for the first American translations of Paavo Haavikko's "Sveaborg," "Fable of the Year 1965," and "Someone's Growing Old Here," vol. 3, no. 4 (1967): 69–71.

Introduction

The present volume derives from the success of the Fall 1970 Finnish issue of *The Literary Review,* an esoteric venture that turned out well. Happily, we are no longer subject to two major restrictions imposed by the magazine format— space and the use of previously unpublished material. We are, alas, still restricted by the scarcity of translators, translations, and by the limits of our personal experience.

A few of the prime movers of this anthology need to be mentioned. Foremost is Philip Binham, who has provided on-the-scene footwork and brainwork as coeditor as well as contributions as translator and essayist.

That highly mobile Finnish poet and translator, Anselm Hollo, was located alive and well in Iowa City, so the anthology is enriched by new and previously unpublished Hollo material.

Pekka Virtanen's contributions—despite the hardships and uncertainties of a year spent being shifted for political reasons between jails, courts, stockades, and military hospitals—have added greatly to both the Swedish and Finnish poetry selections, especially in representing the younger writers.

After considerable debate among the original contributors, it was decided not to expand the volume into the pre-1945 periods. We wanted to, but felt that we could not represent the literature adequately with the few translations we had in hand or knew of, and there was no time to commission or allow for the inspiration of new translations. We hope that this anthology matches the success of its predecessor and arouses sufficient interest in a companion volume covering the first hundred years, 1845–1945.

We have, however, expanded the postwar coverage to include some Swedish-language poetry, prose, and drama of Finland. The representation is token, but we were severely restricted by lack of translations, most noticeably of prose.

A happy change from the magazine format is that the book-printing process can handle photographs. The anthology features a photo essay by Robert Harms, a linguist at the University of Texas who specializes in Finnish and related languages and whose hobby is photography. Some photos cry out to be matched with poems and passages in the stories; however, it was decided to leave the photographs intact. But the images are there: Juvonen's glacial erratic, Manner's boat pulled high, Haavikko's trees, the shorelines of Saarikoski's evening walks, and the ubiquitous duck. The pictures are the physical and, to a large extent, the psychological background of the material in this book: the rural countryside the Finns cannot shake loose—the beauty to which the city people return each summer, the provincialism in which many young residents feel trapped, the austerity described by Knight, and the social organization that frustrates recent migrants to the urban centers.

As Laitinen suggests, the Finns have come from the forest to the city—and in more ways than one. The photograph of the Sevettijärvi farmhouse is not only a beautiful study of textures, but it is also, in a far deeper sense, a study of the textures of Finnish society. Such landscapes are still the home for many of the tough and dour characters we admire in this book, and many of the urban types, as they walk up the stairs to their Helsinki apartments, are still living in that lakeside clearing.

The Harms collection is followed by a few pictures of urban Finland that seek to capture the physical and mental background of the younger writers— perhaps that Finnish sensitivity to contrasts of black and white that William Knight postulates as a thesis at the conclusion of his essay.

The essay section is new, and approaches Finnish prose, drama, and poetry from several perspectives. First, Kai Laitinen's "From the Forest to the City" traces the development of Finnish prose in the sociological context of the urbanization of a peasant society.

Jaakko Ahokas, formerly of Indiana University and now living in Helsinki, offers a traditional genre-and-national-literature approach, comparing and contrasting various writers represented in the anthology. Professor Ahokas graciously adapted his essay, in part, around the projected contents of the anthology.

William Knight's approach is different. A young American writer who discovers Finnish writers striking a chord sympathetic to his own work, Knight offers a frankly impressionistic—though well documented—view of what Finnish writing is and is not. His style is creative and imaginative, his thesis clear and well supported.

Coeditor Philip Binham rose to our need for comment on Finnish drama, and to his essay we have added a footnote synthesizing additional facts and opinions on the subject.

The essays then turn to more specialized topics. Ingmar Svedberg, a young teacher of Swedish literature at Helsinki University and literary critic for *Hufvudstadsbladet,* Finland's leading Swedish-language daily, discusses political poetry in modern Finnish literature. The essay is translated by Dympna Connolly (whose work also appears elsewhere in the anthology) and includes several fine poems that have been left intact rather than removed from the context of the essay to the poetry section.

Kaarina Sala offers a sketch of Eeva-Liisa Manner, whose work is featured in the book.

Coeditor Richard Dauenhauer has prepared some notes on Zen attitudes in the modern poetry of Finland—both of the Finnish and Swedish languages—and has also expanded a slightly revised introduction to the original Finnish *Literary Review* issue into a second essay focusing on a conceptual analysis of Paavo Haavikko in a specific international context.

Finally, Lassi Nummi, noted Finnish writer and critic and chairman of the Finnish Writers' Association, concludes the essay section with comments on one of Haavikko's recent works.

The primary material in translation is too great and varied to comment upon, so a few statistics will have to suffice. The prose section has been tripled by reprinting the stories by Marja-Leena Mikkola, Veijo Meri, and Hannu Salama, with the addition of six new writers: Timo K. Mukka, Eila Pennanen, Juha Mannerkorpi, Veikko Huovinen, Antti Hyry, and Väinö Linna. Diana Tullberg joins Philip Binham and John R. Pitkin as the translators.

Likewise, the drama section was expanded. Haavikko's *The Superintendent* is reprinted, preceded by Eeva-Liisa Manner's *Snow in May*, from which our title derives. The Swedish-speaking theater is represented by Walentin Chorell. All plays are translated by Philip Binham.

Of the poets, only Turtiainen, Pylkkönen, and Salama have not had new additions. The average representation of the others has been doubled. Saarikoski in particular, whose earlier sampling was inadequate, has been greatly increased. Also, five additional Finnish poets have been added: Aila Meriluoto, Lauri Viita, Jyrki Pellinen, Caj Westerberg, and Kalevi Lappalainen.

The Swedish writing of Finland is too often a waif in English translation, excluded from Swedish anthologies because it is not from Sweden, and from Finnish anthologies because it is not in Finnish. This is not the case in Finland, where fine editions are published with the original language on one page, and translation into the other national language on the facing page, often by a poet with a similar style. Thus, Bo Carpelan and Tuomas Anhava might be translators of each other.

The Swedish-language poets of Finland are represented by almost fifty poems by seven poets: Bo Carpelan, Lars Huldén, Henry Parland, Claes Andersson, Per-Håkon Påwals, Th. Warburton, and Solveig von Schoultz.

Translations, alas, cannot be forced. An attempt was made to round out the collection with more samples of Finland-Swedish poets, but the translations would not jell. The Swedish-language poets especially have suffered from editorial imbalance. Parland, for example, is represented by a far greater number of poems than von Schoultz, although von Schoultz is a major contemporary poet and Parland dates from the 20s and 30s and was first published posthumously in 1964. We offer our apologies for the imbalance. But what we do have will give some idea of what the Swedish-speaking poets of Finland are doing, and will allow the reader to gain some overview of the total national literature of Finland, which is, we must remember, bilingual.

This book is the first major anthology of Finnish national writing in English translation. With the exception of some of Hollo's work, none of the material has ever appeared before in English (outside of Finland), except for that which was first published in the now unavailable Finnish issue of *The Literary Review*.*

We have tried to be comprehensive, and the anthology represents work by most translators from Finnish into English working in the postwar period.** We are few in number, and acutely aware of our limitations of time, taste, experience, background, and style. As such, this book is our commentary on the literature of postwar Finland.

---

*This situation has changed during the period in which the anthology took final shape. The plays *Snow in May* and *The Superintendent* appeared in *Modern Nordic Plays (Finland)* published by Universitetsforlaget, Oslo, and simultaneously by Twayne Publishers, Inc., New York (1973) in The Library of Scandinavian Literature.

**Not included are Naomi Walford, translator of Waltari; Alan Blair, translator of Sillanpää; and John McGahern, who translated Meri's *Manila Rope*.

Snow in May

ESSAYS

KAI LAITINEN

From the Forest to the City:
The Great Tradition in Finnish Prose
Translated by Philip Binham

When one comes to Finland by air, it seems at first as if the whole country were covered by forest. Even where people have lived for a long time and medieval stone churches stand witness to a centuries' old civilization, there may be more forest than field. The landscape of the Finnish interior is marked by its lakes, stretching for hundreds of miles, joined by sinuous waterways and broken by hills, forest-clad capes, isthmuses, and islands.

This is the landscape of the classical Finnish novel. Its great tradition begins from the forest.

The Beginning

In 1870 Aleksis Kivi, a poor university student who had broken off his studies, published his novel *Seitsemän veljestä* (*Seven Brothers*). At first it met with adverse criticism, and, indeed, the writer died a madman before it was understood that he had written a classic of rare quality and permanent value. The novel describes seven stubborn brothers who, after their parents' death, come into conflict with the local village community. One of the brothers, Lauri, puts forward his own solution to the problem: "Let's move into the forest, and to hell with the din of the world." And a little later he continues:

Let's do as I say and move with our horse, our dogs and our guns to the foot of Impivaara's steep height. There we can build ourselves a jolly cabin in a clearing looking south and live in peace far from the bustle of the world and spiteful people, hunting game in the woods.

And little by little that is what happens; the brothers rent out their home-farm and move into the backwoods to clear new lands. Though life is not always so "jolly" as Lauri, the keen hunter, would like to suggest, the ten years they live like this is decisive in their development. They mature both individually and socially, and return to society as aware and responsible citizens.

For all practical purposes, *Seven Brothers* is the first novel in early Finnish literature. It is at the same time an admirable pioneering achievement and a stimulating example for later writers. It confirmed the *description of ordinary people* as the main channel for Finnish creative prose. It became a trailblazer in many ways: choice of setting, handling of character, and style. Still today many a Finn may say of *Seven Brothers* what Dostoievsky said of Gogol's *Overcoat*: "That's where we all derive from."

Nature as friend and enemy

The environment of Kivi's novel is at first a thinly populated village community, then the virgin forest, where the brothers clear their fields and build their dwelling. "The forest entices" says the poet Eino Leino in his essay on Kivi. From Kivi's time on into the years after the Second World War, the setting for the Finnish novel has been predominantly rural. In Ilmari Kianto's novels, *Punainen viiva* (*The Red Line*, 1909) and *Ryysyrannan Jooseppi* (*Jooseppi of Ryysyranta*, 1924), the characters live in a remote frontier district of northern Finland. Pentti Haanpää's short stories of the 1930s and 40s are also set against a sparsely populated landscape in northern Finland: "Some little potato patch and shred of barley-field appeared like a nail scratch deep in the endless backwoods. A small haystack on the fringe of a swamp or the bank of a brook looked like the work of mice." In Joel Lehtonen's *Putkinotko* (1919–20), the characters dwell comparatively near to the town, but live, nonetheless, dependent on nature and isolated as people in more remote parts. Nature in the Finnish novel is no decorative backcloth; it may be almost as much a principal actor as the characters, as in F. E. Sillanpää's novel, *Ihmiset suviyössä* (*People in the Summer Night*, 1934). And in some novels the events are regulated and fixed in time by the motion of the sun: both Maria Jotuni's *Arkielämää* (*Everyday Life*, 1909) and Joel Lehtonen's *Putkinotko* (an area in eastern Finland) extend over a single summer's day.

Nature in Kivi's *Seven Brothers* is the characters' ally and protector against society; true, it raises obstacles in their way, too, but these are overcome by work and endurance. In later novels nature may treat people more harshly. For these passive, feeble creatures, nature is most often an opponent, they fight against it and sometimes lose the struggle. Their relation to nature is purely practical or hostile; for them nature is not an aesthetic value. When in *Putkinotko* the author's alter ego, Muttinen the bookseller, wants to plant apple trees in his summer place and dreams of them at blossom time, the other main character in the book, who is his polar opposite, the poor cottager Juutas Käkriäinen, does not understand this picture in the slightest; he only wonders if it wouldn't be better to plant potatoes. This double aspect is seen also in the novel's descriptions of nature: to Muttinen's eye, or as the writer describes it, nature appears like a colorful impressionist painting, but Käkriäinen sees it always in relation to his own life, sometimes protective and concealing, sometimes trying, sometimes menacing.

For a long time the city is a stranger to the characters of classical Finnish novels. When they get there, they generally become confused and do stupid things, as in Maiju Lassila's *Tulitikkuja lainaamassa* (*Borrowing Matches*, 1910), in which one of the main comic elements is the difference between the slow-thinking country folk and the small-town people who think they are better. For Lehtonen the city and especially the suburbs represent moral degeneration. And in Sillanpää's great novels of the 1930s, the city still appears as the place where one goes to buy liquor or have fun with ladies of easy virtue.

Naturally, plenty of descriptions of city life appear in Finnish writing, also, especially in the 1920s, when the expressionistic romance of the machine caught the imagination of young writers. Toivo Pekkanen's novels of the 1930s are chiefly set in towns, and since then urban environments have appeared increasingly in novels. But even in those works where the events take place in the city, Kivi's familiar pioneer motif may appear: Lauri Viita's *Moreeni* (*Moraine*, 1950) describes the life of a working-class family in the industrial town of Tampere, and it first shows how a new settlement is built on a wooded ridge and how the people live in this new community. The novel gives significant place to the boys' fishing trips on a nearby lake and their contact with nature. In many novels of the 1950s and 60s there is a sauna evening, a fishing trip, or a visit to a friend's summer cottage, at least as an episode; this motif appears often in Veijo Meri and Hannu Salama. Antti Hyry's characters remain rural even in the city, and constantly long for the environment of their childhood close to nature. The "asphalt jungle" of the big city is seldom the sole environment in a Finnish novel, although works of this genre have begun to appear in recent years.

The predominance of a rural setting and the big role played by characterizations of "the people" have proved an obstacle to making the Finnish novel known abroad. The environment they describe is strange to many foreign readers, and the text difficult to translate. When the cottager in a Finnish novel leaves home of a snowy winter morning to face an intense frost, puts his fur cap on his head and his *lapikkaat* (high boots that turn up at the toe so the thong that is his ski binding doesn't slip off) on his feet, takes his skis from the sauna wall, and skis across the frozen lake, his world is certainly exotic for many city dwellers. Besides the difficulties raised by terminology, nature, and conditions in the north, the translator must wrestle with dialogue heavy with dialect expressions. All these things will tend to direct the reader's attention too much towards the novel's environment, so that the highly original structure in, say, Kivi or Lehtonen receives too little attention.

The worth of the ordinary man

Another feature inherited from Kivi and prominent in many later novels is the writer's attitude to his characters, his concept of people. Kivi describes the brothers as if he were one of them: at the same level, understanding, giving value to each one. Some of his contemporaries, including his most severe critic, Professor August Ahlqvist, reproached him for this. Ahlqvist did not think it proper that Kivi should choose characters who were uncultured, primitive, and socially undeveloped and—still worse—describe their activities and behavior with obvious sympathy, without condemning their fighting, cursing, and drinking. Kivi described his people as they were, without moralizing. "He shows us the Finnish people of those days in their workaday clothes," as the poet Eino Leino aptly puts it.

This does not mean that the characters in Finnish novels are never criticized. They are, indeed, in many works; but even in these, the writers take the characters as their starting point, describe what they do and are through their circumstances, and allow the reader to formulate his own criticisms. The perspective is more or less defined by Sillanpää in the name of one of his collections of short stories: *Maan tasalta* "from ground level." The reader has to share the lives of these people, to see at least some of the events through their eyes. Sometimes this may lead to a humorous double vision, as in Juhani Aho's novel *Rautatie (The Railway,* 1884), where kindly fun is poked at an old rural couple on their first train journey; but with most writers the result is that the reader, at least to some extent, identifies with the characters of the book. Thus, even such primitive people must be taken seriously; they are not just clowns and yokels, brought on the stage to give the story picturesque local color or to perform a comically clumsy bear dance. They have their own lives. In Lehtonen's *Putkinotko,* the poor, dirty, and unsympathetic Juutas Käkriäinen is just as important a person as his wealthy and comfort-loving landlord, Muttinen. "They have to shift for themselves here," Muttinen thinks. "For their children, and themselves, of course. . . . That's the way it goes . . . as it goes, for those without schooling. They don't know much and they can't do much. It's a hard struggle. . . . And so life goes on from day to day, groping and suffering. Human life all the same, dearer than aught else."

Thus one fundamental problem in the classical Finnish novel is the question of *human worth*. The idea of every person's worth is sometimes justified biologically, almost metaphysically, sometimes socially and ethically. Sillanpää is representative of the biological approach; he speaks repeatedly of the "basic man," and discovers this basic person even in the most pitiable of his characters. For him, people are members of the same kind and tribe, so that at bottom they must have something in common. Other writers, representing the social-ethical approach, emphasize that a person's worth is not determined by his social position, his prosperity, or even his level of culture, but by his everyday activities measured against his conditions and in relation to the world in which he lives. In this sense someone like Ilmari Kianto's Jooseppi, poor and ineffectual as he may be, is a hero. This concept is brought out strongly by Väinö Linna, too. In his war novel *Tuntematon sotilas (The Unknown Soldier,* 1954), the real heroes turn out to be the ordinary men of the people, not the officers who cling to their military values and external formalities. The conflict between two measures of worth, the "real" but unofficial and the "official" but practically invalid, is one of the ironic basic themes of the book.

This concept of the integrity, the indestructible basic worth of even the most insignificant person, is reminiscent of the idea of man in the classical Russian novel. Direct influences can in fact be traced: Arvid Järnefelt, an important depicter of the cultured classes, was a student and kindred spirit of Tolstoy; Ilmari Kianto studied Russian and translated Goncharov's *Oblomov* into Finnish; and Väinö Linna's concept of history has distinctly Tolstoyan features. And there are even earlier connecting links. Annamari Sarajas, Professor of Finnish Literature at Helsinki University, has demonstrated that the central idea of a *type* in realistic literature came to Finland from Russian literature earlier than from France. At the same time the idea of people's fundamental equality, already familiar in Finnish literature, was strengthened. From its earliest beginnings, the classical Finnish novel has been strongly and convincedly democratic. The writer, as it were, whispers to the reader through his main character: this could be you.

The hero of the classical Finnish novel, thus, has for long been an anti-hero: he appears in "workaday clothes," he sees life through hard conditions at "ground level," he is poor and often unsympathetic. But all the time he has a significance of his own, his own unique worth as an individual. The measure of his worth is not money nor outward success. Sillanpää wrote his novel *Hurskas kurjuus* (*Meek Heritage,* 1919) about an insignificant cottager who is executed in the Civil War to show "how significant a man Jussi in reality is. . . ." The main character in one of Pentti Haanpää's short stories is, "Pussinen's old woman, a female worthy of respect," who uncomplainingly brings up a pack of children in the unshakable conviction that "there's more water than shit." The picture is straightforward and caricatured, but Pussinen's old woman grows in a few pages into a mighty monument to the desire for life and belief in it.

The individual and society

The conflict between the chief characters and the community that Kivi describes in *Seven Brothers* is repeated in various forms in numerous later folk portraits. In Juhani Aho, the conflict is given humorous or melancholy coloring, but in Joel Lehtonen and Ilmari Kianto the tone becomes more serious. The spiritual background to their great novels is the War of Independence of 1918, which in reality was a civil war, a traumatic experience for the whole nation. Lehtonen reacted quickly to the events of the war and handled them in some short stories in the same year; Sillanpää wrote "the end of the life-story of a Finn" in *Meek Heritage,* and tried in it to show the tragedy of the losing side in particular. And much later, Väinö Linna returns in his tragedy *Täällä Pohjantähden alla* (*Under the Northern Star,* 1959–62) to the themes of 1918, analyzing the causes and growth of social discontent and depicting its violent explosion. It was 1918 that convinced writers that the conflict between social classes was a terrifying reality and that sharp national self-criticism to reveal mistakes and failures was vital.

Even in those works that do not touch on the events of 1918, the problem of social justice is of high importance. There are two opposing approaches, and they are not easy to reconcile with one another: on the one hand is the humanistic idea of the fundamental worth of every person, the affinity of human beings whether from the highest or the lowest class, and on the other hand is the bitterly realistic observation of the conditions of the poor, their vulnerability to official bureaucracy, or the pressures of the more prosperous. Between these two poles flashes the fundamental tension of the classical Finnish novel. And since the writers regularly come down on the weaker side, they sometimes throw out a direct social challenge to the reader, like that at the beginning of Kianto's *Ryysyrannan Jooseppi*:

> Enter the cottage of the Finnish people and see its poverty, bitterness, and ineffectualness. Criticize, if you can, but don't come to the wrong conclusion: many a stranger before you has made a false judgment, and thousands will follow you, will hold their noses and run away, angrily exclaiming: "It's shameful the way people live!", and at the same time forgetting and returning to their happier lot. . . .

"Even among us farm folk there's like two big parties," thinks Jooseppi as he skis across the frozen lake. "The haves—and the have-nots." The classical Finnish novel has generally described the latter and gathered its characters from the lower social classes—small-holders, cottagers, tenant farmers. forest workers, and, later, factory workers. There may be wealthy people among them, too, as in Sillanpää or Volter Kilpi, "the Finnish James Joyce," who wrote about the southwestern Finnish archipelago, but generally these people are not blessed with worldly riches. Kianto's and Lehtonen's characters are from the poorest rural proletariat, like Toivolan Juha in Sillanpää's *Meek Heritage*. Some are not tied to any place or job; they live a mobile life, without attachments. Such are many of Pentti Haanpää's characters.

The social antithesis in the Finnish novel thus seems clear, almost according to Marxist formula: poor contra rich. But in this antithesis a paradox can be seen. The writers describe their characters sympathetically, emphasizing their fundamental worth, in a democratic spirit, coming down on their side in the social conflict. But what kind of people are these characters? They are often extremely strong individualists, antisocial even within their own social class. These anti-heroes are in no way ideal figures; they are lazy, sly, egotistical, narrow; they are the object of criticism, also. Nor do they show solidarity even with those who share their fate. Their solidarity does not extend beyond the immediate family circle—not always even that far. They keep themselves to themselves; they want to solve their problems alone. Personal freedom is important to them, and they guard it jealously and suspiciously, and defend it hopelessly. These same individualistic features can even be found in novels about factory workers, where the main characters are usually lonely thinkers, not active class-conscious thinkers. Only in the novels of Haanpää, Toivo Pekkanen, and Linna do we find characters who clearly feel they belong to some class and consciously attempt to develop politically and ideologically.

Thus, the relation of most of these characters with society is ambivalent. Poverty, which on the one hand means for them a burden or a cause of suffering, offers them on the other hand a kind of freedom. It is also a protective wall against social pressure, within which they have a chance to realize themselves. It is a role, too, maintained partly deliberately; it enables them to protest constantly against those richer than themselves. Poverty in the Finnish novel has many faces, nor are all of them inconsolable.

Realism and humor

"He shows us the Finnish people in their workaday clothes." Leino's observation about Kivi includes more than the writer's attitude to his characters. It also defines his style: realism. Kivi was in this respect, too, a pioneer. With him, the classical Finnish description of the people becomes established as a realistic one, tinged with humor.

Realism appears usually at three levels: in dialogue, in characterization, and in setting. August Ahlqvist condemned the way in which Kivi's characters spoke in *Seven Brothers,* and accused them of coarseness, swearing, even blasphemy. In other words, he objected to the writer allowing them to speak as young men of their type and level probably spoke at that time. Almost exactly the same accusations were leveled over ninety years later concerning Hannu Salama's novel, *Juhannustanssit (Midsummer Dances,* 1964) . Why does the writer allow his characters to use improper language, why does he repeat the uncensored jabbering of drunks, ask the critics—especially the moralizers and the conservatives. In this respect tradition seems to have been followed surprisingly closely. The speech of characters in novels has, of course, changed over a century, and modern writers make use of spoken language more freely and more consciously than formerly, but the objective is the same: to achieve a characteristic quality and verity through dialogue.

Dialogue is in itself a part of characterization: it discloses the nature of the person speaking. Again the tradition from Kivi to the present day is continuous. The essential characters of Kivi's brothers are disclosed in the first things they say; in Linna's *Unknown Soldier* as in Kivi the center of the picture is filled by a group of young men each of whom speaks in his own way. Linna has even made them speak different dialects, so that the differences stemming from regional background immediately appear.

In some characterizations, realism has meant that no attempt has been made to hide the persons' bad sides; they are openly revealed and demonstrated objectively. The anti-heroes of Kianto's and Lehtonen's novels may be partly intended as a critical study of certain sides of the Finnish national character— passivity, reticence, obstinacy, suspiciousness, fruitless envy. And as precisely as these individuals' negative characteristics are registered, the writer describes their ragged clothes, even their rank odors. In the partly autobiographical novels of Pekkanen and Viita, the characters are more positive—the chief character's inner growth and spiritual development are described, but Salama's first person is at times strikingly unsympathetic.

Kivi's descriptions of setting are not marked by their realism; his landscapes are pictured in terms of lofty beauty. Juhani Aho's nature description is lyrically impressionistic. Kianto and Lehtonen also describe nature in picturesque terms, but everything connected with people and their lives is handled quite differently. The wretchedness of the main characters is described concretely and with a nagging attention to detail: the writer's eye picks out the broken window, the dilapidated building, the untidy yard, the trash and filth in the room, the cockroaches and other vermin, the flies. In later writers the realism of their descriptions of setting is no longer so pointed nor so detailed; the environment of Pekkanen's workers is a joyless but rather indefinite grey, while Haanpää in his short stories selects only a few typical details.

Realism or naturalism? Finnish literary historians have pondered the question and decided to use the term *realism*. Even texts that approach naturalism usually lack its programmatic quality. The wretchedness of the characters is not—as it generally is in the naturalistic novel—dictated purely by social determinism. The classical Finnish novel diverges most clearly from naturalism in its element of humor. In this respect even examples of heightened realism follow the great tradition begun by Kivi. Almost all the novelists since Kivi make use of humor— Sillanpää and Pekkanen the least; Aho, Jotuni, Lassila, Kianto, Lehtonen, Haanpää, and Linna all considerably. This humor finds different forms in different writers. It is often connected with the fantasies of people who live close to nature and their ideas about the world; an individual philosopher of this kind, who molds abstract matters to fit his own forest environment in concrete forms or events, appears as the chief character in Veikko Huovinen's popular novel *Havukka-ahon ajattelija* (*The Thinker of Havukka-aho,* 1952). Haanpää employs humor for the purpose of social criticism; his observations are flavored with bitter irony and paradoxical expressions. In describing the great depression years of the 1930s, he notes in passing that all this happened "at the time when the earth was made, when it was noticed that there were far too many workers, a plague to the country and a terrible scourge to society." Linna's humor also backs up his social criticism and spotlights the disparity between real and apparent values. Veijo Meri's humor is concentrated in anecdotes or appears in angular,

Chaplinesque descriptions of people's clumsy reactions and blunders. In his actions, his self-importance, his self-centeredness, man *is* a comic figure, most writers seem to think; this conception embraces the whole range of society, from the highest to the lowest, in the Finnish novel.

Out of the forest

In an essay, Toivo Pekkanen states that the characters in his novels are not of the same breed as the passive, dreamy figures in *Jooseppi of Ryysyranta, Putkinotko,* or *Meek Heritage.* They rather stem from Kivi's *Seven Brothers:* "They are not the children of the brother who inherited the farm, but of those brothers who built a cottage. Nothing was known about the descendants of these cottages other than their wretchedness, before industry came to the country and established a new kind of society."

It is Pekkanen who has described the development of this kind of society in his works. The most coherent picture of this process of change has been given by Väinö Linna, whose *Under the Northern Star* gives a large-scale cross section of conditions in a small village over a period of seven decades, from its start at the end of the nineteenth century in an almost immobile, patriarchal, rural community to its conclusion during a period of brisk development and economic recovery after the Second World War. The background to recent Finnish novels is the constant process of industrialization and urbanization. This means in practice that the traditional rural picture is becoming relatively rarer and city and industrial settings more common in literature.

Many writers have continued the story from where Linna left off. The characters of Veijo Meri, Paavo Rintala, and Hannu Salama are often first-generation city dwellers who wrest themselves from the old environment and experience the conflicts between the old and the new way of life. In Joukko Puhakka's popular play, *Hyvästi, Mansikki!* (*Goodbye, Mansikki!,* 1968), the country people nail up the doors of their homes, sell their cattle, move to the town, and turn their backs on the past. One short-story writer, Seppo Urpela, has described workers who have come to the city from remote villages and are thrown into hopeless competition with the urban community. "The only things we don't have are half their wages, a home, teeth, and six inches in height," says one such newcomer, a country boy who is beaten in a fight, in one of Urpela's stories. As Rintala says in his novel *Rikas ja köyhä* (*Rich and Poor,* 1955) : "The descendants of Kivi's brothers are still today pushing their brothers around in the Finnish community."

All the same, the tradition that started from the forest continues. The question of the worth and significance of man, and his relation to society, is still a topical one in literature. It may be even more vital today than formerly. The little man comes from the depths of the woods to the city streets, the red tape of bureaucracy, the competitive consumer society, to learn by bitter experience the strange and labyrinthine rules of the urban game—this man needs an advocate or a portrayer who can distinguish the funny side of his plight. The setting varies, society changes, but the theme of human worth and social justice continues in Finnish literature. The new writers whisper through their new characters in a new voice: this could be you.

Of the novels mentioned in this essay, those that have been translated into English are listed in the bibliography.

JAAKKO A. AHOKAS

The Short Story in Finnish Literature

Short stories have been written in Finland as long as there has been a literature in the true meaning of that word in the country—that is hardly more than a hundred years—but there is no author, with the possible exceptions of Juhani Aho and Maria Jotuni, perhaps, who is considered to be a master of the genre. Finnish literary critics and scholars operating with a traditional terminology gave, in general, a rather narrow definition of the short story—called *novelli* in Finnish, from the Italian *novella,* a word used under various forms in many European languages. Like the Italian prototype, a novella was supposed to narrate a new or unusual incident, to concentrate only on that incident and preferably to have an unexpected and surprising end. It was also often considered that the novella was a highly refined type of prose composition and, as such, was beyond the reach of Finnish writers and their readers, who lacked the background of a well-established literary tradition. The typical novella is, of course, as much of a fiction as any other literary model, and it is somewhat curious to see how faithfully both writers and scholars or critics in Finland used it as a standard of literary value, although they were quite well aware of the fact that large amounts of short prose of all kinds were written in their time in every country. Finnish writers have often been of very modest social origin and their attitudes toward their work seem often to be compounded of modesty and aggression. They seem to consider that novels are serious works of art that have to be written carefully, but they mostly describe their short prose compositions as sketches or tales, told, as it were, to a group of friends. However, under this apparent and often quite genuine modesty, there is often, also, the implication that such simple tales are closer to the realities of life than refined artistic texts, and that they appeal to people with genuine and simple feelings and tastes, not to overrefined aesthetes. Maiju Lassila (pseudonym of Algoth Tietäväinen-Untola, 1868–1918) is typical in this respect; his father, a farmer, died when Lassila was thirteen years old, and he had to work as a boy before he became an elementary schoolteacher and, later on, a newspaperman and a writer. He began his literary career by publishing two huge, overambitious, symbolist, and decadent novels in 1909, but then he changed his style and motifs completely, adopted the pseudonym under which he is known, and wrote mostly humorous stories, short and long, about country people in his home region. He speaks, himself, of his style and aims in a manner that is seemingly modest but obviously also critical of more elegant forms of writing: "I do not like the idea that so-called better people would read my writings, for everyone should stay within his own trousers"; or "it would not be very difficult for me to give them (for example, the stories in a collection) the condensed quality required of novellas, but their readers do not understand condensed novellas. Common people with their slow thoughts read this kind of stuff for their pleasure, not to meditate on the intensity of the images in them, and, to them, the main thing is that what they read is easy to understand"; and, to one of his compositions, he gave a subtitle meaning, more or less, "a thing" or "a piece of writing".[1]

Pentti Haanpää (1905–1955), who wrote mostly about small farmers, lumberjacks, and hoboes of his home region, north Finland, insisted that his short writings be called, not *novelli*, but *juttu*, "tales" or "yarns," of the kind told by the characters themselves. The case of Juhani Aho (1861–1921) is rather different; he belonged by birth to the middle class, traveled widely, was a public figure, admired and recognized as a great writer in his lifetime. He expressed understanding, sympathy, and concern for the poor and the underprivileged, but from a socially superior position, and his ideas about his own short prose works were not motivated by an effort to make them accessible to all readers. Rather, he seemed to have considered them unworthy of a serious artistic effort; he said, himself, about them: "When a woodworker is shaping an object, shavings drop to the floor of his workshop. . . . I am offering here these 'shavings' of mine just as they dropped from my writing desk and curled up on the spot."[2] Aho's attitude is, however, somewhat ambiguous, for some of his "shavings" (*lastu*) are very carefully composed, especially those in which a meditative, melancholic mood is projected into a landscape, and that are among the most typical of his writings.

Statements about the short story as a genre have been made by other Finnish writers still, with the emphasis placed mostly on the form, without social implications. Joel Lehtonen (1881–1934), best known as a novelist, said in a preface to his collection of short stories, *Korpi ja puutarha* (*The Wilderness and the Garden*, 1923), that "in the world, we hardly experience anything differently from what we have originally been; almost nothing that could really be called a plot".[3] Among contemporary writers, Eila Pennanen (born 1916) has discussed the use of the narrator in short stories; according to her, "an entirely exterior narrator using the first person, or an impossible and abnormal crossbreed between a narrator and a character . . . seem to violate a kind of ethical principle that has ruled the short story after Chekhov and Mansfield: the writer and the character are members of the human race, brothers and sisters," and, as Mrs. Pennanen says, when the narrator is entirely discarded, the characters become emotionally part of the author.[4] One of the best known postwar writers, Veijo Meri (born 1928), has taken a somewhat aggressive position against the traditional rules on the form of the short story. Speaking of his own writings, he says: "For each short story there is an increase in the number of these hidden patterns and contradictory rules, and each short story is a new and more impressive gesture by which I want to demonstrate how they are abolished, how this short story, too, upsets all expectations and its own prerequisites."[5]

As for their content, Finnish short stories follow the general pattern of Finnish literature; of late, and still today, they often describe rural life, and more often poverty and suffering than happiness. Humorous short stories have also been written, in large numbers even, but the humor in them is often combined with a more serious attitude. It is at times a bitter and rebellious protest against all the meaningless suffering in the world, like in Haanpää, or a cunning way to fool the wealthy and powerful, like in Lehtonen and also Haanpää, or a satire of human foibles, like in Maria Jotuni (1880–1943), or a boisterous joke about all the madness in the world, like in Veikko Huovinen (born 1927), or a desperate and ultimately unsuccessful attempt to find something good among the meanness of human society, like in Sillanpää (1888–1964), or an underscoring of the general absurdity of everything, like in Meri. The short stories of the earlier authors are often largely descriptive; I already mentioned Aho's descriptions of landscapes seen as moods or mental states, but also, when he introduces characters, it is rather for portrayal and observation than dramatic action. In *Vilhelmiina Väisänen* (a woman's name) and also in *Leivänkannikka* (*A Piece of Bread*), he imagines that he is traveling in a train, observing a fellow traveler, and trying to guess what his life might have been; typically, I would say, he makes both of them elderly, so that they are like finished works of art, in which no change will take place anymore, and therefore may be examined at leisure.[6] In *Sasu Punanen* (a man's name), a much admired humorous sketch, the main character is acting and speaking, but nothing decisive happens and no development takes place; he merely reveals himself as a connoisseur and lover of the Finnish sauna bath. Maria Jotuni's short stories are apparently more dramatic than Aho's, for they practically always contain speaking and acting characters (letter writing is, of course, speaking, too), but, within the framework of the story, the action is often set in the past and narrated by the main character in a long monologue interrupted only by such remarks as, "You don't say," or, "Really," or, "Go ahead," made by the listener. Moreover, what is described is not so much action as interpersonal relations, especially love between the sexes, or what the characters call love. The author is very skillful in letting the reader understand what selfish and often crassly materialistic calculation the characters are covering under their sentimental outpourings, but she does not stop at this primary level of satire. Often, her women, who sell themselves to men for the position of a legal wife or a kept mistress, seem not to believe themselves that anybody would take their talk about love at face value, and seem also to be wondering how men can be such fools as to bind themselves to women who want only material security, and to wish, nevertheless, to be told that it all happens because of love.

The short stories of Volter Kilpi (1874–1939) and Heikki Toppila (1885–1963) stand entirely apart from all other similar works in Finnish literature, and probably in the literature of the whole world. Both describe people in their home region, both look toward the past, and both also often draw portraits of old people, who at times die in the course of the narration, and who narrate their lives, thus brought to a completion, in interior monologues or in fragmentary conversations where detail is added to detail till the picture is finished. Both were influenced by their native dialect—Toppila in the northwest, Kilpi in the southwest—and Toppila also drew freely on the local folklore, although his stories are by no means folk tales arranged for publication.

Toppila does not tell ghost stories either; rather, he writes about everyday people and their lives, but, to his people, ghosts, all kinds of apparitions and portents, witches, magic, and the devil are part of their normal life, so much so that there is nothing romantic or beautiful about them; they are ugly and familiar, although terrifying. Toppila also often leaves open the question whether he is describing *bona fide* supernatural apparitions or projections of subconscious terrors, and, when he dwells in unsurpassed graphic and gory detail on violent death, maiming, and dismemberment, it is also often in a manner that purposely leaves the reader in doubt whether the images are supposed to render actual incidents within the framework of the narration, or half-mythical, half-delirious visions. Toppila, like Kilpi, also wrote novels, but his style is better suited for short narrations, because it tends to become repetitious in longer texts.

As for Kilpi, it is impossible to say what his style would be suited for, except for works by Volter Kilpi; he achieved the not very common feat of writing a novel in two volumes and nine hundred pages, *Alastalon salissa* (*In the Main Room of Alastalo Farm*), on a discussion between wealthy farmers, shipowners, and captains, that lasted about four hours. His short stories, published in the collection *Pitäjän pienempiä* (*Small People in the County*), is a contrast to the novel, in so far as he describes in it the poor and the humble, whose work is also necessary to the success of the wealthy. There is no trace of social aggressiveness in them, for Kilpi was ideologically a conservative; they are only analyses of individual defeats, whereas the novel is a description of personal success. Two of the stories, *Merimiehenleski* (*A Sailor's Widow*) and *Jäälläkulkija* (*Walking on the Ice*), consist almost exclusively of interior monologues in which the characters recapitulate their lives, dwelling on past actions and words, thoughts and feelings, and also on what might have been should an incident not have occurred, a word not have been pronounced, an act not committed. Neither of the characters in the stories comes to a satisfactory conclusion; in *Jäälläkulkija,* he is a man whose pride and stubbornness had ruined his life and the life of his family, and who is fundamentally aware of this, although he insists on justifying his attitude to himself and to God up to his death. In *Merimiehenleski,* a poor old woman is trying to find a meaning in all the suffering that life has inflicted upon her and rebelling at times against God, himself, for his injustice, but then submitting; Kilpi, who formulated an aesthetic theory of life in the essays he published at the beginning of the century, was a conservative, as I said, and never criticized openly the church or religion, but seems not to have found solace in the Christian faith.

It is a typical feature of Kilpi's style in his late works that, while it is individualistic in the extreme and aims at the highest artistic perfection, the linguistic material out of which it is built is, nevertheless, everyday Finnish, in conformity with the characters he is describing; the moderate use of local dialect and phraseology, reminiscent of old Bible translations, is normal in the context. The images and metaphors that he uses abundantly are also taken from the familiar surroundings of his characters—mostly sailing, the sea, and commonly observed animals—but he uses these materials to create a vision of the world entirely his own. In his lifetime, he was told that there were some similarities between himself and Proust, and, because he knew French, he read some of *À la Recherche du Temps Perdu* and admitted that Proust's style and his had something in common, but that their aims were quite different.[7] Proust always stayed well within the limits of normal linguistic usage, whereas Kilpi deliberately broke with it, and his intensity of thought and feeling, his images, which are closely woven into the narration itself, the importance that objects take in his world as reflections and projections of the human mind, and his constant gliding from the present to the past, from the real to the imaginary and virtual, from the inner monologue to the objective narration make me think of Claude Simon, in *La Route de Flandres,* for example.

For a long time, Finnish authors wrote mostly about rural life and characters, and the fact that they did this spontaneously, not because they were following a preestablished program or ideology, is nowhere seen better than in the individualistic treatment of the subjects they chose. Pentti Haanpää is entirely different from Toppila and Kilpi and of every other Finnish writer; there might be some similarities between him and Veijo Meri. The action in Haanpää's books takes place mostly in contemporary Finland: the twenties, the prohibition (applied at the same period and with the same results as in the United States), the great depression, the wars, and the postwar time are faithfully reflected in them and influence the lives of his characters, who are everyday Finns, totally free of all superstitions, and who comment freely on the world, in terms that are critical of capitalism but at times also of socialism or communism. In 1928, he published a collection of short stories, *Kenttä ja kasarmi* (*The Field and the Barracks*), in which he criticized sharply the brutality and stupidity that, inevitably, seem to be part of every army in the world, but, because Finland had been independent for hardly more than ten years by then and had gone through a civil war, such criticism was received very adversely, and Haanpää was immediately branded as a communist. For about ten years no respectable publisher would print his books, several of which came out posthumously, but, from the late thirties on, he enjoyed again the position of a well-known author. Haanpää wrote mostly about characters living in his home region and spent all his life there, a fact that had the result that a kind of legend grew around him in his lifetime; he was supposed to be like one of the lumberjacks and hoboes he described, only able to write somehow about his experiences. His father was, however, a well-to-do farmer, who took part in public affairs in his lifetime, and, although he himself never had more formal education than elementary school, he read widely and acquired through self-study a good knowledge of English, so that he had a fair number of books in that language in his private library, including, for example, works by James Joyce (although not *Ulysses*). He modeled two of his compositions on two of Joyce's stories in *Dubliners*, perhaps to see if the literary critics and scholars in Helsinki would notice the plagiarism but they did not, not until a few years after his death.[8]

Haanpää always describes characters in his short stories, which are dramatic and lively, although the point in them is not to narrate a plot and to bring it to a conclusion, but to give the picture of an individual in a given situation and in given surroundings. They are told in a simple and straightforward manner, without any stylistic refinements; inner monologue is not used and the thoughts of the characters are seldom rendered. There is something similar to the American folk ballads in these stories about simple men and women and what happened to them, although there is hardly anything in them that could be called romantic, and unusual or startling elements are also mostly lacking. Haanpää's characters live in a harsh and unfriendly country, north Finland, and struggle against overwhelming odds, without much success, but without surrendering either. They keep their spirits up with the help of a bitter and sarcastic humor, alcohol, and frustrated efforts to shake off for a while the burden of everyday drudgery. Haanpää's works can be read as a protest against a given social, economic, and political system, but this protest is very seldom expressly formulated and the author decidedly does not want to arouse pity or sympathy towards his characters. He describes them as strong and independent individuals who rely only on themselves, and he even implies that help would be useless, for his sarcasm seems ultimately to be directed against the whole world, which is so badly made that man can mostly only suffer in it.

The Nobel Prize awarded F. E. Sillanpää mainly on account of his novel *The Maid Silja* (the original Finnish title of which is quite different) has tended to overshadow the rest of his production, especially abroad, where his short stories are unknown. He began his literary career by publishing two short novels before 1920, but after that year he wrote only short stories. However, because he was considered to be a promising young author, everybody expected him to write still more novels, for a writer, it was thought, could not really be a great writer unless he wrote a great novel, so he finally produced *The Maid Silja* in 1931. It is interesting to compare the novel with a short story, *Huhtikuinen tanssiaisyö (A Ball on an April Night)*, published in the collection *Töllinmäki (The Hill with the Cabin, 1925)*, out of which the longer narration was obviously developed. I would say that the incident described in the short story gives a full picture of the main character, and that the novel only adds incidents to her biography, without saying anything essentially new.

In the short story, Silja, the main character, loses her *fiancé* because she is too honest and good to counter the malicious slander told about her, but which the young man, however, believes; the novel adds the story of her father—a man too honest and good, as she was—to be successful in this world, a romantic and short love story she has with a young man from the city, and her death, young and beautiful, of tuberculosis. I am afraid that the novel was often translated and read abroad because of this rather Segalesque end, and I would agree with the Finnish scholars who say that the story of the father destroys the unity of the novel by giving it two main characters.[9]

Sillanpää's stories are like Haanpää's in so far as the characters in them are presented through their actions and words in their familiar surroundings, but their structure is formally more complex. Sillanpää uses, at times, interior monologue, which is mingled freely with an objective narration, and he also presents, himself, direct comments and philosophical conclusions on the action, addressing them openly to the reader. His characters are much more passive than Haanpää's, they are born to submit and to suffer, and the author attempts at times to demonstrate that it is right for them to do so, for, according to his philosophy of life, men are happiest when following their instincts, not their reason. However, Sillanpää saw clearly that mere submission to suffering does not bring happiness to average people, and he expressed sympathy for their plight, although this sympathy was mixed with a kind of exasperation at their inability to fend for themselves. His humor is also a kind of desperate attempt to tell himself and his readers that his characters are so stupid and helpless that they are funny because of that, like in the novel *Hurskas kurjuus (Meek Heritage)*, for example.

The new generation of writers that appeared about 1950 and gave a new aspect to Finnish literature does not include any typical short-story writers, just as the case was before them. It was almost by chance that they appeared as innovators, for they did not form a coherent group, issue manifestos, or set out to change literature and the world. Through a strange whim of fate, almost all of the Finnish writers who would have been middle-aged by then had died— not in the war, by the way—or stopped writing, so that the young ones confronted the world alone; according to Kai Laitinen's often quoted words, "literature was produced by grandfathers and grandsons; the generation of the fathers was almost completely silent."[10] Among the writers whose first works were published before the fifties, there are a few who have remained active and, without sacrificing to any fads, have produced works that are relevant in the present-day world. Eila Pennanen is one of them; in her early works, there was an opposition between artistry and realism, and an interest in exceptional situations and characters still appears in two—very good—historical novels she wrote in 1954 and 1958, but, by then, she was decidedly turning towards contemporary settings and characters. Her technique is traditional; she does not attempt to create a new vision of the world by the use of a highly individualistic style, but she possesses, nevertheless, a literary personality very much her own. In her short stories (collections *Tornitalo, The High-Rise Building,* 1952, *Kaksin, Twosome,* 1961), as in her recent novels, she describes everyday people in everyday situations, although these situations often illustrate conflicts, tensions, and maladjustments. As she has said in an essay, she "jumps quickly in and out of a character,"[11] that is, she may use interior monologue, relate the thoughts of the individuals she is describing, or present them through their own words and actions. She keeps herself very much in the background and does not offer direct or indirect comments on her characters or on any specific questions related to politics, social problems, or morals. What she is most interested in are situations in which a conflict arises between two persons or a person and a social group or institution through nobody's fault. These conflicts are never dramatic or violent and do not bring about a solution to the problem that created them; what the author is interested in is how the characters become involved in these situations and how they react to them. She seems always to be hovering on the line separating mild satire from subdued tragedy, depending on whether she views the discrepancy between the expressed aims of her characters and their half-unconscious motives as a source of half-humorous misunderstandings or truly negative experiences.

Among the young writers of the fifties who are now fast becoming young classics, Veijo Meri is one of the best known, appreciated both by a large number of readers and demanding critics. Two facts are immediately conspicuous in his production: his interest in military life and war, and what has loosely been called the absurdity of the world he is describing. Absurd and absurdity are words that have been much used and misused lately, and it should immediately be said that Meri's works are basically realistic, not to be compared to Beckett's, Ionesco's, or Pinter's in form. Meri's characters move in an easily recognizable contemporary Finland, or in a not very distant past, and engage in normal everyday activities, or in normal warfare, for a large number of his stories are either about war, mostly the last conflict, or military life. I would, however, not say that they are realistic, first of all because of what Meri has said himself about realism in the modern novel.[12] In the whole essay, Meri argues with unnamed opponents of the modern novel, who, he says, charge it with being full of irrelevant details and not giving due importance to the essential facts of life. Further, he says, the great realists of the nineteenth century are opposed to the modern novelists, because they presented only what was relevant; but Meri contends that these writers (Balzac, Tolstoy, and others) were not realists at all because they created worlds of their own, "the like of which we have never seen." According to Meri, modern novels are more realistic than the classical masterpieces because they reproduce both the irrelevant and the relevant details of life, but, he adds, his opponents would then retort that the main defect of the modern novel lies just there; it is only realistic, a fussy reproduction of trivia.

As for the form of the short story, Meri states about the same well-known facts I gave at the beginning of this essay: Finnish writers in general have refused to submit their short prose works to any kind of formulas and have given them various names, avoiding the use of the word *novelli,* "novella."[13] Here, Meri's arguments seem to be slightly confused, for he appears to be saying that, because of the choice of a certain name, short Finnish prose works have been neglected, which can hardly be correct, certainly not in the case of any of the well-known writers: Aho, Jotuni, Sillanpää, and Haanpää, for example. As for himself, Meri considers that any kind of short prose composition should be called *novelli*, a somewhat pointless request, for this has been done for a long time already. Meri says that he had at first written all of his works as short stories, and then expanded some of them into novels; length seems to be to him the only criterion of classification, because he says that, when he had two versions of the same text, "the longer one could then be called a novel and the shorter a short story."

If there is something absurd in Meri's works, it is not in what is described, although the mingling of trivial details with relevant facts may seem pointless to the readers who are accustomed to neatly arranged traditional compositions. Of course, even the trivial details have their place in the structure of the work because they have been created and selected by the author, and their purpose is not only, perhaps not even mainly, to create the impression of a confused and meaningless world, but also to reproduce in a fresh and vivid manner reality as experienced by the characters, who can not fail to notice a tree or a billboard on the roadside, a car passing in a street, or a man on a bicycle, even if none of these influences their lives in any manner. It is in such passages as these that one finds unexpected pieces of poetic writing, unexpected because Meri's world is generally practical, at times cynical and often brutal, with no time for meditation and beauty, but they are nevertheless there, too. Kalevi Haikara has given a quote from such a passage as the title to his book on Meri, *That Was That Golden Land.*[15] Haikara presents it as an instance of how Meri passes without transition from a description of the external world to a rendering of characters' thoughts and feelings, but I would analyze it slightly differently. In the passage, a few persons cross an expanse of water on a ferry; this incident is first described objectively, but then we have: "The sun cast a yellow shine on the faraway shore beyond the tug and the barge. That was that golden land. It was always so far that, when you got there, the sun had already set; in black houses, which were made of charred wood, sick people were being tarred, children were snuffing out glowworms in the woods, and young maidens were blackening their eyebrows with bits of coal taken from the hearth." What strikes one first is the surrealistic quality of the vision, then the fact that this vision is given directly, without any transition, and then that it is not represented as a traditional metaphor, but projected into the world. There are many other similar passages in Meri's works; I take one at random, from *Sujut* (*Quits*), where a soldier is told that he will, after all, not be shot for deserting but sent back to his unit. When he starts walking and steps into the shadow of a hill, "it seemed that the air was full of horizontal threads, which were so fine that they went easily through him and cut him up into slices so thin that they did not come apart. He started shivering and threw up." In my opinion, this is expressionistic writing in the precise meaning of that word: that is, the expression of a person's feelings, thoughts, and states of mind through a direct modification of the world, not metaphorically or symbolically.

Another question that has been much debated in connection with Meri is whether his characters behave in a rational manner or not; generally speaking, those who are for the irrational interpretation form the majority, but Haikara disagrees with them and devotes several pages to a refutation of their views.[16] It cannot be denied that Meri's characters often act in an unpredictable and apparently meaningless manner, although it might be said that Meri has often made it easy for himself to explain why they do so; they live in wartime conditions, where everything is unpredictable and meaningless. However, it is generally the most intelligent, courageous, and energetic characters who behave in this manner, in protest against an impossible situation that can not be handled in a rational manner. Meri underscores often in this manner the basic absurdity in the philosophy of the armies, which are set up to carry out senseless violence and destruction, but which are also supposed to do this according to precise rules and regulations. The best fighters, according to Meri, are those who do not follow rules and regulations, but they are mostly reprimanded for this.

In civilian life, Meri describes mostly individuals who fail to communicate and to establish contacts with each other; each of them acts quite rationally from his own premises, but because all of them have slightly different premises, they never achieve the goals they are trying to reach. This brings about quite a lot of friction, irritation, and frustration, but never leads to violent tragedies or conflicts; at the end of the story, the characters are quite ready to go on with their efforts as before. This means, also, that Meri's books could, in a sense, go on forever, and that there really is no difference, as he says himself, between his novels and short stories; both are slices of life, cut thicker or thinner, but containing basically the same stuff, only smaller or larger amounts of it.

I would say that Antti Hyry (born 1931) is in many respects not unlike Meri, as far as the form of his works is concerned; there is no basic difference between his short stories and novels, for both deal with the same type of situations and characters and differ fundamentally only in length. However, Hyry's motifs are quite different from Meri's, not only because Hyry always describes peaceful and constructive activities, but also because his characters mostly succeed in what they are attempting to do. One should not think that the story included in this anthology is about a defeat; after all, the dam is built, the waterwheel works, the turbine produces electricity, and the lamp glows; only, the builder comes to the conclusion that he can not make anything really useful with the materials he has on hand, and therefore, quite rationally, takes everything apart again. Another of his short stories, *Kaivonteko (Digging a Well)*, describes the same kind of practical activity, which ends in an undisputed success: two men, the owner of a lot in the suburbs and his friend, start digging a well on the lot and, although largely inexperienced, carry the task through. In the novel *Maailman laita (The Edge of the World)*, a group of men start on a fishing expedition in two motorboats. One of the boats has a breakdown and drifts away in a strong wind, but no major catastrophe follows, and the boat is eventually found next day. Hyry's characters are exactly the opposite of Meri's; they live in a rational world, which they have learned to master, and in which they perform all kinds of simple, creative, and rewarding material work. Hyry's interest in simple everyday things, his matter-of-fact, dry style, and his way of describing apparently unimportant details with the same care as the main facts have puzzled some critics, who have taken great pains to find a hidden message or a new style of writing in them. Parallels have been drawn between him and the writers of the *nouveau roman* school in France, especially Robbe-Grillet, but these parallels are rather superficial.[17] I think that, in Hyry, what you see is what you get, and that he is really not attempting to say anything more than that it is worth while doing simple, elemental things well, because they are the most rewarding and, after all, keep this world going—an often neglected truth in our times. In addition to doing manual work, Hyry's characters also enjoy other basic activities, like eating simple, tasty food, walking in the forests, and feeling the sunshine together with the smells of nature.

As Meri at times has sudden flashes of poetry in his texts, so Hyry reproduces at times the thoughts of his characters that are not necessarily simple and un-articulate; in *Kaivonteko,* the main character thinks and speaks of Bartok's music, modern painting, and Chekhov's works, and, in *Maailman laita,* some-thing similar takes place. There, indeed, the person who is thinking finds his own thoughts slightly unpleasant and disturbing. He realizes at a given moment how vast nature and the world are and how small a speck man is among them, and the main character in *Kaivonteko* has a similar feeling at one time, but they both snap quickly back into reality. It is perhaps here that Hyry comes the closest to delivering a message, which would be that philosophizing is a dangerous and unhealthy occupation (at the International Writers' Seminar in Lahti in 1964, he delivered a surprisingly vehement—vehement for him—attack against the very idea of meeting in public in order to discuss general ideas). At first, it might seem surprising that two Finnish poets and writers have described him as one of the few poets in Finland,[18] but, if one considers what the very widely held standards of contemporary poetry are in their country, this opinion is not surprising. Poetry, according to these standards, should present images, preferably images taken from everyday life, and not add any comments to them, leaving the reader free to draw his own conclusions from them, and that is no doubt what Hyry is basically doing.

Meri, Hyry, and other writers of the fifties are by now the young classics and another literary generation has grown after them. The new writers do not form groups or schools any more than their predecessors, but have, nevertheless, a few common characteristics. They often break completely with all literary and linguistic traditions, something that has not been seen earlier in Finland, they are often openly and aggressively critical of social and political conditions, al-though they do not formulate definite programs or support any established ideology, and they openly violate sexual taboos, respected until late not only for fear of prosecution but obviously also because the earlier writers were more interested in other motifs.

Jyrki Pellinen (born 1940) is one of the authors who have most decisively discarded all traditional forms both in his poetry and in his prose; one of his latest works, *Tähän asti olen puhunut (Until Now, I Have Been Speaking)*, can hardly be classified otherwise than as a certain length of text. It might be called a novel, for the same character moves throughout the sections into which it is divided, or a collection of short stories, because these sections do not have much in common, except just the character of the narrator, or it might be prose poems, for there are many decidedly poetic passages in them. It might be said that, here, Meri's badly built world has got completely out of joint, so that the characters do not even attempt to adjust to it, noting its absurdity dispas-sionately, and that the occasional poetic glimpses of the "golden land" have become the only meaningful part in it.

All the new young writers do not break as thoroughly with traditional forms as Pellinen; Hannu Salama (born 1936), who became famous after having been prosecuted and sentenced for blasphemy, has written both novels and short stories that are formally traditional, but the protest against society is quite violent, although rather loosely aimed, and sexual activities are described very frankly. Salama is in many respects like Pentti Saarikoski (born 1937), who is best known as a poet, but who has written prose as well; both are ill at ease in a bourgeois society and defy openly its conventions, but they cannot find a meaningful alternative to it—Saarikoski for a while tried communism, but seems now to be disillusioned—and end up writing mostly about themselves, young writers who doubt the validity of literature and drift rather aimlessly from alcohol to sex.

Timo Mukka (born 1944) is a very individual author; he can be frankly romantic and writes at times a directly poetic prose, but he also describes, in a realistic manner, rootless modern life and presents a slightly surrealistic but very efficient satire of all the brutality and stupidity of the present-day world. The story presented here has some nonrealistic details, but is basically closer to everyday experience than the others in the collection from which it is taken; however, like the others, it leaves the issues open and does not offer any obvious explanation of itself, a feature that it shares also with most of all relevant prose and poetry written today in Finland.

NOTES

1. Pekka Tarkka, "Novelli," *Suomen Kirjallisuus* 8 (Helsinki, 1970) : 129; cf. Raoul Palmgren, *Joukkosydän* 2 (Helsinki, 1966) : 261. In Untola's lifetime already, "better people," critics and scholars (Volter Kilpi among them), nevertheless read and enjoyed his works, and he is now considered one of the classics of humor in Finnish literature.
2. Almost infallibly quoted whenever Aho's short prose is mentioned; see Tarkka, "Novelli," p. 88.
3. Tarkka, "Novelli," p. 103. When translating the original, I have not tried to improve on its slightly confused language.
4. Tarkka, "Novelli," p. 108.
5. Veijo Meri, "Käsityksiäni novellista," *Kaksitoista artikkelia* (Helsinki, 1967), p. 28.
6. I make some comments on this type of short story in a small essay "Kaksi novellia," *Esseitä* 63 (Turku, 1963) : 45–49.
7. Indeed, in the preface (for which he coined a new word, "Prechapter," *esiluku*) to *Alastalon salissa*, Kilpi says that it is his intention to recall to life people from the past of his home region.
8. In 1962; *see* Kai Laitinen, "Pentti Haanpää," *Suomen Kirjallisuus* 5 (Helsinki, 1965) : 387, 398–99.
9. Rafael Koskimies, in *Elävä kansalliskirjallisuus* 1–3 (Helsinki, 1944, 1946, 1949), V. A. Koskenniemi, in a review written shortly after the publication of the novel, and Alex Matson, *Romaanitaide*, 2nd ed. (Helsinki, 1960). Aatos Ojala, *Kohtalon toteuttaminen*, Hämeenlinna (1969), defended the unity of the novel; cf. Timo Kukkola, "Nuorena nukkuneen kaksiaiheisuus," *Tilanne* 6/28 (April 1964) : 203–209.
10. Kai Laitinen, *Suomen kirjallisuus 1917–1967* (Helsinki 1967), p. 145, (there is no reason why Mr. Laitinen should not have written "grandparents and grandchildren," to include the numerous Finnish writers of the female sex).
11. Quoted in *Tarkka*, "Novelli," p. 108.
12. "Onko uudessa romaanissa realismia?", *Kaksitoista artikkelia* (Helsinki, 1967), pp. 151–58.

40

Much in the essay was suggested to Meri, according to his own words, by Claude Simon's comments made at the International Writers' Seminar in Lahti in 1965 (*see* pp. 53–55).

13. Meri, "Käsityksiäni," pp. 33–34.
14. Meri, "Käsityksiäni," pp. 33, 41–42.
15. Kalevi Haikara, *Se oli se kultamaa: Veijo Meren romaanien tarkastelua* (Helsinki, 1969). The passage from which the quote is taken is discussed pp. 82–83.
16. Haikara, *Se oli se kultamaa*, pp. 81–82, 104–112, 115–17.
17. Laitinen, *Suomen kirjallisuus*, pp. 190–91.
18. Pentti Holappa, "Kertojan nykyiset kasvot," *Uusi Suomi* 225 (21 August 1960) : 14; and Maila Pylkkönen, "Neljä runodebyyttiä," *Parnasso* 4 (1964) : 181–84.

WILLIAM KNIGHT

Some General Notes on What Contemporary Finnish Writing Is Like (It's Like Blueberries) and What It's Not Like

These Finns, like wild blueberries, tantalize me with their elusive taste. I sample and taste again, expecting that with each handful I will mark and identify their flavor. Then, fixed in my mind, I can tire of them and put the berries aside with other familiar things, conquered and discarded, familiarity being the kingdom of the lost. But blueberries escape familiarity. I can never quite name their flavor. Thoreau calls theirs an "innocent taste." It never comes out, clarion. That is why, as they roll around on my tongue, my mind is drawn to their texture, their tiny size, the stain--that scares everyone but children—they leave on my teeth and hands, the small patches where I find them wild up in Maine. I look for them when their season comes and to many they are the very symbol of summer.

If winter had a fruit, I think it would taste something like *Autumn, A Girl and a Bottle,* Virtanen's "Four Poems," and most of the other works in this anthology. The appeal of this winter fruit is strong, but, like blueberries, almost impossible to describe. How the Finns accomplish their result is, however, easier to grasp. Good Finnish writing singles something out (in a special way I will mention in the last section) and penetrates it sharply, as if to sting. This is true for the subject of a story (*The Wolf, Dam,* and *The Killer* come to mind) as well as for a characteristic line within a story: "For he was in possession of his senses, but not of his reason, and that's where the madness lay."[1] Here, the author tells us that his body worked but that his mind did not. He is telling us more than that he was mad. In that same line he defines what one form of madness is: the segregation of mind and body. Take another example: "Slowly he began to rise, as slowly as dough rises in the oven. . . ." Many writers would stop here and quit the metaphor, thinking they had squeezed the lemon dry. But it is typical of the Finns for Meri to hold on. He continues: "Slowly he began to rise, as slowly as dough rises in the oven, forced upwards by the yeast that was the fierce will of the lieutenant."[2] He singles out the act of getting up from a chair and uses it to describe both the slow boil of anger and the determination of the lieutenant, connecting both physical and psychological aspects in such a way that he makes me taste and smell it in my head. He describes the simple act of a guy getting up out of a chair, but he exhausts it, in a few lines, and creates something solid out of his ingredients.

What is singled out, penetrated, and rendered in a few words is done so with reference to specific, everyday things: "Close to the grass, I'm green."[3] "By this time the mad sergeant had lost the last rags of his reason. . . ."[4] "Through the window Viira saw Joose, and in a dither of excitement she straightened carpets, forced more firewood into the range, settled the coffee pot, dragged benches into position, and ran to the sitting room for a clean new tablecloth."[5]

Descriptions absent of such anchors are treated through hints and gestures in

Finnish writing. And its special balance of the specific and the general tends to make fiction in Finland short, and difficult for the novel to flourish. *The Manila Rope,* for instance, is actually a tight group of stories rather than a novel.

It follows that Finnish writing is not generally panoramic. Its effect is not that of Tolstoy's, in whose works all is accounted for, nothing omitted, all, in all its aspects, explained. So that one hesitates to put the book down, fearful that its characters might smother in the paper. It might be the end of life itself since life depends on Tolstoy's telling of it. This is Tolstoy's genius. He absorbs us, he makes us content with our drab lives against which another world, seen through his eyes and heard through his voice, is exciting and sufficient.

Finnish literature on the other hand is meant to accompany rather than to substitute life. It is a companion, a buddy to push against—someone who doesn't bring news or sing a song, but someone with whom you can argue and drink, who says, "Yes, it sure is shitty, isn't it . . . I mean the way. . . ." It's a buddy from wartime when there was no coffee, boots were wet, and you washed your brains and crotch in cold water.

There are no pastry chefs in the kitchens of modern Finnish literature, no jewels on its bookcovers—except an occasional moonstone—no embroidery. Its elegance is that of a mathematical proof or a black goldfish near the surface of a pond. The Finns write about acres of white snow where there are patches of blood, rain, liquor, and remains of dogs and men—footprints made by boots or bare feet. All is on the same plane making similar imprints in the snow along with the sun and giant tree trunks.

What Edith Hamilton said about English and Greek writing and how the Finns are like the Greeks and not the English.

Edith Hamilton wrote:

Everywhere fancy travels with a tight rein in the poetry [and prose] of Greece, as everywhere in English poetry [and prose] it is given free course. Byron [writes]:

—the monarch of mountains.
They crowned him long ago
On a throne of rocks, in a robe of clouds,
With a diadem of snow.

When Aeschylus has the same thing in mind, he will allow himself a single touch, but no more:

the mighty summit, neighbor to the stars.[6]

Plain writing is not the English genius . . . the words are like rich embroidery.[7]

Like the Greeks, the Finns are plain. They are stark and accustomed to reserve. Their fiction moves with subtlety, and their writing is not fancy. One of Meri's most lyrical descriptions is:

The card game continued. Otherwise all was quiet in the wagon, most of the men in sleep or dream. A red glare had crept into the light, the day itself close to the hands of night, but even yet they hadn't reached the old frontiers of Finland.[8]

And this is pared enough to be inscribed on a building without tiring a stone engraver. This is sculpture, not tapestry.

"Greek writing," Hamilton states, "depends no more on ornament than the Greek statue does. . . . It often seems, when translated with any degree of literalness, bare, so unlike what we are used to as even to repel."[9] As this anthology shows, Finnish writing is likewise unornamented. Sometimes its authors prefer to say in two ways rather than decorate it when the plain statement they seek is inadequate: "No shout went up; not even the faintest echo from the forest could be heard."[10] Kirstinä does likewise: "One of her eyes was brown, and so was the other."[11] Note how this beautiful and coquettish line teases with redundancy. Pylkkönen says it twice to say it strongly, and intimately: "The boys were told to go to bed and to shut their eyes."[12] Here again redundancy is effective, although mothers of little boys may deny it. More plain writing: "It has been raining all night. The grass is bending back from your footsteps."[13] He does not say he feels tender, but he shows us that it is with tenderness that he sees her path. In these examples there is no ornament, yet they are not bare. The same is true of most of the stories and poems in this book.

Yet I am sure there are parts of this anthology that will seem to some "bare . . . as even to repel." Some Finnish literature does leave English readers unmoved. Sometimes what is singled out, penetrated, and exploded appears too insignificant to support such excavation. Sometimes the Finnish writer works from too little substance. One may feel the subject is weak, or, if one believes all subjects have equal promise, that they are not made relevant or are not well handled. There are dangers, of course, inherent in any starkness of style. One cloud in a sky is not always an interesting cloud or even a sky. We must judge between what is bare of ornament and what is bare of substance. These Finns acquaint us with such a simple but superb diet that we are disappointed when their dishes are imperfect.

Hamilton uses the verb *seems* here: "It often seems when translated with any degree of literalness, bare. . . ."[14] She wants us to come to like the Greeks as they are, not as Englished ancients, and not as translated by Gilbert Murray who wrote:

I have often used a more elaborate diction than Euripides did because I found that, Greek being a very simple and austere language and English an ornate one, a direct translation produced an effect of baldness which was quite unlike the original.[15]

Hamilton wants us to accustom ourselves to translations as "brief and little adorned as the original. . . ."[16] She despairs because our translators refuse to let them be bare, "The mighty summit, neighbor to the stars."

Fortunately, translators from the Finnish do not set up such a barrier against the Finns. They are not tempted as was Gilbert Murray. This is true probably in part because English has changed in a direction that complements Finnish style, and also because the translators in this anthology seem aware of Murray's mistaken goals.

García among the Finns; on clichés; on nature as the other person in a Finn's life—how he loves nature as a pagan and draws metaphor from trees.

García among the Finns

While reading this anthology, a friend gave me Gabriel García Márquez's *One Hundred Years of Solitude*. Early on I found these six sentences:

By then Melquíades had aged with surprising rapidity. On his first trips he seemed to be the same age as José Arcadio Buendía. But while the latter had preserved his extraordinary strength, which permitted him to pull down a horse by grabbing its ears, the gypsy seemed to have been worn down by some tenacious illness. It was, in reality, the result of multiple and rare diseases contracted on his innumerable trips around the world. According to what he himself said as he spoke to José Arcadio Buendía while helping him set up the laboratory, death followed him everywhere, sniffing at the cuffs of his pants, but never deciding to give him the final clutch of its claws. He was a fugitive from all the plagues and catastrophes that had ever lashed mankind. He had survived pellagra in Persia, scurvy in the Malayan archipelago, leprosy in Alexandria, beriberi in Japan, bubonic plague in Madagascar, an earthquake in Sicily, and a disastrous shipwreck in the Strait of Magellan.

This gypsy Melquíades obviously carried me far away from my blueberries. While reading García, I felt as if I had fallen asleep in a floating garden and just been awakened by the gentle rocking of my boat wedged among thick, perfumed hyacinths.

García collects words, and creates situations for them. His collection is vast, and its effect is accumulative, a waterfall next to which the Finns are an indoor Chinese fountain, a tropical storm compared to a frost. *One Hundred Years of Solitude* is a rich embroidery—English but not Greek. The Finn on the other hand fills up fewer pages because of the way he winnows his language. He selects, scrapes off, and trims everything. He is direct, clean-lined, almost abbreviated. He uses strong verbs (". . . ants struggled through his hair . . ."[18]) rather than verbs lit with adverbs. He is unflorid, and sparing with adjectives—those he uses cling to their nouns like barnacles. His effect, for these reasons, is immediate rather than cumulative. He uses good metaphor to clench descriptions that are exact, quick, piercing, and unromantic. His metaphors can sting like ice water.

García, on the other hand, seems to clench his paragraphs with *lo bizarro, lo fantástico, lo inesperado*. Although sparing of detail, the Finn makes you feel that his stories are true; García's prose brims with detail and intimacy, but it reads like a yarn because he *describes* the world of his characters whereas Meri *defines* the world of his:

They had constructed their field lavatory in a wood, a few hundred feet behind the station. The morning after their departure it too had vanished, without a trace. People wondered what they had done with the pole or the two wooden

sheer-legs. It was generally agreed that they had carried them off with them.
The pit was filled and carefully overlaid with sods of grass. Not a single piece
of wastepaper, not a used matchstick or cigarette butt was to be seen. The pit
near the station where they had deposited their garbage was filled in as well.
They had even buried their stale bread. Like smoke in the wind, the Germans
had vanished.[19]

After reading the Finns, I want to take in my belt a notch; I had gained
weight reading *One Hundred Years of Solitude.*

On clichés

Both García and the Finns avoid clichés. García does so because he is a good
writer; the Finns do so out of a passion to restate the universe, which does
not appear to be García's mission.

Clichés are like static on the radio. If there is enough interference, the effect
is lost and the gist is undone. Falsehood is not the objection to clichés, since
they are seldom false. Rather they are like a record that skips so that you hear
the same part over and over, and after a while you don't hear it at all, or you
become bored and turn it off.

Clichés ruin fiction in a similar way. We stop listening, even hearing, when
we come across them. We begin to skip over phrases and lines, and soon assume
we know what the author means, and before long we are lost. The senses are
deadened by clichés. We become drowsy and our pores clog. Our eyes blur,
our ears stop up, our fingers lose their touch.

In methodically avoiding clichés, the modern Finns tend to search for fresh
descriptions that yield a tight link between the reader and writer.

On nature as the other person in a Finn's life, how he loves it as a pagan and draws metaphor from trees.

At times I have thought that stories and poems are like letters written to
oneself, to a friend, a lover, a parent, stranger, or for a cause perhaps. I think
the "other person" in a Finn's life, those to whom his letters are addressed, are
things in nature, the oracle of his soul.

Upon reading *A Girl and a Bottle, Long Ago, Boy for a Summer,* Haavikko's
poems, I think many readers will feel that the Finnish writer has a special buddy
in nature. I guess that it's from the forests that he has learned his lesson of
balance—the relation of straight line to curved, positive to negative space, the
effect of one color next to or seen through another, the relation of the simple
to the complex, the importance of economy, disdain for ornamentation. He is
accustomed to boldness and now and then it seems he is trying to learn the
language of the trees with whom he would speak. In some places, the author
is absent and only the trees are left. The reason he struggles with written language is that he is trying to communicate with nature and he seeks to hear its
intonations, and to gather its gestures and complements.

The sun, a little time before, had gone behind its tall ridge. Mansard roof
of the world, it seemed from the gable. Between the trunks was this dying
blood red light, as if the forest was on fire, but little by little it weakened.
The forest was locking its gates for the night. . . . And when the far field
rose upright into the night and the forest was close enough to touch, Joose

turned towards the kitchen. As a child he'd always been overwhelmed by this incomprehensible vision, but now that it was dark he was free to give his attention to the things about him.[21]

And in the pagan language of the trees he finds metaphor for infinity and fate:

On the open road each man has to walk, so to speak, under the watchful eye of the world: but in the forest he can feel safe from all eyes, even the eye of God. In a thunderstorm, sheltering under some tree there, we easily start to imagine that it's our own tree that will be struck, and not even Providence will be able to turn it aside.[22]

A note on what a painter told me about negative space and how the Finns often use it in constructing their literature.

When you draw a face on a steamy window with your finger, the face makes a positive shape and the steam a negative shape.

If I stand in the doorway with my hands on my hips and my legs spread apart, you will see not only me, the positive shape, but also two small triangles of space between my arms and my body, the larger triangle of space made by my legs and the floor, and you will see past me through these triangles, these negative spaces that have always been an essential concern of the painter.

The subject of space, of course, includes the problem of optics. Why does the sun appear to be a hole in the sky? Forgetting what we know: Is the cloud in front of the sky or is there a deckled opening in the sky behind which I see the cloud? Which is positive and which is negative space? How are they integrated?

Once the painter learns to see, his work gains form and he sees what is essential to the picture. Then he can eliminate, add, change, imagine. Literature requires this as well. The writer must learn to see what is before him, grasp the whole, the truth, then he can focus, edit, put into relief those things that he singles out and imagines. Sometimes this can be accomplished on the first try; usually it takes great pains and a changed perspective to make irrelevancies fade.

Only certain impressions make up a story and in turn these must be enlivened and built up. It may require a changed mood or a fresh approach to unclutter our impressions and allow focal points to surface. Carson McCullers said she had the whole of *The Heart Is a Lonely Hunter* written before she realized that John Singer had to be deaf-and-dumb.

All literature gathers from experience, but, like Carson McCullers, the modern Finnish writers define their characters with especially sharp lines, set their stories in high relief, and give particular attention to negative shapes. Stroke against stroke, they build balance of characters, characters and setting, parts and whole. They contrast and fit. In *The Dam* the little boy and his work are described with penetration and set in high contrast against the small triangles of the laundress and "them." Look at Antti Hyry's lines:

"You've got a fine place for water there. Goodness me."
And the laundress went down to the brook and put her bucket under the mouth of the sluice. Red-checked kerchief and apron fluttering, she looked at the bucket and the sluice. The water splashed on her apron, her hands held

the handle of the bucket tightly. The bucket soon filled. The laundress went away with her full bucket. . . .

"Funny old bag."

And he remembered the laundress drinking coffee, contented looking, chattering and sitting a bit sideways in her chair.[23]

The old laundress is not just pasted on the page. She is both interesting in herself and essential to the construction of the story about the boy. Without her and the negative space she provides, the story would lack dimension, balance, and dialogue.

García, of course, selects. He does not tell us every single thing he can imagine about every character, yet he paints them with their jewelry on, flags flying, and decorates every edge. Yet, the Finns give their characters just enough air to breathe while Garcías luxuriate in tropical greenhouses.

This special technique of isolating and penetrating the core of a subject quickly and incisively is a talent that unifies the postwar Finnish writing in this book. The style is strong and winning. Even though one turns anxiously from story to story and story to poem, the essence of its talent remains as bold and elusive as transparent Arctic air.

NOTES

1. Veijo Meri, *The Manila Rope*, trans. John McGahern and Annika Laaksi (New York: Alfred A. Knopf, 1967) , p. 79.
2. Ibid., p. 16.
3. Paavo Haavikko, Poetry, *Literary Review*, 14, no. 1 (Fall, 1970) : 91.
4. Veijo Meri, *The Manila Rope*, p. 76.
5. Veijo Meri, *The Manila Rope*, p. 112.
6. Edith Hamilton, *The Greek Way to Western Civilization* (Mentor, Ohio: New American Library, 1957) , p. 52.
7. Ibid., p. 49.
8. Veijo Meri, *The Manila Rope*, p. 21.
9. Edith Hamilton, *The Greek Way*, p. 48.
10. Veijo Meri, *The Manila Rope*, p. 17.
11. Väinö Kirstinä, "Two Poems", *Literary Review*, 14, no. 1 (Fall, 1970) : 125.
12. Maila Pylkkönen, *The School Teacher's Wife, Literary Review*, 14, no. 1 (Fall, 1970) : 115.
13. Pekka Virtanen, "Four Poems," *Literary Review*, 14, no. 1 (Fall, 1970) : 123.
14. Edith Hamilton, *The Greek Way*, p. 48.
15. Edith Hamilton, *The Greek Way*, p. 49.
16. Edith Hamilton, *The Greek Way*, p. 49.
17. Gabriel García Márquez, *One Hundred Years of Solitude*, trans. Gregory Rabassa (New York: Harper & Row, 1970) , pp. 5–6.
18. Veijo Meri, *The Manila Rope*, p. 110.
19. Veijo Meri, *The Manila Rope*, p. 96.
20. Pentti Saarikoski, "Pope and Czar," *Odyssey Review* 3, no. 1 (1963) : 149.
21. Veijo Meri, *The Manila Rope*, p. 117.
22. Veijo Meri, *The Manila Rope*, p. 109.
23. Antti Hyry, *Dam*, in this volume.

PHILIP BINHAM

New Finnish Drama—The Fifties and After

Just as the early fifties mark some sort of turning point in Western drama generally, so the late fifties reveal Finland following the new trends and searching for a more vital theater. Before this, Finnish plays had for years concentrated more or less on representing stark rural life more or less faithfully. At the same time, there had naturally been a sprinkling of drawing-room and barnyard comedy. Now, plays like *Waiting for Godot* were seen in Helsinki soon after their Paris premiere. They encouraged Finnish writers to experiment with freer forms; to make their own use of the theater of the absurd and the epic, Brechtian stage.

It is tempting to trace modern Finnish epic theater back to 1940, when Brecht himself came to Finland as a refugee and lived on the estate of Hella Wuolijoki, socialist and distinguished playwright herself. As the names reveal, Brecht's *Herr Puntila und sein Knecht Matti* is based on his Finnish experience—in fact, Brecht got the plot from Wuolijoki.

After the Second World War, Hella Wuolijoki had a considerable influence on Finnish drama as director of the Finnish Radio. She created a Radio Theater and encouraged such young writers as Chorell and Manner. Radio and TV have been important media for other writers, including Haavikko, Mannerkorpi, Meri, and V. V. Järner.

Among the new writers of the fifties, Chorell was among the most prolific. Like Järner, Chorell writes in Swedish and is consequently well known in Sweden. His early play *Grass* (1958) aroused keen attention, with its deliberate emphasis on "this is only a play, we are only players," and its theme of un-wittingly incestuous love. Later, Chorell has introduced new, usually urban environments and new sectors of society to the Finnish stage. His plays often deal with abnormal or at least unusual persons who reject or are rejected by the community. In *Cats* (1961) all the characters are women workers in a factory; the central theme is an apparently lesbian relationship and the violent feelings it generates among the other women. On the surface, Chorell appears to view his creations with a psychiatrist's air of coolness and objectivity, but at times one feels he identifies strongly with them. He has a powerful sense of the theater, creates challenging parts for his actors, but sometimes seems to have difficulty in sustaining his themes. He is a highly skilled writer, with a range from farce (*The Motherless Ones*) to tragedy (*Madame*).

Chorell is unusual in Finland in that he is best known as a dramatist. Eeva-Liisa Manner is primarily a poet, and not surprisingly her early play *Eros and Psyche* (1959) is written in verse; its texture is as ethereal as its subject. In her later, prose plays the style is poetic but powerful. There is a roughness in *New*

Year's Eve (1965) —a sort of Finnish *Who's Afraid of Virginia Woolf,* although the author did not know Albee's play when she wrote it. In *New Year's Eve* a number of cultured people are gathered together to welcome in the new year; as they get more and more drunk they become less and less inhibited and indulge in a sort of spiritual striptease.

Manner's more recent plays about the problems of very young women, *Snow in May* (1966) and *Burnt Orange* (1968) are more tender. *Snow in May* is a picture of a physically precocious but emotionally childish teenage girl's loveless environment. *Burnt Orange* also concentrates on the destruction of a young girl; here the family environment is sexually stifling. In these plays Manner, like Chorell, shows a preoccupation with psychology. One of the main characters in *Burnt Orange* is a psychiatrist, while the published edition of *Snow in May* is prefaced by this quotation:

I am gradually beginning to get used to the idea that all sexual activity is between four people. We shall have much to say about this later.

S. Freud

Another poet, Paavo Haavikko, has proved a playwright of distinction. In the fifties, along with Chorell's *Grass,* Haavikko's *Munchausen* (1958) was heralded as a signpost of the "new" Finnish drama. Haavikko has a strong sense of history, and in both *Munchausen* and *Agricola and the Fox* (1968) his feeling for political parallels is sharply apparent. For the Helsinki City Theater production of the latter play, directed by the brilliant young Kalle Holmberg, the part of Ivan the Terrible was played to resemble Stalin, with startling effect. Haavikko turns to the grotesque in *The Superintendent* (1968). In this television play psychology—albeit in its early stages—is to the fore again. Haavikko has been accused of lacking warmth; on the other hand, his frosty, ironic approach is especially suitable for satire.

Since so many of the principal playwrights of the fifties and sixties have also been distinguished poets, their dialogue has tended to be highly personal, shifting away from the realistic and colloquial speech of most earlier Finnish drama. But nobody today is writing more individual dialogue for the stage than the novelist and short-story writer Veijo Meri. Along with his ability to write spare, revealing, and amusing dialogue, Meri also has an acute sense for the absurd situation. His *Private Jokinen's Wedding Leave* (1969) is highly effective and wildly funny. Meri is adept at gaining comic effect by juxtaposing the realistic with the surrealistic. *Private Jokinen* describes in brief, episodic fragments the adventures of a Finnish Schwejk, harmless, smiling, and happy-go-lucky, as he makes his way from the front towards home. As elsewhere in Meri's work, the play's message—though there is no trace of open pronouncement—is felt as a comment on the lunacy of war.

Of the younger writers, Juhani Peltonen—a poet once again—is among the most promising. His plays deal with a world of young people of intellectual bent, the sickness of the children of this era, the pressures of the times and between generations. His situations, disconnected from reality, show affinities with the absurd theater, and especially with Polish plays like Mrozek's *Tango.* His dialogue is a skilful blend of poetry and everyday language. *The Birthday*

(1968), a play about a young man who commits suicide, is perhaps his most complete achievement.

Towards the end of the sixties, studies of the recent political past, plays based on documentary material as well as purely political theater, reached the Finnish stage following the trend elsewhere. These plays are often characterized by a trenchant, cabaret style, with the numbers played straight to the audience, and an unconcealed intention to influence the spectator's opinions directly. The best example of this genre, as yet unsurpassed, is *Opera of Lapua*.

Some plays seem—at least when they first appear—more important than their authors. This was true of *Opera of Lapua* when it was performed at the Helsinki Student Theater in 1965. A serious musical dealing with an extreme right-wing attempt at a takeover in the Finland of the early thirties, its extreme youthful vitality, aggressive questioning of older beliefs, and simple political message stirred up controversy far beyond the theater. It was the joint work of the left-wing poet Arvo Salo, who has spent much of his energies in politics, Kai Chydenius, a gifted songwriter, the members of the Student Theater, who were deeply involved in the play and its ideas, and Kalle Holmberg, the director. Holmberg is the most conspicuous of a number of young men and women of the theater—left wing, socially conscious, and highly intelligent—who have striven mightily to bring the Finnish theater closer to their ideals and to a wider public—sometimes at the risk of deafening or boring their audiences.

Few other playwrights have dealt with the Finnish political past directly, but there have been several adaptations of novels for the stage, such as Väinö Linna's *Here Under the Northern Star*. Ilmari Turja's *Headquarters* (1968) is based on documentary material: the central figure is Marshal Mannerheim and the subject the cracking of the Finnish front at the Karelian Isthmus in 1944. The events of the same critical period are the basis for Pekka Lounela's *The Man Who Shot a Cat* (1970), but here the writer examines the aggressiveness and behavior in war of a single, violent individual.

Along with these serious, sometimes gloomy studies of war and the past, there have been plenty of brighter plays, some of them touching lightly but keenly on social problems. The most popular Finnish play in 1970 was *Goodbye, Mansikki* by Jouko Puhakka. It is an amusing portrayal of the "developing" areas of northern Karelia, from which the rural population is drifting away. Mansikki is a familiar Finnish name for a cow. . . . Conditions in Lapland are described in a playful, fantastic vein in *Hell 16* by Oiva Arvola and Jorma Etto. In cabaret form, this play imagines a Lapland that has cut itself off from the Finnish Republic—it is left with its tourists and its reindeer, but also with its chronic unemployment.

Absurd, epic, individual, social, protesting, pitying, documentary, fantastic, tender, grotesque, realistic, surrealistic—the Finnish drama seems to have covered most of the international trends and emotions in the past two decades (has the theater of cruelty failed to appeal to Finnish playwrights?). Together with their awareness of what the world is thinking, Finland's dramatists—like her poets and novelists—are still keenly interested in their own, specially Finnish experience. The combination has a tang all of its own—it is high time that audiences of the English-speaking world were given a chance to savor it.

Footnote on Finnish Drama

Richard Dauenhauer

Philip Binham's essay happily replaces my apologies for inadequate treatment of drama in my introduction to the Finnish issue of *The Literary Review*. I would, however, like to add some meager comments as a footnote, and to those add a few excerpts from a subsequent article by Jaakko Ahokas.

What little secondary literature exists on the subject leads me to conclude that the mainstream of Finnish drama, unlike the poetry and prose, is derivative and firmly entrenched in the naturalist-realist tradition. It is, for example, perplexing yet typical that while a play by Ionesco had its world premier in Helsinki (although in Swedish, by a Swedish-speaking company) in 1955, two years before it reached Paris, Finnish writing and productions remain for the most part traditional. Mrs. Ritva Heikkilä of the Finnish National Theater notes in one of her articles[1] that their repertoire consists mainly of translations and nineteenth-century Finnish favorites by Aleksis Kivi and Minna Canth, who are considered unsurpassed. An example of this realistic strain even in experimental Finnish theater is the world famous outdoor summer theater in Tampere, in which the audience rotates and the action takes place along the perimeter. The longest run has been a dramatization of Linna's novel, *The Unknown Soldier,* which has used real airplanes in some of the battle scenes. Other well-received Finnish plays would be of little interest outside Finland: for example, the very popular play *The Unknown Patient (Tuntematon Potilas)* is a commentary on Finnish conditions and relies, as the title suggests, being a pun on *Tuntematon Sotilas—The Unknown Soldier,* on the audience's knowledge of things Finnish.

Prof. Jaakko Ahokas's article of ten years later speaks frankly of the problem:

> It is very strange, with all the interest in theater in Finland, there is not a single great dramatic author in the country. . . . There are many remarkable novelists, poets, and short-story writers in Finland, but no one person you could call a playwright, who has written mainly . . . or only plays. Almost all have been written by persons who wrote mainly novels, short stories, or poetry and who once or twice tried their hand at writing drama.[2]

The bulk of Ahokas's article demonstrates the public interest in theater in Finland. For example, one table illustrates how ticket sales outnumbered the population for nine of the largest cities in Finland. In Joensuu, with a population of 30,000, 50,000 tickets were sold in 1958; the 1958 population of Helsinki was 430,000, and 490,000 tickets were sold. Much of the article deals with technicalities of construction, financial support, and business management, after which the author returns to the playwrights, and their reception by the public.

Minna Canth (1844–1897) is considered, after Kivi, the second greatest playwright. Ahokas writes of one of her plays:

The public protested so violently after the first night that the Board of Trustees

ordered the performances be discontinued. . . . Today her plays are not much performed in Finland and are not found radical at all. They are felt to be a bit naive. . . .[3]

Changing times seem to have affected the public reception of Hella Wuolijoki (1886–1954). Ahokas writes that her plays

were thought to be very radical at that time, (the late 1930s) and the author herself had political left-wing sympathies for which she was jailed during the last war when Finland was fighting the Soviet Union. Now it is difficult to see where the radicalism is.[4]

Ahokas argues that many Finnish plays are well written, but do not seem to work out well on stage. For example:

Technically, there is nothing wrong with it or Mrs. Wuolijoki's other plays. It's the contents that do not seem quite convincing. [or] Paavo Haavikko has written two plays which present a very personal and poetic view of the world— so personal and poetic they have not had much success on the stage, although admittedly they are beautifully written.[5]

Writing of one of Eeva-Liisa Manner's plays:

It is written in beautiful language, but lacks action because the characters speak about their feelings rather than act. It is justly admired as a work of art but it has never had any success on stage.[6]

Because the Manner play mentioned above is not the one included in this anthology, the reader is left with the Haavikko play alone to consider in light of these comments. Professor Ahokas concludes his article with the following paragraph:

As yet, Finland is still waiting for a truly great playwright. One could say that everything has been done to make things easy for him. The theaters are there, the actors are there, the money to finance the production is there, and the audiences are there. One day he or she will surely appear.[7]

NOTES

1. Ritva Heikkilä, "The Finnish National Theater," *American-Scandinavian Review* 49, no. 4 (1961) : 365–73.
2. Jaako Ahokas, "Finnish Drama and Culture," *Michigan Academician* 3, no. 3 (Winter 1971): 45–53.
3. Ibid.
4. Ibid.
5. Ibid.
6. Ibid.
7. Ibid.

INGMAR SVEDBERG

Political Poetry in Modern Finnish Literature

At regular intervals the question of politics, or commitment, in literature comes up for discussion. The opposition between Jean Paul Sartre and Claude Simon, between Peter Weiss and Hans Magnus Enzensberger, a few years ago, naturally has its counterpart in Finnish literature. This article is an attempt to comment on the committed poetry appearing in some Finnish collections of poetry published in the last few years. The survey does not claim to be exhaustive.

It may be necessary to define at the start what we mean by *committed* poetry. The term is frequently used to describe certain kinds of poetry. There are many different kinds of commitment, and there is no reason why one should be worse than the others. I suggest that instead of *committed* we should use the term *political,* for it is less open to misunderstanding. But what is a political poem? Some people claim that all poetry is political. Their argument is based on the idea that human intercourse is a form of *politics* between the individuals in a society, that poems are an instrument of this intercourse, and must also, therefore, be political. Here, the word *political* is used in such a wide sense that it almost loses all meaning. It is considerably more reasonable to use the word in the generally accepted sense; a word concerned with the State and its functions. In this sense, at least three qualities of political poetry can be distinguished: 1) it reflects a political situation, 2) it is an account of certain political attitudes and stands, 3) it suggests a certain form of political action. These distinctions may naturally overlap, they appear in differing degrees, and in some cases one of them may not be present at all.

In the mid-60s, discussions on cultural policy frequently put the young generation of the sixties in opposition to that of the fifties. In the early fifties, lyrical modernism made its final breakthrough in Finland. This modernism sometimes went too far in its scepticism, sterile intellectualism, and hermeticism. Some of the young lyricists of the sixties wanted to act in conscious opposition to the lyrics of the previous decade, while often they built, unconsciously, on the work of the modernists. Pentti Saarikoski, one of the lyricists who benefited from the teachings of the fifties, and developed them further, wrote a much-discussed essay in 1963 called "On Dialectical Poetry." This proved the starting point for many aspects of Finnish political poetry. Saarikoski's argument goes roughly like this: we live in a time of many fast changes. The present is the past, shattered into pieces. A new future is built up out of these pieces, a future we cannot yet experience. In this situation we need two forms of poetry: a complicated poetry, that analyzes the dispersal of the language, and a very simple poetry that builds up a new language. The new/restored poetry advances on two fronts: destructive/constructive. Saarikoski maintains that the characteristic of dialectic poetry is that it puts the classless society into practice in the language. All works and senses are of equal value, but the poet must make a conscious choice between them. Saarikoski's collection *Mitä tapahtuu todella?* (*What's Really Happening?,*

1962), perhaps the most influential collection of the decade, evokes a political reality throughout. The everyday idyll of the poems is interrupted by dry comments on high rents, the Berlin crisis, domestic policy. The same rare blend of opposed elements appears again in the next collection *Kuljen missä kuljen* (*Walking Where I Walk*, 1965). Compared with the fifties, Finnish poetry has gained a much wider and more varied reality. For some years, Saarikoski was the leading figure in political poetry, and his publications included socialist agitation poems, meant to be read to large audiences. He has since become more introspective, writing polished miniature poems on life and death.

Väinö Kirstinä's poems have also shown a change to more and more *impure, unlyrical* reality. Big city civilization, technology, and advertising slogans play an increasingly important part in his poetry. His collections *Luonnollinen tanssi* (*Natural Dance*, 1965) and *Pitkän tähtäyksen LSD-suunnitelma* (*Long-range LSD Plan*, 1967) discuss man's helplessness in the waste land of technology in ironic, dadaistically playful leaps. Kirstinä, too, takes a stand on the big questions of the day, although he does it indirectly, with a surprised, sceptical smile.

The sixties have also brought forward a demand for the expansion of the very idea of poetry. Arvo Salo, author and cultural debater, claims that it should be possible to use the poem for widely differing purposes. It should be possible to combine the poem with light music and protest songs. He recommends that poetry should be written in a popular, journalistic style, in the idiom of the day. Salo himself has put his ideal into practice by writing great quantities of occasional poems to order. The collection *Tilauksia* (*Commissions*, 1966) consists of pungent cabaret songs and political poems on current events; the language is such that it can reach a large public. His musical *Lapualaisooppera* (*Lapua Opera*, 1965), describing the struggle between fascists and socialists in Finland in the thirties, is of greater and more enduring worth. The finale of the opera is a mighty plea for nonviolence, an expression of the idealism of the younger generation. Three authors ran in the 1966 parliamentary elections, and Arvo Salo was the only one of them to be returned to Parliament.

Finnish lyric poetry developed in the main along the lines predicted by Salo. The poets set enthusiastically to work on song lyrics and cabaret texts. Within a few years a lively, fresh cabaret tradition, following in Brecht's footsteps, had been created. Marja-Leena Mikkola wrote many of the texts for the cabarets written for Finnish radio and television, presenting pointed, droll criticism of defects in Finnish society, such as housing policy and restaurant regulations. The television cabaret, Circus Europa (a traveling circus), is an attempt to discuss the gap between the rich and the poor nations of the world in a popular, easily comprehended form.

Student radicalism, familiar throughout the world, came to Finland much later than to other countries. Awareness of the problems of the Third World has thus been very slight. This has been reflected in literature, which to a large extent ignores international conflicts completely. It is hardly surprising, then, that the first attempt at an internationally aware poetry should come from a poet who spends most of his time traveling abroad. Matti Rossi first made a name as a translator of Spanish and Latin American literature, before publishing his first collection of poems, *Näytelmän henkilöt* (*Dramatis Personae*, 1965). The characters are de Gaulle, Ulbricht, Erhard, Khrushchev, and the Pope, all appearing in different poems. In the last section of the collection, a group of

American soldiers from Vietnam talk about their life and their situation. Rossi's independent, unusual poetic temperament unites a knowledge of the international lyric tradition and up-to-date reportage. His second collection *Leikkejä kahdelle* (*Games for Two*, 1966) is all about love, its appearance and gradual fading. The third collection, *Tilaisuus* (*Occasion*, 1967), turns outward again towards the world: the pressure and the economic system that keep the poor sections of the world down are critically examined. He seems, like Shakespeare, to see the world as a machinery of power, where actors and spectators are equally fettered victims of their destiny.

The events of August 1968 in Czechoslovakia left many traces in Finnish poetry. Rossi's *Käännekohta* (*Turning Point*, 1968) is a bitter indictment of the double morality of the great powers and the lies they use to mask crimes. As a left-wing intellectual he takes a coolly critical look at the crisis in world Communism following the invasion of Czechoslovakia. In his closely packed prose poems he uses his biting satire to comment on the ends and means of great power politics.

Eeva-Liisa Manner, the unobtrusive lyricist of the fifties, is not as intellectually analytical as Rossi. In her collection *Jos suru savuaisi* (*If Sorrow Smoked*, 1968) she expresses her sorrow and despair over the world situation after those same events of August. As one of the poems says, there seems to be *eine kleine Machtmusik* playing everywhere.

Ever since the thirties there has been an unbroken tradition of radical left-wing proletarian poetry. Arvo Turtiainen belongs to the older generation, but his poems have experienced a renaissance in the sixties. His Helsinki poems in particular, written in slang, have captured the fancy of the young public, while his poems of social criticism have gained a new relevance. The collections *Hyvää joulua* (*Merry Christmas*, 1967) and *Puhetta Porthaninrinteellä* (*Speech on Porthaninrinne*, 1968) are stamped with humor and a warm acceptance of life, but the old radical identity also makes its appearance in some poems with a social and political emphasis: the privileged society and its extravagance in a world of starving children comes in for its share of criticism.

Lassi Sinkkonen is an heir of classic Finnish worker poetry, and continues its traditions. Almost all Sinkkonen's poems are strongly realistic; in his first two collections he creates small portraits, and tells life histories or anecdotes. In *Sinusta huomiseen* (*From You to Tomorrow*, 1967) his grasp has become surer and more personal. In his poems he asks the questions that have become increasingly important for the workers' movement in the society of the sixties. In the collection *Meitä kohti* (*Towards Us*, 1968) he searches for an undogmatic openness and a living warmth. His most caustically ironic poems with the heaviest content of social criticism, nevertheless, have at their core a tender, loving relationship to the world and environment. The collection *Minä maani maailmassa* (*Me, My Country, in the World*, 1969) takes up the questions forced on a socialist poet by the events in Czechoslovakia. Sinkkonen has also published a highly acclaimed novel with a factory setting.

Claes Andersson, the Finland-Swedish poet, sprang a surprise with his fourth collection of poems, *Samhället vi dör i* (*The Society We Die In*, 1967), by displaying a completely new character as poet. The international perspective has become more and more important in his poems. The experience of death, hunger, and suffering in the world has resulted in a way of writing free of all illusion,

where once or twice Andersson simply gives a documentary catalogue of dry facts.
He, too, has written cabaret texts and television plays with a content of social
criticism.

All poetry translated by Dympna Connolly

Eeva-Liisa Manner—"If Sorrow Smoked"

If sorrow smoked, the earth would be covered in smoke.
It is covered already
and returns to its ancient form, to the heart of night.

The conquerors come, the Middle Ages have returned
but without their medieval light:
not even the sky is clear any more.

The trees are bare.
Autumn
leads its misty horses to the river.

Distant dogs bark, distantly.
Small carts come through the gate,
alone, driverless, and vanish.

They say that's how ghosts ride
if the heart lies under a holm oak.
But ghosts are only memories.

Night comes early.
Soon it will be winter
like a well, deep and cold.

Matti Rossi—"Turning Point"

What is the Finnish way of life, and why should it be preserved,
    the issue is simply what should be preserved, how long, for whom,
        and who pays, the one with the most to lose
            thinks up the reasons for preserving things.

We'll preserve the graves, the stones and inscriptions, many
    have nothing more durable, then our own ground's paid for, inalienable.
        We'll preserve the churches, they're valuable, and the bells, they bring in
        the weekend, the souls like their clatter.

                The earth is conserved, the Finnish bedrock, a bit of soil, then
                    stone upon stone, the cities stand there
                        squarely, you just have to enjoy yourself,
a flock of Finns nesting in holes and money flowing like honey

into the coffers of the banks and private capitalists, conservers of the forms
of life
and the most eager conservers already own so much of Finland
that defending it they can truly say they fall for their own land,
and their lives were far from cheap.

Lassi Sinkkonen—"Me, My Country, in the World"

We talk of changes, we demand changes.
Changes we are not ripe for
are violence.
Changes without love lead to hate.
Changes without development are just changes.
Something carefully seen and said
is just seen and said.
Analysis of power is not power.
Human progress is a slow-growing tree,
sensitive to changes of season.
Let's read the old books, to find out
what's new in the new ones.

Claes Andersson—"The Society We Die In"

At the political meeting they said, for example,
that there's broadmindedness and broadmindedness
Your broadmindedness isn't worth much
But mine is a different question
The radicals said that being a liberal
meant being a slippery customer
the others said it was simply stupidity
I walked slowly home through a frozen city
thinking about what had been said
and everything left unsaid
although it was important
But once you've been to a political meeting
you aren't a liberal any more
and you're rarely at rest
Where did that nonpolitical birdsong get to?
What is "freedom with responsibility?"
For whose freedom am I responsible, to whom?
But there is still a dream
of living an evening
"that smells of books"
I'm on the way home from a political meeting
Frozen streets
I run with the wind

KAARINA SALA

Eeva-Liisa Manner: A Literary Portait

Eeva-Liisa Manner is one of the most international and individual poets in Finland. She is best known as a lyricist, though her literary output has also included plays, prose, and translations. When Eeva-Liisa Manner's fourth work, the poetry collection *Tämä matka* (*This Journey*), came out in 1956, it represented the breakthrough of Finnish modernism. Manner's highly original imagism was felt to be something new in postwar poetry. The poem was built up of images, and the contrapuntal construction of Manner's lyrics was a new advance in Finnish poetry. In fact *Tämä matka* meant a move towards a greater cosmopolitanism in Finnish poetry and a clear association with European modernism. Paradoxically, this breakthrough by Eeva-Liisa Manner's lyric poetry was perhaps most influenced by two prose writers; the imagery of Hermann Hesse and the Swedish-Finn Oscar Parland played a part in liberating Manner's own power of expression and the former's *Der Steppenwolf* and the latter's *Den förtrollade vägen* are, in fact, among her most important translations. As far as form is concerned, she has probably been most influenced by T. S. Eliot of all European poets, and the musical multilevel quality of his poetic form is reflected in other postwar Finnish poetry, too.

Eeva-Liisa Manner's childhood was spent in an international atmosphere, as the poem "Lapsuuden hämärästä" ("Dusk of Childhood") in *Tämä matka* and the prose fantasy *Tyttö taivaan laiturilla* (*Girl on Heaven's Quay*, 1951) show. She was born in 1921 and brought up in Viipuri, which her family had to leave during the war. Her first collection *Mustaa ja punaista* (*Black and Red*, 1944) was written in the middle of the dislocation of the war, and *Kuin tuuli tai pilvi* (*Like Wind or Cloud*, 1949) is still the same kind of traditional mood lyric. A portrait of Eeva-Liisa Manner has much in it of a Cassandra, foretelling mankind's disasters, as the name of a collection of poems from 1960 *Orfiset laulut* (*Orphic Songs*) indicates. The collection *Niin vaihtuivat vuoden ajat* (*So Changed the Seasons*, 1964) contains the most natural philosophy of all Eeva-Liisa Manner's poetry, and reflects the seasonal rhythm of Finland's lake landscape, its trees and birds. *Kirjoitettu kivi* (*Written on a Stone*, 1966) gets its mood of international nervous tension from the Mediterranean scene: Eeva-Liisa Manner, in fact, works part of the year in Spain, a country whose atmosphere finds powerful expression in the collection *Fahrenheit 121* (1968).

Eeva-Liisa Manner's individuality lies in both the mastery of form and the variation on the philosophy of loneliness that extend throughout her output. Sleep, play, space, and music are the most recurrent themes in her poetry. Her verse also reveals some of her spiritual kin through the centuries, such as Descartes, Spinoza, and Simone Weil. Eastern philosophers and Chinese poetry are also close to her. Eeva-Liisa Manner has said that Bach's music is the key to the clarity and logic of modern poetic expression; she has also dedicated some light, figurative poems to Mozart. Antique mythology is also one of the sources of Manner's inspiration and material. She has herself said of her verse play *Eros ja*

Psyke (*Eros and Psyche,* 1959) that she had "discreetly twisted the legend to make it more impressive," and the result is a very consistent and subtle series of variations on the consequences of the lovers' fancies and reserves. This verse play has been produced in the theater and on the radio, but proved particularly good material for the latter because of its ethereal effect and its dependency on the spoken language.

Of Eeva-Liisa Manner's plays, that with most dramatic power is perhaps *Uuden vuoden yö* (*New Year's Night,* 1965), which is about a party at which a number of intellectuals—a married couple, a clergyman, a scientist, a writer, and an actor—reveal that they are unhappy and insecure under their sophistication. These people's problems and their developing relations with each other come close to Albee's *Who's Afraid of Virginia Woolf,* which is purely coincidental and merely shows the urgency with which similar problems find expression in different writers at the same time. The central figure of the play *Toukokuun lumi* (*Snow in May,* 1966) is a young girl, as in *Poltettu oranssi* (*Burnt Orange,* 1968), a work parallel to the poetry collection *Fahrenheit 121. Poltettu oranssi* is the case history about the problems of a schizophrenic girl and her parents, set in the days of Freud. The bulk of the play's action is linguistic—even abnormalities are skilfully built up and expressed through the language. We are here approaching the very peripheries of linguistic creation. Study and mapping of the limits of the human mind and fantasy are, indeed, also characteristic of Eeva-Liisa Manner's other work.

Eeva-Liisa Manner is a unique writer ever capable of self-renewal. The first great change was from the playful, lightly poignant mood of the *Kuin tuuli tai pilvi* collection to the modern style of the "brain poetry" in *Tämä matka.* Her present deliberate orientation towards the drama shows the same individual strength, though the poet has so far always been central to this writer's literary being.

For a recent essay on Eeva-Liisa Manner, *see* Jaakko Ahokas, "Eeva-Liisa Manner: Dropping from Reality into Life," *Books Abroad* 47, no. 1 (Winter 1973): 60–65.

RICHARD DAUENHAUER

Some Notes on Zen Buddhist Tendencies
in Modern Finnish Poetry

There is a strong Zen Buddhist tendency in modern Finnish poetry, and it merges with the "objectivist" tendency or stylistic trait (discussed at length in the following essay) in the problem of the dichotomizing intellect of Western tradition, especially as it comes to bear on cold-war politics and attitudes toward nature. Like the Zen thinker, many of the Finnish poets (and some Soviets, such as Voznesensky, and several Americans as well) are searching for a truth that transcends dualism. William Barrett writes "what Zen seeks above all is the concrete and the simple that lie beyond the snarled tangle of intellectualization. Zen is the concrete itself."[1] And in much of both modern Finnish and American poetry we see a return to the concrete itself,[2] as in W. C. Williams's famous imagist poem about the red wheel barrow.

The passage about the noise made by the Golden-eye Duck in Snyder's *Myths and Texts*[3] parallels the Zen story about Hui-neng (639–713) who brought an abstract debate over the physics and philosophy of a flapping pennant to a quick halt by commenting "it is neither wind nor pennant but your own mind that flaps."[4] This endless flapping is perhaps the point of the otherwise pointless dialogue and monologue by the various characters and personae in much of Haavikko, such as in "Im Rovajärvi. . . ." Certainly such a poem, in which an East German statesman refers to the World War Two German dead in Finland as West German soldiers, and whose Germanic thoroughness extends only to the precise location of the graves, illustrates one of the basic objectives of Haavikko's style and work, as I see it, which may be described in the words of D. T. Suzuki:

To see dualism in life is due to confusion of thought; the wise, the enlightened, see into the reality of things unhampered by erroneous ideas.[5]

Once the duality and conceptualization are abandoned, once the desire to see one thing in terms of something else is given up, an awakening is experienced, as well as an increased ability to see things clearly.[6] The experience is beautifully put by Robert Bly in his poem "Watering the Horse":

How strange to think of giving up all ambition!
Suddenly I see with such clear eyes
The white flake of snow
That has just fallen in the horse's mane![7]

The process of awakening is long. Suzuki quotes one Zen master's description:

When I began to study Zen, mountains were mountains; when I thought I understood Zen, mountains were not mountains; but when I came to full knowledge of Zen, mountains were again mountains.[8]

Two Finnish poets describe the experience. Kalevi Lappalainen writes:

> There are many degrees of consciousness:
> I see a bird, I see a bird, I see a bird.

An example from Bo Carpelan, who writes in Swedish, reminds us again that Finnish national literature exists in two languages and demonstrates a conceptual similarity despite the language difference:

> Wintry trees,
> brittle, their stillness
> I saw, I didn't see
> when young.

Prerequisite is the absence of ambition described by Bly. Tuomas Anhava describes it, thusly, in a haikuish poem:

> I have stopped
> longing.
> I can't any more.

The result is reflected in another of his poems—a postawakening, nondualistic poem:

> I look out, it's very calm:
> a leaf falls, and a second leaf,
> and a third.

The Swedish-language poet Lars Huldén celebrates the same delight and satisfaction of mere perception of the concrete that we have seen in Williams, Bly, and others. His poem "On the Day of the Apostles Peter and Paul" describes two fish, and concludes

> never before had we seen
> perch glide so, as
> these did.

A poem by Pertti Nieminen provides a transition from the idea of delight in the concrete itself to pleasure derived from awareness of impermanence:

> The world full of gazelle tracks:
> let them be mine
> until the next rain.

The concept of impermanence is one of the common denominators in Haavikko's imagery—the house, real estate, the tree, the road versus traveling on it. For Haavikko, permanence is an illusion. His personae are obsessed with fixity and are unaware that their existence is one of fluidity and, as such, is as ephemeral as Nieminen's gazelle tracks. Haavikko is fond of emperor images and personae, and R. P. Blackmur's comment on Wallace Stevens's famous poem is also a magnificent statement on Haavikko:

> "The only emperor is the emperor of ice cream" implies in both stanzas that the only power worth heeding is the power of the moment, of what is passing, of the flux.[9]

Compare Haavikko's lines from "1960":

> . . . the decade changed although there's only one
> decade, only the one we're in,
> speech is as little a world as I am, changeable,
> fearing eviction from history.

that typically combine a number of his themes—themes that are also central in Buddhist thought; and in the essay, "The Analytic and Synthetic Approach to Buddhism," D. T. Suzuki touches upon some of these.[10] He proceeds from commentary on impermanence, per se, to the concept of new order deriving from the old in a never-ending flow. Suzuki writes that "affirmation and negation . . . must all be taken as the whole which is going on every moment in our experience."[11] This point is central to Haavikko's political poetry, but is more easily excerpted in Saarikoski. Suzuki's point pertains directly to Ingmar Svedberg's comments on Saarikoski in his essay "Political Poetry in Modern Finnish Literature," where he discusses the concept of "destructive/constructive" in Saarikoski. According to Svedberg, Saarikoski's argument in a 1963 essay runs thusly: "The present is the past, shattered into pieces. A new future is built up out of these pieces."

This is, of course, similar to the IWW (International Workers of the World) slogan, and Gary Snyder unites it with Buddhism in his essay "Buddhism and the Coming Revolution."[12] The concept underlies his *Myths and Texts*, where it surfaces in natural, political, and religious forms. A central image is the lodgepole pine, which reseeds after the cone is passed over by fire; a line such as, "Shiva at the end of the Kalpa," capsulizes the "destructive/constructive" in Snyder; and, finally, the following lines from *Myths and Texts* are similar in style, tone, and concept to Saarikoski:

> "Forming the New Society
> Within the Shell of the Old"
> The motto on the Wobbly Hall
> Some old Finns and Swedes playing cards
> Fourth and Yesler in Seattle.[13]

Haavikko's lines from "Sveaborg," a poem referring to a fortress in the Helsinki harbor, also call for a new society created from the old. Haavikko would prefer gentle passage rather than violent destruction and re-creation. His lines "a mind full of clarity and well equipped, an unconquered fortress that surrenders. . ." call to mind Robert Frost's meditation following his reluctance to end a walk:

> Ah, when to the heart of man
> Was it ever less than a treason
> To go with the drift of things,
> To yield with a grace to reason,
> And bow and accept the end
> Of a love or a season?[14]

In traditional style with description followed by a moralizing "punch line," Frost articulates a major conflict in Western thought. As a literary theme, the conflict is as old as *The Gilgamesh Epic*: man seeks after permanence, but there is no permanence. A major contribution of the Finnish political poets of the mid century is their coming to grips with the social conflict capsulized in Frost's rhyme of "reason" and "treason." This aspect is more fully developed in the following essay.

Suzuki discusses another theme close to Haavikko—language and words.[15] This point, as well as Haavikko's concept of political change, is discussed in my essay on Haavikko, but I would like to develop the theme of language in a different direction here, namely the similarity between Zen thought and the style of modern Finnish (and American) poetry itself.

Suzuki comments on the confusion of linguistic symbol with reality, and discusses the potential of Buddhism for delivery of the thinker from "the tyranny of language." Suzuki's wording is similar to Haavikko's line "syntax that has only a few exceptions," and Haavikko's line explains in part the modern poet's preference for direct presentation of concrete, nonconceptual images, so that ideas formerly presented through discourse (in the manner of Frost's presenting images and leading the reader to a logical conclusion stated by the poet) are now left for the reader to experience directly or derive intellectually for himself by finding the common denominator. The technique is described by Haavikko in *Winter Palace*: "side by side:/ the images./ to have them tell you. . . ?" and by Gary Snyder in *Myths and Texts* as: "Poetry a riprap on the slick rock of metaphysics."[16]

The purpose of the style, then, is to liberate poet and reader from "the tyranny of language." The philosophy is very Zen, and is described by Snyder as "carefully avoiding any direct thought of it, attentive to the real world flesh and stone."[17] The technique of avoidance of direct thought is the same as the Zen technique of instruction by means of the Koan.[18] Thus, we have come full circle to the problem of intellectualization. Snyder has more to say about the problem than Saarikoski, but their techniques are similar. Saarikoski has some lines such as:

> The wine had time to evaporate in the glass
> before I understood
> it was useless to converse with him.

or:

> When petals close
> he still quotes Rilke.

but he talks little about the problem. He proceeds to present his images directly, as in the samples presented in this anthology from *What is Really Happening?*,

"The High White of Winter," and others. Both Snyder, and Saarikoski—and an entire range of modern poets—favor a direct record of nonconceptual observations uncluttered by words of transition, elucidation, or conclusion, which are for Snyder just so much intellectual toilet paper:

> Again the ancient, meaningless
> Abstractions of the educated mind,
>   wet feet and the campfire out.
> Drop a mouthful of useless words.
> —The book's in the crapper
> They're up to the part on Ethics now.[19]

The meaning of Saarikoski, as of Snyder and many other moderns, is derived from the pattern the reader constructs of the images—most often images of daily life experience—presented without comment: the concrete, stripped of the "snarled tangle of intellectualization."

It is ironic that in contrast to Saarikoski, who says very little if anything about Zen in his poetry, yet is very Zen in style, Eeva-Liisa Manner is most un-Zen in style when she is thematically most concerned. While talking about Zen, she employs a style that begs interpretation of images dualistically on a symbolic plane. Only after her thematic resolution at the end of her book *Orphic Songs*, does her style turn, in subsequent collections, to a more nonconceptual attitude toward natural imagery.

Manner is concerned in *Orphic Songs* with the failure of Christianity as a true ethical force in Western civilization. The situation is complicated by man's desire to turn to the past for solutions for the present, as if the past mirrored the present. Her poetry as sampled in this anthology traces her thematic concern through several books with recognition of the void, of flux, and of death as a life process to be viewed not dualistically but as a continuity.

Manner considers the concept of mirroring and finally rejects it as illusory and dualistic. Mirror images and conceptual alternatives on various levels—personal, historical, mythical, optical—predominate in the poems from *Orphic Songs* ("Shore and Reflection" to "The Bones of Chuang Chou"). The collection finds its resolution, after Cassandra-like predictions of the decline of the West, in Buddhist thought with its absence of stress on power, dualism, and rivalry. Her poetry, in turn, abandons the ambition of *Orphic Songs,* and in the samples included here from three of her following collections turns to concrete imagery with no pretention to symbolism.[20]

Finally, one of Haavikko's poems may be read from the Zen perspective of Karma as the seeking of truth in order to end the cycle of rebirth:

> In this cruel world, it is useless to ask
> not to be reborn.[21]

Stylistic simplicity and directness, then, and thematic concern with change and the road to enlightenment are some manifestations of the Zen tendency in modern Finnish poetry. And now, after all these words and flapping of typewriter keys, after a paradoxical, snarled tangle of intellectualism advocating just the opposite, perhaps it is time to end, and end on a Koan-note with a poem by

Tuomas Anhava, which may well say it all, and therefore should be handed to the reader like a flower:

Everyone who believes what he sees
is a mystic.
In the dark
move slowly.[22]

NOTES

(No reference is made to those poems cited that are published elsewhere in this volume.)

1. William Barrett, *Zen Buddhism: Selected Writings of D. T. Suzuki* (Garden City, N.Y.: Anchor Books, 1956), p. 14.
2. In Barrett, 1956, Suzuki writes (pp. 136–37): "The worst enemy of Zen experience, at least in the beginning, is the intellect, which consists and insists in discriminating subject from object." I do not see this comment as being in conflict with the thematic concern with perception of reality–even at its most intellectual, as in Wallace Stevens. I see the intellect as being used to eliminate distortion so that things may be seen clearly.
3. Gary Snyder, *Myths and Texts* (New York: Totem Press & Corinth Books, 1960), p. 21.
4. Barrett, 1956, p. 72.
5. Barrett, 1956, p. 73.
6. This also seems to me to be the point of Voznesensky's poem "Antiworlds."
7. Robert Bly, *Silence in the Snowy Fields* (Middletown, Conn.: Wesleyan University Press, 1962), p. 46.
8. Barrett, 1956, p. 240.
9. R. P. Blackmur, "Examples of Wallace Stevens," in *Form and Value in Modern Poetry* (Garden City, N.Y.: Anchor Books, 1957), p. 191.
10. D. T. Suzuki, *The Field of Zen,* ed. Christmas Humphreys (New York: Perennial Library, 1970), pp. 44–51.
11. Suzuki, 1970, p. 51.
12. Gary Snyder, *Earth House Hold* (New York: New Directions, n.d.), pp. 90–93.
13. Snyder, 1960, p. 40.
14. Robert Frost, "Reluctance," *The Poems of Robert Frost* (New York: Modern Library, 1930), p. 31.
15. Suzuki, 1970, pp. 44–51.
16. Snyder, 1960, p. 43.
17. Snyder, 1960, p. 34.
18. Carlos Castaneda discusses a similar experience in his apprenticeship to Don Juan. Perception in a state of nonordinary reality, whether induced by drugs or meditation, seems to involve either optical or intellectual diversions of focus. This is in contrast to Rilke, for whom direct focus and concentration comprised the vehicle for insight and establishing the reality of the object. Castaneda writes: "Whenever I tried deliberately to trap the voice, it subsided altogether or became vague and the scene faded. . . . The voice was like . . . a . . . shape that can be seen as long as one is not looking at it directly; but the moment one tries to look at it, it shifts out of sight with the movement of the eyeball." Carlos Castaneda, *The Teachings of Don Juan: A Yaqui Way of Knowledge* (New York: Ballantine Books, 1969), pp. 162–63.

19. Snyder, 1960, p. 7.

20. For a recent essay on Eeva-Liisa Manner, *see* Jaakko Ahokas, "Eeva-Liisa Manner: Dropping from Reality into Life," *Books Abroad* 47, no. 1 (Winter 1973) : 60–65.

21. Some Zen poems, in turn, compare strikingly to Haavikko, and as an example I would like to footnote one from a book published after this manuscript was completed: *Zen Poems of China and Japan: The Crane's Bill*, by Lucien Stryk, Takashi Ikemoto, and Taigan Takayama (Garden City, N.Y.: Anchor Press/Doubleday, 1973; p. 46). Stryk's preface illustrates four dominant moods of Zen poetry and one of the poems he uses as an example seems very comparable in tone to Haavikko. It is by a contemporary Zen poet, Shinkichi Takahashi:

> The wind blows hard among the pines
> Toward the beginning
> Of an endless past.
> Listen: you've heard everything.

22. There are many other fine examples of this Zen attitude in the poems translated in this anthology. For example, Nieminen writes:

> The fog of talking hides the scene:
> where should the hunter aim?

We shall leave the rest of these poems for the reader's discovery and pleasure.

RICHARD DAUENHAUER

The View from the Aspen Grove:
Paavo Haavikko in National and International Context

I:
The Literature of Finland

In a recent review, Ivar Ivask refers to modern Finnish poetry as the secret treasure of contemporary European literature. His term is appropriate, for postwar Finnish literature, like most small-nation, small-language writing, remains a very esoteric subject. Linguistic obscurity and the resulting dependence upon translation into the profitless and hostile markets of major languages, often prevent the very exciting and significant—and, at the very least, interesting—literature from reaching an international audience.[1] Let us look at this "unlocked treasure," first in a very general and introductory way, and then in a more specific analysis of one or two writers.[2]

Finnish literature is a young literature, and its written tradition begins, for practical purposes, with Dr. Elias Lönnrot's collecting trips through Finland and the publication of substantial portions of the national oral epic, the *Kalevala,* in 1835 and 1849. Finland's first great creative writer is Aleksis Kivi (1834–1872), whose novel *The Seven Brothers,* published in 1870, remains the most popular book in Finland and the second great foundation of the national literature. In his *Lion Among Roses,* David Bradley introduces Kivi to American readers with a very interesting and appropriate comparison:

> Finnish writing begins with Alexis Kivi in much the same way that American writing begins with Mark Twain. The two were contemporaries. *The Seven Brothers* and *Huckleberry Finn* were published in the same decade, and in many ways the books and the men are remarkably similar. Both writers broke so completely with an overelegant tradition that the tradition ceased to exist. Both gave tongue to backwoods men and boys. Neither overlooked brutality or stupidity or failed to ease us toward the truth with humor and sympathy.
>
> Finns automatically turn to *The Seven Brothers* for a mirror of themselves: "Read this," they say, "if you want to understand us."[3]

Kivi possessed both a passion for his native language and a matchless "ear" for poetry, with the result that he was able to reject Swedish and German models, and experiment in his poetry with living Finnish speech rhythms. Kivi was followed, in the words of the Finnish poet and translator Anselm Hollo, by

> three or four decades of nothing until Eino Leino (1878–1926) . . . going by instinct, with no clear sense of what a Finnish prosody could be . . . became the first and perhaps only Great Romantic Master Craftsman only surpassed, in terms of that craft, by Otto Manninen (1872–1950).[4]

Manfred Peter Hein, the German poet and critic, and important translator of Finnish poetry, includes V. A. Koskenniemi (1885–1962) along with Kivi, Leino, and Manninen as one of the four prime movers of traditional Finnish poetry.

Modern Finnish poetry is young in that it dates not from the first decades of the twentieth century, but rather from the 1950s. In the superb introduction to his anthology *Moderne finnische Lyrik,* Hein gives an excellent example not only of the difference between Finnish and other European writing around 1920, but of the striking difference between Swedish- and Finnish-language writing in the national literature of Finland (which, we must not forget, is bilingual).[5] Edith Södergran, for example, (1892–1923) was, like many of her compatriots, a Finnish citizen who wrote in Swedish. Her poetry is modern, in the European sense of the word, whereas that of her Finnish-language contemporary, Katri Vala, is not. Hein writes:

> The birth date of newer Finnish poetry lies between 1947 and 1951. More than in the rest of Europe, World War Two must be considered as a decisive turning point in the Finnish-speaking area. Only since 1945 can we speak of modern Finnish-language literature in the true sense of the word.[6]

Likewise, even such Finnish "expressionist" poets as Uuno Kailas are not "modern" in the sense that Swedish, German, English, Russian, or French poetry of the same period is "modern." Hein, again, discusses the styles involved in some detail, and I refer the reader to his book for the specifics.[7]

It is interesting to compare the Finnish experience of 1950–1970 to European literary activity between 1910 and 1930. In 1922, for example, *The Waste Land, Ulysses,* Rilke's *Sonnets to Orpheus* and *Duino Elegies,* and Pasternak's *Life—my Sister* were either completed or published. This twenty-year period in Anglo-American literature alone saw either the emergence or maturity of such diverse groups as the Imagists, Fugitives, "Objectivists," and such figures as Frost, Williams, Lawrence, Joyce, Eliot, Pound, Yeats, Lewis, Woolf, Cummings, Stevens, Dos Passos, Fitzgerald, Hemingway, Faulkner, Auden, and Zukofsky. These same years witnessed the development of European Expressionism, Futurism, Acmeism, Surrealism, and numerous other literary experiments that have been continued, modified, or reacted against in more recent writing. But it is only in the postwar period that comparable activity in styles that can be called "modern" flourishes in Finnish writing. An excellent example was given by Professor Esko Ervasti of Oulu University when he mentioned, in conversation, that "Haavikko's *Winter Palace* (1959) is our *Waste Land.*"

Thirdly, Finnish writing is young also because the writers are young. A sampling of the ages of twenty-one of the most prominent poets writing in the past decade shows one in his 60s, three in their 50s, eight in their 40s, and nine in their 30s. Whereas in America most poets, whether new or established, publish poems first in magazines (both "little" and "reputable" ones), in Finland—which justifiably prides itself on its phenomenally high literacy rate and per-capita book production-consumption—publishers will generally accept and print entire books of new poems by unpublished poets. As a result of this policy, there are few literary magazines in Finland, but there exists an entire range of talented poets in their 20s who have already published numerous books.

Finally, the poetry of Finland is nonacademic. Many writers are employed as literary critics by the major papers, but few if any of the postwar poets are associated with the universities. Most have never set foot in one.

II:
Prose in General

Two directions seem to be evolving in postwar Finnish fiction: one in the traditional realistic vein, and another tending toward the "new novel." These two directions may be best illustrated in a discussion of the two prominent writers Väinö Linna and Veijo Meri. It is interesting that the most well known of Finnish writers in English translation, Mika Waltari, is probably the least representative of the style and content of contemporary Finnish prose.

Linna's *The Unknown Soldier* was published in 1954, and remains outsold in Finland only by the Bible and the Almanac. It is about a machine-gun platoon in the Continuation War with the Soviet Union, and, as a war novel, has been compared to Mailer's *The Naked and the Dead*. Linna's representation of the Finnish soldier aroused much controversy. The debate over the accuracy and favorability of his presentation seems to be between those who were there and say the description is perfect, and those who favor a more idyllic depiction. The novel makes extensive use of dialect in character portrayal. The war is shown from the point of view of the average soldier, and critics such as Kai Laitinen see its realism and humor as clearly in the Finnish tradition of Aleksis Kivi. No small part of the controversy aroused by the novel surrounds national self criticism over Finland's alliance with Hitler to wage an offensive war beyond the former frontiers.

A few words on the historical position of Finland in World War II might be of help here. The Finnish participation is divided into two shorter wars—the Winter War and the Continuation War. The Winter War began on November 30, 1939, with the Soviet invasion of Finland, and ended on March 13, 1940. The name accurately describes the war—105 days of combat in weather often dropping to forty below zero, during which time the Finns held out on the famous "Mannerheim Line," fighting the Soviets to a standstill, and winning the admiration of most of the world. The Finns were unbelievably outnumbered, having, for example, ten divisions as against the Soviet twenty-six, forty tanks against 2,000, 114 aircraft against 800, and 486 artillery pieces against 3,780.[8] The Finns, however, were fighting on their own soil, and, secondly, demonstrated the superiority of ski troops over long columns of tanks in the forest.

The Continuation War was a Finnish offensive to regain territory lost in the Winter War, and was launched on July 10, 1941, two weeks after Hitler's attack on the Soviet Union.[9] The Finnish drive took them back into their former territory, and then continued into Soviet territory, developed into over two years of trench warfare, and turned into a retreat in the face of the Soviet offensive following the break of the sieges of Leningrad and Stalingrad. After a series of negotiations, Finland was fortunate enough to secure a separate peace with the Soviet Union on September 4 and 5, 1944—the Finns being required to cease fire first. The Finns were indeed lucky that, as Stalin is reputed to have said, "Berlin is a bigger city than Helsinki."

Finland's foreign and domestic policies of the present day, as well as its economic situation, are directly linked to the continuing provisions of the peace treaty. Also, much of the Finnish concern with neutrality and national sanity on the part of the major powers in the nuclear age may be directly attributed to the Continuation War, which was clearly an avoidable disaster entered into because of the Fascist mentality that had been brewing for over two decades in Finland.

In 1959, 1960, and 1962 Linna continued his analysis of the Finnish social structure with the publication of his trilogy *Here under the Northern Star,* which treats several families of tenant farmers and their descendants from 1880 to the present day. The second part of the trilogy has caused the greatest excitement because it deals with the previously taboo subject of the Finnish Civil War of 1918. The outcome of the war, with the White victory and the subsequent incarceration of the Reds in concentration camps—with tens of thousands executed or starved to death in this "White Terror"—created sores in Finnish society that remain unhealed to the present day. Linna is credited not only with being one of the first to take up the subject, but also with helping to give rise to a new and more realistic view of the complexity of the Civil War and social conditions that led to it. He is sympathetic to the Red cause, and views the Reds as downtrodden and exploited rather than as unthinking dupes stirred up by outside agitators.[10]

The third novel of the trilogy examines Finnish democracy and Fascism in the 1930s, the culmination of the decade in the Winter War, the start of the new decade with the Continuation War, and follows through to the present. Linna won the literary prize of the Nordic Council in 1963.

While there are certain modern aspects of prewar fiction, such as the experimentation by Sillanpää (who, in 1939, was the first Finn to win the Nobel Prize) with simultaneity of action and intersections of time and place in his novel *People in the Summer Night,* the work of Veijo Meri illustrates a type of Finnish modernism that may be compared stylistically and thematically to writers such as Faulkner and Sartre, to recent German writing by Böll, Grass, and Johnson, and to the French "new novel."

The central stylistic device in most of Meri's writing is explained very early in Sartre's *Nausea,* in the entry entitled "Saturday Noon."

> A man is always a teller of tales, he lives surrounded by his stories and the stories of others, he sees everything that happens to him through them; and he tries to live his own life as if he were telling a story.
> But you have to choose: live or tell.

> Nothing happens while you live. The scenery changes, people come in and go out, that's all. There are no beginnings. Days are tacked on to days without rhyme or reason, in interminable, monotonous addition.

> That's living. But everything changes when you tell about life.[11]

Excellent examples of this style are the grotesque *Manila Rope,* now available in English translation, and the novel *The Woman Sketched in the Mirror,* available in Swedish and German translations. For Meri's characters, the act of telling gives shape to otherwise formless experience, and, by extension, gives order, control, and meaning to events otherwise in flux and therefore beyond order, control, and meaning. The structure of a Meri novel such as *The Woman Sketched in the Mirror* is one of the most important analogies the author draws to the problem of perception and ordering of experience that he examines in much of his work. Random events of the present are explained and ordered by the authority of the past; the present moment itself gains form and meaning for the characters either in its identification with a story or tall tale of past experience, or, ironically, in becoming such a story or tall tale later. Either way, the present moment is essentially unnoticed, unappreciated, seen in terms of something else rather than itself, and is therefore not really experienced. Conversation and narration typically reflect this contrast in Meri between moment and monument, reality and perception, experience and ordering. The imagery of the novel supplies further analogy, and the perspective, focus, and narration are constantly shifted and reexamined. *The Killer* is an excellent example of Meri's ability to manipulate conventional stylistic technique into an initially perplexing, but typically Meri-an commentary on human behavior.

Observing first that Linna was born in 1920, and fought in the war, whereas Meri was born in 1928 and was therefore too young to have fought, Laitinen compares his two favorite writers thusly:

Linna sees war as an absurd phenomenon but the behavior of the men is, according to him, in itself meaningful: his basic problem is life versus death. But in the work of Veijo Meri both the framework situation and the activities of all the people are absurd—absurd with a wonderful perfection.

Linna has certain social and historical intentions in his words: he wants to show "how it really was," or how it probably was. In visual art, Linna would be a realistic painter, but Meri a caricaturist.

The works of Linna are important because they revaluate and correct the conception of Finnish social history. The works of Meri are important because they show the loneliness of man in a world where nothing is certain and nothing can be taken for granted.[12]

Some of the stories and essays included in this book illustrate another aspect of contemporary Finnish writing: namely, that it is still, as the Finnish critic Pekka Tarkka has pointed out, very much agrarian.[13] Although Salama's works are anything but idyllic, they do often treat the average Finn in a rural situation. In a letter accompanying his translation, Philip Binham writes:

I'd like to add that one of the reasons I chose this story is its full picture of how it feels to be one of the many young Finns still stuck in a rural community that offers them so little, though the industrial world they'd like to move into doesn't seem to have much more to offer them either. The juxtaposition of "modern" life and the old Finnish "kurjuus"—the almost-enjoyment of hardship and misery (leading to harshness of character) that Sillanpää catches very well, and that still exists in the Finland I know—is something a lot of people—publicists like Jörn Donner, writers like Salama—are concerned about. No proper education for youths like Lahtinen, even if they want it. No technical schools within perhaps a hundred miles. What can they do? And the Raijas drift off to the towns and get pregnant at fifteen, and who cares? And the old people who have the fine old Finnish sisu only blame the young people for having the courage to protest.

I think these are some of the things Salama is on to, and he here typifies a lot of Finnish thinking and writing just now. I think also they (the Salamas) are like older Finns in their total dedication, inability to compromise, and readiness for "civil war" on the cultural front.

We have to add that he (Salama) has a strong feeling and understanding for the country world as well as the city—he is a "real Finn," but sees the plight of those for whom this lovely, romantic countryside (that the summer cottage people get all gooey over) is just a prison. This may be a universal theme, but I believe in Finland it is pointed up with special poignancy.

Salama is best known in Finland because of his trial for blasphemy on charges brought by a bishop of the Lutheran (State) Church. Salama was fined and imprisoned, and the publisher, Otava, was also fined. The novel in point, *Midsummer Dances* (1964), was re-issued in a censored edition with very effective white spaces replacing the objectionable dialogue ordered stricken by the court. The blasphemy trial and the language in the sample included here are two specific illustrations of Philip Binham's general comment in his letter that Salama's language is "rough," and his style "powerful, rich, sullen, accurate, compelling, and sometimes nauseating." The Salama story here is taken from a collection called *Kesäleski,* in which "many of the stories deal with violence and lack of love in the Finnish community."

III:
Poetry in General

Two predominant themes in current Finnish poetry are nature and politics.[14] Much of both, in my opinion, too often reveals the situation of too many people living in the same geographical and cultural environment and writing the same thing. Much of the nature poetry is conventional versification, and much of the political poetry fails to rise above grumbling about the very real problems of Finnish provincialism, parochialism, and, above all, the lack of opportunity for either meaningful work or self expression felt by many young people. Apropos of expression, for example, Saarikoski mentions almost in passing in one poem: "Finland's Finland, the birds are flying, criticism is impossible." Two poems by Väinö Kirstinä may well fall in the category of grumbling, but they nevertheless reveal the state of mind of young writers. In a group called "Word-ing," Kirstinä plays with words and sounds in his indictment of the Finnish national mentality; the poem called "Culture" goes "Car culture/ garden culture/ fur culture/ sauna culture/ restaurant culture/ buttermilk culture/ cemetery culture." Another poem is called "Milk" and reads, "it's a milk man/ and a milk mirror a milk tree/ . . . / a milk swamp and the finn-maiden/ fears the network of roads above her/ and milk tires." A classic of haunting and powerful political poetry is Matti Rossi's Vietnam poem, which I include here in Anselm Hollo's translation.

The Lord Revealeth Himself to the Senator
Yes, says the Senator, we used that bomb: the trees
of Vietnam shed their leaves, and behold, each tree had its
burden
of Communists, sitting there, necks hunched into their
shoulders,
their pockets full of rice,

Gentlemen, come and see: from California to Kuwait
these branches, bending, under the weight of those little men
rifle in hand they sit there, wait for the night to descend
on the Western
World

At its best Finnish poetry and prose manage to combine politics and nature, both of which are immediate and real to Finns because of their physical and economic location, into a profound view of the ambiguities of Finland's total "ecology"—both natural and political—in such a way that the national poetry has meaning beyond the national boundaries. Paavo Haavikko is an excellent example of this, and his work will be discussed later in detail.

While it was the postwar era that witnessed the emergence of a truly modern style in Finnish poetry, and the emergence of a younger generation of writers using it, there are many figures whose writing spans both sides of the social and literary upheaval of the war. One of the older poets whose work became more widely recognized in the postwar period is Arvo Turtiainen, head of the radical-left "kiila" writers' group from 1936 to 1951 and a political prisoner from 1942 to 1944 because of his refusal to take part in the offensive Continuation War against the Soviet Union. For a description of his work beyond the samples in this issue, as well as for a fuller description of the poetry of the 1940s, of other transition figures such as Viljo Kajava, Lauri Viita, and Aila Meriluoto, as well as of other important prewar figures such as Hellaakoski and Mustapää, I again refer the reader with knowledge of German to Hein's introduction.

Two other poets of the prewar generation who were prominent in the 1950s are Helvi Juvonen (1919–1959) and Eeva-Liisa Manner (1921–   ).[15] Hein, discussing her work in the Finnish and wider European contexts, cites Juvonen's "dissolution of the lyrical self into the object" as one of her major stylistic contributions that serve to link postwar Finnish poetry to both earlier Finnish poetry and European modernism in general. Like most of her fellow poets, Helvi Juvonen translated widely—in fact, another general characteristic of the contemporary Finnish literary scene that should be mentioned is this great activity in translating. Helvi Juvonen's death in 1959 is considered a great loss to the literature, and, in another respect, exemplifies a generality that may be stated about Finnish poetry—the sad tradition that poets die young.

The most influential book of poetry in the 1950s is generally held to be Eeva-Liisa Manner's *Tämä Matka* (*This Journey*, 1956). The poem "Here" is taken from this collection, along with the Ruth Ellis poems, all three of which show her thematic concern with the nature of human ego, the emptying out of the self, and ultimate transcending of the ego by death. These themes are continued in her next volume, *Orfiset Laulut* (*Orphic Songs*, 1959), which was less enthusiastically received than *Tämä Matka*. Her ensuing volumes have failed to match the success of her 1956 collection, and one gets the definite impression that her once profound influence is on the wane. At her weakest, she seems to be repeating not only herself, but—and too closely on their heels—Spengler and Rilke; in fact, she has been accused of "stepping on the grass" in her drawing on the ideas of other European thinkers. Also, I find her use of Buddhism less successful than the grafting of Oriental and American ideas in the works of Gary Snyder—specifically in *Myths and Texts*. At her best, however, she creates a very sensitive synthesis, or argument for a synthesis, of Eastern and Western attitudes toward "progress," "ego" and "reality."

Another of the "prime movers" of the 1950s who continues to be of considerable influence as a poet, critic, editor, and translator, is Tuomas Anhava, who played a major role in introducing new criticism, many important Anglo-American poems and poets, and traditional Japanese verse forms to Finland. While Anhava translated Japanese poetry into Finnish by way of English translations, the Finnish poet Pertti Nieminen, widely recognized as a sinologist, has translated numerous books of poetry directly from Chinese. The Oriental influence on modern Finnish poetry is widespread, and is especially seen in the poetry of Anhava and Nieminen.

A very different kind of poetry is written by Maila Pylkkönen—a "mind poetry" that either explores or presents psychological problems. One of her poems, for example, is entitled "Poem as a Time of Psychoanalysis," and treats schizophrenia, from which the poet suffers. Her poem, "The School Teacher's Wife" is an intriguingly simple presentation of a complex problem that at one time or another rises to haunt the happiness of most marriages.

IV:
Saarikoski

One of the most interesting and certainly popular figures on the contemporary literary scene in Helsinki is Pentti Saarikoski, who, since his first work appeared in 1958, has been variously known as the *"enfant terrible* of Finnish literature" and as "Finland's funny Communist." Like other modern Finnish poets, he, too, has translated widely—from Catullus to Joyce's *Ulysses* to *The Catcher in the Rye* and *Herzog*. His most significant book, *Mitä tapahtuu todellä? (What's Really Happening?,* 1959), has been translated into English by Anselm Hollo and is available from Great Britain. It contains one of the most striking political images in modern Finnish poetry—Pentti Saarikoski's vision of Finland as a bird flying backwards calling *Kto Kovo Kto Kovo*—the declension of the Russian pronoun "who."

Saarikoski is the subject of much current folklore, and his style the object of some parody by his fellow writers, such as Väinö Kirstinä's comment, "Read Saarikoski for ten minutes and you start to smell like wine, paper clips join everything from Venus de Milo to the pisspot." His more recent works have been reviewed and received as good Saarikoski, but suffering from hasty composition and the poet's concern with his image more than his poetry. Saarikoski would probably respond to these criticisms with lines such as these, from his poem "Idylls":

Someone said I'm a beatnik since I don't write literature any more.
    I took an evening walk with Marjukka, my wife,
                the drain pipes pissed,
      she had on rubber boots, but I had my brown shoes on
        that I bought brown laces for
          on Runeberginkatu yesterday.
I'm really very happy.
I know my house is built on sand, but whose isn't?

I don't like those kinds of parables any more;
Jesus is out, Tarzan's in.
Rejoice, I rejoice, I babble nonsense, I enjoy the mildness
of the air, spring evenings, the flowers.

Perhaps Saarikoski is overly concerned with his image; certainly, there is a greater frequency in his more recent poetry than in his earlier poetry of lines such as "I've got some red wine, I'll try and drink a little, just enough/ to put me out of it, to make me sleep . . . /" or, "On Sunday afternoon I work, I'm translating a book, Saul Bellow's/ *Herzog*, Marjukka's watching Hertta. . . ," but I think this is Saarikoski in search of a middle way between idea, thing, and experience.[16] There is certainly an enormous gap between conceptualization or intellectualization and the objects and experiences that face us every day, and Saarikoski is exploring the role of the average human being that, not only in the twentieth century, but in all history, is, in the words of his 1959 collection, to find out "what is really happening." How is the average person to find meaning in his experiences and in the objects and other people around him without either falsifying or missing the meaning by delusion or abstraction? How is a person to find meaning in his experience when faced with the overwhelming realization that he is all but helpless in the face of world events, when he knows

> the experts lie, they've got the right to,
> they know what it's all about, they know
> what's really happening.

The poet offers an example:

> in Nuremberg one night I suddenly knew
> that no one had been executed
> that all verdicts were still to be carried out
>
> radicalism and retrogression
> two sides of one and the same
> such as buying and selling

Accordingly, in Saarikoski's poetry, objects as well as experiences are not symbolic of anything. "Snow's melted by the statue/ of Alexander the Second: spruce branches are lying around it," and "A right-triangle shaped shadow, on the facade of the Building/ of the Council of State, Katajanokki Canal was open/ mallards floating around in the middle," are matter-of-fact, almost Robbe-Grillet-like images of Helsinki. Elsewhere in his poetry, Saarikoski not only delights in absurdity as it exists, but contributes what little he can to the destruction of any possible arbitrary meaning in computerized society:

> Things are complicated, . . . I impale
> bills, stacking them on the spike,
> I really dig the little holes
> you can peep through.

V:
Haavikko

First place in modern Finnish poetry is generally ceded to Paavo Haavikko, who, in the words of the Finnish critic Kai Laitinen, sprang into Finnish literature full blown and completely developed, like Pallas Athene. After half a century of the "Finnitude" described by Anselm Hollo in his introduction to *Paavo Haavikko: Selected Poems* (Hollo, 1968), Paavo Haavikko appeared in 1951 at the age of twenty with his appeal to see things clearly and in perspective, and to examine the very processes by which we perceive and order human experience. In one of the poems translated by Hollo, Haavikko says

> And if you can't see any longer
> What we see very clearly
> I'll blend the words with the hymn-tune.

Another poem presents for critical analysis by the reader the absurd situation that an emperor is the kind of image that is seen most clearly in the dark. The poem concludes:

> I have misled you.
> Open your eyes now
> Don't listen to me:
>
>
> The Empire is built and destroyed
> By blinking an eye.
>
> And it dies
> When eyes are opened.

Haavikko's poetry may be viewed as a two-pronged attack on the style and content of most Finnish poetry prior to 1950. While the details of many of his poems are drawn from and therefore are peculiar to Finnish history and culture, most of his poetry is truly international in concept. Haavikko's style and thematic content combine in an attack on positivism and national romanticism in particular, and on the irrationality of human perception and social and political ordering in general.

Whereas nationalistic or positivistic poetry is rationally structured in syntax, but has what the modernist would consider a nonrational and uncritical relationship to reality, Haavikko makes a rational break between the world of the poem and the external landscape—be it political or natural—and, by the use of nonrationally structured poetry, treats the problem of perception and social and political ordering of human experience.

The long poem, or nine-poem cycle, *Talvipalatsi* (*Winter Palace*, 1959) is one of the landmarks of modern Finnish literature, and firmly established Haavikko as the most original voice in postwar Finnish poetry. The poem (see Hollo, 1968, for a translation) is in many respects the culmination of several themes of the first decade of Haavikko's writing. For example, one of the first poems in his first book, published in 1951, contains the lines

> Our generation jokes. We hear its questions
> long after demolition, asking
> what kind of a house it was
> and was it ever built.

The house image is one of the many analogies Haavikko uses to treat the problem of change and the relationship of ego and present generation to the total history and gene-pool of man.[17] Other closely related images are of real estate, ancient ruins, territorial wars, refugees, and highways. The image of an ancient highway such as the Appian Way illustrates Haavikko's method of blending images and themes: for example, any road exists in time and space, and stands in a simultaneous relationship to the traveler such that the traveler exists at one moment in one place, whereas the road exists at any given moment in its total length and total physical history, thus being many places at one moment, and one place at many moments, having borne the footsteps of soldiers and refugees both ancient and modern.

Like the stones of the ancient highway, the juxtaposition of which creates the path, Haavikko's style is modern in its use of the associative technique common in twentieth-century poetry and described in the opening lines of *Winter Palace:*

> Side by side:
> The images.
> To have them tell you. . . .[18]

And, apropos of this technique, which places the burden of interpretation on the reader's ordering of the images, Haavikko joins many of his fellow modern poets in questioning the tyranny of language and syntax, viewing them as some of the many arbitrary conceptual categories that severely limit our perception and expression. In anticipation of the reader's bewilderment at the poet's rejection of the conventionally structured poem, Haavikko raises the questions "And what/ is poetry?" and "What is the subject of this poem,/ And is it a poem?" The answer to his second question was clear: one young Finnish poet published a book of blank pages to dramatize the impact of Haavikko's *Winter Palace* in forcing the younger poets to redefine their conception of lyric poetry and to begin from a new starting point.

"There are a few recurrent subjects in Haavikko's verse," writes Kai Laitinen. "Again and again, four matters occupy his mind: history, poetry (and language), love, and death. They are, of course, not separate, static elements, but changing themes, all can exist in the same poem, blending with one another. . . . His artistic solutions are never simple."[19] Haavikko's stance is basically one of questioning the validity of the arbitrary structures we erect, or our ancestors erected, to give us a semblance of order, stability, and security. He would argue, as in the poem, "If there's nothing else. . . ," that these structures are useful and convenient—perhaps even necessary to stave off insanity—but are valid and healthy only to the degree that we are aware that they are false constructions, and become dangerous to the extent that we lose sight of their arbitrary nature and of the void they conveniently obfuscate or fill. Words themselves are a prime example of such convenient and arbitrary structures that Haavikko is constantly examining; however, while he continually questions the validity of words, Haavikko's poetry still does convey conceptual meaning: that is, Haavikko does not treat the word as a sound-object, as some modern American poets such as Louis Zukofsky do.

For Haavikko, as Laitinen states, man's position is one of insecurity. There are no authorities to which he can turn; rather, as the poet states in his poem, "Speech flows in the floating world," man has to know everything for himself. The four themes Laitinen mentions are likewise never static, but always in flux—in flux in two respects: first, that they are historically changing at every moment, and second, that they are being realized in many different images in the poetry. Laitinen states that "two important poles of his poetry are given. On the one hand, the world is real, unavoidable, but difficult to understand. . . . On the other hand, man cannot expect permanence or stability."[20]

One of the central images of Haavikko's poetry, and one which illustrates both his blending of themes and his conception of permanence and stability, is the tree. Laitinen notes in his essay that Haavikko "doesn't 'observe' the world, he *lives* in it." The tree image illustrates this cognitive stance, and, indeed, one of the difficulties in beginning Haavikko's poetry is that the persona in many poems is a tree. In contrast to the structure of a more traditional poem such as a Rilkean "Dinggedicht," the object is not transformed in Haavikko, or revealed through intense study and concentration by the perceiving subject. No single poem views the tree as separate from the persona or perceiving subject; rather, the point of view in Haavikko's poems is established *in medias res* as that of a tree.

The equation of the tree with the persona reinforces and in turn is reinforced by a pun that underlies much of Haavikko's poetry and point of view: the name "Haavikko" means, literally, "aspen grove," much the same way as "nurmi" means "grass" and "nurmikko" means "lawn." This pun is stated most clearly in the poem, "Old names taste like ashes," which raises a group of interrelated problems concerning the meaning of words and names, and the ultimate inheritance of sounds and letters that have long since lost their original relationship to an object. This wordplay adds another dimension of complexity to Haavikko's tree imagery, in that the word itself is an example of the arbitrary structure for which the poet is using the tree image as an analogy.

Having the persona as a tree is puzzling only because it upsets our conventional attitude toward an object such as a tree; and, indeed, the effect of Haavikko's taking such a stance is the creation of a superimposition or juxtaposition of the two stances—the traditional and the unusual—in such a way that a three-dimensional perspective is created that allows for a richer perception of experience. Haavikko, then, joins a number of other European and American poets (such as Stevens and Williams, and the American "Objectivists," for example) who are concerned not only with the object, but with the problem of undistorted human perception of it. Haavikko's technique reinforces his content by leading the reader to a questioning of the nature of his own perception.

The double exposure works in the following way: a person's attitude toward an object may be either a sentimental extension of his own ego, a deliberately imaginative or stylistically metaphorical distortion of the object, or, lastly, an attempt to preserve the integrity of the object—in this case the tree—by rigid discipline and intellectual austerity. The tree is a good example because it is striking in its seasonal change. Human sentimentality identifies the loss of leaves with death and sadness, whereas, botanically, the loss of leaves actually insures the *life* of the tree by preventing evaporation. Therefore, leaf-loss is clearly a life process and not a death process. However, the conventional, preconceived attitude toward the tree fails to perceive the life cycle of the tree accurately, because the tree is seen in terms of an individual human.[21] Thus, as Wallace Stevens says, sentimentality becomes a failure of feeling. The tree is seen not as itself, but as something else. The problem holds true for the perception of all objects, but the tree may be studied as especially significant as an analogy to human experience. If we are to view the tree botanically, then the life cycle of the tree must be seen in larger perspective—the perspective not of a given year but rather of the entire history of the organism; likewise, a larger perspective on human life would view the ego-generation in its relationship to the entire race. Haavikko's superimposition of perspectives asks us to see our place in the world naturally, *as it is*, rather than emotionally, selfishly, and egotistically. The poet is asking the reader to reconsider his conventional perception and see the passing of a given generation as necessary for insuring the further life of the race. If the tree were, in one season, selfishly to refuse to lose its leaves, the entire tree would die because of the lack of cooperation of a given generation. Haavikko asks the reader to consider the perspective gained by voluntary dissolution of the ego. The analogy of the tree, and of various other images, especially the historical ones, illustrate how the failure of one generation to yield to another— the failure of one generation to recognize the true nature of change in a given social idea or structure—may result in the death of the entire organism—be it botanical or social or political. The double exposure in Haavikko's poetry, using natural images to speak to domestic and international social and political issues, is typically Finnish in its plea for sanity, objectivity, and the use of two eyes and examination of two sides of a problem for proper perspective and depth perception in the handling of human affairs.

VI:
Gottfried Benn

Haavikko's thematic and stylistic concern with perception places his work in an international context best demonstrated and documented by comparison with some of the major poets of Germany, the United States, and the Soviet Union with whom he shares this conceptual attitude. The following comparison is purely synchronic: no argument is made for "influence" as it is traditionally understood; indeed, were such a study of influence to be made, it would best proceed from analysis of the influence of certain ideas and philosophical concepts on a number of poets, rather than of one poet on another.

The departure point of Haavikko's poetry, in general, seems to me expressed in the thought of Gottfried Benn as capsulized in the following lines from "Verlorenes Ich" (1943) and "Nur Zwei Dinge" (1953):

> du möchtest dir ein Stichwort borgen—
> allein bei wem

> you want to borrow a slogan—
> but from whom

and

> Es gibt nur zwei Dinge: die Leere
> und das gezeichnete Ich

> There are only two things: the void
> and the sketch of the self.[22]

I suggested earlier in the essay that Haavikko would probably argue (most succinctly, for example, in, "If there's nothing else") that the social, intellectual, and aesthetic structures we create are arbitrary, useful, and convenient, perhaps even necessary, but are valid and healthy only to the degree that we remain aware that they are false constructions, and that they become dangerous to the extent that we lose sight of their arbitrary nature and of the void they conveniently obfuscate or fill. In short, we must never lose sight of the concept of the void and nothingness.

This starting point is essentially the conclusion—as I understand it—reached by Gottfried Benn after a career typified by confusion of life and art, poetry and politics, configurations of the mind and structures of the state and society—in other words, by losing sight of those concepts. His political and philosophical flirtation and subsequent disillusionment with the Nazis (climaxed by their accusing him of writing "Jewish poetry" when Benn himself considered his work the philosophical quintessence of Naziism) is reflected in the development of his poetry.

Beginning with the shock effect and cynicism of the Morgue and Doctor poems of 1912–13, bench marks of Benn's thought may be excerpted from "Gesänge", (1913), from the many fine poems of the 30s and 40s such as "Ikarus" and "Karytide," from the increasingly conceptual articulation in "Verlorenes Ich," and from its culmination and most succinct expression in one of Benn's last and finest poems, "Nur Zwei Dinge," both as cited above.

Benn's final enlightenment contrasts sharply with the germination of his philosophy as shown in his early poetry. Because of its shock effect and philosophical stance, "Alaska" (though in many respects a humorous poem) is a fairly representative example of a Benn escape attempt.

> Europa, dieser Nasenpopel
> aus einer Konfirmandennase,
> wir wollen nach Alaska gehn.

> Europe, this snot
> from the nose of a confirmation boy,
> we want to go to Alaska (GW, 20).

In the second and final stanza, Benn's alternative to and escape from the insignificant Europe of metaphorical snot, or snot-nosed kid, is Alaska—the traditional "great land", home of the noncerebral, nonconceptualizing, "rugged male"-"heman," who operates according to such instincts as his belly and sex drive, "slays bears" and "sticks it into women."

> Der Meermensch, der Urwaldmensch,
> der alles aus seinem Bauch gebiert,
> der Robben frisst, der Bären totschlägt,

der den Weibern manchmal was reinstösst:
der Mann.

The sea-man, the jungle-man,
who gives birth to everything from his belly,
Who feeds on seals, slays bears,
who sticks it into women now and then:
a man. (GW, 20).

I take "Meermensch" here to have evolutionary overtones—primordial man, and "Urwaldmensch" to be primitive man: both are stages on Benn's scale of intellectual awareness to be discussed below in "Gesänge," which parallels the ideas in "Alaska."

"Alaska," in its concern with ego and escape, provides an extreme contrast with Haavikko's poetry, whereas middle and late Benn will offer close philosophical comparisons. At risk of extending an overlong excursus on Benn, I will sketch the high points of his development as they ultimately come to bear on Haavikko.

For Benn, contemporary Europe was "zerdacht"—thought to pieces—cerebral to the point of impotence. The alternative was nonconceptual or even anticonceptual activity, a lust for "Rausch" or activity, involvement, action, and a nostalgia for a primordial existence of mere process without even the rudiments of conceptual awareness. This is most clearly expressed in "Gesänge" (1913):

O dass wir unsere Ururahnen wären.
Ein Klümpchen Schleim in einem warmen Moor.

O that we were our great great ancestors.
A little clump of slime in a warm bog (GW, 25).

The desire is to be, at most, a leaf of algae; any further development would be too complex, too cerebral:

Ein Algenblatt. . . .
. . . .
Schon ein Libellenkopf, ein Möwenflügel
wäre zu weit und litte schon zu sehr.

An algae leaf. . . .
. . . .
A dragonfly head, a seagull wing already
would be too far and would already suffer too [very] much (GW, 25).

Benn's life and art record his various poetic and political attempts at escape, prior to a final synthesis and compromise. By 1945 he had not yet arrived at his solution, but was painfully aware that there existed no possibility for escape. The dilemma is handled magnificently in "Verlorenes Ich," one of his finest, most exciting, and most seminal poems, the opening stanza of which presents the intellectual and identity crisis of modern man:

Verlorenes Ich, zersprengt von Stratosphären,
Opfer des Ion—: Gamma-Strahlen-Lamm-
Teilchen und Feld—: Unendlichkeitschimären
auf deinem grauen Stein von Notre-dame.

Lost ego, split [fragmented] by stratospheres,
victim of the ion—: Gamma-ray-lamb-
particle and field—: infinity chimeras
on your gray stone of Notre-Dame (GW, 215).

When we consider the widest range of associations surrounding each word, we are able, in the manner of the arithmetician doing fractions, to arrive at a poetic common denominator. The contrast here is between Notre Dame, with its associations evoking a bygone period of intellectual, religious, and cultural endeavor in which man's ego and identity were not lost, and the rhyme with "Gamma-Strahlen-Lamm," evoking its associations of intellectual development exemplified specifically in the stanza by physics, chemistry, and technology. The contrast is one of anxiety versus confidence, insecurity versus security, relativity versus the concept of an orderly "Alpha and Omega."

The images and ideas in the opening stanza of the poem are paralleled in the opening of another Benn poem, "Fragmente"—"Fragments":

Fragmente,
Seelenauswürfe,
Blutgerinnsel des zwanzigsten Jahrhunderts—
. . . .
die historischen Religionen von fünf Jahrhunderten zertrümmert,
die Wissenschaft: Risse im Parthenon,
Planck . . . mit seiner Quantentheorie

Fragments,
souls' discharges,
coagulations of the twentieth century—
. . . .
the historical religions of five centuries demolished,
science: cracks in the Parthenon,
Planck . . . with his quantum theory (GW, 245).

The accumulated intellectual upheavals culminating in the first decades of the twentieth century have taken the intellectual to the existential point reached in stanzas five and six of "Verlorenes Ich."

Die Welt zerdacht.
. . . .
Die Mythe log.

The world thought to pieces.
. . . .
Myth lied.

Woher, wohin . . .
kein Evoë, kein Requiem,
du möchtest dir ein Stichwort borgen—
allein bei wem?

Wherefrom, where to . . .
no Evoe, no Requiem,
you'd like to borrow a slogan—
but from whom (GW, 215).

Religion is a myth that no longer has validity. We can return neither to Bacchanalia nor to Christianity. Modern man is detached, alienated, without an identity and realizes there is no easy answer, no place to which he can turn to regain what he has lost through the recognition of his plight. In short, he can no longer turn to the world of Notre Dame described more fully in the final stanzas of the poem as a time:

. . . als sich alle einer Mitte neigten
und auch die Denker nur den Gott gedacht.
. . . .
Oh ferne . . . erfüllte Stunde,
die einst auch das verlorne Ich umschloss.

. . when everybody bowed to one center
and also the thinkers only thought of God,
. . . .
O distant . . . fulfilled hour,
which once embraced the lost ego as well (GW, 215).

The modern intellectual can no longer return to an age in which all activity was for the greater glory of God; but modern man is nostalgic for an era in which his now lost or fragmented ego and identity once occupied a recognized, fruitful, and harmonious position in the practical, intellectual, and transcendental life. Deprived of such an era, man seeks to create meaning through various concepts and causes.

For Benn, then, the problem was coming to grips with the impossibility of escape—"die Welt als Flucht"—"the world as escape," as he writes in "Verlorenes Ich." Benn finally arrives at the awareness that there is no escape: there is escape neither into nor away from the world. Indeed, he is trapped in the dilemma of being caught or trapped by his intellect precisely in attempting to escape from his intellect. His solution is ultimately artistic and philosophical, and is put forth in the concluding lines of "Nur Zwei Dinge" quoted above, where Benn postulates that only two things exist: the void, and that as which you see yourself, or sketch yourself. The essential thing is that it is an "as if" conclusion: by this I mean that Benn's solution allows for the individual to create illusory barriers between himself and nothingness, allows for the individual to act, play roles, or view himself according to various images; but the essential point remains that the individual beware of the arbitrariness of his intellectual construction, and be aware that no cause or preexisting or doctrinaire construction of "external reality" is an adequate equation or expression of a construction of the human mind. Moreover, constructions of the human mind are equally inadequate for filling the void. The void exists, and cannot be filled, nor escaped from. The individual must come to grips with it, and Benn suggests that this be done through simile rather than metaphor—simile retaining the integrity of the compared entities, metaphor obscuring them. In practical terms, it was a mistake for Benn to assume that the Nazi movement equated to his poetic concept of "Rausch" or noncerebral involvement. The specific "sketch" will vary according to each individual and is not important; what is important is the concept of the sketch—the awareness that it is distinct from the ego—if, indeed, the ego can ever be ascertained in any human being—the awareness that it is an aesthetic construction, with no intrinsic relation to anything.

The theme of alienated and fragmented modern man is now familiar to us as we approach the latter part of the twentieth century. A major difference between Haavikko and Benn is that in Benn we see the discovery of alienation, and in Haavikko—first publishing forty years later—the a priori assumption of it. It is possibly this a priori assumption that contributes to the low tone of Haavikko's work, similar to George Oppen's "Forms of Love." For the purposes of this essay, Benn, then, in his final synthesis and resolution, arrives at an insistence on awareness of the disparity between object and perception—arrives at a solution based upon rigorous awareness and analysis of the process of perception.

VII:
William Carlos Williams

It is precisely such an awareness of the process of perception that underlies William Carlos Williams's poem "Youth and Beauty"—a poem strikingly similar to Haavikko's "If there's nothing else," and a poem by which the comparison of Benn and Haavikko may be extended to American poetry. This is a major point, and it is time to set both of these poems on the page, first Haavikko, then Williams:

Jos ei ole muuta, niin kanna pari valkoista kiveä vuoteeseen,
meri on tehnyt kivet valkeiksi,
        ne hengittävät, niissä säilyy tuoksu,
pari valkoista kiveä on neuvoni,
jos vuode on leveä sinulle yksin.

Sinä tahdot elää omaa elämääsi. Hyvä. Sinä tahdot olla oma itsesi.
Varo. Sitä juuri madot odottavat. Sinä haluat elää kun vielä
        olet nuori.
Erehdys. Tuhannen sokeaa silmää kalvaa kuvasi rikki.

Sinussa on lapsen pelko pimeätä hengittävä, kun leikit ovat
    kesken.

If there's nothing else,
        then take a few white stones to bed,

the sea has bleached them white,
        they breathe, retain aroma,
a few white stones—my advice
if the bed's too wide for you alone.

You want to live your own life. Good.
        You want to be yourself.
Be careful. The worms are waiting for just that.
You want to live while you're young. Mistake.
A thousand blind eyes will gnaw your image up.

There's a child's fear inside you
of fear-breathing darkness when games are interrupted
and illusion breaks that you made believe.[23]

A different kind of distinction between object and perception is established in Williams's "Youth and Beauty," and may be compared to that established by Haavikko.

Youth and Beauty

I bought a dishmop—
having no daughter—
for they had twisted
fine ribbons of shining copper
about white twine
and made a tousled head
of it, fastened it
upon a turned ash stick
slender at the neck
straight, tall—
when tied upright
on the brass wallbracket
to be a light for me
and naked
as a girl should seem
to her father.
          (CEP, 219)

The poem is an argument for a distinction between object and perception, but it allows for an imaginative vision of an object provided that the perceiver's imagination is equalled by a rigid self-discipline and awareness that the imaginary distortion or comparison is arbitrary and illusory.

The effect of each poem relies on an awareness of disparity or potential disparity between perception and the object perceived. Both poets allow for an imaginative vision or distortion of an object provided that the perceiver's imagination is matched by rigorous self-discipline and an awareness that the imaginary distortion or comparison is arbitrary and illusory. The potentiality for self-deception must be at least equalled by the potentiality for self-discipline.

Williams's persona is aware of the disparity from the outset; likewise, in the Haavikko poem the disparity is established in the opening lines, although it is the poet rather than persona instructing the reader. Whereas the Williams poem is on the whimsical side, Haavikko austerely warns the reader to be aware of the possibility—imminent rather than remote—of illusion and self-deception. The poem concludes with Haavikko's emphasizing the disparity between object and perception even more vividly by suddenly coming to focus on the immediate sense of fear and terror that arise when self-deception is disclosed: "sinussa on lapsen pelka . . . kun leikit ovat kesken"—"there's a child's fear within you . . . when games are interrupted." Professor L. S. Dembo has described the psychological austerity in Williams's poem as "an objectivist experience approaching epiphany."[24] I submit that this "psychological austerity" is Benn's "gezeichnetes Ich," that the experience is shared in the Haavikko poem as well, forms the conceptual basis of Haavikko's poetry, and that it therefore provides the major point of comparison between Haavikko, William Carlos Williams, and a number of other American poets, most importantly Wallace Stevens.

VIII:
Wallace Stevens

The more I consider the affinities, the more convinced I am that among American poets, the one Haavikko most closely and consistently resembles in underlying concept and frequently in surface comparisons as well, is Wallace Stevens. Tone, also, is strikingly similar, but impossible to demonstrate adequately in the present essay. Both poets are thematically concerned with seeing things clearly. Because metaphor is a stylistic device that perceives one thing in terms of something else, and in that sense may be considered a failure to distinguish and retain the identity and integrity of the object under study, Haavikko's poetry, like Stevens's, is a stylistic rejection of metaphor, although Haavikko does not philosophize about metaphor.

Comparisons abound, and the primary example among these is the concern with the awareness of the contrast between things as they are and things as they are imagined. "The Man with the Blue Guitar" and "Study of Two Pears" are well-known poems on the subject, and in the first stanza of "Study of Two Pears," Stevens argues:

> The pears are not viols,
> Nudes or bottles.
> They resemble nothing else.

The poem concludes

> The pears are not seen
> as the observer wills.[25]

Stevens focuses in his "metapoetry"—poetry about poetry—on metaphor as an evasive device that is essentially dishonest because it not only fails to come to grips with the object itself, but also destroys the distinction between the object in itself and the object as imagined—a distinction Stevens rigorously maintains.

It seems clear that lines from poems such as "The Motive for Metaphor," "Credences of Summer," and "Someone Puts a Pineapple Together" may be introduced into the discussion of Williams's "Youth and Beauty" and Haavikko's "If there's nothing else," and also ultimately of Benn, to the degree that we consider "Nur Zwei Dinge" a rejection of metaphor in the broadest philosophical sense, when metaphor is viewed as an escape.

Consider these passages from "The Motive for Metaphor":

> Where you yourself were never quite yourself
> and did not want nor have to be,
> . . . .
> The motive for metaphor, shrinking from
> The weight of primary noon,
> The A B C of being, . . . (CP, 288)

from "Credences of Summer":

> II
> Let's see the very thing and nothing else
> . . . .
> Without evasion by a single metaphor (CP, 373).

> VII
> . . . It was difficult to sing in face
> Of the object. The singers had to avert themselves
> Or else avert the object . . . (CP, 376).

and from "Someone Puts a Pineapple Together":

> II
> He must say nothing of the fruit that is
> Not true, nor think it, less. He must defy
> The metaphor that murders metaphor.[26]

Although Haavikko has many metapoetical poems, I can think of none that treat the subject of metaphor by name as a rhetorical device. However, I feel that the underlying concepts are the same—namely, poetry as the subject of poetry and concern with accurate perception of reality; indeed, lines from "An Ordinary Evening in New Haven" come very close to literal equation with Haavikko's wording. First, Stevens:

> IX
> We keep coming back and coming back
> To the real: to the hotel instead of the hymns
> That fall upon it out of the wind. We seek
>
> The poem of pure reality, untouched
> By trope or deviation . . . (CP, 471).

Compare Haavikko's "What kind of a man.":

> And if you can't see any longer
> What we see very clearly
> I'll blend the words with the hymn-tune.

In the context of the Finnish poem, which Anselm Hollo compares to the Cree Indian singer Buffy Sainte-Marie's "The Universal Soldier," the hymn tune is equated with the forces of "trope and deviation"—emotional obfuscation as opposed to clarity—with the forces of war propaganda, mass hysteria, "flag waving," "God and Country" jingoism and xenophobia, all as opposed to rationality. In another comparison—fundamental as well as superficial—both Stevens and Haavikko are fond of paradoxical and ephemeral emperors:

> Let be be finale of seem.
> The only emperor is the emperor of ice cream . . . (CP, 64) .[27]

compares to Haavikko's "Now as I tell you of the emperor," with its paradoxical imagery of the emperor's being seen clearest in the dark or with eyes of the perceiver closed. The conclusion of Haavikko's poem:

> The Empire is built and destroyed
> By blinking an eye
>
> And it dies
> When the eyes are opened. . . .

conveys the same freshness and excitement of a first, accurate perception—perhaps "an objectivist experience approaching epiphany"—as do the last lines of Stevens's "Not Ideas about the Thing, but the Thing Itself":

> It was like
> A new knowledge of reality (CP, 534) .[28]

Likewise, even random lines from Haavikko and Stevens show their concern with poetry as the subject of poetry. From Stevens's "An Ordinary Evening in New Haven":

> XXVIII
> This endlessly elaborating poem
> Displays the theory of poetry
> As the life of poetry.

and from his "The Man with the Blue Guitar":

> XXII
> Poetry is the subject of the poem
> From this the poem issues and
>
> To this returns (CP, 176) .

From Haavikko:

> . . . when poems are shown to mean nothing. . . .

and

> This is a poem I am writing. . . .

and

> . . . like symbolism that proposes to irony. . . .

or

> This poem wants to be a description
> And I want poems to have
> Only the faintest of taste. . . .

or

> I am only an image in this poem. . . .

or

> Tourist, listen, perhaps you don't know
> I hardly meet expenses writing these poems. . . .

As indicated earlier in the essay, the total inventory of Haavikko's work is concerned to a large degree not only with poetry, but with the related theme of language. *Winter Palace* is richest in easily extractable lines, such as in the "5th Poem":

> O syntax that has only a few exceptions.
> You slyness of sincerity,
> You rule

> I wanted to know:

> why are you praising the language that rules?
> I would like to teach this poem a lesson. . . .

The theme of language, and especially the word, is widespread in modern poetry, is easily the material for a book in itself, and accordingly lies beyond the scope of this essay. I would simply note here that the theme connects a number of poets: Germans Benn, Krolow, Enzensberger, and Celan; the Russian Fet; and the Americans Creeley, Zukofsky, and Gary Snyder, among many others. The appeal of the theme derives from the contrast between the vocal noise and semantic referent of a word. Meaning is derived on the basis of common agreement on verbal symbols, not because of any intrinsic connection between sound and referent. Thus, the theme becomes connected with the greater theme of arbitrary structuring of society and social experience.

For example, Haavikko is interested in family names, and the extent to which they may have had some meaning at one time, but no longer do. Thus, "Cooper" survives as a family name for thousands of persons today who no longer earn their livelihood by making barrels. The combination of sounds refers to the bearer of the name only by common agreement. Closely connected with the theme of language and word is that of communication, though Haavikko seems most concerned with social communication (as in "Sveaborg") rather than with personal communication, as in, for example, Paul Celan's *Sprachgitter*. Whatever the specific theme, its underlying position in the total structure of Haavikko's poetry is that it is a specific example of an appeal for self-conscious awareness of the arbitrariness of the organization of human activity.

It is the appeal for self-consciousness that creates a tone in Haavikko similar to that of Stevens—a tone difficult to document by the citation of words, lines, and passages. Compare, for example, "The Death of a Soldier," "Metaphors of a Magnifico," and "Martial Credenza" with the tone of Haavikko's many poems on war and politics, such as "Sveaborg," "Im Rovajärvi," "Silence please," and "My Grandfather the Emperor," "Now as I Tell You," "What Use a Man," "But What if the Good Days."[29]

Far more important than superficial matching up of lines, however, is a further comparison that demonstrates a functional similarity on the conceptual level. In form and content, the poetry of Haavikko, like that of Stevens, is a rejection of conventional poetic catharsis and all rhetorical devices that contribute to such catharsis. If there is catharsis for the reader of Stevens and Haavikko, it is intellectual rather than emotional. Conventional, emotional, suprarational catharsis is prevented because the reader—as the above excerpts demonstrate—is constantly made aware that he is reading a poem. Conceptually this is the same technique used in modern non-Aristotelian, or "epic" theater, and is a critical aspect that should be considered in study of "neo-epic" poetry.[30]

Indeed, Haavikko himself compares his poetry to a play. "The Seventh Poem" of *Winter Palace* begins:

> This poem,
> A short play
> And the year, and the years
> One short line, . . .

and continues with such lines as

> Scene Two: light on the branches
> by the riverbank. . . .

and

> And this is Scene Three;

up to the beginning of the fourth part, which I will quote at some length:

> Scene Four, she said:

How do I know what is a dream
And where does the shoulder end, the breast begin?
Make me this poem, make it warm enough for winter,
Make it cheap to live in, with closets for things
And with a room for the soul,
And I will inhabit this line for a long long time,
In a poem that does not shed its leaves,
That is a voice I can live in, a house.

I said, this is Scene Four,
I am constructing a poem
Out of what, do you think? Out of nothing?
A short poem, to be spoken standing up
Or lying down, alone. And are you not
Your own house?

. . . .

And then this woman wanted to know,
What are you mumbling? can't you understand
I want a place, to live in?

This is Scene Four, Five begins here, I said
I, too, would like to live in a house, with my belongings,
A spacious house; and yet, they want one word to be
A complete sentence—they, even they are hoping
For the preservation of productive speech—
I am leaving this poem, against all sense,
It is a poem, no well-built sentence to isolate me,
I am not protesting, I am not negotiating,
I'm simply going, going through it all, it is open, closed,
Like these decades
And that was Scene Five; the seventh poem,
The end
Of the play.

Many of these lines, such as "It is a poem, no well-built sentence to isolate me," are reminiscent of the rejection by Blok, Meyerhold, Brecht, and others of the "well-built play".[31] "The Eighth Poem" of *Winter Palace* continues the description of the poem and the persona's desire to exit:

This is descriptive, and everything is as usual. . . .

or

And it fell silent, the greedy poem. . . .

or

And here, the few lines
That were to have been a catalogue:

. . . .

But I am now leaving this poem.

One of the causes for the persona's desire to leave the poem is expressed thusly:

This noncommercial world makes me ill at ease, . . .

. . . .

Let me go, . . . I don't feel at home here
In this noncommercial world, constructed at random.

These excerpts from *Winter Palace* show how Haavikko is continually playing the concepts of intrinsic order and arbitrary order against one another, contrasting the overwhelming human desire for the confidence and security of what Benn calls "Stichwörter" or slogans with the equally overwhelming human realization that the security and confidence are false, and the "slogans" deceptive. The last line quoted above demonstrates the degree to which the average person considers the commercial or "real" world *not* constructed at random. The "Real World" makes sense, even if poems do not. The average man—whatever his walk of life—sees no necessity to question or critically examine either the existing structure of his society or the means by which he perceives and structures "reality." By extension, art and literature make sense to the degree to which their structures coincide with that of the reader's "Reality".

In Haavikko and Stevens, then, there is continual emphasis on self-conscious perception not only on the thematic or content level of their poetry, but to an equal and perhaps even greater extent in the poet's technique, and, by extension, in the technique required of the reader.

The technique is continually reinforced: neither Stevens nor Haavikko lets the reader forget that he is self-consciously reading a poem that the poet is self-consciously writing, that the object before him is simply an arbitrary verbal construction relating to an equally arbitrary natural or social construction in the "real world." The reader's chief problem—one consciously presented by the writer in his belief that form may be as important as content—is that the construction of the poem does not follow the forms to which he has become accustomed through training and previous experience. Hopefully the reader does not abandon the poem, but proceeds to examine its form, its content, and ultimately the structure of his world and his perception of it. In other words, Stevens and Haavikko are alike in that their thought and poetic styles proceed from a phenomenological rather than from an empirical basis.

This, then, although many other writers and themes could be brought into the comparison, is the immediate international context of Haavikko: Benn's life and work record one man's coming to grips with the problem of distortion of perception of reality by ego; such phenomenal concerns are central in the poetry of Williams, Stevens, and Haavikko, who all attempt to avoid Benn's error by making a poetic appeal to see things clearly and in perspective analyzing the phenomenon of perception itself.

IX:
Conclusion

Awareness of the disparity between the object itself and the perception of the object has been central to the concepts and techniques of modern poetry since the Romantics and the time of Kant, and two opposing conceptual and stylistic options are derived from this distinction between object and perception. The first option is the use of distortion to reveal or disclose the essence of the object under study; the second option attempts to eliminate distortion by rigorous self-conscious analysis. The opposition is represented 1) in the work of those poets who feel that distortion of the object by perception is either, on the one hand, unavoidable, or, on the other hand, highly desirable, not only conceptually, but stylistically as well, and 2) in the work of those poets who disagree. The first group is composed of, among others, poets traditionally identified as symbolists, surrealists, and expressionists. The second group, the opposite of the first, is comprised of poets who share a common attitude that has been called "objectivist" for some of its members. The style of the second group is typified by thematic concern with perception and self-conscious awareness of the integrity of the object, and by refusal to distort the object by conceptualization or by the technical device of metaphor, which would amount to seeing one object not in terms of itself, but in terms of something else.[32]

A glance at Sappho, John Donne, and Basho will demonstrate vividly that poets throughout history have differed drastically in their attitudes toward metaphor and conceptualization. Only relatively recently, however, (since the Romantic period) have poets concerned themselves *thematically* with the problem of self-conscious awareness of conceptualization, and with the closely related problem of the disparity between object and perception.

In philosophy, such thematic study of consciousness is called *phenomenology*. In literature, there are numerous poems with such study of consciousness either as an implicit base or explicit theme. Even though we may not wish to argue that certain poets have been directly or indirectly "influenced" by philosophers such as Kant, Schopenhauer, or Husserl—and I certainly do not wish to undertake any such rigorous thesis in the direction of "influence"—we may certainly concede that the theme of self-conscious perception is central in many modern poems and in the work of many modern poets. This philosophical attitude, then, and its spectrum of stylistic reflexes, may be identified internationally as one of the characteristic features of modernism in poetry, and also provides a critical framework for placing Haavikko and Finnish poetry in general in a comparative context.[33]

NOTES

Reference is made throughout this essay to Gottfried Benn, Paavo Haavikko, Wallace Stevens, and William Carlos Williams. Texts used are:

Gottfried Benn, *Gedichte* (*Gesammelte Werke in vier Bänden* herausgegeben von Dieter Wellershoff), vol. 3 (Wiesbaden: Limes Verlag, 1963).

Paavo Haavikko, *Selected Poems*, trans. Anselm Hollo (New York: Grossman, 1968).

94

Wallace Stevens, *The Collected Poems of Wallace Stevens,* 12 ed. (New York: Alfred A. Knopf, 1972).

William Carlos Williams, *The Collected Earlier Poems* (New York: New Directions, 1951). "Youth and Beauty" reprinted by special permission of New Directions Publishing Company.

1. "Only God spoke Finnish," writes Väinö Linna. Finnish is the language of some four million people in Finland, Karelia, and settlement areas such as northern Wisconsin, Minnesota, Upper Peninsula Michigan, for example. Finnish is closely related to Estonian, more distantly to Lapp and Hungarian, and a number of languages spoken in the Soviet Union. It is *not* related in any way to Russian or Swedish (although there are loan words from each); rather, it is a member of the Finno-Ugric subdivision of the Uralic branch of the greater Uralic-Altaic group. Structurally, Finnish is similar to Turkish and Mongolian. Finns are intensely proud of their language, perhaps even more so because of its obscurity and difficulty for foreigners to master; but at the same time they are soberly aware that their mother tongue presents a major psychological and linguistic barrier to easy social and commercial intercourse with the world at large.

2. Fortunately, this essay no longer provides the entire critical commentary for the book. The present essay is a greatly enlarged version of the original introduction to the Fall 1970 Finland issue of *The Literary Review.* Revisions of the original material are minor. I am happy to delete my inadequate comments on drama. I have, however, retained my section on prose, for I feel it does not duplicate other essays in the anthology, and is useful as background to my discussion of poetry. The major change is the addition of the comparison of Haavikko to Gottfried Benn, William Carlos Williams, and Wallace Stevens. The focus of my essay, then, has changed from that of a general introduction to Finnish literature—though many vestiges of that remain—to discussion of a particular aspect of Haavikko's writing in the Finnish and international context.

   The conceptual approach I attempt to apply has intrigued me for the last few years, but I have had no opportunity for dialogue on the thesis or method—dialogue that would certainly have improved it, because I consider myself a translator trying my hand at criticism, rather than a critic and scholar trying my hand at translation. Since my work in Alaska takes me more and more into the moribund languages and oral traditions around me, I feel it is time to give literary birth to this essay, even if premature and with its various imperfections.

3. David Bradley, *Lion Among Roses* (New York: Holt, Rinehart, and Winston, 1965), pp. 13–14.

4. Anselm Hollo, *Word from the North* (London: Strangers Press, 1965), p. 4.

5. Dr. Karen Beebee of Alaska Methodist University translated a draft of Hein's essay for this anthology, but it proved unsalvagable without the numerous examples of complete poems cited in support of Hein's theses. Because there was not time to allow the translations to jell, we decided to omit the essay completely.

6. Manfred Peter Hein, *Moderne Finnische Lyrik* (Göttingen: Vandenhoeck and Ruprecht, n.d.), p. 13.

7. Kai Laitinen makes a similar observation in "Finnish Literature Today," *PEN Bulletin* 16, no. 1 (1965): 7:

   To be sure, some modern and even avant-garde poetry had already been written in Finland, but mainly in Swedish. The main proponents of modernism of the 20s were Edith Södergran, Elmer Diktonius, Gunnar Björling, and Rabbe Enckell. . . . Naturally the Finnish-language poets who began their careers in the 50s could not directly continue the heritage of the Swedish language modernists of the 20s.

8. Austin Goodrich, *Study in Sisu: Finland's Fight for Independence* (New York: Ballantine Books, n.d.), p. 54.

9. The distinction between the two wars is crucial in Finnish thinking. Consider, for example, the case of Arvo Turtiainen who, as noted in the biography section, fought in the Winter War but refused to fight in the Continuation War. Both wars were against the Soviet Union, but the second war was offensive and as a cobelligerent with Fascist Germany.

10. Linna is represented in this anthology by an excerpt from the trilogy. See *The Eviction*.

11. Jean Paul Sartre, *Nausea*, trans. Lloyd Alexander (New York: New Directions, 1964), p. 39 in the 1969 edition; *see* pp. 56–57 in the 1959 edition. Original French edition, 1938.

12. Kai Laitinen, "Väinö Linna and Veijo Meri: Two Aspects of War," *Books Abroad* 36, no. 4 (Autumn 1962): 365–67.

13. Pekka Tarkka, "Finnish Literature: The Great Tradition," trans. Meri Lehtinen, *Odyssey Review* 3, no. 1 (1967): 264–69.

14. *See also* Svedberg's essay on political poetry. Although the adjective "Finnish" here meant Finnish-language writing in the original version of this essay, the samples of Swedish-language poetry show that we may now consider—for this trait at least—"Finnish" to mean "poetry of Finland." More in-depth study of the national characteristics of Finnish poetry through comparison of Swedish- and Finnish-language poetry is a project I have not yet found the time and energy to undertake. The samples here suggest much similarity in style and content despite language difference, whereas that does not seem to be the case in the prewar period, as noted by Laitinen and Hein.

15. *See* this essay section for a *Literary Portrait* of Eeva-Liisa Manner.

16. This aspect of Saarikoksi's style has much in common with recent American poetry, such as Gary Snyder's.

17. Concern with permanence in Western literature is as old as *The Gilgamesh Epic*, likewise, it is one of Haavikko's favorite analogies—the house. On tablet X, column vi, line 26 of Heidel's translation, Utnapishtim asks rhetorically of Gilgamesh: "Do we build a house to stand forever?"; and in line 32 answers his question: "There is no permanence."

18. This and all excerpts from *Winter Palace* are from Paavo Haavikko, *Selected Poems*, trans. Anselm Hollo (New York: Grossman, 1968).

19. It seems to me that Benn's trouble was that his solutions—though bewildering and obscure to the reader at first—were ultimately oversimplified. (This note anticipates some of the discussion that follows. Rather than to break the continuity of the original portions of the essay, I have left most of it intact, and have elaborated in the expanded portion.) Kai Laitinen, "How Things Are: Paavo Haavikko and His Poetry," *Books Abroad* 43, no. 1 (Winter 1969): 41–45.

20. Ibid.

21. As an equation to the individual life, the analogy of the tree is widespread in Finnish riddles. *See:* Elli Köngäs Maranda, "The Logic of Riddles," in Maranda & Maranda, *Structural Analysis of Oral Tradition* (Philadelphia: University of Pennsylvania Press, 1971).

    Professor Maranda writes: "Taken together, the transformations of the basic riddle seem to explore the possibilities of the original riddle metaphor, which simply says that a human being is like a tree" (204). She summarizes her discussion of the transformations of one riddle metaphor: "Thus we have observed the whole human life cycle described in terms of the life of a tree" (204).

    In "Theory and Practice of Riddle Analysis," *Journal of American Folklore* 84, no. 331 (January–March 1971): 51–61, Professor Maranda points out the universality of the tree as a riddle comparison. "While common sense in all languages maintains that people are totally distinct from trees, riddles in perhaps all languages compare trees to people and people to trees" (54).

    But the following important observation is also made: "Where myths prove . . . the authority of social and cultural rules, or the fitness of . . . conceptual classifications, riddles make a point of playing with conceptual borderlines and crossing them for the intellectual pleasure of showing that things are not quite as stable as they appear" (53).

    The device of the tree in Haavikko's poetry seems either coincidentally or deliberately connected to the logic of riddle metaphor in Finnish tradition. I am not sure if, and it is also unclear to me at present if, should this line of logic be pursued, Haavikko's device should be considered an inversion of the equation of man and tree in the first three Maranda excerpts cited above, or an expansion of the riddle logic suggested in the last quotation. I am not arguing that Haavikko has been "influenced" by Finnish folklore, but the relationship between Finnish riddles and Haavikko's poetry seems worth looking into.

If not at present, riddles were, at least until recently, quite viable in Finnish oral tradition. Finnish scholarship has been seminal in folklore research, and the genre is well collected and documented. Both of Maranda's articles contain further references to trees in riddles, Finnish riddles, and riddle analysis in general.

22. All excerpts of poetry by Gottfried Benn are from Gottfried Benn, *Gesammelte Werke in vier Bänden,* ed. Dieter Wellershoff (Wiesbaden: Limes Verlag, 1963); all references are to volume 3, *Gedichte.* Translations are my own. Notations will be abbreviated: for example, first excerpt, (GW, 215); and second excerpt, (GW, 342). All others as noted in the text.

23. Paavo Haavikko, *Runot 1951–1961* (Helsinki: Otava, 1962), p. 165.

24. L. S. Dembo, *Conceptions of Reality in Modern American Poetry* (Berkeley, Calif.: University of California Press, 1966), p. 55.

Professor Dembo has put considerable effort into documentation of this problem in American poetry, and I am indebted to his research for inspiring the critical approach I am experimenting with in the expanded essay. My original concept was for a detailed comparative study, but circumstances have forced me to abandon it—at least temporarily—in favor of this more superficial essay that greatly condenses what I had already completed and alludes (largely through the footnotes) to the directions in which my research was taking me at the time I decided to cannibalize my original project for this essay.

Another of Dembo's publications on the subject is: "The 'Objectivist' Poet," *Contemporary Literature,* 10, no. 2 (Spring 1969, Madison, Wisc.: University of Wisconsin). The issue features interviews with George Oppen, Carl Rakosi, Charles Reznikoff, and Louis Zukofsky.

25. Wallace Stevens, *The Collected Poems of Wallace Stevens* (New York: Alfred A. Knopf, 1954; 12th ed., 1972), pp. 196–97. All others as noted in the text.

26. Wallace Stevens, *Poems by Wallace Stevens,* ed. Samuel French Morse (New York: Vintage, 1959), p. 136.

27. A point also made in my essay on Zen is worth repeating here, namely, that R. P. Blackmur's comment on the Stevens poem applies to Haavikko as well. Blackmur writes:

"The only emperor is the emperor of ice cream" implies in both stanzas that the only power worth heeding is the power of the moment, of what is passing, of the flux.

R. P. Blackmur, "Examples of Wallace Stevens," in *Form and Value in Modern Poetry* (New York: Anchor Books, 1957), p. 191.

28. Finnish poets other than Haavikko could be connected here. Compare, for example, a poem by the Swedish-language poet Bo Carpelan, beginning "at the table your figure" and ending with the words ". . . the use of things and clarity." Carpelan is very similar to Anhava, Manner, and Haavikko, who are not by accident his chief translators into Finnish.

29. Compare Stevens's "The Snowman" with Haavikko's "Lingonberries" and "Snowman," all of which reject a sentimentality that results from projection of the ego onto the object under study. It is also important, I think, that both Haavikko and Stevens are fond of the device of using a persona to present an ego that embodies an attitude contrary to that which the poem ultimately communicates. Haavikko's various speakers and Stevens's artist in "So-and-so reclining on her couch" are examples.

The theme of rejection of ego is found throughout Haavikko and Stevens, both of whom would reject the "ego concept" or "Ich-Begriff" endorsed most emphatically and in the extreme by the persona of Benn's "Synthese," an egocentric celebration of the primordial delights of masturbation that concludes:

. . . es stinkt kein Staub
mich, Ich-Begriff, zur Welt zurück.

. . . no dust stinks
me, ego concept, back to the world (GW, 57) .

30. In this context, consider also Haavikko's predilection for monologue and dialogue in his shorter poems as well. Vilho Viksten, in addition to his discussion of Haavikko's images, the concept of flux, etc., notes the dramatic aspect of Haavikko's poetry in: Vilho Viksten, "Analogian ja relaation mestari," *Parnasso* 6 (1965) : 244–55.

Professor Esko Ervasti's special interest is the influence of German philosophy on Finnish literature. He has written a number of articles that touch on Haavikko, placing him and other Finnish writers in the context of European and Finnish intellectual history. Among these are: "Erään kuolemantapauksen anatomiaa", *Kiila* 30 (1966) : 38–47, and "Lumoutujat," *Pohjoinen* 4 (1966) : 112–17.

These have been superceded by his monograph on the neo-epic in modern Finnish literature: *Välivaihe: Poimintoja Suomalaista nykyepiikasta* (Forssa: 1967) , 123 pp.

We had hoped to include translations of the essays by Ervasti and Viksten, but those of us available to translate had no time to do justice to Viksten, and after discussion with Professor Ervasti, we decided not to translate those essays he considers superceded by the monograph that is obviously too long for inclusion.

31. Consider, for example, these lines from Reinhard Sorge's *The Beggar,* a German expressionist play of 1912:

Well?! Well?! Was Miss Gudrun well built? Did she have her decent climaxes, hah? Did she go down nicely at the end?!

Translated in W. Sokel, *An Anthology of German Expressionist Drama* (New York: Doubleday, 1963) , p. 29.

32. Eventually, one must come to grips with the nineteenth-century philosophical backgrounds as they bear upon the problem discussed in this essay. Such a project is beyond my reach at the present time, and lies outside the scope of this paper. In the meantime, I have had to rely on various studies on symbolism and expressionism, as well as on more recent movements. The three most valuable to me have been:

Ralph Freedman, "Refractionary Visions: The Contours of Literary Expressionism," in *Contemporary Literature* 10, no. 1 (Winter 1969, Madison, Wisc.: University of Wisconsin).

Edgar Lohner, "Die Lyrik des Expressionismus," in Hermann Friedmann and Otto Mann, *Expressionismus: Gestalten einer literarischen Bewegung* (Heidelberg, 1956) .

Walter Sokel, *The Writer in Extremis* (Stanford, Calif.: Stanford University Press, 1959).

33. This comparison could be extended very productively to Eastern European poetry as well, especially to the Russian tradition extending from Fet through Pasternak to Voznesensky. But essays must stop somewhere. If I were to continue the Eastern European comparison beyond Russian poetry, I would expand the study of metaphor and perception in the direction of some modern Polish poets–Czeslaw Milosz and Zbigniew Herbert, especially, and some of Tymoteusz Karpowicz. I find their poems, at least as sampled in translation in the Penguin edition *Post War Polish Poetry* very similar to Stevens and Haavikko. I think the French poet, Francis Ponge, might also be added to our list for further study. His poem "Rule" suggests thematic concern similar to Wallace Stevens.

I would like to note a book here that came to my attention too late to be considered in this essay: Suzanne Juhasz, *Metaphor and the Poetry of Williams, Pound, and Stevens* (Lewisburg, Penn.: Bucknell University Press, 1974) .

LASSI NUMMI:

At the Sea Gate of the Palace

Translated by Dympna Connolly

When we approach Byzantium we approach the throne: the Emperor. When we approach the Emperor, we need caution and flexibility, the right direction and manner of approach, the right distance. If we try to get too close—if we try to find the answer to the Emperor as if to a riddle—we may be lost in the labyrinth of the palace, the labyrinth of Byzantine power. If we stay too far off, all we can see is the splendor surrounding the Emperor, the contours of the palace: the Emperor remains a blur of splendor, the palace structures are in shadow.

I am talking about Paavo Haavikko's sequence of poems *Fourteen Rulers,* its images, themes, atmosphere. The narrative content (and the form carrying the idea) consists of references to the chronicles of Michael Psellus, the Byzantine scholar and politician of the eleventh century; specifically, the section dealing with the transfer of power from Michael VI (1056–57), successor of the Empress Theodora, to Isaac Comnenus.

When we come to the sea gate of the palace, where are we? Obviously, in the middle of power struggles in the Byzantium of nine centuries ago; in the middle of urgency and exhausted conflict. And also wherever this conflict is waged: in men's minds, the web of mind and action, the community, society. And, quite certainly, in the present as well, which is only unique in the human conciousness.

Byzantium itself, of course, is an incomparable image: the meeting and section point of East and West, an ideological synthesis. The words and expressions of modern language, the references, analogies and anachronisms, bloom into a luxuriant foliage round the historical trunk. Or, on the other hand, the true trunk is modern political and economic thinking, while the images of ancient Byzantium form the foliage.

These two levels are involved and act as sounding boards for one another; the basic form of the sequence is their loose yet articulated contrapuntal correspondence.

The first of the "Fifteen Songs" concerns the instrument: poetry, language. The poet takes leave of the muse, whose task it is to combine and compile too many things that are too distant, to answer too many questions.

Here we must accept (or at least appear to accept) the agreement proposed: we are no longer (this time) concerned with the poet, but with the chronicler, the analytic, the philosopher.

A lyrical pattern begins to be built up—magnificent, sovereignly simple, and uncomplicated. Byzantium is built, in the "Second Song," rapidly and splendidly: by knocking at the gate. In this miniature epic, the imagery is less dense than in some earlier Haavikko, but there are rich comparisons, symbols, metaphors; the poem blooms with them like summer that gently becomes autumn: summer with a thousand breasts.

The essential content of the poem, offering itself for interpretation, lies in the comments and observations concerning property and ruling. They are straightforward, often shaded with irony, but not vanishing in irony; frequently exaggerated into paradox. Through them a political philosophy takes shape, consistent and free from any hint of credulity.

The central problem is the question of power, its significance and relativity, its attainment and loss. The political, military, economic, and psychological aspects of power are involved; the might of word, gesture, negotiation, and weapon. And, in the last analysis, the question is whether power is truly power, whether man can influence the world, whether even rulers are nothing but stamps in the hand of history. The question is whether men direct matters or matters men; to use the classic expression, a question of free will:

It seems we have been very carefully programmed.
But we have perhaps a two percent margin.
Yet the basis of all action
is that we ourselves determine things . . .
Certainly man cannot act without believing in free will.
Or succeed, unless he knows that the world has its way.

Side by side with power, the significance and relativity of ideals and weapons is considered: *neo-Fascism* and the fight against it. Here, too, the poet's ironical, elliptical approach leaves room for interpretation. Even so, I assume that this concept is fairly precise in content, at least in one aspect: doctrines of violence, the hard line on left and right alike, in politics and the labor market, in East and West.

The reflection becomes sceptical:

And, very much alone, I consider, that in this struggle
against fascism there is no point wondering who are allies,
they may be the same themselves, no reason to be pedantic.

Most of the concepts are still more open to interpretation: just when you think you have grasped concrete historical content it slips from your grasp. One can, of course, play with putting symbolical interpretations into the language of the poems: could Michael VI mean a liberal trend followed by tougher doctrines, or perhaps great power policy of today, or maybe even the question of who will be Finnish president after Kekkonen? Sooner, or later, experimenting like this, one feels oneself to be, in the poet's words,

a bird that once again from its hollow bones
assembles proposals as clear as the raven's croak from
the forest verge.

The emperor nods; everything fits, and nothing; the writing of a transparent, unambiguous allegory would hardly suit Haavikko's work.

A political scale of attitudes handled by Haavikko in prose, plays, and poetry is that of realist—opportunist—courtier—toady! We meet them again here. Isaac Comnenus is the kind of realist who ends up ruling. But Psellus, the chronicler, courtier, and opportunist, seems to be still more of a realist, for he lives under eight rulers and always becomes advisor to the new emperor. When the ceremonies begin he is always "close to the center of power."

Should anyone ask whether Haavikko is a radical or a conservative, I should reply that he is a radical conservative, a realist. And a critic of concepts and attitudes, an ironist whose irony is directed at the same object as defined in "Trees and All Their Green," the content of the world's speech: "about every-thing at the same time."

If people were suddenly to come to their senses
It would cause irreparable damage.

But at the same time, between the time-bound and timeless human observa-tions, analysis of the community, illumination of language and thought, there is always one theme: the tapestry and the theme of its patterns.

Of course, the "tapestry," too, as a symbol, may reflect many things simulta-neously: the development of political philosophy, history, and the interpretation of history, art, poetry. History narrates, interprets, and jests; and "strikes us if we do not laugh." Political action, economic action, any kind of practical action or stage of history links the community or the individual with the field of deeds and responsibility: Byzantium moves to the sign of the Rat, and that means

. . . direct action, rapid decisions, efficiency,
belief that there are things and things that need fast decisions.

And the sign of the Rat means darkness of the soul. But

on one side was a picture of Byzantium
working at full capacity.
On the other side its two heirs, East and West,
and at their feet a black woman.
The heirs were quarreling furiously. The black woman was huge-eyed,
her breasts like hanging mountains or gardens.

We are here, here and now. "I looked at all this for my own pleasure." The perspective of the moment also becomes involved, coolly and certainly, in the web: a deep doubt as to the possibility of stabilization is reflected in the next, "Ninth Song," describing the spacious ritual of negotiations that "serves the idea that things can be mastered."

But the "Eighth Song" is the heart of *Fourteen Rulers*; in its web there breathes the second dimension of the poem, conceptual, irrational. Identity, solitude.

I went round to the other side of the tapestry. Sat down.
And there I saw how Byzantium moved imperceptibly into the
sign of the Rat.
I said to myself that Pisces is followed by Aquarius, which means
solitude, the spirit, introspection.
After Pisces comes Aquarius.
But the tapestry went on. . . .

It is unlikely that the age of Aquarius is at hand. And "irrational" must not be misunderstood; it is not a question of a casual mental vacillation, but the expression and emphasis of an extremely aware poet. Of a realist: Aquarius is a reality, part of the world. So is the Rat. Action; and awareness, spirit.

Thus, a poem of this kind is not empty words, elegant lies. On the contrary, it is good sense, directly expressed. Unshakeably direct, since it is not a question of commerce or art, ideals or policies, but of the world, where all these aspects act and interact simultaneously. For its content is not action or identity, not myself or others, but the tension between them. The irreduceable world.

POETRY

Poetry translated by Richard Dauenhauer unless otherwise credited.

Finnish-language Poets

ARVO TURTIAINEN

FOUR POEMS

To Saliini from Jail

Translated by Lassi Vakkilainen and David Bradley

You grub and sweat eight hours every day,
you sleep thirteen,
and three hours you spend in eating
and telling filthy stories, sitting on your cot.
If I say to you, My friend
read something,
you're wasting your life,
you come back with, That much at least
Is mine.

Saliini   Saliini
Must the world be changed for your sake?

They Threw Me in Jail

Translated by Lassi Vakkilainen and David Bradley

They threw me in jail.
Yes, they threw me in jail.
They didn't know—the fools—
that they can't keep a free mind in irons.

They gave me a world I didn't know,
          new reasons, new ideas.
They handed me a crossbarred lookout
                    with a pinch of sunset on it,
                    or a squeeze of morning on it.

They gave me friends, crowned
                    with the leaves of fate.
In the dim glass of their eyes I found deep words
                    written by life.
Their names I read scratched on the stone walls.
I talked to them,
ate their kind of bread, lived their kind of life.
And I got to know the word Freedom,
learned to know the meanings of Freedom,
the many kinds of Freedom.

And I learned to love:
a spear of new grass alive in my cell,
a flower blooming in the shadow of the wall,
a summer cloud reflecting on my crossbarred opening,
the song of a bird in a birch beyond the walls,
children shouting in the road outside the gates.
I learned to love—
everything,
most of all Freedom.

They threw me in jail—the fools,
for the soldiers of freedom,
they hammered me into a sword,
they tempered me into an arrow of lightning.

Forty Below Zero

(The Winter War)

Translated by Philip Booth, with the help of
Soini Pirttila and Patricia Rosenbröijer

          Those January nights
          the stars' teeth
          crunched
          the crusted snow.

          Those January nights
          the moon was a coffin
          slid into
          the heavens' dark vault.

The black forests
spasm'd, the forms
of the Northern Lights
were stilled.

That old dagger
—frost—flashed
in death's hand
those January nights.

Spring

*Translated by Philip Booth, with the help of
Marjatta Utriainen and Patricia Rosenbröijer*

Spring climbs on apartment roofs
    to waltz with the wind;
Spring opens housewives to fling open windows
    and beat their rugs on balconies;
Spring tugs husbands to island harbors, tidal
    with pints of bourbon;
Spring is a flat-out motorbike, with
    a half saddled girl hanging on;
Spring makes trees in the park bud red,
    and girls in its long twilight;
Spring comes home at five in the morning,
    its high heels clicking on asphalt.

AILA MERILUOTO

Wallis

(to the memory of Rilke)

Translated by Philip Binham

Narrow long glass tipped
against the lips: O this wine:
full honey-gold of evening,
burning the surprised mouth
with Rhone's bitter green, and cooling
towards the sides to mountain ice.
O this trinity from which bouquet arises,
the fine bouquet of memory, threefold too:
once, now, never—or not like that:
shyer, wordless, a stranger to the senses.

That which remains, the final sediment,
that was higher, above the valley poetry
and beyond iridescent colour—separate:
a bare husk on the mountain-side,
a poet's grave
windy, gray.

LAURI VIITA

Happiness

Translated by Philip Binham

Narrow path from well to door
grassed over.
Before the window
a dried-up apple tree.
Bag on a nail by the door,
a bird's nest there.
When I am dead, when I am dead.
Summer will continue. Summer.

HELVI JUVONEN

FIVE POEMS

August Evening

A red dragon
roams the summer evening,
lashing clouds
with its tail.
They flee in terror
and the dragon looks,
and ponders—then
swallows the moon, and

satisfied, it beams
with a full belly
over the land.

The Boulder

Erratic
split from the mother rock,
carried far by glacier,
abandoned by the ice:
alone in the forest,
I am alien and rare.

I don't mind it
if children play around me,
I don't mind it when the snow
settles on my back. But,
never cut me
just because I stand
and ponder, looking like a bear.
I am not cold. I too am warm
when the sun shines.

The Bear

Alive? In the land of the living,
shaggy, with corny claws.

His ear can't comprehend the word,
his eye seeks an eye, and reads the emptiness.
The door to the forest never opens,
the sky never spreads
a sheet of snow: light-foot, heavy-foot,
he goes where he goes with the land.

How was his fur
lost? his claws ripped out, the teeth
slowly broken from his mouth?

The wind laughs
when I dance a dance with it,
the day laughs
when it shines in my eyes, and I
laugh when I laugh when I want to.
When I laugh I laugh
in my bear-skull.

The door to the forest never opens.

* * *

The time of the melting of the snow
when rocks become
visible, I see carved into each
the features of my mother, striated
by age and worry, warm in the shining day
when love has melted ice.

*Helvi Juvonen's last poem
dictated, September 9, 1959*

And some of these, too—
tiny, well-formed, green fall-poems
I would like to give you still
did you hear how the words
ran
they were all like songs
each sang
in a leaf chorus
in a leaf chorus
when autumn blew
——

EEVA-LIISA MANNER

Peace Piece

Translated by Liisa Luomi

The town dozes in April rain,
Boats glide down the river, housegables
Slide over the languid water. And from that upside-down world
Other sounds come, as from sleep or very far away:
Someone is singing in a boat
Under the awnings. I do not remember more:
Nur diese zärtlichen Töne:
dich zu lieben, dich zu liebkosen, und über dich weinen.*

The image fades in the rain,
It is the tenth of April
And that day also vanishes
And joins whispers from 50 years ago.

*Only these tender sounds: to love you, to caress you, and to cry over you.

I can no longer keep this undulating world apart
From the world I have made,
And from what lies hidden in all other worlds.

The wooden town is grey in foglight.
A little child walks on the street with his blue reflection
Surrounded by rain, drowsiness.
Suddenly I am awake:
I see that face again drifting farther away
die zärtlichen Augen, still, ohne Hohn,
auch der Regen gehört dem Geschehen an.**

Aber in welcher Stadt das passiert ist
hab' ich vergessen.***

Here

As loneliness extends itself from me,
bushes die away,
trees flee, and the house martin's white
is lost in black.
Coldness of the night advances slowly
        and covers tiny bodies
like a sheet of ice.
Distant trees support
the emptiness,
and loneliness is born from tree
to naked tree
like a rock. Infinity

and snow.

Ruth Ellis's Prayer

I reach my fettered hands; proud
I didn't ask for help. I stood the trial
dumb, a human animal,
waiting forgiveness in the end,

I didn't ask for peace; for
peace will come to me only when my body
has been stripped, only when these limbs,
these limbs, are stripped away.

**the tender eyes, quiet, without scorn, also the rain belongs to this event.
***But in which city it happened I forgot.

And Morning Lightens
(from the Ruth Ellis cycle)

The land is bleak. The sky
bright, and morning clears and deepens
   like a great restrained expanse.
Only the dark hanged figures sway,
softly, and make their sounds. The wind rises
and falls. Silence. And begins again:
nothing but this simple act
   of dying, into a distant dawn,
when empty bodies echo like organ pipes
   or ring like bells for their deaf creator.

Shore and Reflection

When shore and reflection are settled to the same,
a calm and perfect marriage of water and the sky,

when illusion is deep and clear and
clouds and wildlife roam,
and the dark forest hums in its depths
from wind in the air,

we need only the just-wetting tip of the wing of a bird
to shatter—Light and water delightedly confess
illusion to the world: thin as silk,
with surface tension thin alliances.

And the world, as fresh and beautiful
as after rain, creation, change of mind,
or fever break, is pregnant and unique,
and, limb from limb, alone.

Sub Rosa 1

We met on a reddening path,
the flowers weaving carpet, and the sun
and shadows speckles
torn in the breeze

We embraced the green, and light
diffused it to the trees
We gave each other flowers
crushed by kisses

and we saw
everything
for the first time: the land,
translucent, humming groves,
and the twisted trees
wound in death
to sculpture
by the wind.

Sub Rosa 2

We wander past the seasons,
wade through leaves
like old letters,
the squandered
currency of trees.

We caress the skin
keeping us apart;
and wandering, are lost
in the never-changing past.

Sub Rosa 3

What happened was—a swallow flit through the air
and now: silence.

The shore is empty, and the wind
slips back and forth
through the cove of my arm
and up and down the bay like a
stray dog companion.

A blue feather, the broken
speculum of duck, stuck to my sleeve
lifelessly, a spot
splattered on a stone.

Sub Rosa 4

My boat is pulled up high. The wind
will not repair its sides, the water
now ignores it. It's getting colder, I
am all alone.

Let Us, Accordingly, Forget

Trees relinquish their September burden,
and gaze into the distance.
Clearsightedness.
Light, a dark forest, desolation,
and under everything, the dreary bottomless.

Let us, accordingly, forget, and walk lightly
through strange times, changing dusk,
the sensitive forest and yearning autumn days,
not blaming our sorrow, for it is ours, and still warm.

Linen Window

The golden branch of juniper, the fragrant
ashes. In the forest, rain
and yellowing ridges. Sunset lifts
breezes from the lake.

I listen to a wild duck. A shadow
passes on my door, and I recall
time of illusion, my source of strength.
The linen window faces the darkening west.

Orpheus in the Underworld I

You turned, and she solidified. The past
is never mirrored, refracted, never veers;
and yet, it's real,
thicker than your hand, translucent
against the sun.

You never try to grasp
an echo, like a heart-
beat, enclosed within itself.
The minutes close within her hand,
becoming tangible; cold as time she lets them
fall: cities, years, echoes.

You keep on walking,
and are still
wounded by the rocks
which stay behind.

Orpheus in the Underworld II

From loneliness, no road
will lead you back
to the hard, clear past.
Euridice,
    a sister, longing,
a wife, perhaps a mother,
an omniscient follower,
but she won't understand you
if you speak.

A road that hears, but doesn't wait to hear,
footprints show, it doesn't miss them,
it recalls a memory, repels
your person; you enchant the trees,
with an instrument you carry in your breast,
not her.
She always follows equi-
distant, locking herself in her knowledge
like a statue.

You look; you see a face: it's
dead; you touch it: empty.

    A shadow moves
along your puzzled hand,
and in your heart,
from auricle to ventricle the tiny
echo of a sob.

Dionysus, Orpheus, Psychopompous
(for Paavo Haavikko)

If all dreams are born of desire, then isn't springtime also half dream? He's
dressed himself in grass, verdure personified; when he wanders to the shores of
May, he's pretty as a picture of an ox. His shoulder's straight as a chariot axle,
the Gemini sparkle from his eyes. He has a thousand forms, and every spring
he's new, Orpheus the Enchanter, the resounding stag of the woods,
the sprite holder of supernatural games;

and every fall he's crushed,

tossed away, and the green scatters on the wind like a drowning hair, and the
coldwater fish swim in the empty chamber of his head and through the sub-

merged sides of the lyre. He sings and wanders, in his mouth—the money of his soul, obulus, animula, repeating, resounding;

until May

he carries virgin flowers, fragile and red hot, to the feast of the resurrected body, he dresses up in leaves, adorns his waist, takes dionysian cover for the dance; oh, isn't this change profound and beautiful, a metaphorical rain, a nightingale and victorious peace, Siegfried, Sigismund, Sigmund Joy.

The Tired West

> Ej Norden finns mera
> si jorden har dött
> Den nya Solens uppgång förkunnas
> av heliga Foglar*
> —Murnis

It will redden and grow dark when the tired west
is put to rest, and the ripe season
drops into the boundless chalice of the sky;
when they break their swords, opening books,
a hum will descend like the fluttering of wings
and things will rise from their traps like spirits
as if clearer, united, after rest,

a snowy horse, having
struggled on the steppes, wades
to a field, his blaze another star, and with him a
child: a naked warrior; and they run
over the flowering land, sea-
like, surging, boundless and blue,
like the Virgin's robe, woven
from emptiness
and light.

And endless
in all cooperations are their beauty,
tenderness, delight, friendship,
recreation, peace.
And translucent morning after morning rises,
and birds to the trees.

*The North exists no more
 the world has died
 The new Sun's rise is foretold
 by holy Birds

Come to the Yard of Reflection

Come to the yard of reflection
    when the sky is deep-pearl
and the hour of the summer day, warm and quiet
sleeps in seven birds in the shade of seven trees
and seven waters sleep, gathering a dream.

Until light moves an inch
    and colors fall from their prism
tinkling into the trees and casting their net.
You hear the swish of water, the humming of trees,
birdsongs, and the voice of many Buddhas

Chang Heng: The Bones of Chuang Chou

I, Chang P'ing-Tsu, who journeyed through Nine
Deserts and saw their wonders;
and walked man-made roads on the eighth continent,
I who saw the Sun and the Stars on their heavenly paths,
who saw the Roaring Dragon and the flaming flight of the Phoenix,
I who suffered thirst in the red waste-land
and waded through winter villages from Yu to the north,
I wandered in the west through the valley of the Night
and came in the east to the farthest point of the Sun,
which is a bent Mulberry Tree.

Thus the seasons changed: weakened fall died
and the light touch of the breeze awakened winter freezing.
And now: I rein one horse in and urge the other,
I turned my wagon with the tent again facing west.
Thus we drove moving slowly
past ditches, meadows, mountains and sand dunes.

—Suddenly I saw the bones of a man at the roadside
scattered on the bare ground.
Dark frost covered them, and with sorrow in my heart I asked:
"Dead man, how did this happen?
Were you fleeing with a friend from famine
and a troubled land, and lost?
Were you buried here or did the river bring your bones?
Were you rich and wise or poor and foolish?
A warrior or a woman?"
—Then a miracle occurred, from the silence a voice spoke,
weak as an echo, strangely telling:
        "I was a native of Sung
and of the family of Chuang, my name was Chou.

Even though I dwelled in thought high above the commonplace,
it could not save my soul.
Finally, when my long life had run out,
I got to bend as others, I left the big burden of my knowledge.
Old age drew me to the dark hills of Death.
Why, honorable one, do you ask me this?"

Then I said:
"Let me speak on your behalf on the fifth mountain peak,
let me say the word to the gods of Heaven and Earth
so that your bones will be gathered together
and your limbs will be born again.
The god of the land of the north will give me back your ears,
I will march to the south to inherit your eyes,
from the Sunrise I will pull your legs
and I will force the Sunset to relinquish your heart.
All your organs will be gathered, all put in their places
and each of your senses will regain validity.
Isn't this exactly what you want?"

The dead man answered:
"My friend, your words are vain and useless.
What was my life but struggle and pain?
Death gave me my peace.
Is the armor of the winter river better
than the spring which comes of it?
And doesn't all the pride the body knew
equal only ashes?
Who am I to wish
what Ch'ao and Hsü rejected,
what Po-Ch'eng fled—
me, already buried by the side of the Eternal Highway,
where Li Chu cannot see me
nor Tsu Yeh hear me,
where neither Yao nor Shun can eulogize me,
tiger or wolf tear me apart,
spear or ax inflict a wound?
My body has been changed to spirit
where Darkness and Light can interplay like ripples.
The Creator of All is my Father and Mother,
the Sky is my final resting place and the Earth is my pillow,
thunder and lightning my drum and fan,
the sun and moon my fireside and torch,
the milky way my tower, and the stars my jewels.

I have walked back the Natural Road,
I have relinquished all desire. I didn't suffer.
Wash me now and I won't turn white,

smudge me and I am still clean.
I have not come, yet I am here,
I won't rush off, though I am fast."

The sound dies, and everything is silent.
The ghostlike luster fades.
I look at the dead with sympathy and sorrow.
And then I call my servant. I ask him
to wrap the bones in silk
and cover them with the warmness of the earth.
And I myself shed hot tears on the grave of the bones of Chou
as I sacrifice for the soul of the deceased.

FOUR POEMS FROM *Thus the Seasons Changed*

1

No paths in the rushes.
From the openings of shore
no boat slips away.
Frosty morning, undivided days,
loneliness, the soft forest.

2

All day—the sound of wings, migration's
underway. A noise
from the forest: falcon
or the wind? The sound of autumn,
rain-full.
From the eaves a black
and airy bird
        falls away.

3

Morning again, and warming.
A loosened fog belt
rises from the shore.
From the forest the gentle
hooting of an owl.

4

Footsteps whisper at the gate.
They come and go, the footsteps
but never his I need.

TWO PROSE POEMS FROM *The Inscribed Rock*

I: Thus the Season Changed

Spring, summer, and autumn divide the year among themselves. Winter doesn't really exist. Days when it rains, autumn's come from the north. Rain rushes past me like an endlessly long Madrid express train, at night there's distant thunder suggesting earthquakes. Matches won't light, and there's water under the crystal of my waterproof watch. A butterfly is crawling on the wall, big and frightened as a child's face.

When I look at the mountains in the morning, they aren't there. Emptiness has thrown its cup, mountains have disappeared as if a gigantic hand had moved them from here in Spain to Africa. Nor is it a runway, only a chasm of the mists. The pearl cover of the rain covers my door, the doorstep is scattered with flowers. The yard is round and has risen like a loaf of bread.

II: The Inscribed Rock

It's a flattened cup-shaped object, and judging from the surface, brittle and granular, very old; it's beautifully eroded like the beautifully eroded language on its edge: Arabic, with rare softness and elegance in the vine of writing, perhaps a chapter of the Koran, it too is worn. It's a dark heavy rock, yesterday it weighed a kilo, today 900 grams; because I've slept half the day and am happy and a kilo weighs 900 grams today. They say it's from the eleventh century.

When I raise it against the light, clear houses rise around it, houses with bright shutters, and on the balconies waterfalls of flowers. From the next house a song: "Your heart is rock, and I inscribe it." I don't see the singer, the words stem from ivy. A crazy girl, a girl who lets the ivy cover her window, maybe she too is looking at the moon through glass, a crazy girl.

TUOMAS ANHAVA

FOUR POEMS

1

I look out, it's very calm:
a leaf falls, and a second leaf,
and a third.

2

A cold night, fog
on the bay, a sound from nearby:
a boat rowing past.

3

Fog turns green on the thick grass,
on the cold sand, yellowing,
on the shore, four mallards sifting mud.
My house is open everywhere into fall.

4

I have recently stopped
longing.
I can't any more.

TWELVE POEMS

Translated by Pekka Virtanen

1

Ten thousand songs
flew over this morning.
I am moving away.

2

A sprout of birch. In the wind
a big shaggy leaf
tumbles, head over heels.

3

The house, the spruces,
rainy days around them.
The lake shines dim through the woods
like a constant sorrow.

4

I come and go.
It's harder and harder
to say anything.

5

From eight to six.
From eight to six.
I wouldn't know my children any more.

6

I don't remember.
Summer, like a woman next to my skin.
It is November, now gone.

7

Not a single person
      has ever seen him except
before or after a meeting.

8

It's the first time I built a room for myself.
It's low. It's good to look at in. It didn't cost much.
And the door almost pierces the ceiling.

9

Was born to be a mother for the Gracchi*, gave birth
to two foresters
and an M.A.

10

My hand is open, I remember
you with my fingers,
distracted.

*Roman family of statesmen, 2nd century B.C.

11

You have these charges . . .
    What is it?
That everything around is of nature.

12

This spring I, in my turn,
see how spruce branches have
green candles.

FOUR POEMS

Translated by Anselm Hollo

1: The Birds

When a bird goes
    it is different
when a bird goes
    it is a light fall
when a bird goes
    it is an easy flight
when a bird goes
    it is quite different

from the departure of one dead: he drags himself
away, crumbles onto the road, piecemeal,
and nothing remains to be buried but his corpse.

When a bird comes
    it is quite different
when a bird comes
    it is light knuckles on the door
when a bird comes
    it is a foot stepping lightly away
when a bird comes
    it is different

from the arrival of one dead: in pain, he is removed
from the dying, a cry, from the cry—
out, onto the road, from the dust, to dust.

2: May, 1964

I

A night in May, in the May of nights
out of the day gone west into the sea
      out of the day, and sweet now, with an offshore wind,
      smoke rising out of the ship,
      sails of darkness, remote islands,
      star-studded masts and shores and horizons,
northern,
      budding forth from the cold,
      a youth, a maiden
      and the tree's maidenhair rustle so green! so light!
      the earth, now moist and open,
May, gone now,
time without time
      of the northern night,
      high, leisurely, a migrant hawk
      gliding at twilight speed
      a waking dream
      and the dew on the roads
      stretching towards the morning and the city,
morning, holding its breath
        rooftops, mirrors
        ablaze like the open sea
        a youth as old as the sun
everything held
in its eyes,
      the true, the green, the grey
      the eyes, gazing far out to sea;
wind on the forehead
and transience,
proud as a ship

II

The moments, like statues, and the statue

      its eyes blinded by distance
      its breath becalmed
      the marble heartbeat within the ribcage
      the hand's gesture, casting no shadow
      the frozen step
      the elegance of nudity

incontrovertible as dreams
as youth, there is no return
who would not find it beautiful
to die into memory
to be forgotten eternally
when youth dies
it makes us feel so immortal

III

Who is young, who would go
would do every thing, everywhere
say this and say that, meet others, always in new frames of mind,
then sleep, in his sleep, in a peace of this world.
Not having acquired that skill of statues, spectators
of freezing into stillness,
for a moment it takes your breath away, eternity,
then gives it back,
it is not in the fire, but the flesh is alive,
it has its desires, its fears, it is at one with all living creatures,
whenever the sky is ablaze, the sea rises, the wind
touches his forehead
and transience, a message: the heat of crematoria.
His pores are open, the world moves in and out
in him who is young, most alive, most mortal,
but we know that our peace is anguished
and this certainty makes him uncertain, this skill makes him clumsy,

wealth impoverishes, cleanliness soils him
and our shame forces him to avert his face,
this labour, so productive, yet so useless in so many ways
makes his heart sink, and the freedom he is permitted
turns into anxiety in his mind,
our dwellings force him out into the street.
One sees a migrant hawk and decides to follow it, into extinction.

But most of them follow us, well, what about us;
some follow those who do not want anything any more,
who don't even want to die, members of no class,
there aren't many of them, anywhere, there are a few everywhere,
a harmless amount of activity, in our bones.
Who would not like to set his course the way youth does,
the cunning radical, the middle-aged, the jovial bishop at the bazaar,

and old age, guided by right and might and reality, faith
and beauty and terror, all the sisters of our dreams
and finally, always, indifference,
the sister no one invited.
Not a springtime, no sea, no creature
left unpoisoned. And it is only twenty years, now.
We ask what is going on, the world replies,
it is all of it going on, it is, all of it, real.
No one would like to wait for that answer.
The songs have died. I grieve,
grieve for Scylla and grieve for Charybdis,
both of them sirens, both of them choked to death.

IV

The immortals? I do not think of them often.
I think of the others, all the others

one cannot remember, only consider,
cannot imagine, only know. The mortal ones,
more and more often I think of them. *Manes et maiores.*
Just names, if that. Dates, if that,
but years, yes, endlessly, years. Gone with their days
and with those who did remember,
if they ever had any of those.

But not as you would think of a procession,
of some frieze of anonymous exaltation.
Among them, perhaps,
      an old man who kept telling his ailments like a rosary.
      A difficult child, subnormal, pacified with cold water.
      The nurse who told me about it and smiled.
      The polite young man who had a few rare words in his vocabulary.
      Two women who used to read their newspaper every day, from the first
                           to the last page.
Workers idlers finger-tappers talkers runts gluttons blondes pedants hotheads
                                          rawbones.

From morning without morning
until night without night—see, there you are,
even you can be buried under a phrase.
Farewell
Goodbye
We'll come as soon as

V

The last day of May
of the last May?
the invisibility of tomorrow
but this May is pushing its leaves into June
in the morning, the rock dove
covered in dust, turned its head, trembling
the sun was out, the air was blue to breathe
the sun is still out, the air is bright
and in the midst of this day, this pay-day, the daily reckoning
I appear in the doorway of the Bank
suddenly filled with wonder at all that goes on
with tenderness
the women! the women, like perennials
the men like wardrobes
their steps in the street
the sun is out, howl of cars
trams lorries ignorant armies
      If rain has fallen,
      where will our nostrils meet with the scent of that grove?
      how does the twig lie across the path?
      where does the cloud go? when there is no one there
      and what is blue?
I go in through the door

the lift squeaks to a stop, the doors slam
the world is a city and does not cease
these rooms where I live receive it, the surge of the surge
      What did you say? it does not cease?
      and suddenly all is quiet:
      sometimes, it is.
And that, too, is received here,
through the open window.
Then you hear it again. Someone whistling.
A boy. Down in the yard. No tune.
Just whistling. His own.

3

I thought how each
              tree, house, man
stands apart when there is no one to see them

      Such a *callous* thrill
when plant roots tangle and grope the Earth

And is there a sky; and what does it feel like
           if one is a horse

4

Everyone who believes what he sees
      is a mystic.
In the dark
      move slowly.

PERTTI NIEMINEN

SIX POEMS

Translated by Pekka Virtanen

1

Flesh grows
inside it a butcher's knife:
day after day the bones loosen,
they will be heaped in piles, crumble.
O my beloved.

2

As little reason as for life,
as little import
from morning to night, month to month,
year and year, from birth to death.
Nail up the instant, live
up the sun fixed at its zenith
an endless syllable in the mouth
eternity as in a photograph.

3

Su Tung-po used to live here
nine hundred years ago:
perhaps we both saw the same stone
even though we went entirely different ways.

4

The talk's fog hides the scene:
where should the hunter aim?

5

The world full of gazelle tracks:
let them be mine
until the next rain.

6

The wind blows, in passing,
times of the year touch the empty ground:
the runes will be carved, stones piled,
the sun goes up, goes down
far away, far away.

TEN PROSE POEMS

Translated by Pekka Virtanen

1

I love the plain most when lightly covered with snow. Leaves of grass rising all over, brown and black; under the trees, the earth is bare. The sky arches deep and blue, the noon sun shines cold, frosty. The frozen grass, soughing, frostwork on the bank, bright and cool like the air. Smoke like an uncanny pine, God's lonely tree, it rises from the hunter's cabin across the river. On a day like this the mountains disengage from the haze; one might think a stone would fly some ten, thirteen miles. The slaves and the beasts of burden tug timber from the mountains, load after load they strain to the city. I turn to the river, walk along the bank for a while, upstream. The osier sprigs do not quite give way under the snow, not yet, the shadow of a maple dips its top to the stream. From behind one can every now and then hear the elephant's trumpet: it crushes the air to crack, then falls to the plain snow and rolls to the end of its rate. The snow clings to the shoes, my footprints are almost black. The wind is rising. I am thinking of you. The river runs, dark. I am thinking of the king and the chase.

2

And I, I am thinking of you. I wouldn't care for dying but that is the rule. Last night it was snowing and today, the king took off to hunt. The king could be eaten by a tiger: this or that, there will be a new king always at hand but not a new me for you to be true to.

The king will love me until death; I, you.

3

I am the king. The chase does not please me though the forefathers have always been for it. One can do nothing about it.

Woodcutters' ax blows have been left beyond the range of my ears. The pines rise high up to the skies, the sun, between the trunks, pokes one in the eye. One cannot ride at full gallop on the mountains, the game tracks lead to the rocks. I let the deer pass and I believe I am after a tiger with a black and golden fur.

I love my beloved, she loves hers, and the history demands me to slay her. And if the tiger will kill me, the king to come will execute the seer too; how could he trust a seer who couldn't tell the king's death. I feel so sad. The wind slashes through my mantle, the sun begins to set.

I may not see a tiger today; perhaps it only sees me.

4

The king lays down his beloved for his country, he is a humble and loyal king, just in every respect. Many a country has been ruined because of a beloved.

How beautiful, the plain. Single tracks lead to the bank and along it, upstream. The wind has shaken the snow down from the osier sprigs, the shadow of a maple reaches the other bank. The whole city is covered by a thin smoke. The king has not been back yet. It is told the woodcutters have been involved in accidents on the icy mountain paths. The tigers might have food enough.

5

We could run away, the king is gone: flight from the realm of the Gods means human fortitude, the courage of our forefathers was different, the times have changed, now, they are Gods.

I still hear the elephant's trumpet. Dry leaves and needles have fallen to the river. I predict the tiger will tear the king to pieces, I will take you down the river to the big forests and to the sea, Gods we shall unclothe for the billows to carry away, and I shall lay you out.

If you care to leave.

6

I know lots of fellows who can talk only about one thing; sometimes it's quite vexing to talk with them. Last time we met, I said that boys, please, let's not always think bawdy, let's talk about something else now, and so we started talking about women.

One said he liked that kind and the other this kind, a third one thin ones with high breasts, and I said I love all ripe and wonderful:

the neck and breast white, honey-colored legs, thighs firm except for the inside end, soft and velvety, not too thin; the back and shoulders like in the Venus before the mirror by Velázquez, the belly like in Dürer's Eve, breast the like you can get hold of; I won't utter a word about the face, beautiful faces are of so many kinds.

The boys went off their ways and I went to my beloved, and when I told her what I had said, she said: why didn't you describe my face, now they'll undress all the women before they'll find me.

7

John asked me why do I write. First I said I don't know, and I really wasn't sure of it. Then he asked whether I wrote to see my name in the papers. Hell, of course, I said, and even more: I praise my own intellect and scoff the others, I have no other natural need, purpose, nor end in view.

John said that he had thought so, too, and my wife fully agreed.

8

Professor W. Barnstone, Indiana State University, interviewed me once in a restaurant. What kind of poems do you write, he asked me, he was young and comely and always like a bit drunk, he had many collections published and had been busy translating besides; he showed me pictures of his children. I said well glad and sad and from between; he went on inquiring and finally he asked me whether I had a dream not yet come true. I have, I said, I would like to see some time a woman with hair aplenty growing in her mouth. Professor Barnstone said uh and turned his back to me; and I had been altogether honest, however.

9

Quantz is teaching Frederick the Great how to flute; he's just come from Dresden where he had heard concertos composed by an excellent Venetian abbot, pater Antonio Vivaldi; Frederick sees behind the pear trees the moon on its back, he's thinking of the Venetian moon and then the pears are hanging from the branches upside down and the king has the taste of their white flesh on his tongue; he decides to go south.

Those maps! Those kings!

Quantz longs all his life for Venice and, yearning, composes some 500 pieces for flute. In Poland, Frederick gets the gout.

10

Christiane Eda is a charming dear lady, listen to the voluptuous trills she twitters in the holy scenes. Still, I'd rather hear Ambrosina; she's singing Gloria's soprano solo, a long swinging air; it rings, the wind rings in the orange trees and vines, and Ambrosina, she's no countenance, behind the golden lattice; the oboe carries her voice, Ambrosina hushes and the oboe rings like a bird in love; and then, does Ambrosina know the trills? If I were the cardinal, I'd tell her not to; she'd come by night and sing for me only, and we would be like the wind and the grass, like the wind and the grass.

PAAVO HAAVIKKO

Someone's growing old here,
walking blind around a pond, amazed
    by the silence of the water, amazed
by all the water.

Our generation jokes. We hear its questions,
long after demolition, asking
    what kind of a house it was
and was it ever built.

*   *   *

Every house is built by many people
    and is never through,
history and myth are told and told again,
contradicting halls lead to understanding
of an error, lead to remembering the sole
antiquity echoed by the rooms.

Flowers reproduce, planted by forgotten gates.
Irrigation fails, doors rust shut, a silver pond expands.
Someone's intrigued by specialized machinery
    and looks for tools,
or spends the epoch of a morning
laughing over sherds of schedules.

* * *

On days foretold by ravens, conquerors march by,
oh victors, I won't be with you then
oh victors, more than happenings and people
    I love objects, I prize old cars
more than modern ones, and olden times
more than our own; I praise mercenaries and old
    soldiers, I value houses that imitate the old
ones no one builds today, no one builds today . . .

oh victors, I will not march through the sunflower fields
    those days.

* * *

Wind and wind but spruces listen silently
    without surrendering to the storm.
Birch and aspen cover the slopes, leaves
    yellow in the time of change.
The changeless gloom named weather
    settles into spring or fall.
Waters flow darkly in these northern regions
    where the birds sing,
where birds sing in the forests
    and where birds fly
to other compass points and over other lands.

* * *

Eternal highways sent in all directions
    from the Forum
far to the east, to the sea in the west,
in the north to forests, to deserts in the south

brick and flagstone joined without a seam,
a junkman's load, a floating load, drifting;
kinship, fate and family tree
define no connection
inns follow the same road, relay stations,
merchant, soldier, and long wandering,

the wind a legend and a song
cities of the wind.

A Flower Song

Translated by Anselm Hollo

The fir-trees at play;
cones raining down
ceaselessly;
O you, the wood-cutter's
daughter,
steep as the mountains,
as gruff and as gorgeous,
listen,
if you never loved, if I
never loved (your
bitterest words
when we parted), O listen—
the cones, raining down upon you
abundantly, ceaselessly,
without mercy.

*   *   *

Where will we end up, oh where will we
end up, like tired animals
in valleys of grace
without a god without gods

where we're coming from: from the bliss of the sea
as the sea first came
without being the sea, invited by no one
from the bliss of the sea
from the bliss of the sea.

The Bowmen

FIVE POEMS

Translated by Anselm Hollo

I

Statecraft, sagacity
Gone to the mountain council

My lord has planted his banner
We must not go there

And clearly
Alone I am nothing
Come read it now—

Returning to Worms
I take nail and hammer

The hand touches sky
The foot presses down on the ground
Henceforth may nothing divorce
The hand from the sky
The feet from the ground

On the mountains forever
Winds water and fire
Scorched earth
The elements bringing forth bloodshed
Rebellion war
Plague evil sudden death

Statecraft, sagacity
Reappear
And also the men in black
Honour cries out for violence
Sagacity's foresight improves
When the glasses are reddened by flames

We have not come here
To look into wisdom
But into our hearts
We have all of us come here
Not to display sagacity
But the willingness
To make sacrifices.

II

Now, as I tell you
Of the Emperor
You see him
The Emperor, *in medias res*

As I tell you
The Emperor, you see it is winter,
The Emperor lonely,

The Emperor is an image
Becoming clearer
As darkness descends

The Emperor is an image,
Dusk is falling,

A thicket grows on the slopes
Like an eagle's eyrie,
The dense dryness of branches

And the Emperor
Is alone
And clearly seen

He is in his hunting lodge
A cold place in winter

He is the one
Best seen in the dark

And the thought, the bird, the owl
Your blindfolded thought
Yet sees him, even now, in the dark
The Emperor.

I have misled you.
You stand at the foot of a mountain
It is winter
You try to peer through the branches
At an Emperor who is not

But again when you close your eyes
You see him there in his lodge
And his image is clear

I have mislead you,
Open your eyes now
Don't listen to me:

The Empire lies in your heart,
There
It has power

The Empire is built and destroyed
By blinking an eye

And it dies
When the eyes are opened.

III

What use a man if he isn't a soldier
No use at all
What use a soldier if not a creature in irons and chains

What use such a thing
No use: board him up dig him down
Under the ground to push up more trees

And land you were promised land you shall have
Open your hand receive your reward
A handful of land

Open your eyes and you'll get it into your eyes as well
I can tell you your land
It lies from North to South under a certain firtree

And if you can't see any longer
What we see so very clearly
I'll blend the words with the hymn-tune for you to hear

We stand here close by as darkness is falling
Turning to see
Where it comes from

The rest we know
But wherever we are
At the edge of what forest

It makes us rise
The darkness
Most longed-for sight to our eyes

And go.

IV

The bastard son, born with a tooth in his mouth,
Hair on his head,
Sits in the corner, not in the cradle,
Not on anyone's knee,
Ruddy his hair like the firtrees in winter, and in that glow
The bastard son goes through the woods, no cap on his head,
He takes to the open road, is a giant,
One inch tall, he takes to the road.

Ten years have passed, the Beauty is sleeping, the giant grows,
He grows in his sleep, goes on growing, another ten years
And the giant is a giant, full grown,
He goes through the woods.

In his dream he sees three men who carried the world on their shoulders,
He is struck with awe, and awe-struck he laughs,
Laughing falls down and falling down falls down like an oaktree,
Oaks falling crash to the ground in all their length and height,
Then lie on the ground, sleeping,

They sleep, they dream, they fall, the bearers of the world.

V

In the dream
A golden vessel
In the dream
An open sky

The vessels were gold

The King's men tied us
Ankles to treetops
Bent the trees down

The trees' green
Bursts into rage
We rage
Against life everlasting
And it is torn

The green
Greening inside us

We fly
Against the doorjamb
Of the air

The air
Weeps for us

We were the King's bowmen
We are leaves on the trees

The leaves
Touch air

Not heavy
Like the King's treasure

We go
Trees
Into the reddening glow.

Birthplace

FOUR POEMS

Translated by Anselm Hollo

I

And yet, we must have a word with happiness,
Build the house to catch the sun's light,
Open our windows on the valley;
So, be seated under the tree and listen to it,
Exchange pleasantries, talk to it,

Give up all hating, see the fir growing, and the rose
How it flowers there, by the field,

Before the lake freezes over you hear the horsemen
On their way to the forest, before the mountains grow dark in Bohemia,
The Bohemian mountains, the Bohemian forests,
Deep down to the forests of the Balkan,
Deep down into Balkan dust
Where pine, fir, and willow rise out of the sand, a white bird perches
On the far side of the Danube, utters a pitiful cry.

II

But what if the good days should strike us dumb,
How can we endure without falling silent,
How can we endure without falling silent when poems are shown to mean nothing,
This, for the present generation's praises:
We wrote it, that poetry, then we fell silent, listen:
Now it is time for the drums,

It is the time of the drums,
And drumming's a sound when mute darkness precedes it,
Sheer darkness that cannot carry a voice,
Twice, no,

Seven times the Black Regiment has been gathered here, under black banners,
And it is not the same, here it was gathered, but this is now
And only now the drum-sound has this to say:

Now is the time, now is the time before death,
Before the trees burst into flower,
The time of the drums,
And thus, even this golden decade has begun and is drawn to a close,
Scarce friendship becomes exhausted, gold is exchanged for steel.

III

The wood of the pinetree, used with great care,
All the way from the Balkan forests to these woodlands, here
With care, the dampers are closed before dusk, to keep the heat in the stove,
How immutable this world is, terrifying, it is here, always here,
Only we move,
And I have to make up my mind what to do, what to begin
Waiting for the letter that will not come,

Bring me the dead man's letter, gilt-edged, through the forest
It is a great forest, its greatness reaches from the Balkan to this wood,
It is the inheritance of generations, the poets, also, rest there,
Oh, at last I can say it, they rest there,
Dug down, squeezed down with great effort under the sod,
It is true: they are resting,
I envy them this great forest, the wind makes me bend forward
And take up my staff in the endless storm,
The wind blowing across their graves,

But the dawn, the dawn, most important of all: weak glimmer above the treetops,
While we, ourselves, move across the frozen lake, going where? to a flowering.

IV

Heavy, the humid sky, but the earth is not heavy here,
The earth is light,
Light lies the humid earth on this son,
His hair alone well worth a whole forest of firtrees,
His voice is heard from out of the ground, the voice a root gives
When it is torn from the earth.

Poem o poem, my only birthplace, I speak of,
It is my beloved, flowering into song,
But I also long for myself, for the place where I am, an empty space,
A soul in a field of flowers,

Oh I long for an end to changing, to stand where I am,
The soul is an empty space,
A field become barren from too much tilling and reaping;

There are twelve of us here, of whom one is only half a man
And one of us only a pair of hands with a rifle;
We, the misshapen, start marching and march away into dusk
Now that our missing shadows no longer cry out from the earth,

Now see us standing among the sunflowers, within the dusk,
Among the black, broken stems,
See us, twelve empty spaces where we stand
In the field of flowers.

> If there's nothing else,
>   then take a few white stones to bed,
> the sea has bleached them white,
>   they breathe, retain aroma,
> a few white stones—my advice
> if the bed's too wide for you alone.

> You want to live your own life. Good.
>   You want to be yourself.
> Be careful. The worms are waiting for just that.
> You want to live while you're young. Mistake.
> A thousand blind eyes will gnaw your image up.

> There's a child's fear inside you
> of fear-breathing darkness when games are interrupted
> and illusion breaks that you made believe.

* * *

> Flood tides and ebb, rain, and a needless wind
> make black a color too; a black color that shadows eyes
> and lets us mark on paper:
> there's a mountain here, its toes
> penetrate a cloud, it watches
> over four dominions. Four shore villages
> turn desolate, the refugee goes far,
> the mountain stays, a mountain, eternal,
> only this poem of black letters, this breathing,
> that'll then be blown to the wind, this absolute poetry
> will also be blown to the wind, these names of things,
> black characters, like the mountains, black.

* * *

Once I was an object, and I
opened up, and took up words to that degree
and built with them. The land
doesn't crave clarity.

The landscape is a dream.
Wheat like a thousand autumns rises from the void.
Wind and weather, water and the land won't
linger in us long, I can't
keep up this talking long.

* * *

When I move, a bird, leaving the world, books
remain, books, difficult to move are
addressless letters, the wind tears
and when a book is read, its leaves are leaves.

* * *

Where does the voice in us come from?
     what does an eye say?
speech flows in the floating world,

speech flows in the floating world,
     what everything is not from
you have to know for yourself.

THREE POEMS FROM *The Finnish Cycle*

I: The Prince Speaks

With all due respect, Finns hang on tight to the wind.
People standing by the Porvoo gates: hello,

Good Finn, good morning, I said,
how are the pigs? the chickens? how's the wife?

I've taught myself to talk to the people
in their own language, but no people doesn't talk,

Finnish isn't a language, it's a local custom
of sitting on a bench with hair over your ears,
it's continual talking about the rain and the wind,
it's inborn table pounding,

Sire, it's the kind of language you can't speak,
it's nothing but endless talking,

We're here on account of original sin when March turns
to spring, March is incomprehensibly mild
and turns into spring,

Sire, please say that half-baked talk fits into a bag,
a prince, if he's a prince, is a prince and a poet,
dines on roasts, delights in giving after-dinner speeches

(gets his kicks and eats that way)
drinks hot broth and burns his mouth.

II: Spontaneous Toast

Your Majesty, Tsar and Grand Prince Alexander,
Prince whose virtue is support of half the world,

Helsinki burghers, pour that sugar in your red wine
to keep the blood from tasting bitter,

Sire, the way to do right by tradition is to misunderstand it,
here there's a traditional custom too,
it loses everything in translation,

it's come here through Bothnia, Your Excellency, say:
Suomalainen, Savolainen, Pohjalainen, Perkele.*

Now you know Finnish. I'm on a journey into the language
of this people, let me drink and be quiet,

let me play cards and gamble, let me drink
and keep on singing my song,
the voice of a dead man
always praises this country and its name,

this people's primer is carved in rock on the roadside
west of the Kymi River, Welcome, it reads, Welcome.

Welcome carved into rock is absurdity.

III: Sveaborg

A person's livestock all agrees, all the pretty horses,

---

*Finn, Savo-ite, Northerner, the Devil. As the persona suggests, it doesn't really translate
at all. Perkele means "the Devil" and also "dammit" or "oh, hell!"

a chicken and a sheep of equal mind,
isn't it fine we disagree, unity—diversity,
a people of one mind is a people without a mind,
it goes wherever horses, chickens, sheep are led,

a generation marches against itself and marches underground,
isn't it nice we have the multiparties,
there's life in a generation as long as it lasts,
and the way it keeps its voice is language,

let laughing while you're marching
be a splendid way of marching, to march but to think,
a mind full of clarity and well equipped,
an unconquered fortress that surrenders.

* * *

The sea full of seeds
and the oceans
and the moon, eye of the unborn,
we sail
and I conceive we're spirits
moving into being emptied.

* * *

A woman strips, rain, wind and darkness rise,
when she's full, a child arrives,
children, children bring poverty,
we take in guests: darkness, poverty and wind.

* * *

The Greeks populated Mycenae,
the poets of Rome in their turn
filled Greece with shadowless beings,

there is no night when no one wrote
someone's writing into these rooms too,
poem-dressed lovers, when we're not saying

the room is not free but full of breathing
and embraces, light sleeping, hush,
be still, so we don't wake, someone's writing
    into the night.

* * *

Traveling and time
(Land and Tree, too)
are known, and go together,
there's reason to be bitter
when we're still not trees,
don't compare, don't restore, don't hope

advice is brought too simple to implant.

The December Poems

FIVE POEMS

I: The Old Man and the Child

I go where I'm going through December
    arm in arm, an old man and a child,
I walk, while day is getting shorter,
    the old man and the child
through December,

the world is in a long night the twenty-second day
    and stops
and turns away from death, the time of which
    is emptiness and dark.

II: Lingonberry

From the forest, a child brings a bouquet:
a pine twig, some hay, and a lingonberry stem
    with a berry still surviving,
poor forest, wind passes through, the breath of the year
and spring, summer, fall,
    and winter go hand in hand through the trees.

I eat the lingonberry and spit away the skin
    to keep my sense of taste,
there's snow enough in the wind, I know
    how the cold tastes.

III: The Snowman

The snowman fell to his knees, everything's
    a little terrible, I thought of a candle

as the snowman's soul when day is short, when shadows
    and bones of the unborn are equal shadows,

my eye's an expanse of calm open water.

IV: Old Names Taste of Ashes

I have seen the year flower, ripe and hollow

and full of darkness, darkness in this fruit
    and the fruit: is time and place
and in this land a hundred years ago my Father's Father
    made another branch
an owl maybe, who fled the darkness
    who flew in the winter into this time.

Leaves are raked into piles, cover for my multisoul.
    Close to the grass, I'm green.

V: 1960

December's gone, left last night toward midnight
1960, the decade changed although there's only one
    decade, only the one we're in,
speech is as little a world as I am, changeable,
    fearing eviction from history.

THREE POEMS ON A CLASSICAL THEME

I: Ownership

The moon will grow no rounder than it is . . .
    the sound of a song and words, full of feeling.
The grasshopper and the ant dispute the ownership of fall.
    The great and the great can find no room here.
Time's not getting cheaper. The earth gets more expensive
    toward the fall.

II: The Fortunate

    The voice of autumn will not break
    off, the voice of autumn's

low in the trees, and when I open my mouth
I'm a screeching bird! I'm flesh!
I move. Trees are standing
latent reserve. They work, dropping
needles, cones, seeds, water
to the fortunate.

III: Metamorphoses

Grass turns to snow,
                  the grass, the grass,
and so,
      immortal.

*   *   *

Trees, all their greenness.
I wanted to extend a lawn to you
              on the palm of my hand
        because it was spring.
I didn't make it in time.

*   *   *

Hay flowers. A rose flowers.
    It's that time,
the time of a rose when a rose bursts open
    and sometimes
makes the rose rot, its bud dries up
    like a certain kind of girl, of woman,
like symbolism that proposes to irony, and,

and from this decade the smell of roses will remain.

*   *   *

Rich people, a husband and a wife
    side by side, profiles in a car by the front side window
so
    that the man's profile's in front, and further back
the woman's covers his ear and . . .
    they've got empty rooms already waiting,
        their curtains are ordered.
There's so much money between them
    it's immaterial what they do

in order to prevent the natural passing of inheritance.
Did you remember to order the drapes? Yes.
>They're ordered. They'll come gathered in with leather,
>priscilled on the side so they'll sweep in widely
>from the top and then fall straight down from the side.
Darling.

Did I forget to mention: they're young. It'll be a long time.

* * *

Translated by Anselm Hollo

Equal parts of courage—full of courage—equal parts—much
>roundness—cheerful roundness that eats sweet pastries—
coffee—while male companions have a Coke or imbibe a cup of coffee—
their ears cocked as if they were listening—
>she laughs—she is full of laughter, too.
She eats a pastry that costs many square feet of land—
>the equivalent of a cemetery lot—she eats it,
>>once and for all,
cheerfully, in passing.
>Then she walks on by.

* * *

Translated by Anselm Hollo

Autumn comes, apple pastries, covered with coarse burnt sugar.
>Inside, there's a sour apple.
I think about all the things I did not buy
>and the things I have sold.

* * *

GDR noncom Egon Schultz, 21, teacher by profession, was
>murdered. As far as I've read,
>a cordial person, an incomparable noncom.
I'm not a cordial person, as a noncom I'm not incomparable.
>I may even be incompetent
>at putting commas between these words
to make some sense out of them.
>Wise, unassuming, helpful, aways friendly,
this concerns him.
>While he was alive he was very friendly and helpful,
also to people from the west, and the west agrees.
>It doesn't matter.

Foreigners are always suspicious.
 I should have been able to tell him so he'd have known
to be careful.

*   *   *

When the German priest, black hood on his head,
  rode along the Multala road and jumped off his bike
  like an old infantryman
and asked directions, murdering Finnish . . .

I don't like it.
He's running a boys' camp somewhere not too far from here.
 I think he's the devil himself, and what he's doing here
is the devil's work.

Fable of the Year 1965

Silence please. I'm telling the best German joke in the world,
 with von Papen's ok. In loose translation:

the greatest—and time is not important—the greatest
 is to serve the power of government
it doesn't matter who.
 It's as if you served your country.

Wasn't that a gasser? Pretty bad, I guess.
 Parody's been impossible for a long time now.
They're doing it themselves.

*   *   *

Im Rovajärvi liegt, nein, beim Norvajärvi liegt, nämlich,
 ein Grabplatz der gestorbenen westdeutschen Soldaten,*
the GDR statesman sent here clarified.
 The German's mine.

*   *   *

Translated by Anselm Hollo

Old Grandmother Rothschild, ancient Jewess, lovely.
 Like a silver coin that has traveled through Africa

*In Rovajärvi lies, no, near Norvajärvi lies, namely, a graveyard of dead West German soldiers.

in black hands, payment for many things,
      still bearing the likeness of Maria Theresa.
Lovely, this woman, a grandmother, gray hair,
      and she has ears, and cannot be overlooked.
Lovely
because she has changed totally,
      become storehouse and wisdom, winter and greed.
Ancient.
Covered with wrinkles, alert and perceptive,
      not so much in regard to ideas,
but in regard to people.

*   *   *

Praise of real estate might easily come of this
if I hadn't seen too much of it.
There's work there all the time.

*   *   *

Translated by Anselm Hollo

The years are your heartbeats, short, as those of a man who has just committed murder; nor does "when you first met her" seem any farther back in time. She is there, within range of touch; if only time were to reverse suddenly, you would meet, embrace, and say goodbye for ever. The way one lets go of a good book for a short while, not caring to read on, life stops when the world races at full speed through the dragon's tail.

*   *   *

I was born in a northern country called Hysteria.
      But nothing much is left of that, only an expression of a kind
when at times I get up at night
      and hunker in front of the fire.

*   *   *

After trees and bushes
      face and body, skin and hair
         are most expensive.

*   *   *

My grandfather the emperor, was, as you know,
      crazy as a loon. He wrote poetry, with other people watching.

You want to have a war?
  it can be arranged.
   You walk with rigid steps
like soldiers, always hysterics before an attack:
Hysteria's a sickness that never improves.
An hysteric's a victor, he never gives in.
   It's useless for me to talk. I'll read his poem:

The fog is so thick you can't see the water from the bridge.
Flowers begin to rise up
   when they have to die
without any rhyme or reason.

*　*　*

In this cruel world, it is no use asking
not to be reborn

*　*　*

When women are pictures on a wall
   and men shadows
walking under trees, negotiating
perversities—
   to be born again, not to die, to rise again—
the shadows of the trees on land, on the snow
are dead branches. Some would like to saw them up, others
say it can't be done.
   He's still a sceptic.
Every time they're walking in the shadows
   they're afraid of the snap.
It never comes.

*　*　*

Translated by Pekka Virtanen

Leave me alone, you say. It is no business of yours to say that.
She is a woman you look at, and your teeth begin to feel cold.
You say she is young.
You ask for one thing, wish for another.

*　*　*

To converse with the wind is fruitless, to argue
with the waters, to question trees, and give answer
to the grass.

*　*　*

There are many wise men, but, on the other hand,
     there's not a single
crazy tree. After writing, reading
    is hardest.

* * *

Translated by Anselm Hollo

Do you know summer's so late this year many trees are still in full bloom.

* * *

Translated by Anselm Hollo

I was to have one highball per evening,
    sitting at that marble-topped table,
and you were to keep your things
    in the wardrobe we painted the color of rosewood.

* * *

Translated by Anselm Hollo

Of course I had to show off: look, that's where we now have
    a bit of a field, and over there
        I planted two hundred young aspens, in May.
Of course I had to remark on how fast they had grown.
    They don't seem much taller now.
Only the grass
        has grown, this high.

* * *

Translated by Anselm Hollo

Why aren't you using your clothes.
    Each dress reminds me of
        some summer.
Whenever I open the wardrobe, it is you,
    taking them off.
        The moon is quite thin.
Call. Write sometimes.

* * *

Aspen seedlings, hybrids—I promised you
    they'll grow in our time to trees.
We're always in such a hurry.
    The house is finished now.
Today the shingled roof
    of one of the sheds was finished.

* * *

Translated by Anselm Hollo

What can I do with these hairpins? They are so thin,
    intended to hold together
        only that one head of hair.
At the bottom of the drawer
    there also remain some lead weights sown in silk,
        three of them, meant to improve
            the fall of long hemlines.
A receipt from Stockmann's, indicating that something cost 5.85.
And what about the two small pieces of mosaic,
    pried out of the wall in Caracalla Terme.
What about these rocks from the shore of the Black Sea.
    They are black.
From such desolate places.
What about the piece of Chinese Wall.
        When you keep moving things
    from one drawer to another
you feel you aren't really destroying them.
    They just disappear, one by one.

* * *

Translated by Anselm Hollo

The towel I bought in the summer of '58
    had been torn in two, while I was gone.
It was black, orange, and white
    in equally wide,
        wide stripes.
A bath towel it was.
    It was summer.
True, it had worn quite thin
    in places, but I thought
that kind of weave is so strong.
Even the colors are as good as new.

Song Thirteen

FROM *Fourteen Rulers*

Translated by Dympna Connolly

The true history of every reign is the battle over the next ruler.
The interests of parties and power-seekers are primed. They are stored,
   to be used when the time comes.
The reign of Michael the Sixth meant that I planned the reign of Isaac
   Comnenus soon to follow.
Thus, I took little note of the messages foundering heralds brought from
   the capital.
Saying Michael had been overthrown, had fled. News rained like heavy
   drops on the brink of a black storm
when I came to Comnenus's tent. He was dictating a letter to the
   Emperor.
He did not believe in this sudden abdication, did not approve. Then—
   it was not yet sunset—came a messenger with confirmation. Michael
   had abdicated.
A galley was ready to take Comnenus to the capital. Another messenger
   said the same; he had hardly finished
when a third brought the same news.
   Finally came a scholar of intelligence and discrimination
whom we had to believe.
So I was there when the reign of Isaac Comnenus began.
And now it was the night of September the first; I wakefully reviewed
   the situation.

My old patrons had fallen, my services to the new were slight.
   Best for them to destroy me, like any nobody.
I gritted my teeth, expecting a step from the darkness.
   Byzantium had learned, surely. The upper jaw is Thrace,
the mouth the Black Sea, the lower jaw Anatolia.
   Teeth clenched together in the Bosphorus.
I thought of horrors. If people ate one another, they would not treat
   their food so badly. It would spoil their appetite.
Now I realized that power is that with bad eating habits. I had seen
   it eating, beginning a meal, growing hungry, but I had not thought
   of everything.
   Now I had good reason to think of this.
To this new emperor I had publicly proposed compromise, moderation,
   planning, waiting. Retrospectively the time could not have been
   worse for me.
Alliance with an enemy is possible, for enemies are equals.
   But now I was in no camp.
Neither laying aside nor taking up power.

As day dawned I peered out from my tent.
I saw the guard-fires round the Emperor's tent, the lamps.
The army was ready to march to the capital.
The Emperor led his army.
We followed with the rearguard.
I expected him to command my attendance during the march to
explain myself.
I would have to explain the motives for my advice.
I did not try to work out what to say, that would depend on the
moment.
But to my amazement Isaac spoke completely unexpectedly: sincerely.
I was prepared for rhetoric or, still worse, all his logic.
I thought he might pretend to think up his platitudes on the spot.
But no. Not a mention of earlier discussions.
He had his plan, of course. Byzantium was in his charge.
He asked what I thought he should do
to make his reign a competitor for high fame.
My courage returned. This hinted at continuity.
He did not want generalizations, either, but tried to make things
concrete.
So we decided on his immediate policy.
And the sun rose, began to warm us after the cold night.

MAILA PYLKKÖNEN

The School Teacher's Wife

1

Sometimes I wonder how it would be in the home
of a teacher of literature, or if I were married
to a minister, or if my husband
taught literature.
I'm married to a historian, I've been married
for ten years—by my own choosing, I want to make it clear.
Ten years isn't very long, the past is short and quick,
but the future looks so empty.

2

I know him by heart. He's studied himself like a book.
He doesn't need years any more, or seasons, or semesters

or holidays. He is thoroughly prepared.
He doesn't even need speaking any more. As he would say,
he's reached the point of diminishing returns.
He's reasoned himself completely out, he can't change anything
from his room. He owns his own reference works,
evenings, lightly, as if caressing history, he revises what he knows,
he expands his soul by an inch or two of note cards,
sighs if he finds a new legend, like what William Tell's son
is said to have said after the apple incident.

And he gives his whole knowledge of it
to his students who take in the past in the local
schoolhouse that rests on cornerstones.

3

And on his vacations, he also tours through history
and hunts in the archives of Europe, eats national dishes
and injects life into himself with the taste of old wines.
I went along with him in the beginning, Europe
was a billion monuments. This battle took place here,
this was signed there, and these are so-and-so's descendants,
these are monuments and what they have to do is stay there,
and if they don't last, then a monument is made for them,
these are old pictures, portraits in which beauties have to stay
separated for all eternity. I went along, educated and with interest,
I stood in the windows and noticed that the window-feeling
is always the same: the view is an eye's circle, here,
as if a home were always here.

4

I like domestic things, rugs, warmth. My home's complete.
There isn't any room for a new doily or pillow.
I've got two boys, they began to run and play
and were told about the Trojan horse,
a little education, the home environment,
we taught them hymns, how to pronounce Ararat,
they got tricycles, we let them go to town alone,
they bought bubblegum, got invitations, read books,
did all the things boys do, and were told to go to bed
and shut their eyes.

When we stand admiring our boys when they're asleep,
I can tell you what he's thinking, how he's thinking
a thought, which is the only thing that's born of him:

"The children will come to learn brilliantly. They will get
my world view, they will get everything. Cornerstones,
and national history, European history, trips to the monuments,
trips to other parts of the world."

I never say that I am full of the future and empty.
In the evening I listen to him turning the pages,
leafing through a new history book, doing his research.
Our boys are as ordinary as two intelligent lingonberries.
Only sometimes does it come to mind to ask
if they've gotten any warmth.

5

When I think of travel, I think of comfort and discomfort,
the minor points he has to know,
the locksystems of the entire world,
traffic, expressions of courtesy, misunderstandings,
people muttering in languages you can't understand,
discouraging discomfort and needless luxury,
before he feels he should start to change to a human being again;
alienation is the whole point of such an existence.

But then: Europe is full of people.
Two trips, a billion monuments, but a dozen people.
Two or three of them.

And one of them,
it should have really been the future
and would be the present if I had wanted.
He was a physicist. When he talked about the future
I felt at home. Life is chaotic.
You can't figure out the future,
but then the future was not empty, it existed.
He touched it with his fingertips all the way.

6

When I was young, I wasn't much of anything,
I was nothing special,
I was very plain, I kept a diary,
the only thing I wanted to know next
was what I should have wished for,
I was insecure, I despised the ordinary,
the mediocre, but I never really knew for sure
just what mediocre was,
there was nothing in me but good taste and a little imagination.

There was nothing I could have known for certain.
Then it happened.
I didn't want a love triangle.
It's the first thing I ever came up with on my own, the idea that
freedom is something you can't dispense with, you can't get rid of,
just as you can't cure it along with your health.
From entering into the spirit of freedom, I think I found
something of myself, an impression of myself,
a characteristic, an element,
I don't know what I'd call it, maybe peace:
at any rate, an idea, a solution, an out perhaps
for which I didn't need
someone's blessing or approval.

I wouldn't have been afraid to make the break.
I didn't love my habits.
When I met him, everything changed, conscience changed to love,
history to a great childhood you slowly walk away from.
And just by that I was free in a certain way: I was nowhere.
The ordinary person wishes what he has to. The taste
of acting according to freedom is cool and fresh.

And so I returned with my historian, or rather
I can almost say I fled with him, free, empty.
I am the middle generation. I have nothing to teach my child.
They themselves will get their soul,
the future is natural for them, without dramas,
history for them is a natural distance, a father's work
like the work of all other fathers,
it is a story, a row of books.

7

I've met my childhood friends from time to time, my schoolfriends,
I listen without trusting myself. I am sure.
I am this. I am by no means unhappy.
Maybe I'm slightly depressed, but maybe it's the frame of mind
of the middle generation, sad to the extent of the suggestion,
and slightly sublime, elevated, reserved,
because I wish for nothing.
An understander, like the pillow that receives
night-cryings is wordless but not unkind.
Emphasis in a worn-out life
is where each person wants to put it.

I'm on the go from morning to night.
My home is above reproach. No longer any loose threads dangling.
There could be glass doors on my closets.

There's a view from my balcony that can't be reduced
or widened. Forests, houses.

And ten years will come,
                    everything will come.
How would it be in the home of a teacher of literature?
Of my own free will, I want to emphasize.

VÄINÖ KIRSTINÄ

FIVE POEMS

Translated by Pekka Virtanen

1

I step into a shop. The saleswoman looks at me, she sees me, I her.
One of her eyes is brown, and so is the other.
    I say: "A pear, may I." She answers: "You can have big ones
and small ones, which would you like?" I say: "That one." And I pay,
saying: "There you are," and she says: "There you are."
    That's how it goes. And off I go. I run through the corridors,
I come home. I take the pear from under my coat like a hidden heart.

2

I cough.
The draught leafs through the books.
Pages open and close.
I walk in my room
towards the night;
the sun sets.
An old man looks in from the door, he smiles.

You can crack like a pot, a window glass.

The flags flutter.
A shadow is thrown over the city.

3: A News Agency

Heat in the world's telex network
steady clink:

it's a son
Elisabeth is well

4

The window is open.

Somebody walks in the park,
somebody feels so sad.

A baby,
her face
upright
like a small sphinx.

Somebody has found a prehistoric pot;
it has a picture of her and her husband on it.

5: Mao's Thought

Revolution
is not a dinner party,
it's not vignette carving.

HANNU SALAMA

Translated by Pekka Virtanen

smell of smoke
fishermen's cries in the haze
drizzle has glued the girl's hair to her cheeks

the cartwheels sink in the slime
leaves are falling as if somebody were altogether gone

NIILO RAUHALA

THREE POEMS

Translated by Pekka Virtanen

1

I went back to the University
after a pause of couple of years.

The same porters, sitting there, they looked the same,
    in the same places as before,
the same smell and buzz of talk in the corridors.
    I found it pleasant so.
I had some practical errands,
    theology as a science didn't interest me.

2

It began to rain in the evening after blowing all day.
    I wonder whether Israel will attack over Suez or not,
and if it does, what will happen then.
A powerless thought weighs on many a heart and a dark rain.
    The rain wets the grass and all the trees,
what does it look like, in the morning,
        when the children will wake up?
    De Gaulle has recently disclosed
that he takes a most pessimistic view
    of the world's future.

3

Year after year, the summers get shorter:
    the morning, green day, bird singing above the window.
The words feel useless, like a forest
    that grows to be felled.

PENTTI SAARIKOSKI

Beyond Toijala, there's not much of anything.
Northbound express leaving from track two.
In the windows: stocky faces, rocky fields
and children like chubby cucumbers.

* * *

The Finn-nation reads,
drinks near-beer in the coffee shops,
fans out from bus stops into places

where only some spruce is listening
or nothing,

spruces,
under the spruces
little spruces listening
to the big ones

"Little Connections"

SEVEN EXCERPTS FROM "OVID"

1

When petals close he still
quotes Rilke.

2

Trees are wrong, you're right on
they don't fit in here.
I noticed it from the car.

3

These poems are little connections,
rocks, needles,
I am a hopeless attempt.

4

Stores are full of irrefutable facts,
what are you talking about?
Capitalism? Socialism?

5

The wine had time to evaporate in the glass
before I understood
it was useless to converse with him.

6

Before, I considered sleeping inconceivable.
But now, after having looked into the matter,
I know that it is unavoidable.

7

I've been delighted with rocks or flowers
in this countryside, and with the woodsmoke.
And we go out visiting.

The Running Dog (Conclusion)

            i walk the street
        it's been raining
                the wind is blowing
    i'm cold
        Newsweek in my pocket
    dreams   misconceptions   beliefs
            the thick cloud of tyrannies
        on a moving mind
            clicking heels clickety click
    hot on a chick's tail
                in a tunnel
    where a warm train-smelling wind blew
        i'd like to get into her

        me
            and the baggage
    a knapsack and a knapsack
            i rested against a wall

    it's jumped up to the sky bigger than the sun
        bigger than the shadow of the earth on the sky
    a bird
      our ruler
            black immoveable
    come down
        to our level
      eat us
        you're not a dove

    i found the address # 42 and opened the door
        in a small round aquarium
            happenings before

```
           and after
        green expanses
              and the shadow of an airplane
                 over the grass one a minute
           wood to the sawmill
   i'm sawing wood, my heart
              beats in time

           from   here
                    in all directions
```

SEVEN EXCERPTS FROM *What Is Going On?*

1

I live in Helsinki.
Helsinki is the capital of Finland.
It is situated on the shore of the sea 120 miles west of Leningrad.
Helsinki is a growing city, and the rents are high.
We sit here in the middle of our forests with our back to the giant
     and look at his picture in the paper. He has a dark suit, a white
     shirt, and a silver gray tie. In his country, everything is
     different from here; there people walk on their heads or
     without a head.
We sit in the middle of our own forests,
but far away in the west there is a land in whose coastal waters
     float huge eyes, and they're looking here.
Helsinki is being rebuilt according to Alvar Aalto's plans.

2

```
        I've been listening for a long time
                 to my heart a white screen
                     a discus thrower's motions
              Tarquinian graves

        The Pope and the Tsar
        Metternich and Guizot
        French radicals and the German police

                 the nation that lives like this is dead
```

ETERNAL PEACE. . . .

3

Now I'm alone by the wall
          and disaster is unavoidable
               jeder, der sich uns entgegenstellt, wird vernichtet*
               **Wir weichen hier keinen Schritt zurück

4

in the evening smoke looks cleaner
          and the wind is heard best

     let's make some coffee

a boulder sticks out of the ground like somebody's fist
                    I'm thinking about Finland
     I've been thinking about everything and now it's evening
                    I'm tired
               and there's sand in the bird's wing

5

          I love you
               like a strange land
                    boulders and a bridge
          like a lonely evening that smells of books
               I walk toward you in the world
          beneath the atmosphere
                    from the space between two lights
     my thought which is sculptured and of you

6

the boys were playing hockey
the flag was straight as a window in the stiff breeze
the step-van backed out of the garage
the woman parted the curtain and looked if it was cold outside
far away on the field there was a thin cover of snow
in the paper a picture of two statesmen going to a conference

*Each one who opposes us will be annihilated.
**We will not retreat one step.

7

they speak of free-market economy, and justice
whatever they happen to talk about, the western nations
i will talk a long evening away

THREE EXCERPTS FROM *What Is Going On?*

Translated by Anselm Hollo

1

                    what are they talking about
Freedom ·
            and Democracy
                        if it isn't one then it's the other
what's the use what is it they want to save
            Occidental
                    Civilization
they never understood for one minute
                            until it was later
            letem
one word
        all it takes
                to knock them down

2

            slowly it's getting colder
        and that there is heaven
                seen as an equilateral
                        triangle with an eye in the middle
                                looking
        like a spot of thaw
    and that was my friend the artist
                bounding down the street
                                    now in winter
                            arboreal structure becomes
                                    very clear
killing
            that's like when you drop a whole load of thin glass

3

       some clergyman writes in the paper
how would it be if Jesus Christ
    put in a sudden guest appearance in Helsinki
surely then even the humble waitress
        would be rid of her inner burden
            rid of the need to make
                a little bread on the side
  what are they
talking about   a kite
              like a kite rising

   I want to give up existence
and I want to live
    in a communist world that is one animal in its body

SIX EXCERPTS FROM *Still Have A Few Things To Tell You*

Translated by Anselm Hollo

1

remembering you   how you were
you had eyes
like an afterthought

2

don't let me die
get me some soup
a couple of eggs
I still have a few things to tell you

3

there is a substance
makes me light up

when you look into my eyes
you can be certain I love you

4

the world shrinks when the flowers fade
why did you leave
why was the room so vacant so suddenly

5

of animals there are
the elephant the monkey and the snake
the monkey lives in the tree
Tarzan appears and grabs the snake

6

today it is quiet here in the bar
I am the only customer

got a letter it said
"you are Rimbaud"

The High White of Winter

Translated by Anselm Hollo

the high white of winter
cold as Xtianity*
shape of my breath like a tree-climbing primate
Verwoerd**
        allow me to raise my voice once more
        in the cause of progress
"The one thing I regret is that I didn't get married sooner"
          —Harry S. Truman
sentences out of sentences
moods out of opinions
a certain number of thoughts
the temperature just about sufficient for me to remember
the one or the other
a few fragments of myself
and of events

*When I wrote this poem, it was winter, and Vietnam was ruled by Madame Nhu. Now it is summer, and Vietnam is bleeding under Air Marshal Ky.
**Prime Minister of South Africa, assassinated 1966.

the woman lies on her back
moves her feet
blurring
spidery twilight
pitch dark
and all of a sudden it is night
things I can't get into words
people I do not like
or plants that don't grow here

life is shabby and futile he said
nothing pleases me any more
most of the movies depress me
nothing in them seems to happen
in any comprehensible order

work and dedication
the only way out
reaction—what is it? a question
to be asked time and again
the defenders of invalid arguments
to be pilloried time and again
unexpected
are the positions they take

sun raining through
the cypresses with a tinkle
last summer

I have arrived at this point
and there are plants that don't grow here

I'll write no elegy on the death of
Mr. Edwin Linkomies
pseudo-Hellenic boss of the University of Helsinki
nothing sad about that
sad
the blue streetlight flowers in this city in winter
hanging from their wires
staring down
Poverty and Fear
Reaction
is a crow
its feet stuck fast on the tar-covered boards
of a wooden bridge
or some such metaphor
B. B. soon *passé*
the songs no one hums any longer

morning
on the lake

> bright dew on the grasses
> cobwebs
> strung between thistle-stalks

other men's mornings
"I am the dead hero of so many futile wars"
Finland
> and its edifices
the mobility of flesh that has just begun its decay
the intellectual vigor
in that old man
his alert rabbit eyes
seeing back and forward
all excess
> is anathema to him.
8:31 P.M.
> one of the most horrifying moments
> every night.
I have
no intention.
> I am
> with you.
And I'm not afraid of Amerika, I push my way through the crowd

TEN POEMS

Translated by Pekka Virtanen

1

> So sad, the biographies.
> Ought to write . . . make big money.
> Out of mere habit
> > you'd think it would deliver from evil.
> Well, that's not how it is.
> Everything is in such a false order,
> > it calms you down, at times, to realize this.
> In these circumstances
> > is it possible to take a stand?

2

> This world in me, dying.
> I look at the houses people used to live in.
> Sorry, what did you say?

3

Naked,
        I see you from before and behind. Boats on their bellies,
it'll be spring soon,
                beyond the trees, the woods.

4

I was on my way through a forest
        to a rendezvous
When my ears went up in the air, stayed there
(well, that's what they claim anyway)
to listen to the forest voices for a while

5

I'm reading your letter. Fall,
you've got it too.
Soon we'll be the only ones left.

6

In your eyes, the city going to lie down
                proud candles
horses sunk in our dreams

7

go fuck yourselves see you don't come here to give me that shit
all blue i want my skies to be cloudless
i'll come right there, right there, Your Sadness
i put nettles in your armpits snow your eyes
i too have my right to a garden and apple trees

8

The fall is near. It's spring, early summer.
That's when you'll see it.

9

You need glasses.
Take them off.

10

I came here, with an errand.
People didn't like it.

JYRKI PELLINEN

SEVEN POEMS

Translated by Pekka Virtanen

1

Secretive experiences move around the house,
                like childhood memories,
the wood rises up with husks in its hair.

2

Some 35 feet from the wall to here,
that's my house,
the original idea has vanished into space,
the baby has time to be born,
                the baby has time to grow old.

3

Time is different,
and the social classes are
                different,
and the volumes of social poetry
                hang in the wind,
there's nothing sadder in them.

4

At times a word may get a meaning too grand.
Hurrah, I think, it is better to sit down and sing.
And the songs last longer and mean less.

5

I look on nature, always. You have a good example in it,
any time you may see something going on.
I think of it as such then I am not afraid of saying
that year after year autumns and winters
                become more and more strange to me.

6

The money is dispersed in the room, like a woman's
                                        voice
—a new silence, like before,
                but the voices in the street move my thoughts
                                beyond days past

7

In the evenings, I work at the table. At times I fall asleep,
and, in the morning, the sky is clear and cloudless.

PEKKA PARKKINEN

THREE POEMS

Translated by Pekka Virtanen

1

From among the falling leaves of autumn I look for
Rilke's heart

2

There were no marks of battle any more.
As if they wanted to forget it all.

3

If I loved my country
I'd burn its flag
to let the wind flutter
freely in the air

VEIKKO POLAMERI

THREE POEMS

Translated by Pekka Virtanen

1

And I thought strange this sound
                of the rain against the windows
and found it appropriate to say: the apparatus of rain wrote on
        them.
                Where is this metaphor from?
the kind the Czechs—Wolker, Nezval, Halas, and Orten—
                knew how to use properly,

and then,
in the midst of all, we who for a long time now have taken all
                in consideration
were able to see the worst happen
and it was not a murder, it came by night, the phone rang,
and in the morning the whole world knew it,

and now, my friends,
we can already say, actually,
nothing has happened.
Somebody had only been dreaming of spring
on a dark winter night.

2

The baby cries.
I know how it is
when I look through the rain
at the garden wall

against which a leafless
creeper is like a cleft.

3

No I didn't say anything.
And it's needless to maintain that the rain
would call somebody's voice to memory.

This Hymn Is Still Missing

Translated by Dympna Connolly

This hymn is still missing.
I owe those who come after an explanation. Not you.
Good. Now there is storm and thunder.
A great hill chain surrounds you.
The sky is distant, like blood in fire.
And I hurl myself down from the hills.

You are not naked. Sorrow has clothed you in black
to the neck, to the neck.
Killed up to here. I must cry love
over the four winds.

I learned to hear your speech. It was difficult.
I scarcely believed I had folded your hands on your breast,
that I had smashed the bones of your insteps
and invented witchcraft, as food for fire and water.

The night strikes against my face.

This night with you I shelter from the fury of the skies.
I have hurled myself from the hill granted me
two thousand years, my God,
do you see how the wind strips the hills of their
jagged silhouette.

The grave is open, I speak to you, back turned. Come.
And hands meet. But you suddenly
start jerking along the slope towards me.
The hill arches so steeply above, I can see it
without turning.

This morning all the landscape there is bewildered.

KALEVI LAPPALAINEN

FIVE POEMS

Translated by Anselm Hollo

I: Photograph

That is grandfather.
That is grandmother.

That man was a boy.
That woman was a girl.

What did the boy do?
What did the girl do?

They played in the back yard
and went to the movies.

Later they lived
in this house.

They had this photograph taken.

Look at this photograph
and tell me how they lived.
They did likewise,
while they still lived.

II: Reminder

There are many degrees of consciousness:
　　I see a bird, I see a bird, I see a bird.

III: The Faithful

The blue eye likes
the red one.

The dog
has red eyes.

How old is the dog?

Its mouth does not open.
The blue eye

mists over. We must be
growing old,

says the dog.

IV: Caveman Brain Spasms
Or
Notes Found In A Bottle

I

It is a pleasure
to stop and

let the buffalo run

he said

II

Yesterday I learned how to

whistle

make love

Heaved some rocks into the lake

III

When we watch the birds
we dance

When we fall off a high place
we Die

(A dream, was it?)

IV

Far off in the grove
the trees are flowering

Besides me she sleeps
in the rock hole

V: All Wrong

1

I sit on the table
squeezing my
own thing

2

The bus
blue as
the wind

3

The man said hello
to me out of
the photograph

4

The radio is yellow
I
wear black

5

Someone is looking through my glasses
just a moment ago
I put them into the case

6

When I light
a cigarette
I paint my lips

7

Picking my nose
I'll eat either the next
poet or

8

I pick up the axe
darling
the flower I pick

RISTO AHTI

TWO POEMS

Translated by Pekka Virtanen

1

20th century.
The country was governed by hobgoblins and two big bogles
and no-one was able to do anything to them.
And a metaphor, after last century.
The hen is taken by surprise, in the sky, it sees it is a hen
and crashes to the ground like a stone and gets instantly killed.
Half way down it has no past
and an inch from the ground
it lays its whole life before the upheavals of the future.

2

There'll be this violence for the sake of violence,
immense heat without object,
discharging senselessly in languor,
suicides, murders, mere languor and expiration.

PEKKA VIRTANEN

SEVEN POEMS

Translated by the Author

1

January, all bright; a green leaf
    grew on a bough, 1960
the one, the broken one, from the realm of dreams.

2

It has been raining all night.
The grass is bending back from your footsteps.

3

Sierra de las Minas; Melpomene
    at our heels
we started off to garland Guatemala.

4

Guevara has been murdered.
It snows on the thighs of the field,
    a squashed dream.
The eyelids of the night will be closed.

5

His family's services are well known for 380 years now. But all of a sudden, in the midst of all, 1918, it was decided that he will not rise again: and just like that, it was forty-eight, he was beaten down once more. 1967: they write some nasty stories about him in the U.S. Names like die dicke Bertha, und so weiter* . . . Max, Gustav. And now it was Alfried when we last praised him. His value has been estimated roughly at 4 billion dollars. That is probably why we haven't been able to get rid of it all.

*Big Bertha, and so forth.

6

She stayed home this morning.
The sheets made pleats
on the hill of her belly.

7

— Was it of me or women in general? you
asked me, in your dream. Your soft warm skin
had kept me awake, blood-hounds
were running, in my mind, eyes gleaming.

Of you, if you asked me: what do I know
of women in general, now?

TWO POEMS WRITTEN IN ENGLISH

I: I'm Just Walking Around

1

I would like to hear why I'm staying at Geneseo,
while I have two eyelids elsewhere,
       People travel to learn,

reading papers, bobolink, bobolink, it suddenly
                                    struck me,
and a soldier carries a wounded baby in his hands,
    the wind takes pages, Let Hertz put *you*
in the driver's seat, Xerox, give that man
a ceegar!
              Travels! bureaux! agents
Rice sparrow, rice sparrow, in its own country,
                    could be a legal bird.

2

There is nothing to declare, the air is clear;

Thoreau, thoreau, toro, Nubar Gulbenkian,
    John Paul Getty, Hieronymus Bosch,

everything happens from Salvador Dali to the CIA,
     Gestapo, I remember her, 40 wars since 45,

Mr. Emmet Mulkin is taking my ears off,
what can I do: I am only a guest here, in an enemy country?

3

I lay my nights under a heetaire; winters in Finland
are like branchy breasts, apples of papal time Rome,
    a woolen sock,
nights are cold over here, winters, weathers, leaves.

The next day I met the rich man's hollow-legged son,
How do you do,
we were introduced,
      but later on he got mad at my talks
about the elbows in his family tree,
     he drank pink champagne his head full to the knees,

firs, pines, eyes, poplars, cypress, brooms, nails.

4

Laocoon! Laocoon! When it snows up in the mountains,
    it snows up in the mountains; Mrs. Smith has a nice
and intelligent husband or father,

We keep on forgetting things,

Quidquid id est
    timeo Danaos et dona ferentes. Ils n'apportent pas
de cadeaux, c'est vrai!* Turn it off, anyway.

5

I'm just walking around. I push my hands deep
              into my mind's
    pockets. I am one of us,
      arranging ugly things into a funny little row,
commanding Asia back from the corner.

*"Whatever it is, I fear Danaos and those bearing gifts. They do not bring gifts, it is true!" or
perhaps more freely: "I fear the Greeks, even though they offer gifts. They don't bring gifts,
it's true." (Latin from Virgil's *Aeneid,* Book II, line 49)

II: A Poem

There is no light in the room, their eyes
have hardened in the darkness,
and as the day soon passes by,
there is only a new day in their memories.
They cannot urge anything, what shall be
shall be on its own time.
The sun has gone out,
their shadowless union governs the room.

First the gate dips into the solid haze,
then the wall, then the other gable of the building,
the building, and after the building the ridge.
Slowly it sinks to the dell.
Behind the barracks the swampying earth
ranges to the edge of the woods.
Covered, he says, staring at a net of squares in the window,
so that one cannot tell what's really behind it,
and he draws with his bony finger more squares,
they are side by side as to prop each other.
He waits for an answer.
But he doesn't say it aloud, it is a plan
reminding the clearing of the haze.
And first he sees the gate, through its eye,
then the wall, then the other gable of the building,
the building, and after the building the ridge.
He has his answer as the haze gathers
into the bottom of the dell.

The garden fulfills imperfectly its function.
Soon, no one knows how to use it;
the bullace grows its fruit in vain,
and the green bean-sized drops underneath the leaves
shed despondency on the environment.
The dead serious families, like pale maids
behind the thick walls,
eat their hearts out for the light
shot with yellow through the window.

The brown brim hat, hanging slack in front,
imprints a shadow into his cheek.
There are deep grooves in his face,
it is like a field,
three rocks sulk in the field,
on the edge of the ditch blossom gray tufts.
He walks with high steps in through the stable door,
carrying his years with him,
a little man black as a shadow.

He has his fortune making a big mechanism go round,
his family whirling at his feet.
But he will be hustled to a damp garret,
that's his 75th birthday,
and his money will be robbed bit by bit.
He has raised his family all by himself.

CAJ WESTERBERG

EIGHT POEMS

Translated by Pekka Virtanen

1

as one visits somebody's place for the first time
and sees
       how things are

2

i left her
as if the stairs were climbing up
under my feet

3

"Do you realize we're living wholly different times at one time?"
he once asked an obliging man,
and as he answered: "Yes, I do," I found out something was
badly in the wrong.

4

From an ice-field of years ago wades a man, a gun on his shoulder, wade men, guns on their shoulders. They wade from the future, this way begging the right to live. There hangs on the wall a picture of an important-looking man, Stalin perhaps, perhaps Mannerheim. From afar, a choking dog barks.

It's difficult to stay quiet or still. The days slide, all days of existence slide like copies from a rotary machine and are left heaping between and on top of each other.

The glass is broken. The sound is a clash. I sit wordless in a wordless world;
like in a tree a branch that seems to be extra, unfit, a mistake, and into which
a bird, surprisingly, an oriole, sets its nest and starts a song to last the summer.

5

But which realism, and how, dear Messrs. academicians,
when the words and the sound mix nicely like a breaking glass
and when the hand is bleeding.

6

Death, that is the one thing in life one cannot have
any personal relation to, the only thing.
One can see it from outside as one sees a corpse.
One can take part in it, by mourning or by killing.
One cannot experience it in itself, no one can.
It starts living only after one self is dead already.

7

And we went away, each our own way, everybody somewhere, and when we
met, it was very toilsome and grotesque. A shoe, thrown to the bottom of the
sea, the despondency of which falls upon the diver's mind is the mankind into
which somebody sends his consciousness, wearied but, at intense moments,
dashingly diving. When this consciousness carries too much love directly to
destroy, however, the man carrying it, it gives birth either to a rage or aesthetics.
It'll be receptive but barren, I suppose.

8

The superstructure of the well had become rotten,
it was broken up, the pieces were thrown into the well,
and there were thrown leaf piles, nettle roots, earth.

Simo suggested the topmost cement ring
be picked apart
and be made into a grill for the yard.

I was thinking how would it be
to live here in the slum area as a local abortionist
grilling embryos on my yard all days long
and feed them to my fair cat.

Life is a present.
It's too much for me to make out.

Swedish-language Poets

TH. WARBURTON

FOUR POEMS

Translated by Pekka Virtanen

1

The best age:
the day's open, though
beginning to close in.

2

You read,
move and re-move papers, write,
it is as if you were thinking.

3

People in a theater,
representing people in a theater
—the milieu demands it.

4

Outside the scene
we, quite consistently,
stay outside.

BO CARPELAN

1: The Mute Grass

The heart does not agree with its bounds,
the poem with reality,
nor reality with God's dream.
What kind of a dialogue is this, which changes you
without your changing yourself?
Don't seek in the mute grass,
seek the mute grass.

2: Skiing

I have followed my fate,
the snow drives me over the coarse sand,
the ice track is not seen, there are no years,
the visible is not seen, you see your self
in flashes, pushing along
between the left-over stubble and poems
where not even the snow is enough for some rose fire
in your confirmed soul or in the dark December.

3: The Boy Who Ran Through
The Flowing Water

The boy who ran through the flowing water
has disappeared into the mountain. He calls no more.
You see him perhaps yourself but do not hear his voice.
Perhaps you do not see him either in the summer dusk.
His mother calls for him.
Now all the flowers stand brittle from frost.
It is winter's snow that falls on the other side of the mountain
and someone who already awaits his image impressed on the mountain side.
That is in the shadow of the unchanging landscape
where the birds of death raise their light song
reminiscent of his voice.

4: At The Table Your Figure

At the table your figure,
above your hand the shadow of a child's head, a fruit,

your gaze through the window fixed on the movements of the trees,
the movement mirrored in the knife that cuts the bread,
the use of things and clarity.

5

Listen,
in the silence,
there is no silence:
the nails,
the wall.

6

Who has said
that silence bears witness
to the unsaid.
The absent words
are absent.
So speak
in proportion to that
which you cannot say.
Nothing
can remain unsaid
unless because of lack of skill
or
wisdom.

7

Trees?
They remain.
He who journeyed from his home
saw what I have not seen
for a long time.

8

What evening said,
that which died out close to you,
leaves that fell, you forgot.
The wind, greater than the birds,
bore you away
lighter than the words that say
that it is so.

9

When summer was dripping its rain like leaves
and even the leaves had fallen, September entered,
I saw a bird glide over my head,
a shadow moving away from me who lived on the earth,
October's harbinger, wordless, but itself a song.

10

Over the grass
suddenly snow
as if it had been in bloom long enough
for your lifetime.

SEVEN POEMS

Translated by Pekka Virtanen

1

One can believe only in what's left over from belief.
It is a security, like quietness in
                                    a lonely table.

2

The sea
a human dimension:
that of drowning.

3

A tree,
a branched out
light

4

Veins
under the thin

skin,
hand
on the quilt,
the day
at its end,
unfinished.

5

Regret,
connect.
An island
sways
like a leaf
above the darkness.
Come to me.
See: the trees,
saying
goodbye.

6

Blue snow,
day's
dim

7

Wintry trees,
brittle, their stillness
I saw, I didn't see
when young.

LARS HULDÉN

SIX POEMS

1

On this pastoral isle in the Gulf of Bothnia
I saw some scattered signs of empire:

the grass cut short,
juniper bushes closely clipped round.

There is probably something romantic in
that the land is dotted with pearls
of sheep.

And what is this but a renaissance,
when the young studs dance the bunny hop
on a summer night so the alders break,

while a steamer slowly
becomes a point and disappears
on the yellow Gulf of Bothnia.

2

And so I carried home
my half loaf of limpa*
it was very clear to me
that no stone
either is or ever has been
baked in it.

Hence I cannot reasonably
have any aversion whatsoever
to any baker.

That is my problem.

3

One of the philosopher's students
(I don't remember what his name was
but he was crazy)
had a tree hollowed out
and closed himself up in it
in order to study more closely in this way
what life is all about.
The tree died however, little by little,
and of the philosopher's student
never a sound
is heard.

*Rye bread made with molasses or brown sugar.

4

A new reminder
was given to me today
when I saw my overcoat
lying lifeless on the floor
with a broken hanger,
a new reminder
not to stuff so much
trash in the pockets.

5

I am standing on the shore of a bird marsh.
I am alone and still yet not alone.
A thousand gulls swarm over the water.
A thousand voices shriek:
We want to see our king!
I arise from the bushes.
The jubilation nearly deafens me.
Only the cranes' republican club
banks in silence toward the north.

6

On the day of the Apostles Peter and Paul
we saw two perch gliding
through the clear water
at our summer house.
Never before had we seen
perch glide so, as
these did.

PER-HÅKON PÅWALS

THREE POEMS

Translated by Philip Binham

1: Salad-green Mistress

I press the pedal with care
someone might bump me
my salad-green mistress

stops soft as a cat
the lights show red

I look up through the screen
the sky is grey, a deep color
beginning from the nervous system
in a window in a flat
I see a mummified head
an old person
by a flapping curtain

I see myself
in an anonymous future
the children grown-up
and become strangers
my salad-green mistress is scrap
and I myself
an old man with
prostate trouble

the lights turn amber
I press the pedal hard
to get there first.

2: I Killed a Moth

I killed a moth
like that pam!
like that
without thinking
like one kills a moth
that's what we do
and must do
no compunction here
no tears
no prayers
he who created the insect
in his own image
is sleeping
snoring
and if he wakes up
it's too late

3: Reality

Reality smells raw
intoxicating

and repulsive
scent plus stink
amber and urine

you stand on the sidewalk
somebody shoves you
sharp elbow
reality

maybe a woman with a diadem
dangling breasts
cheap heavy perfume

maybe teutonic
red fleshy face
stinking hide

you see pearls gleam
round the swan throat
she is raw and naked
if you wish

choose a dream
choose death

CLAES ANDERSSON

TWO POEMS

1

The cat comes in with a bird in its mouth
        the USA is sinking in the sea with Asia in its mouth
In Africa black men are heating soup water
        in a big stew pot
The North is an ice box bristling
        with light pink pigs
Every time a pig grunts
        a Chinese is born, an Indian, an African
with a soup knife between his teeth

2

How much has a normal individual
in 60 years

eaten and drunk in his life?
One can estimate the following figures
for a person living in Scandinavia:
20,000 kilos of bread
15,000　　”　　”　vegetables
7,500　　”　　”　potatoes
6,000　　”　　”　fruit
1,200　　”　　”　pork
500　　　”　　”　butter
12,000 eggs
9,000 liters of milk
6,000 kilos of fish
500　　　”　　”　sugar
200　　　”　　”　salt
All this a 60-year-old person has eaten

HENRY PARLAND

FOURTEEN POEMS

Translated by Pekka Virtanen

1

I went out to get some cigarettes.
Meanwhile
they beat him to death.

Now, somebody says:
they wouldn't have beaten him to death—
but I say:
they would have anyhow
and I
would have been left without cigarettes.

2

I am used to eating.
Maybe somebody claims
so are we all.
Is that any objection?

3

At times a sun rises,
it darkens in your eyes,
you come to think: the night
— t h e n i g h t d a z z l e s

4

Coffee or tea
(Hamlet said it more eloquently
—but I am not Hamlet)
He said much more, too
—it won't make it any clearer
—it won't be any clearer now
but
we can always choose

5

On the phone,
it was hell, coming down to me,
an even stream
from the receiver.

And I thought:
hell,
why not?

6

Naturally
the sea is like a woman
in spite of the oil flecks and floating canisters
— — —
It courts
the sun willingly
and strips
in the moonlight.

7

A horrible hangover:
when the stars have the hiccups

and all the archangels drink Vichy water
we gather in a restaurant,
tune in
to women's legs.

8

My hat,
run over by a streetcar
yesterday.
This morning,
my coat
walked away.
My shoes
were attacked,
it was afternoon.
—That I'm left?
T h a t ' s
i t.

9

She asked me
to send the telegram:
"Come to me or send me money!"
I did it
without hesitation
because she said to me:
"Come!"
and to him:
"Come to me or send me money!"

10

How strange:
First, she called him
(every day).
Then he called her
(every day).
And finally
the phone rang
by itself.

11

They say
I'm constantly
lying.
And yet I lie
as little as possible.
People around
bury their lies
inside them
and that's why
they think they are right.

12

I've got
this cold again
and I stay home
sneezing poetry
all over the desk.
The bacilli and the poem microbes
shoal around the room;
I cannot tell
which
is
which.

13

I mean
it's all the same,
after all.
I couldn't afford
to live
however cheap it were.

14

Money—
why do I love it
most of all?
Because it's the only kind of knuckle-duster
to bite
life's snarling bulldog muzzle.

SOLVEIG VON SCHOULTZ

Three Sisters

Translated by Philip Binham

A woman bent and lifted her child
and hair fell over her face
and within her a little old woman
clear-eyed and dry
with trembling head
bent for her knitting
and within her
with tender hands
bent a girl for her doll

three sisters
who would never see each other.

PHOTOGRAPHS

Photographs by
Robert Harms (H)
and
Richard Dauenhauer (D)

Kaisa, a Skolt-Lapp storyteller (H)

Farmhouse in Sevettijärvi, with hay drying (H)

Two boats on Lake Inari (H)

Woman and boy fishing on Seurasaari, one of the many islands comprising the city of Helsinki (H)

Seurasaari shore, Helsinki, near the couple fishing (H)

Birch leaves (H)

Forest and boulder (H)

Two mushrooms (H)

Adder, the only poisonous snake in Finland (H)

Farmhouse with grain stacks (oats) in central Finland (H)

Solarization: Farmhouse (H)

Solarization: Duck on Seurasaari (H)

Solarization: Arctic tern (H)

Solarization: Fishing (H)

Solarization: Farmhouse in Lappland (H)

Solarization: Reindeer (H)

Birch-lined country road (H)

Lake grass, which lies flat on the surface of the water (H)

Twisted pine tree (H)

Running reindeer (H)

Solarization: Skier in Lappland, with Pallastunturi in background (H)

Solarization: White reindeer (H)

Helsinki open market, with fisherman selling from their boats (D)

Streetcar stop in downtown Helsinki (D)

Market in Turku (D)

"The changeless gloom called weather"—Gulf of Finland, late fall (D)

Feeding the ubiquitous mallards at Lauttasaari (D)

Finns are tough: a Helsinki baby getting the daily complement of three hours of fresh air (D)

PROSE

Finnish-Language Prose

JUHA MANNERKORPI

Autumn

Translated by Philip Binham

Autumn again.

How many autumns has Jallu seen—five and seventy for sure. But not one of them has Jallu admitted yet. That the birches yellow in their beauty and over the grey reedy shores moves the redness of death—rubbish, fairy tales! Potatoes up out of the ground, there's your autumn. Whitefish nets still in the lake and that's enough to remember.

Only that son-in-law of his, that Matti, had taken the nets to the neighbors' to look after when he left the cabin on the island. So an old man couldn't go out on the lake again this autumn, of course. Even if they hadn't put it quite that way, that was what they all meant, let 'em say what they please. Those nets, what'd Matti want with them? Hiding 'em from thieves for the winter. Load of old rubbish, eh? If he wanted to hide them, then why not here just as well, at his sister-in-law's, when he had to come this way into town anyway? But that was it, they'd hidden 'em from him, from Jallu, secretly, while he was lying in the hospital in the summer.

Yes, Jallu had been lying in the hospital, if not for the very first time in his life, still not far from it. Started to get very giddy in the summer and short of breath, whatever it was; must be the blood getting thin or something. They'd rowed him over from the island here at first, Matti and Leeni, his daughter that lived in the town. And from here, his other daughter's home, he'd been taken to the hospital, where they'd put him straight away into one of those special rooms. The special rooms where they put those who were going to die.

But Jallu had recovered, in the way an old man recovers of course, and he'd started to talk the doctor round: "Let me out, doctor, let me out so I can leave my footsteps on that lawn." The girl could feed him and make him better just as well—that widow, the one that always came to see him, the doctor must have noticed her. And anyway, what'd he need with feeding, he could hold a spoon in his hand all right, was fit enough again, and no great age with twenty years to go for the hundred. And the girl needed him as well, with her having to go out to work, and who was there at home to chase after the children? Five little bundles of mischief, and her left a widow.

That was the way Jallu talked to the doctor, and in the end they let him go. Bad it had been to lie there, with not even a clock to watch the time go by.

But somewhere from the muddying waters of his spirit had risen a bubble of playfulness, spinning up from the hard, strong core of his younger days. All the same, Jallu knew the doctor wouldn't have let him out "just from talking, but you could have a chat with him, and like I'm telling you, they don't want to keep people with nothing wrong with 'em wrapped up in cotton-wool there."

Still, his daughter came pretty near to giving Jallu a taste of his own medicine and repeating his "load of old rubbish, eh?" For a fit man Jallu was not, as anyone could see from looking at him. It was as though, after getting out of the hospital, to add to his ailments, something else had been inflicted on him. He was restless as a dreaming dog, lying on its side with its paws running in their own time and its mouth jerking, trying to bark. Where the order of life said things should be done this way, he did them that. When it was time for meals, he wandered off into the yard or the attic, where somebody had to go and find him. Sometimes he dozed all day, but then pulled on his boots in the evening, sat on the edge of the bed late into the night with his elbows on his knees, and stumbled in the small hours between woodshed and kitchen, leaning on his stick, a few bits of firewood under his arm. He snuffled and coughed, heart thumping like a threshing machine, but still he refused to understand why he should fall over the threshold.

"Damn that," he grunted and explained to his daughter as she hurried to help him: "Didn't see the pattern of that carpet—catch hold, don't pull, don't I say—I'll manage all right, just don't put them carpets over the threshold." And when he'd got over that, he started to boast: "Like last spring, I could still carry them big pine logs. Carried one from the forest. That Matti came along, wanting to help again. Huh, I never needed people like that hopping round me." But that the work had had to be done in two parts—Jallu said nothing about that. He didn't remember it any more. He would have thought it was some women's nonsense if he'd been told that to mend his efforts he'd had to lie on the bench in the cabin for four days. In the meantime, Matti had sawn the log in half and carried it to the woodshed. But Jallu had had another one the same size over his shoulder when Matti met him coming along the path one morning. Matti came near to losing his temper: "Why don't you saw them up smaller in the forest and carry them a bit at a time?" Jallu only grunted, "Don't get in my road," and added later at the lunch table: "Just thought I'd see if the old back was still bad."

Now the back was no longer bad and, if Jallu's word could be believed, nor was any other part. All the same, everything seemed to go curiously dark. Jallu's mind was like a lonely rower in the fog, hearing the rattle of duck wings and seeing the bird only if it flies straight toward him, but seeing or hearing nothing spontaneously. But from the reaching tongues of mist he can read the direction to row in, and row he must when panic rises with the fear of not coming to his destination. You could guesss this from Jallu's face; it was too miserable, too stubbornly set. The children especially sensed it. Jallu wasn't any more the strong, safe grandpa, but a frightening black object you preferred to keep away from. His hand was like a cold grey frog, it made you nearly scream when it suddenly caught hold of your hand and from unknown hollow depths rumbled: "Whose little girl are you then?" Jallu meant no harm and awaited no answer; he only asked when from the fog dived forth a fair, human head, a girl, a little girl, "Whose little girl?"

Then a hole was torn in the fog. That evening it was almost as if Jallu was reconciled to something and someone. From the bedroom could even be heard scraps of song, from which could be clearly distinguished the good-humored verses of Jallu's prime: "The captain scanned the stormy seas. . . ." And when his daughter's boy came to call him for evening coffee, Jallu was again momentarily the grandpa of old: "Go on, don't tell me lad, you've never made that coffee." There was a reason for his good humor. Jallu had again found what he had started to look for, all on his own, soon after he got home: the key to his boat.

While the others were away he'd searched for it everywhere he could think of—in cupboards, boxes, store rooms, and over and over again in his pockets. Finally it had appeared before his eyes in a dark corner by the stove, on a nail: "There 'tis. And me thinking. . . ." Covetously he had put it in his pocket: "What in hell they want to hang it there for?" The key was his, his and nobody else's; the boat was his, his. Key, boat, whitefish nets.

And who guaranteed the nets were being looked after properly? Them neighbors? A good pike there to look after a minnow. If they'd even been Matti's nets, but they were his, "mine, my nets they took there, and it's a rotten shame if I say it right out."

Jallu's good humor was only sufficient for one evening, for in the quietness of his mind he wasn't so sure of his strength as he tried to make out. But little by little compulsion grew from the key. Key, boat, nets, whitefish. In the darkening autumn the whitefish gleamed like a miser's silver, most-coveted still. Wet nets, whitefish. Whitefish that struggled when you picked them from the black web of the net, twisting, springy as the biceps in a man's arm. It didn't matter that his daughter's family had never cared for fish, his daughter not at all, and the children with their complaining: "Don't want any, it's all bones." Never mind them. The birch leaf was already on the ground, and that was a command: whitefish nets in the water.

There came a night again when Jallu was awake from evening till morning. He turned from side to side, kicked the covers off when he was hot and pulled them over him again from cold. The whitefish gleamed before his eyes in a sleepless dream. Every now and then he got up, groped round the door frame, found the switch and turned on the light: only two o'clock, three, half-past four. Piece by piece he pulled on his clothes, first trousers, socks, boots, then sweater, jacket. When his daughter came into the room around seven, Jallu was sitting at the table with an expression that gave her cause to ask: "You going somewhere, with all your clothes on already?" "Couldn't sleep so I just got dressed." "What kept you awake?" "Why don't you get on and make the coffee?" The coffee boiled, they drank it, and still the daughter kept on: "You going to the market again? You're not to go anywhere, with you tired like that." Jallu tried to shoo her away: "Go on, go on off to work and don't talk rubbish."

The daughter left. The door was hardly closed before Jallu's hand plunged into his pocket. There it was, safe enough, in its thick wad of cotton waste. Jallu pushed it back, found his old black overcoat, a hat for his head, a stick for his hand. From the window the children saw him turning towards the shore and starting up the hill beyond which was the boat shed.

Halfway up the hill he was already stumbling to the roadside to sit down; he got his stick under his arm for support and leaned on it with all his weight. Ten, fifteen minutes passed before his heart stopped pounding, then he got up and managed somehow to reach the top. After that it was easier going, and within an hour he was on the shore. Two, three passers-by had shown their surprise at his efforts: "Well, well, Jallu, morning to you—must be a bit tired then, wandering all over the road like that." But Jallu had managed to counter their inquiries with a joking reply: "Just thought I'd try and see if the old feet'd go up the hill as sprightly as they go down." And on the downhill: "Had to sit down here a minute—only way to put the brakes on."

The lock on the boat opened, the plug thudded in with three blows, and when Jallu had pushed and jerked a few times and rested in between, the boat began to obey and finally slid into the water. Jallu waded out after it. His boots leaked a bit; he felt his ankles getting cold and tried to hurry. The boat rocked. At last Jallu got one leg over the side, but the other got caught on the rowlock, and he fell forward into the bottom of the boat.

A long hour passed. Jallu lay, half unconscious, just as he had fallen—one torn trouser-leg caught on the rowlock and his leg hanging over the boat's side. Then an obscure need for haste stirred in him; someone might come and see. He shifted on his hands and one knee, almost fell again, swayed and staggered. Then his trouser-leg ripped. Jallu got his other leg into the boat and managed to sit. The boat was already far out; it had slipped off the shore when he fell and now the wind was already catching its flank. Jallu raised the oars to the rowlocks, first one, then the other. His whole body shivered, but the oars began to rise and fall just the same. The bow of the boat turned towards a nearby point.

Jallu became calmer. Nobody had seen him leave, and rowing was familiar work. The tense shaking of his arms was relieved by the gentle swinging they had learned over the years. There was some wind, but the point gave shelter, the boat kept on its course, and in the momentary calm of his mind, Jallu again lowered his nets and pulled in the whitefish. He felt something near to well-being. Not so well that the well-being would reach out to warm the blued backs of his hands or soften the sullen glare of his lumped features. But there was some sort of grumbling content in having your old hat pulled right down, your coat collar up to your ears, and knowing that how far you went or didn't go was your own business.

Beyond the point stretched an expanse of water unbroken by islands, and Jallu's boat began to meander. The waves were not big ones, but they came awkwardly from the side. They tried to push him off his course. One oar needed to be pulled harder than the other, and Jallu lost his rhythm. For a while he left his right-hand oar floating from its rowlock and rowed at the left with both hands. It didn't help much. The bow turned in the right direction, but at the same time the boat drove more and more toward the left. When an hour had gone by and he was in midwaters, Jallu had to pull hard against the waves. The boat kept better in that direction; one oar was content to do the same as the other, and Jallu's arms found their rhythm again.

But the distance grew no shorter. Another hour went by, and still Jallu rowed across the open stretch. The backs of his hands had changed color from blue to white, but he did not feel how cold they were; his toes in the wet boots were numbed and stiff, but it did not come to his mind to try and move them; the sky was covered with grey cloud, there was a drizzle of rain and fog, and the old black coat, wet through at the shoulders soon, might as well have covered the bow as Jallu. The field of his thoughts narrowed and clouded like the misty waters around him, the horizon of far treetops was dimly visible as a mere outline, and the only clear direction was felt in the arms that, stubbornly and blindly, turned the boat into the headwind. When the swell finally settled, Jallu no longer knew where he was; he did not even suppose he had got anywhere. It had only become calmer, and his numb hands surrendered. There he sat; the wind had driven him into a sound on the other side of the open water, therefore the calm. But gentle puffs of wind entered even there, and the boat floated through, to a new open stretch.

By then it was evening. Jallu woke up when the waves began to play tricks with the oars again. Some question that did not reach his conscious mind bundled together the scraps of his dogged will, and slowly, very slowly he stumbled to his feet. It was like a sleeper turning, slumber on either side, a low hillock of wakefulness between. He did not manage to get upright, for he did not let go of the oars, but somehow, for a moment, he was standing there. A moment only; before his eyes from that higher level were able to descry a single landmark from the gloom, an oar bumped against his thigh and he fell back on the seat. At the same time the rowers changed finally: the waves pressed against the oar blades and started to row Jallu. The handles were still in Jallu's fists, and against them he leaned his chest, and whenever a bigger wave came he shifted slightly.

So they found Jallu at last. By midday the daughter had guessed what had happened from questioning the children, asked leave from her work, and got help from her neighbor with his motorboat. First they had driven out to the island cabin, then made a wide circle back with the wind. And Jallu was found, not dead, but hardly alive, not ill nor well. Weeks went by without getting a single word from him. Some flickering scrap of fancy urged him one day to feel around the corner of the bedroom stove. But the key was no longer there, and outside the frost was already in the ground.

—1956

EILA PENNANEN

Long Ago

Translated by Diana Tullberg

I went there and decided to speak my mind to her.

I'd found out in advance where they lived and found my way easily from the station to the cottage. Or rather, to the house, because it was a neat and tidy place, and rather big. The building itself was quite new, still not weatherboarded, and unpainted. Oho, have they run out of cash, I thought, as I walked along the field path to the house. Making my way through the yard, I kept my eyes on the ground so as not to appear inquisitive. It was early autumn, a fine clear day, and when I glanced at the rose bushes I saw there were fat red blooms on them. The path through the yard had hardly worn a track through the yellowing grass.

I raised the latch and went into the hall. There were colorful striped runners on the floor, in pale shades. Somehow the sight of those runners made me angry. My heart started thumping and I stood still for a moment looking at the various doors, until in the end I knocked on the one I thought led to the kitchen.

"Come in," someone shouted. Was it her? I wondered. Am I in the right place after all? But that's what they said, those two strangers on the bus.

As soon as the door opened I saw that it was her. I started to weaken and hesitated shrinkingly on the threshold. "Come in, come in," she repeated. "Could I have a glass of water," I asked as nicely as I could. "I'm lost. I'm on my way from Villilä, and I was supposed to get to Laukeela station. I don't know where I went wrong, but I seem to be on the wrong road altogether. I'd like to rest a while."

"Of course, rest your legs, sit down—no, not there, the rocking chair's better for resting in. I see, Laukeela station, was it? Well, you've certainly missed your way. But you can get to Kulju station this way if you can manage another five kilometers. Dear, dear, your shoes are all muddy."

"Yes, they are," I said. She brought me a glass of water, and had even put a saucer under the glass. She stood in front of me, staring at me while I looked back at her. I thought: you're rosy cheeked and well covered. Good God, it makes me feel ill. A smooth skin like that and bright eyes. A woman like you. I'd never have thought it.

She was chattering on all the time. "We've got good water in the well. Clear as anything, never leaves a stain on the bucket. Just have a look." She came over and showed me the white bucket, and there wasn't a stain on it, just as she said. This annoyed me, too, and I could have grabbed the bucket and flung it at her. . . . "So you're on the way to Laukeela . . . and from Villilä. . . ." "I missed my bus," I explained quickly. "There's only one a day into town." "Oh well, you can still get there from Kulju," she said. "You've plenty of time to walk, and you'll still have to wait at Kulju. No, I know, I'll make some coffee. I dare say you wouldn't say no after all that walking?" "I dare say I wouldn't," I replied and thought: oh, am I going to get a cup of coffee out of you? Just wait.

She began to busy herself with the coffee, and I looked around me like a thief planning what to take. Here, too, there were rag rugs side by side, well washed, colorful. The whole kitchen was cheerful with big windowsills and geraniums still flowering even though it was autumn. There was an old-fashioned clock ticking on the wall—now where did she get that from? Most of the stuff was new, even so . . . or then if not exactly new, certainly not family heirlooms. She sang as she made the coffee, took the canister from the shelf, burnished up the side of the copper pot a bit. Then she added some splits to the stove, where a fire was already burning. . . : she must have had some casserole or other in the oven, since there were no saucepans on the top. Yes, of course, the family were at work and would soon be in for supper. . . .

Then she started to chatter again. "I thought as I saw you coming through the window, who's that then, a stranger, we don't get many visitors here, set back like this. . . . It's lonely . . . I'd be proper glad to pack up. . . ."

This gave me the opportunity I needed. "You're a Karelian for sure?" I said, like the folks back home did.

She was thrilled to bits. There was just some small doubt that stopped her from falling on my neck, or did I just imagine it? "Are 'e, too? Well, well, fancy that. . . ." Her accent deepened in a flash. Then she slipped back into standard Finnish and it was a good thing—my heart had started to thump again so hard. Yes, I had a weak heart even then, though the doctors kept telling me there was nothing wrong with it.

"Where are you from?" she asked.

"I'm from the Koskisalmi area myself."

"Koskisalmi. . . ? Never. . . !" she exclaimed. Her eyes were beaming at me. "What village?"

"Valtala, before we had to leave in the war. Where are you from yourself?" I asked and looked her straight in the eye, twisting my water glass between my fingers. Oh yes, she jumped a bit when she heard the name *Valtala*. Familiar, was it, I thought to myself. Just wait, there's more to come.

She didn't say anything for ages. Picked up the rug she was making, sat down, and stared at the rag strips as if wondering how to tackle the next bit. But she did nothing, just stared, and I could guess why. As she said nothing, I started for her.

"Yes, we had to leave Valtala. And you, were you a refugee, too?"

Now she had to say something, because my question just hung in the air and waited.

"No, I wasn't a refugee myself. I left Karelia a long while ago." And she repeated: "A long while ago," and stared at her rug.

"Oh yes, the years slip by," I said in the kind of voice the workers' institute principal uses when he's making a speech and gets carried away. "We've got to get older, on strange soil."

She jumped again and looked at me—quite a different look from before. Older, in a way. I looked back at her, studying her, and waited to see the marks of guilt on her face. But none came. Then she started to talk in a low voice, and hesitantly, as if feeling her way in the dark.

"Yes indeed. On strange soil. So you're from Valtala . . . I've. . . . I've been there occasionally . . . long ago. Good farming land. Big wide fields, you know, rolling. As if a wave had swept over the fields and frozen there. . . . But what am I chattering on about. . . ? It was a pretty village though. . . . Rowan trees in every yard. . . ."

Then she fell silent, and I just said, "yes, yes," when I couldn't think of anything else. I couldn't help it that my voice hissed in a nasty way, like a cat's— "yes, yes." She turned her head away from the window and faced me.

"I'm sorry, you were saying? Yes . . . yes . . . in Valtala you had a lovely open view from the window—didn't just face straight into the forest, like here. When we first came here, I said to my old man, cut those trees down and make some space. . . ."

"The old man, is it?" I thought. That wastrel.

She glanced at me, and finally came out with it. "Were the Härkönens still alive in Valtala, when you left?"

"The Härkönens?" I repeated, gaining time. "They were . . . well, the Härkönens . . . they could never have moved from home. Of course when the war came we all had to move. And old Mrs. Härkönen died on the way."

"What, Milli Härkönen? Is Milli dead?" Her voice trembled. "But then Milli was getting on, a lot older than me. And how about Vihtori Härkönen?"

"Old Mr. Härkönen died a long while ago. Ten years before the war," I said.

"Oh, both gone then . . . Milli and Vihtori. . . . And what about the folk at Nirkkola? How are they doing? And the Putkinens?"

"But you know everybody in the village!" I said. "Your coffee water's boiling."

She hadn't even noticed. Now she went clumsily towards the stove, not as nimble on her feet as before, when I arrived. Aha, my dear, I've swept your feet from under you, I thought.

She measured out the coffee and seemed to give full measure. Then she stopped and asked, "Do you know anything about Mikko Tuomaalainen?"

"I think I heard him spoken of when I was a child," I answered. It annoyed me that she didn't respond to my comment about how well she knew the village.

"He was a really marvelous fiddler, was Mikko. He was getting on then, when I saw him, so he must be dead by now. He just fiddled away. And we danced. There was always dancing and fun and games going on at the Härkönen house. And the crickets chirped at night, coming home."

"You must have been a young girl in Valtala," I commented. I had to get her into the trap cleverly, so she couldn't deny it. So, dancing and fun and games, was it? Good, good.

"A young girl . . . yes . . . I used to visit the Härkönens . . . just occasionally." She was standing with her back to me, watching over the coffee pot. Then she threw over her shoulder, or shouted really, "What do you know about Viljami Tarkiainen?"

Is she nibbling, I thought. I got up and put my glass on the table, then sat down on the bench. I don't like rocking chairs, they don't let you think straight.

I said, "I don't think I remember him. Which village did he live in?"

"Oh, you must remember him," she replied. "Lived right next to the Härkönens. Just a bit of a way up the road, on the other side, that was the Tarkiainen cottage. Oh, you must remember the Tarkiainens if you remember the Härkönens. Painted red, the house was, with white roses in the yard and a white swing. Two big fir trees at one end. Really big ones. . . . Don't you remember? A rusty old weather vane on the roof. . . . always creaking and squeaking at night."

My throat was absolutely choked now. So, the bitch remembered as well as that. Now I had to watch my tongue.

"I remember the house," I admitted. "One just like that. One of the firs was felled a couple of years before the war. Going rotten. But the Tarkiainens?" I pretended to think. "Viljami? What did he look like?"

"Tall and powerful, a real bear of a man, a bit on the fat side . . . oh, he knew how to get things done, kept the house in good condition . . . everybody respected him . . . on the council, too. . . . Oh, I'm sure you remember. . . ."

Now she turned to face me, with the coffee pot in her hand, shifting it from hand to hand because the handle was hot. There was a searching look on her face. She'd obviously noticed something, and guessed. . . .

"Oh well, perhaps Viljami wasn't in Valtala any longer in your day. Perhaps he'd moved away? How old are you?" She was measuring me up with her eye, but I didn't answer. I just asked, "What kind of family did this Viljami have?"

"There were two children—then, long ago—toddlers, a boy and a girl. The girl was three and the boy two. . . . "

"And what was Mrs. Tarkiainen like?" My voice was hissing again. She stared at me.

"Mrs.?"

"Yes, maybe I'd remember her better. . . . I don't pay much attention to men."

I said it in an angry voice, choked. But *she* looked alarmed, too, and stood there like a fool.

"You mean Viljami Tarkiainen's wife? You couldn't have known her. She left home a long time ago. Left and never went back."

"How come?"

"Just left . . . and didn't go back. Left the children."

She was recovering now, though I was just about dying. She started to bustle about again, set the pot on the table next to the cups, with the sugar and cream. Moved nervously back and forth. I, myself, couldn't have moved a step. All I was thinking was how I could have been so mad as to come like this . . . at least I should have brought Väinö along with me . . . he would have cried and babbled and perhaps she would have given in more easily. . . .

"Help yourself," she said in a firm voice. It was too confident to be an old woman's voice, I thought. There's life in the old dog yet. But this thought sharpened my resolve. After all, I was owed some kind of compensation, I thought, and went to the table. We sat facing each other.

"Oh, so Viljami Tarkiainen's wife left just like that," I began. I didn't feel choked any more, and my hand didn't tremble. "Left all alone, did she?"

"No," her reply sounded out sharply, like a fist thumped on the table. She took a bite of bun and stared at the table.

So she'd decided to talk, I thought; and I went on: "Oh, who with, then?"

"Their hired hand."

"Oh, the hired hand." Frank, aren't we, I thought. I tried to laugh, but it sounded like a poor effort. "The hired hand, eh? Oh well, young and foolish, no doubt. I suppose the wife was still a girl and the husband was a lot older? That's usually the way. . . . The other man was the wife's age and managed to talk her into going off with him?"

"No, it wasn't like that." Her face softened again. She was thinking back—it was laughable. "The hired hand was a boy of twenty, and the wife was thirty-five. The wife and husband were the same age . . . they'd been to confirmation class together."

"Ah, to confirmation class together," I said, when she dried up again. "Couldn't have been a happy marriage. The husband must have beaten her or been unfaithful. So she ran away. . . ."

"It wasn't like that, either."

"Well, how was it then?"

Now she looked up at me. Quite some eyes she had, they drew the strength out of me.

"Who are you?"

"What, me? Nobody really."

"You know Viljami."

"I did. Viljami's dead."

"And who are you?"

"I'm Viljami's daughter."

She was staring at me—I didn't have the face to stare back. I knew, though I didn't look, that tears had risen to those old eyes. I didn't want to feel sorry for her. How could you feel sorry for someone like that? She was nearly in tears. Now she was taking out a handkerchief and blowing her nose. I didn't say anything. She went on weeping. Finally, I was the one who had to say something again. We couldn't sit there forever. Her family might walk in, or the man of the house, or whoever it was she was expecting.

"Yes, Viljami Tarkiainen died a couple of years back and they can't settle his estate because they can't find his wife. She disappeared, and though there've been notices out for her and she's been looked for high and low—by the police, too—she's nowhere to be found. They couldn't declare her dead because there's no proof of demise. Her children have a mother who's neither dead nor alive. They haven't been able to divide up the estate and the son's wife is demanding that it should be divided—and soon."

She just went on crying. Not quite sobbing out loud, but with tears running down her cheeks. I began to get annoyed.

"Now stop that crying. Crying won't help. Here's your daughter sitting in front of you and there are things we must clear up. You're not going to deny it, are you? That'd be no use. I recognize you from pictures. Otherwise I wouldn't have known you. I wouldn't know my old mother otherwise. Yes, Valtala sends its love. And the Tarkiainen house. One fir was felled when I was a little girl and father thought about you then—you'd liked those trees. Don't just sit there crying. Answer me—will you sign the papers or not!"

She just wept on. I was furious and started to dig the papers out of my bag. I'd had them drawn up by a lawyer, and they meant that she surrendered the entire estate to her children. But she couldn't hear or see, just went on crying. So I had to start lecturing her again: my heart was hurting.

"For twenty-five years we've been searching and looking for you. . . . I got on your trail quite by accident . . . some complete strangers told me. Two women . . . started staring at me in the bus and whispering among themselves. Eventually one of them asked was I so and so. When I answered, they both said, 'You go there if you want to find your mother.' I didn't know what to say, they were staring at me and their eyes were glittering. But I guessed that they were telling the truth, and they certainly were. . . . I'd never have found you if it hadn't been for the war mixing everybody up. . . . Well, is he still alive, the fellow you ran off with? The hired hand? Is it him you're living with now, or have you found someone else to keep you? Father always said that he wouldn't have minded otherwise, but you went off with such a weak little knock-kneed character. Why? Father didn't understand, anyway. He used to go on when he was drunk about what he'd do to his old hired hand if he got hold of him. . . . He thought you'd gone mad. You'd been gloomy and talked strangely for a long time before you left, father said. Well, tell your own daughter what happened, why you ran off like that."

No answer.

I poured myself some more coffee in my annoyance. I took a bun, too, and dunked it in the coffee. She just went on crying.

"Did father treat you badly, or what? Were there secrets, the kind a father wouldn't tell his children? Though he told us all about what had happened between you. . . . When he was drunk he used to go on about that bed business between you. . . . How could a woman leave her own children? There must have been some reason. Little children—a girl of three and a boy of two. Have you thought of that? Or of what would happen to them? How they felt when they grew up to hear that their mother had gone off like a tart with the hired hand?"

Now she came out with something. Gasped between her sobs, "You're still so young." That's what she said. They were the first motherly words I had heard from her—I don't recall what she may have said to me as a child.

"Oh, young, am I? A fine young thing I am—near thirty. I look older and I'm getting older. Everybody thinks I'm forty. I'm thin and dried up like an old stick, sour like a pickle. The juice all ran out of me as a child, when I had to act the housewife in a house without a wife. Father didn't want any women messing about the house. He hated women. Evil-tempered to all of them. He said he'd beat the whore out of me. . . . Not that there was much in me to beat out, so he needn't have bothered so much. . . . I suppose he meant well, and I'm not ungrateful. I've never been one for flightiness. My days were spent working, being a mother to my brother. I'm not young any more, I'm old, older than you. I don't talk like a young woman talks, the principal of the institute said so. Yes, I've been through college and studied at university, too, though I am such a poor little motherless thing. Yes . . . and another thing I'd like to know is whether I've got any brothers and sisters—has your hired hand fathered any bastards on you? Just tell me—I know the facts of life, though I am so young."

I ranted and raved and all the time I was softening without realizing it. I wouldn't have let it happen, but it just did. The old woman realized it, and stopped her sobbing. She just wiped her face and sighed. I tried to go on, but there was no heart in it:

"Oh, I've had to suffer so much because of you, I've never had a chance to be a proper person, growing up like that without a mother . . . that's the psychology of it. . . . I've read all about it. It'd do you good to find out what it's like . . . you've been all right, anyone can see that. But now your neighbors are going to hear that you're not married, that your children aren't legitimate. . . . You have got children, I can tell by the things hanging on the pegs—you don't wear trousers like those there. . . . Yes, you've made your bed—now you can lie in it. . . . What was wrong with father, he was a good breadwinner. . . ?

After you left he went in for cattle dealing and things went very well for us. . . ."

She was looking at me quite calmly now and broke in: "Ah, Viljami was always one for cattle slaughtering, even in my day."

That's all she said, but the word rang in my ears. Did she mean that it was a bad thing that father slaughtered cattle? Father was a good slaughterman, everybody knew that, and he knew how to geld them too. Hadn't she liked that? But her face was expressionless. It was just as if she'd said what popped into her mind. I tried to go on as before, but everything got mixed up.

"You've just got to surrender father's estate, you don't deserve it, running off like that, and the law. . . ." I didn't really dare talk about the law. The lawyer had gone on to me about all kinds of things that I never managed to get clear. "Yes . . . the law, and you owe Väinö an apology, too. He's the one who really suffered on your account; he never grew up into a man, just a weak slug he is, whining away under his wife's thumb. . . . I know it's all your fault, I've read all about it. . . . An unnatural mother, to leave her children."

It had seemed such a good sentence when I made it up walking from the station, but now it rang false. She was looking at me with complete indifference, and I knew that I had lost. She started to talk.

"If I told you why I left, if I explained everything, what good would it do? There are some things that don't show on the surface, and things that all happen inside you. When life loses its flavor, when you start feeling the grave gaping before you and don't want to go on, you start to think you could start afresh. That's what I thought then. I couldn't go on with Viljami . . . so I left. I know it was wrong. You can't start afresh. Don't think that I haven't had my own cross and punishment to bear. For twenty-five years I've hankered for the place where I was born and thought of the children I left behind. But I've done what I had to and worked for those that came afterwards. This time I learned to be humble, if nothing else."

Humble? I wondered what she meant. I mean, she didn't have to be humble— she could have left her hired hand. Anyway, my revenge had been taken from me, my words had faded into the air where I was sitting, and that slut, my mother, showed no shame at all. I tried again.

"So, it was all father's fault, and I've often thought that, too, but surely things could just have gone on as they were. Go on, admit it, it was the lust of the flesh that drew you to that young laborer."

But I heard, myself, that there was no strength or heart in those harsh, forced words—they just sounded silly.

Not that she paid any attention to them. She just stared at me, remotely. I saw the look of a stranger in her eyes and shrank further down over the table. So, that's how it was, I thought. I tried to get up, and then she stretched out her hand—her old, veined hand, which still had firm, plump flesh over the bones.

"Don't go, daughter. Sit down."

I guessed what she was up to. I should have got up then and flung out of the house, but I couldn't. I sat there and my docility angered me. Just what did I want of this stranger? She went on:

"They'll be here in a minute, I can see them coming through the window. Him and the boy. Two boys I've had with this second one, and one daughter."

"Oh."

"Your visit's turned out well for all of us. You didn't mean well, but it's turned out that way."

"Don't you believe it."

"You can get to know your brothers and sister. . . ."

"I've got a brother."

"But now you'll have a sister, too. You'll be grateful to me yet. . . ."

"No, I won't."

"Be nice to your stepfather; he's always been afraid that you'd come—you or your brother. . . . Or Viljami. . . . But Viljami's dead. . . ."

"You can get married now. . . ."

"Yes, yes, so we can. . . . Been a long time moving from place to place under a different name. Always well-off the beaten track. . . . Always moving on when somebody starts asking questions. . . . It was good you came . . . makes it easier. . . ."

"I don't believe you've suffered," I burst out. I could hear the stamping of feet in the hall. I would have liked to leap out into the yard through the window, I was so appalled.

"You just wait till you see your sister. She's always asking about her big sister and wondering why you don't come and see us."

"You mean they know?"

"How could it be otherwise?" She looked astonished. "But they don't know we're not married. Young people—they don't understand."

"Oh, I'll soon enlighten them, you can be sure of that."

"No, you won't. You'll do the right thing by them."

Someone had already taken hold of the door handle. And there they were, my mother's present—I was just part of the past, and it wasn't worth bringing it back to life. I did nothing at all, just sat, stared, and even smiled.

So that was our meeting. And it took no time at all before she had persuaded me and my brother to give her her share of the estate, though I'd planned something quite different. She just twisted me round her little finger.

But I haven't gone so far to please her as to start hanging about there fawning over that famous sister. I've kept my distance. My brother visits them, but you know what he is.

My mother still keeps on trying, but it's a waste of effort. Not with me. I gave her her share of the estate, but not myself. I mean, she left me before. . . .

But I can't help thinking, even now; I wish I knew why she left home, when everything was all right. A good husband, a good house, and she just ran off. That's what I don't understand.

—1957

ANTTI HYRY

Dam

Translated by Philip Binham

It was late September and it had rained for many days. The water had risen; it flowed plentifully in the stony bottom of the brook. It had cleared and the rain had stopped.

"You could get electricity from that brook," the boy thought. Now it was morning, he had come out and stood by the brook looking at the water. "The brook would turn a water mill and the mill would turn a dynamo."

The boy walked across the yard to the house, found a spade, and took it to the brook. He began to dig turfs from the ground. With his spade he broke the surface of the earth into square-shaped pieces and twisted them out of the ground, beginning from the bank. The boy dug out the turfs from different places, wherever they came out most easily, carried them to the bank of the brook, and put them in one pile. He should really have had rubber gloves; the ground was wet and black water dripped from the turfs.

The stones at the bottom of the brook were covered with brown rust. The water ran over them dark and living. It wasn't like sometimes in summer, when the water only ripples forward, and if there is more water somewhere you can find tadpoles. There was not a single leaf on the willow shrubs growing along the brook; the stream made the branches touching the water tremble.

They were calling the boy from the yard.

"Light the fire under the copper and fill it up with water. The laundress will be here right away, now it's such nice weather."

The boy thought the best way to get away from them was to carry the water and light the fire.

He fetched sticks of spruce from the woodshed and took some birchbark for tinder. He lit the fire under the copper, and he carried water from the brook in two buckets. The boy thought as he carried the water that each time he carried twenty liters. The copper was full after the fourth time. The spruce burned poorly under the cold and sooty copper.

The boy went away to make the dam. He took off his shoes and socks. He turned up the bottoms of his trousers and the sleeves of his jacket and stood in the water by the pile of turfs. He took a turf from the pile, pushed it down to the bottom of the brook and put his foot on it to keep it in place. He pushed another turf under the water and put his other foot on it. The water tried to push under the turf. The boy stamped down the turfs in the brook and kept standing on them. The dam rose, the water rose above the dam; the water running over the turfs was cold and smelled of rain.

When the dam was high enough the water stopped flowing; it stayed there, rising; it was dammed. The boy quickly made a plow-shaped sluice from boards. With the heel of his axe he drove two posts through the turfs on top of the dam and nailed the sides of the sluice to them. He sawed off the posts level with the sluice, and he put turfs on both sides of the sluice and pulled up stones from the bottom to weigh down the dam.

The water rose; above the dam it formed a narrow, standing pool. Willow branches, stones, and grass were covered by the water. Then the water reached the level of the sluice, it came smoothly to the wide end of the sluice, flowed spinning to the narrow end, and fell to the bottom.

The laundress came from the yard. She was carrying a bucket in one hand, in the other she had a packet of washing powder. She noticed the dam and the boy and said:

"You've got a fine place for water there. Goodness me."

And the laundress went down to the brook and put her bucket under the mouth of the sluice. Red-checked kerchief and apron fluttering, she looked at the bucket and the sluice. The water splashed on her apron, her hands held the handle of the bucket tightly. The bucket soon filled. The laundress went away with her full bucket.

The boy laughed to himself.

"Funny old bag."

And he remembered the laundress drinking coffee, contented looking, chattering and sitting a bit sideways in her chair.

The boy started to make the water mill. With axe and saw in his hands, boards under his arm, and pockets full of two- and three-inch nails, he went to the back of the woodshed. He remembered there was the broken handle of a pitchfork in the cowshed, which would do for the axle. He fetched it, took a bicycle wheel from the wall at the same time, and carried them to a door lying on the ground beside a log at the back of the woodshed.

In the corner of the grey door under the log there was a damp dark patch left by the rain. On the horizon high clouds could be seen. Higher in the sky there were white clouds that didn't stop the sun's light. The sun shone from a clear patch of sky. The dogs were loose; they had fun doing all sorts of things; sometimes they barked in the woods at the foot of a tree and smelled the wild ducks in the evening in the dark fields. When it was raining they lay in the cowshed, and in bright weather found shelter by the wall, where they lay snapping at fleas.

The boy sawed six pieces of five-inch board, each thirty centimeters long. He nailed one piece to the center of the axle and another in the opposite direction at the same point on the other side of the axle. Then he nailed two pieces of board at equal intervals on both sides of the axle between the two opposite vanes. The boards now formed a radial structure round the axle.

The boy stood up and wheeled the contraption in front of him on the door. It did not feel really strong and steady. This upset the boy; it was as if something had stung him in the back, the shoulders, and the arms. In the center of the axle he had to hammer a lot of nails, three two-and-a-half-inch nails for each piece of board. They all went through the axle and weakened it.

The boy fetched a drill from the cowshed. He sawed two rectangular pieces of board and through the center of them drilled holes the size of the axle. He put them on either side against the vanes, so that the axle came through the holes, and nailed them fast to the sides of the vanes. This strengthened the contraption.

The boy made two-inch-high sides for the vanes; each vane was now like a little box.

The bicycle wheel was a back wheel from which the back-pedaling brake in the hub had been removed. The axle of the mill fitted into the hole where the brake had been, after the axle had been trimmed a little. The boy hammered the hub onto the end of the axle, where it held tightly. Round the other end of the axle he wound some some wire tightly, coiling the strands neatly side by side. He drilled holes in the ends of the axle with a fine bit and hammered long screws into the holes. The ends of the axle did not split because the brake casing was round one end, the wire round the other end.

The boy took hold of the axle between the vanes and the wheel and carried the mill to the dam. He fetched an iron bar, took it to the brook, and went off to look for suitable posts.

"Go and carry the wash to the clothesline," the boy was told.

"All right," he answered.

The laundress and the boy carried a tub full of freshly washed laundry to the line. The line was stretched from tree to tree.

"It's really good weather now . . . and good water," the laundress said.

"Here's the clothespins, come and get them," they shouted to the boy.

The laundress hung the clothes on the line. She put the shirts to hang from the bottom, the towels side by side so that every clothespin held the corners of two towels. She hung the heavy underwear over the line and doubled the sheets over. The clothes hung heavily, water dripping down to the ground. The line sagged down; the lower ends of the clothes, from which drops of water fell to the grass, almost touched the ground.

With the iron bar the boy made two holes in the bottom of the ditch below the dam, the length of the axle from each other, at the mouth of the sluice. With the bar he knocked upright posts into the holes, and sawed them off a little below the sluice mouth.

The boy put a turf in the sluice, and the water stopped running. Then the boy took the mill and fixed it on top of the posts on the long screws at the axle ends, so that the vanes of the mill reached to the mouth of the sluice. And he hammered nails into the top of the posts to keep the long screws in place. He spun the wheel with his hand and the mill revolved, and at every moment one of the boxlike vanes was at the sluice mouth.

The boy lifted the turf from the sluice. The water flowed again, it went to the narrow mouth of the sluice, fell onto a vane and filled its box. It weighed the box down, filled another box, weighed it down and filled another. And the mill started to turn. The wheel at the end of the axle turned with it.

The boy made a hole with the iron bar in the bottom of the brook near the hub and hammered in a post on which to fasten the dynamo. He went in and took the dynamo from the wall of the cowshed, and from the drawer of the sewing machine he took an empty thread spool, a needle, a reel of strong thread, and some narrow oil-lamp wick.

The boy unscrewed the dynamo head, the part that rubs against the tire on a bicycle. In its place he pressed the empty thread spool, so that the revolving axlehead of the dynamo armature came through the hole in the spool.

A turf was placed into the sluice, the water stopped running, and the mill stopped turning. The boy nailed the dynamo to the top of the post so that the spool was close to the revolving hub. He twisted the lamp wick round the wheel and the empty spool at the end of the dynamo, pulled it tight, cut it off with a knife, and sewed the ends together with the thread. The lamp wick acted like a belt. When the boy spun the wheel, the belt turned the spool, the dynamo armature turned with the reel, and electricity was generated in the dynamo.

When the boy took the turf away from the sluice, the water began to flow again. It turned the mill and the hub with considerable force. The belt from the hub turned the reel. The dynamo screeched. The spool did not keep in place, it twisted sideways and came off, the belt fell onto the axle of the mill and began to twist around it.

The boy shoved the turf back into the sluice and stopped the water mill. He wound thread round the head of the dynamo, coiling it evenly and tightly, and he pressed the spool firmly back into place. He untangled the belt and put it back into place. And he took the turf away from the sluice.

The water pushed the mill round. A continuous swish and splash was heard, as the radial boxes filled, weighed down, emptied, and rose again. The dynamo whizzed round on top of the post.

Evening had come, and dusk, for it was autumn. The sky was an even cloud, but no rain fell.

"Come and have your dinner," they shouted to the boy, who was standing by the brook.

He went in. There was mutton broth with barley grains, bread and butter, milk, and beetroot.

"Couldn't see you anywhere. Where have you been?" they asked the boy.

"Outside."

It seemed a bit strange to have the laundress eating there. Nobody behaved quite normally. It seemed to the boy that the laundress ate her bread and butter especially quickly. Suddenly she seemed to him quite helpless, and he felt so sorry for her that he could hardly keep sitting at the table.

By the telephone there was a hole in the wall for the telephone wires. The boy pushed two leads through the hole. He fetched a dynamo lamp bulb, twisted one bare end of a lead round the bulb, made a hole with an awl in the soft metal at the base of the bulb, and inserted the end of the other lead there. And he fixed the bulb by the telephone in a good position so that it was held by the leads. The other ends of the leads were outside on the wall, where they hung free.

The boy went out. From the cowshed he gathered a bundle of telephone wire, and from the lead ends coming out of the wall he ran out two lines to the water mill. He bared the ends of the leads and joined them to the ends of the wires running to the mill.

The laundress came out of the door and stepped on the wires.

"What are these wires doing here? How do you get over them?"

She was going home. She lifted her skirt with one hand, her bag in the other hand, and off she went.

The boy reflected that the wires would have to be raised up in the air later.

At the water mill the boy wound the end of one of the wires round the nails that fastened the dynamo to the post. He hammered in one more nail, so that the wire would certainly contact the dynamo. With pliers the boy coiled the end of the other wire into a little ring, and put it under the coupling screw of the dynamo, twisting the screw tight with the pliers.

The boy went in. The bulb was burning. The spiral-shaped metal filament inside the glass bulb glowed red; it lighted a small area on the wooden wall behind the bulb and around it. The light dimmed and brightened at an even rate, as the water-mill boxes filled and emptied. It wasn't bright, but, when he looked really closely at the hot filament, it diffused a reddish, inconstant light; it was the same as when you looked at the phosphorescent numbers on a watch, and you could see a pale light like the daylight that comes through the roof into the room.

"Can't see anything with that," the boy thought.

He went out. He coiled up the telephone wire into a bundle and took it to the shed.

He took the mill and the dynamo off the posts, carried the dynamo to the nail on the cowshed wall and stood the mill with its wheel up against the wall at the back of the shed. He went in, took the bulb from the wall, pulled the leads out of the hole, coiled up the leads, and put the coil and the bulb into the washstand drawer.

The laundry hung outside in the darkness. The spruce and birch trees stood there holding up the clothesline. Near the line the air smelled of freshly washed laundry. The water flowed into the sluice, fell into the bottom of the brook, and ran between the stones into the river.

It was morning.

"Go and light the fire under the copper and fill the copper," they told the boy, "The laundress is coming first thing this morning."

We went out. A dazzling sun shone from the autumn sky, its light warmed your hair and the back of your jacket, the smell of sunlight was in the air. The laundry had dried and become lighter, the line had risen higher. The white linen and sheets hung from the line. The water in the brook had dropped during the night. It flowed cold and bright through the sluice. The boy filled two buckets from above the dam, and he carried them to the copper.

—1958

VÄINÖ LINNA

The Eviction

Translated by Philip Binham

Väinö Linna's trilogy, *Here under the Northern Star*, deals with the fortunes and vicissitudes of the Koskela family and of socialism in Finland from 1884 until the end of World War II. In Book One, from which *The Eviction* is taken, Finland is still a Grand Duchy under the Russian Czar. The central figure is Jussi Koskela, an orphan who has lived most of his life at the Parsonage, first as a shepherd boy, then as a farmhand. He persuades the minister to give him a piece of swampland to clear as a tenant-holding, and works himself sick before he completes the job. Later a new minister confiscates part of the land that Jussi has cleared with so much labor. Jussi's eldest son, Akseli, is very bitter about this. He comes under the influence of Halme, the village tailor, an idealistic socialist, and becomes a fiery supporter of the workers' cause.

Anttoo Laurila, who is evicted from a small holding, is a bullheaded, simple peasant. He has proved too outspoken and happy-go-lucky for his landlord, Töyry, to stomach.

The day of the eviction happened to be at the weekend, when many of the tenant farmers had already done their "work days" for their landlords. The farmhands at the Manor were reluctant to be away from work, but Halme argued that they too must play their part, and only a very few did not come.

They gathered at the workers' headquarters, the Fire Brigade building. Akseli was given the task of flag bearer. There was even a little ceremony of honor.

"Akseli Koskela. I give into your hands the noble flag of our Union. Carry it high today, in honor of our first battle."

And Akseli took the flag, after which with obvious pleasure Halme started to explain how he had designed it. It was, of course, red, and within a green wreath was embroidered in gold the motto of the Workers' Union: "WU Forward!"

There had also been consultations with Anttoo. Halme had asked Janne what would happen to Anttoo if he did not obey the orders of the police, and Janne assured him that this would mean prison. Halme had then gone once more to Anttoo to explain this, and proposed that Anttoo should leave when he was ordered to do so. Janne actually was of the opinion that it would be better to get the police to use violence. It would give strength to the cause. A month or two's imprisonment wasn't so hard after all.

But Halme could not take such a burden on his conscience; he even reproached Janne for being too ruthless. "You would sacrifice this unhappy family, my boy, for the sake of election agitation. So far we surely need not go."

Anttoo's attitude decided the situation, however.

"We fights on the threshold like I says."

Halme was shocked when Anttoo stuck to his intention. He even looked fearfully at the axe in the corner by the door.

So there was nothing to do except wait for what might come. The people's restlessness reflected the atmosphere of tension. Wasn't it time to leave yet? Which song should they sing first?

Then Kankanpää Elias, who was on guard, came running from the crossroads. "A gentleman's coming in a sleigh. But e's coming here and not taking the Töyry road."

It was true: a sleigh was coming. A young man who looked like a gentleman was sitting at the back of the sleigh.

"Good day. Could I see Comrade Halme?"

"He's inside. Halme. . . ."

"Halme, here. . . . Hey, tell him!"

Halme came out. The gentleman greeted him and introduced himself.

"I am from the 'People's News.' Comrade Hellberg advised me to speak to you. I intend to make a report of the eviction and the demonstration. May I march with your body at first, then I will go on to the scene of the eviction."

The reporter raised their spirits. It was as if he brought support from some higher and more powerful level. Halme wished the man welcome; he could not have asked for anything better from life at the moment. The man even had photographic apparatus with him.

"Welcome. May I express my pleasure that the Party has not forgotten us in our lonely struggle."

And then more privately:

"I expected Comrade Hellberg to come. But it seems to me that, as a candidate for election, he will not endanger himself. Well. I must lead the struggle alone, then. I have no such position for which to safeguard myself."

So it was. In Tampere they had pretended not to know anything about Halme when the candidates had been chosen.

The reporter said that the police would soon come. He had left the village before them. There were a dozen horsemen, and the Chief of Police and two constables were coming by sleigh. At the same time Elias, who had returned to his post, brought fresh news.

"They're a-coming. . . . Got to Mäenpää Hill. Horsemen and two sleighs. Bloody fine horses."

"Form up behind the flag. Akseli, march in front at an easy pace. Younger boys at the back, and women also. If anything happens, keep calm. And above all: no shouting whatsoever."

The reporter shouted for his part:

"If they try to break up the group, do not be afraid. They will ride toward you, but then they will start to press the people back with the horses' flanks, but they will not ride us down. So just keep calm."

Kivioja Vikki stood in the ranks in his fur coat and roared:

"Damn that, why din' us bring horses—I could 'a ridden one. Other people have bloody horses, too."

"Comrades. Forward, in the name of truth and of justice."

Akseli started off, tense with excitement; he tried to get the flag to flutter, but there was not enough wind.

They turned down the Töyry road, where the police had already gone. The road led also to the Parsonage, and from this road the actual farm road to Töyry turned off. Laurila's cottage was at the fork.

The song Halme had started began softly. The excitement rose higher and higher. Never before had they experienced anything like this. Fear, too, dug into their hearts, and therefore they put more into the song, finding security in it:

"You Sla-aves of Labor from the night
Of harsh Oppression rise. . . ."

From a turn in the road, coming towards the procession, appeared Susi-Kustaa, a frozen fish trap over his shoulder.

"Kustaa in the ranks. Come on."

"Go by yer fucking selfs. Go on then. . . . They'll chop the tops offen yer with their swords, every mother's son."

Because of the song Kustaa's mutter couldn't be heard clearly, but enough to know it wasn't anything good anyway, and there were shouts of:

"What's that Kustaa mumbling. Ain't workers' company good enough?"

"No it ain't. Go on, roar your heads off, you silly devils."

There was still some muttering and cursing as Kustaa passed the end of the procession. He went off with his net, grunting in his anger.

The reporter ran in front of the procession and quickly got his camera ready. Halme moved up beside Akseli from behind the flag, and others in the front rank tried to come out of its shadow. The scene was repeated two or three times.

Then they could see the Laurila cottage and people in the yard. The procession turned off the road in the agreed manner and plodded through the thick, lumpy snow, making towards the little hill that had been chosen for the demonstration. From there Laurila's yard could be seen well. When the singing procession came into view, there was movement in the yard. The Chief of Police came over accompanied by one constable. Halme broke off the singing and told the others that only he would speak.

The Chief of Police strode angrily towards them. He was still a long way off when he demanded:

"What is the purpose of this crowd? And by whose permission has it assembled?"

Halme took several steps towards the Chief of Police, greeted him by raising his hat, and pronounced in a clear voice:

"Sir. The purpose of this gathering is to be present at the destruction of the home of one of our comrades. And it has assembled according to the right which the law of Finland grants to every citizen."

"The law also requires that notice be given of public assembly, but I have received no such notice."

"Sir. This is not an official occasion. People have been in the habit of gathering, for example, for the Whitsun Bonfire, and there has been singing at such occasions, but this has not been considered unlawful."

"There is no Whitsun Bonfire here. This is an obvious demonstration." The Chief of Police looked at the group for a moment and made his decision:

"I warn you solemnly against interfering in any way with the activities of the authorities. I forbid you to come closer than this to the eviction premises. Otherwise you will have to answer for the consequences."

"Sir. We are not here to interfere with the authorities. We demonstrate against the general state of affairs, whereby occurrences of this kind can take place in this country."

The Chief of Police looked at the crowd doubtfully again. Everyone tried to look solemn and businesslike. Probably even the trace of a grin would have influenced his decision, but since he saw nothing of that kind, he went away, saying as he left:

"I warn you once again. The slightest trouble and you will be liable for and accused of interfering with a government official in the execution of his duties."

The Chief of Police returned to the yard. The Laurila family stayed inside, and the police only waited for Töyry's arrival, for the landlord must be present when the official order to vacate the premises was given. The reporter followed the Chief of Police to the yard, where the latter asked:

"What are you doing here?"

"I am a representative of the press. Here is my card. After all, this is a public eviction."

"Very well. You will remain aside from the proceedings, also. You intend, of course, to write an account disparaging the authorities."

"The editor is responsible for the legality of the matter, as the Chief of Police must know."

The Chief of Police shouted to the constables:

"Men, remember to behave in a manner fitting a government official in the execution of his duty."

At the same moment Töyry drove into the yard. His wife was with him; she had not been able to overcome her curiosity in spite of the unpleasantness of the occasion. She remained seated in the sleigh, however.

The Chief of Police spoke in a low voice to the officer commanding the mounted police. Then the officer ordered the horsemen to place themselves facing the demonstrators. Töyry greeted the Chief of Police. He looked gloomy and upset, but said in a determined voice:

"Very well. In you go then."

The Laurila family were sitting in the living room. The boys and Aliina were in the corner by the stove, but Anttoo himself was sitting on the long bench by the table. The Chief of Police greeted him, but received no answer, only sullen looks directed at his boots.

The Chief of Police took a piece of paper from his pocket and read the eviction order. Then he turned to Töyry.

"Does the landlord demand that the order be carried out?"

"I have said my say and I stand by my word."

"Anton Kustaa Laurila. I urge you with your family to move out of this building, at the same time taking with you all the livestock and chattels that do belong to you. In accordance with the eviction order issued by the courts of law, I inform you that if this does not occur voluntarily, I must perform the eviction through the instrument of the police."

"Kill us here then. Kill the whole lot, kids 'n all. But I ain't leaving my home. 'N that's my last word."

"Laurila. I must point out for the sake of clarity, also, that if I am obliged to perform the eviction by force, this will incur the charge of resisting a government official."

Aliina began to laugh, a hysterical and malicious laugh, but with tears just behind it:

"Then there'll be a home for us somewhere. Better be in the jug than on the road."

Töyry, flushed and nervous, said to Anttoo:

"Listen now. I'll give you this last chance then. If you promise me now to take everything away inside three days, then I'll give you them three days' time. You can find somewhere to live around here iffen you just look for it."

"Not in three fucking years. You know I ain't leaving my home, you bloody thief. You won't move me 'cept in little pieces."

"All right, if that's it. If a man can't listen to reason, there's nothing for it but to let the law take its course. There's still a law in this land for all your shouting."

The Chief of Police decided it was useless to continue the discussion, but, because of the reporter, he said:

"I ask you to inform me of the place to which you wish your property and livestock to be taken. Otherwise they will be left outside."

"I ain't got no place. Take 'em to the Finnish highway. That's a place where even a poor man can be, 'long as he keeps nicely out of the way if a gentleman comes along."

"Raitamo and Saari. Take the tools and remove the doors and windows. The stove should be demolished, also, so that it cannot be used. Order two mounted police to carry the things out. And Mrs. Laurila. Dress the children ready to leave. I warn you not to make trouble."

"Let 'em freeze! What'll they do in this world for Christ's sake? Let's all go to hell together. . . ."

Aliina burst into tears, took Elma in her arms, and sat there, her body rocking, her face pressed into the girl's back. The child started to cry, too. The policemen fetched the tools; they looked harassed, chiefly because of Aiina's crying. Töyry said he was leaving because he wasn't needed there any more, but the Chief of Police, who was beginning to get annoyed, said angrily.

"You will remain here. The work of demolishing will be to your account, and you are also responsible for it. The police will follow your instructions in this matter."

It had been decided beforehand to perform the demolishing so that Laurila would not return to the cottage, and the Chief of Police had then insisted that Töyry must be on the spot to give permission for all breakages.

One window after another was removed, and the cold air streamed into the cottage. The doors were taken away, too, and then from the hill the demonstrator's song sounded:

". . . whe-re our fla-ag is flying . . . our country's honor is sa-a-afe. . . ."

The mounted police began to carry the things out. There wasn't much. But when they started to empty the baking room, the lunatic fastened to the wall started to bellow and wrench his chains. The chains were long enough that he could lie down on the bunk by the wall. This unfortunate had a name, too: Antti. He was a horrible sight with his unkempt hair and beard. On his forehead, just by his "madman's wrinkles." was a big birthmark. Rags had been wrapped round his wrists so that the chains would not chafe.

When the police started carrying out containers and bowls for mixing dough, the lunatic stamped his feet, clanked his chains, and laughed. Evidently he felt some kind of desire to be part of what was going on. Through his laughter, confused and unclear words could be heard:

"Aaa . . . a . . . ntti. Dough . . . dough. . . ."

One of the mounted police asked the Chief of Police what to do with the lunatic.

"He must be unchained and dressed to go out. Because they have not procured themselves any place to live, he must be taken to the poorhouse."

"But isn't special authority required for that?"

"We cannot leave him loose. In this case no authority is required, because they have not looked after him themselves. . . . But what a state of affairs."

All the time Anttoo had been sitting on the bench without saying a word. Clenching his teeth he tried to smile mockingly. Aliina was still crying with Elma in her lap, and the boys had moved behind her. Then there was nothing left but Aliina's chair and the bench Anttoo was sitting on.

"Laurila. Get up off the bench. It must be taken out."

"Can't you see it's staying under my arse?"

"For the last time. Stand up."

"Fuck off."

"Constables! Conduct this man out. Put his hat on his head and take him out."

One of the policemen found the hat and tried to put it on Anttoo's head, but he swept it off onto the floor, and so the game began. The policemen grabbed hold of Anttoo, but he got up and began to struggle his way free.

"Jesus Christ . . . Christ almighty . . . go to hell the whole bloody lot of you."

Elma screamed frightfully. Aliina started to swear on top of everything. The policemen lost their calm and dragged Anttoo out, and though they were two strong men, they were shaken by his arms so that the door frame trembled.

"Fetch the handcuffs and some rope from the sleigh. You can't leave this one loose."

One of the mounted policemen brought the handcuffs and the rope, and Anttoo was tied up. Töyry's wife in the sleigh began to cry and carry on, and the landlord walked feverishly back and forth in the yard, repeating over and over:

"It's like I said, the law's the law and you can't change it. . . . I said my say, and there 'tis."

Anttoo cursed and roared, and that was all he could do with handcuffs round his wrists and rope round his legs.

The crowd of demonstrators could not see the drama clearly between the horses, and in the middle of a song were heard shouts:

"What're they doing there? . . . Not killing 'em surely? . . . They hitting him. . . ?"

The women began to get upset, some of them were even sobbing. Akseli looked round, his teeth clenched. He turned towards the crowd, offered the flag to Halme and said:

"No, by Christ. . . . I can't watch that. . . . Never mind what happens, I'm going."

"In your place. . . . Stay in your place. . . . Remember what you have promised. . . ."

Otto stepped over to Akseli, shaking his head angrily:

"Boy, boy, boy. . . . Keep some sense in your head."

"Damn them . . . hitting people. . . ."

Women began to shout between their sobs, too:

"Go on Halme and say something. . . . That's terrible that is. . . . Oh God, what's happening there. . . ?"

Halme began to feel afraid of the crowd's excitement. His voice shook with agitation and uneasiness as he turned to the crowd, his hands spread wide, and shouted:

"For God's sake, comrades. . . . Keep quiet. . . . Otherwise something terrible may happen. . . . Some of us are almost children, and you think of going against horsemen. . . . Let us sing . . . do you hear me comrades? . . . 'Forward now children of your land'. . . ."

The crowd began again to release its feelings in the "Marseillaise," but Halme followed the situation out of the corner of his eye. In the middle of the song he said to Akseli:

"You are making people restless. . . . I order you to obey. . . ."

"Who can look at that. . . ?"

"One must. . . . Can't you see what it would mean? There are children behind . . . little boys. . . ."

Halme's pleading voice made Akseli control himself, but now a miracle occurred. Powerfully, though terribly out of tune, Akseli began to sing:

". . . To a-arms, you citizens. . . ."

In the yard the drama continued. Anttoo had been lifted onto the police sleigh, and from there he kept up a constant racket:

"Knock 'em all down for Chris'sakes. Chuck the kids out then. . . . Get the poor lunatic, too. . . . Kill 'em all in one bunch."

The cows were let out first. The cowshed and the stable were emptied, and the animals began to rush about stupidly here and there, bellowing. There was a young bull among them; it stared round and then let out a tremendous roar and started to gambol round the field so that the snow flew wildly. And soon the sheep were baaing outside, too.

Anttoo's bench was brought out at length. There was still the chair in which Aliina was sitting. But there was no trouble over it, for Aliina stood up of her own free will, wrapped a blanket round Elma and went out accompanied by the boys. She came into the yard, crying, but when she saw Töyry's wife carrying on in the sleigh, she put down the child and rushed towards the other woman:

"Christ. . . . Just you look . . . look at them kids, driven out in the yard. . . . Laugh you devil . . . laugh . . . till you got what you want. . . . I'd tear yer eyes outer yer head, but yer such a poor thing . . . dried up codfish . . . stiff-neck. . . . And yer arse as thin as a piece of string. But I'll show you me own and then you'll see."

And Aliina bent over, jerked up her skirts, and raged through her tears:

"There y're then. Take a look at that. . . . There's two good cracks . . . see which one you want."

Töyry's wife covered her face with her hands, but then started to scream hysterically through her fingers.

"Filthy . . . filthy . . . look how filthy . . . look."

She was beside herself with the insult. The landlord grasped the situation, ran to his sleigh, turned it on to the road, gave his wife the reins, and told her to drive home. He came back and shouted to the Chief of Police:

"Can't you do anything then. . . ? Letting that sort of indecent behavior go on at an official occasion. . . ."

But Aliina had crossed the line beyond which people are no longer tied by any scruples. She turned her backside and showed it to the Chief of Police, too. He was nonplussed for a moment but shouted then:

"Reporter . . . now you can get a picture, come and take it."

The newspaperman, with a smile on his face, had been taking notes all the time. He did not start photographing Aliina, however, but said to the Chief of Police:

"Interesting sight . . . don't you feel ashamed?"

"Do not meddle with my business. Otherwise you will have to leave. I shall require the photographic plates for inspection, also."

Aliina ended the show and snatched up Elma, who was screaming at the top of her voice. With the girl in her arms she flew at the Chief of Police:

"Cut-throat swine. . . . Ain't you got nothing better to do than drive children out in the snow? Shame on you, you buttoned-up bastard."

"Woman. . . . Clean your tongue."

But Aliina wept and was about to fling herself at the Chief of Police, who ordered a couple of policemen to restrain her. The boys, who had up to now stood aside silently, went wild when they saw the policemen grab hold of Aliina's arms. Lumps of ice, bits of wood, even frozen horse dung began to rain down on the police. One of them went off after the boys, who started to run away; as they went, one boy shouted, sobbing and breathless:

"Cunt . . . unt . . . nt . . . ucking swine . . . shit, shit, shit. . . ."

The cows, sheep, goat, and bull were still rushing about. There was shouting and confusion. There was struggling, thumping, storming. In the midst of all this they brought Antti out, wrapped in Anttoo's fur coat. Antti guffawed and bawled and started to jump around in his chains in excitement at all he saw.

"Take him to the sleigh."

Then Aliina let out a terrible shriek. She tore herself loose from the policemen's hands and tried to get to the lunatic. At the same time Laurila's bull thrust its way towards the spot, snorting and throwing its hind legs into air. The policeman in charge of Antti turned instinctively towards the bull and loosened his hold for a moment. The lunatic pulled away with a triumphant bellow and started to run after the bull. In summertime one of his greatest joys had been the animals moving in the yard. He had watched them through the window and bawled out his interest in them. Now, his chains dragging across the ground, he ran wildly behind the bull. The heavy-moving policeman could not catch the lunatic, who—clad only in his shirt, fur coat thrown aside— was running with incredible speed, hair flying, joyfully shouting at the bull, which charged on in front of him, frisking up its rear, and uttering bellows like those of its chaser. Yelling, weeping, and cursing were mixed with the furious commands of the Chief of Police, as he ordered the mounted police to catch the runaway. And above all this, from the nearby hill could be heard the heavy notes of the "Internationale," with the women's voices from time to time rising to painful heights.

"Hunger always living here beside us, but like vultures from their prey. . . . One day we will drive them from us, and the sun will shine again. . . ."

All this was too much for the Chief of Police, who lost his temper:

"Lieutenant Grönberg. Disperse that screaming crowd. Order them first to go peacefully, but if they do not obey, then use force. But as little as possible."

"Mount! Slow trot, forward!"

One of the mounted policemen was chasing the lunatic, but the other nine began to trot toward the crowd, past the well, and over the little field beyond which the crowd were singing.

"The Cossacks are coming. . . ."

This caused a little stir, and the women were alarmed. Halme knew, however, that they would not ride into the crowd without first giving the order to disperse, and he shouted that the people should remain calmly where they were.

And the Lieutenant did stop his men about thirty meters away, and—he was a Swedish-Finn—shouted in poor Finnish:

"Crowd to disperse at once. Everyone to home peacefully. If not this one command is obeyed, then I order my men into crowd."

"Let 'em come. . . . They won't kill you. . . . You women get behind." Halme was faced with a hard choice. He understood very well that it would be best to leave, but he did not wish to do so without protest. He stepped forward several paces and answered:

"Sir. The assembly is peaceful and is observing law and order. It is in no way interfering with the authorities."

The Lieutenant understood this as a negative reply. Moreover, he was uneasy and upset.

"Forward! You know what to do, men."

When the riders began to move, women's shrieks were heard. Some of them began to run towards the road, but the front rank stood fast. Akseli pressed the flagpole to his chest, twisted his wrist around it, and stood sideways to an approaching horse. Halme stood in his place, pale, as if waiting for the riders to stop their approach, as if the whole thing were not true. His mind searched for a quick decision, but he was unable to make one. He had expected that after some discussion, they would have been able to withdraw peacefully and honorably, but the rapid decision of the officer had changed the whole situation. He understood that they must go away, and moreover he was personally timid when faced with physical force. But it was as if he were paralyzed. Fear demanded that they should leave, but the picture of an ignoble flight troubled his self-esteem. He got as far as opening his mouth to give the order to disperse, but left it unsaid when he saw that Akseli, in front of him, was being pushed by the first rider. Halme held his breath, shut his eyes, and turned his side towards the approaching rider. He could not leave when he saw that the flag bearer was resisting. The horse snorted just in front of him as Halme heard Janne's shout:

" 'Song of Our Land,' boys . . . sing to these Russian serfs. . . ."

Halme opened his eyes. In front of him was a horse's head and, as if braced by Janne's shout, he began:

"Land of our fathers, native land. . . ."

The horsemen were already pressing against the crowd. The trained horses walked sideways on, with small, dainty steps, as if taking care not to tread on people's toes. The crowd had joined in the song. True, the ones at the back had retreated to the road, but they were singing there. Some woman's cries could be heard:

"Jesus have mercy. . . . They're trampling. . . . Come away. . . ."
*"With plows, with swords, with solemn thought
Our Finnish fathers fought. . . ."*

The police officer tried to shout over the song that they should disperse, but his words had no effect.

*"The flowers in their buds that grope
Shall burst their sheathes with Spring. . . ."*

The song was becoming confused, as the front ranks tried to catch their breath in their efforts to stop the riders.

". . . So from our love to bloom shall ope
Thy gleam, thy glow, thy joy, thy hope
And higher yet some day shall ring
The song to thee we sing. . . ."

Kivioja Vikki caught hold of one horse's mouth:
"Fine bit o' horseflesh you got. Why 'n't you sell it? Give you seventy-five.
. . . Just step down. Vikki'll count the money out."
"Let go . . . let go at once. . . ."
The policeman raised his whip, and dust flew out of Vikki's coat. At the same time, from the back of the crowd, Kankanpää Elias threw a lump of snow that hit the officer on the shoulder. The officer struck out, too. When Halme was struck lightly, he lost his fear completely. Now it was really happening, it was not so terrible as he had imagined. But the blow made him decide to give the order to retreat. He felt as if the moral victory were his, and in a cracked voice he shouted:
"Comrades! Back to the road . . . Akseli, take the flag . . . take the flag to the road. They're whipping us."
Akseli, teeth clenched, was pushing against a horse's flank, which step by step forced him back. He felt someone grab his shoulder and heard Otto's words:
"Take the flag to the road . . . t'others'll follow."
"By Christ, no."
"You go on there. . . . No good in this. . . . They'll break up soon anyway."
Akseli went off with his flag, and at Halme's urging the others followed him. The little boys made faces at the policemen, and some jeers were heard. Halme trudged through the snow to the road, and ordered the boys to be quiet. The police officer had the sense to allow the crowd time to gather together, and ordered his men to stay on the hill. He himself rode down to the road to Halme.
"You leader?"
"I have the honor to enjoy the confidence of my comrades." Halme spoke in a voice still trembling with indignation; he stood purposely erect and looked the officer straight in the eye.
"You take at once crowd away. Go with flag allowed if obey."
"We will withdraw behind our flag, but I shall lodge a protest concerning the behavior of the police. Today for the first time I have seen free citizens of Finland struck with a whip."
"You not struck. Only touched. Police act according instruction. But you resisting police. I inform legal proceedings due to resisting police."
"We can bear that, too. Comrades! Let us march back to the Fire Brigade Headquarters. We must fetch horses and see that this unfortunate family is rescued from the cruel snowdrifts."
The procession moved off, and the "Internationale" was struck up with great demonstrative vigor.
The police waited until the crowd had clearly gone away, then returned to the cottage. Antti had already been caught, and was put into the sleigh together with Anttoo. Aliina sat on a bed in the yard and wept. The boys lurked behind the corner of the cowshed.
Anttoo threatened to kill Töyry, whereupon the landlord said to the Chief of Police:

"That kind of talk on an official occasion is too much. . . . He must be arrested. There's no knowing what 'e might do."

"He will be taken for interrogation in connection with the legal proceedings. But after that he will be set at liberty, providing, of course, that he no longer utters such threats."

The Chief of Police demanded the photographic plates from the reporter, but the latter explained that this was impossible. The negatives might be spoiled, and he referred to the law concerning the press, according to which all such matters were the responsibility of the editor. He was allowed to keep his pictures in the end, especially because he had not managed to photograph the breaking up of the crowd.

Then they went off. Aliina remained with the children and the things in the yard. Antti jumped up and down in the sleigh, shouting confused words in his joy:

"Antti . . . Antti . . . gee-gee . . . moo-cow . . . moo-cow . . . moo-oo-ooo. . . ."

Töyry had managed to get away before the Union men arrived to collect the livestock and the things. The cows meekly allowed themselves to be caught, but the bull had to be chased and cursed for a long time. The family was taken to Kankaanpää, along with the milk cows. The other cattle and sheep were taken to other small tenant farms.

The last loads were carried away in the dusk of evening. Silence reigned over the yard of the grey cottage. The beginnings of a storm blew snow in through the empty door and window frames. And little by little the snow covered the traces of turmoil in the yard and in the field.

—1959

MARJA-LEENA MIKKOLA

Boy for a Summer

Translated by Philip Binham

They had met by the river one day. Seija had swum to the boom; a little boy was sitting there. Seija had asked whether the boom went far.

"As far as Lehtisaari," the boy said.

They'd walked along the boom all the way to the island. It was a calm evening and dragonflies flitted by at eye level. They'd stopped to look at a couple of water fleas as if there were something remarkable about them. Seija had pulled up a water lily and made it into a necklace, which soon went limp and useless. They'd gone on to Lehtisaari, picked spotted orchis, and looked to see whether there would be many wild strawberries.

"The strawberries come late here," the boy said, "because it's so shady. There's a lot by the barn, they'll be ripe all right by tomorrow morning."

The sun had gone down slowly behind Hovi's mill; it had been quite silent, only the clip of horse's hooves sounded from the direction of the bridge. Gradually it became clear that the boy lived on the other shore of Seija's lake. There were no other houses on the lake shore, only her mother's summer cottage and this other one. They'd swum back against the current; Seija was nearly all in when they reached the landing, but didn't want to show it because the boy was so much younger and managed the swim without any trouble. Seija had combed her hair on the landing, while the boy threw ducks and drakes. He always made them jump six or seven times, but looked quite indifferent.

Seija had put her bathrobe over her shoulders—it was a rather super one. She'd got it when her mother came back from France, when she'd got into fifth grade this spring. They'd walked past the mill, then along the edge of a field on the other side of which was a damp and shady wood. There were always lilies of the valley there; it was curious. The boy looked for birds and their nests to show to Seija, but didn't find any. It was early twilight now; almost no sound could be heard. They sat down for a little while on a gate without speaking. Seija had been quite weak from the silence and the sweet scents, and then the cuckoo had called heaven knows how many times. They'd started to count but got mixed up and then the boy had run off as fast as he could along the lake shore toward home.

Seija had gone slowly along her own path to the sauna, cleaned her teeth, and walked to the veranda as slowly as she could. Saara was sitting on the porch with a white bonnet on; she had made tea for Seija.

"You don't need to wear that bonnet when there's nobody here except me," Seija had said. Saara hadn't answered, she'd turned the pages of her home magazine and looked for cake recipes.

The next day they had met by the barn. Seija had come to see if there were any strawberries there, but the boy had already picked them all and strung them on a stalk of grass. Then he had given the strawberries to Seija. Seija hadn't wanted to take them, but the boy said he didn't want them, they'd already got a bit dry. They had looked at a field of buttercups and jumped over into it, it looked so inviting. By the ditch there was a mole hole.

"It doesn't bite," the boy said, "it won't even come out."

"But supposing it's a field mouse's hole," Seija said, but the boy said it didn't look like one. Seija had picked a big bunch of buttercups; the boy had helped.

"These will look nice on our porch," Seija said. They'd crossed Hovi's bridge to the other side of the river and come to another lake, a really big one. There was a meadow sloping down, the edges white with daisies. Seija had gone down on her knees and started to pick them with one hand. The boy had picked three stalks of strawberries in the meantime. Seija had picked as many daisies as her hand could hold.

Seija had arranged the buttercups on the porch in a big brown vase and the daisies in a blue glass jug in front of the fireplace. Saara was cross: "They make a mess," Saara said, "and they don't smell nice."

"Don't fuss all the time," Seija said, "they're gay flowers."

In the evening they had swum to the boom again and with the current to Lehtisaari. When they got back to the landing, the boy started to fish.

"You catch more fish here than in the lake," the boy said. He caught a couple of minnows, but threw them back. They heard big splashes, but the big fish didn't bite. The boy didn't care, but ran back and forth on the way home with his rod. From the lake shore they'd collected bits of cork and mussels.

"Just look around you always," the boy said, "you'll find all sorts of things."

Mother always came on Saturdays; sometimes she had a woman friend with her. On Sunday morning Seija sat drinking coffee with them on the veranda.

"Seija's going wild here," Mother said, and the friend smiled and swung her foot, on which was a ridiculously high-heeled shoe.

"Isn't Seija going to Paris to your friend's? She's going to study French at school in the autumn isn't she?" the friend asked, with a smile on her painted mouth.

"Yes, I've thought about it," Mother said. Seija got up and ran to the shore. The boy was sitting in a tree and listening to a woodpecker. Seija climbed the tree. She had a couple of books with her and she gave one of them to the boy.

The boy was small for his age. He had dark brown hair and light brown eyes and very narrow features. He was thin and brown. His legs were peculiar, they must have been ten different colors. They were covered in mosquito bites, scars, new pink skin, all kinds of blotches and calluses. The boy's skin was dark; he probably didn't wash it except in the sauna. He always wore just swimming shorts, with a check shirt if it was raining. Seija was wearing shorts and a brown striped blouse; if it was cold she wore jeans and a big grey sweater. When they went swimming the boy didn't have any trouble, he went straight into the water in his swimming shorts and got out again in the same clothes—they soon dried. But Seija had to go behind the bushes, undo buttons and hooks, pull one garment up and another down, squeeze into her swimsuit, and fight with the zipper. Every time Seija swore softly.

Seija said to Saara one day that they might invite the boy over.

"What boy," Saara asked in alarm.

"That boy from the other side of the lake, he's a nice little boy."

"Huh, so you've found yourself a boy for the summer," Saara said. "But there're lots of big boys and little boys there. It's a big family and very dirty. When you go past it really stinks there, they've got the outhouse right by the road, but they don't always use it."

"Don't talk nonsense," Seija said.

"I'm not talking nonsense," Saara said, "it's a very funny family, a bit queer. Their father's been in prison, so they say."

"So what," Seija said, and went out on the veranda. Mother had brought her *Elle* magazines, and she glanced over them. Stone-faced mannequins put one foot in front of the other, their mouths open in surprise, their fingers stretched out; they looked silly. Seija threw one leg over the arm of the chair and tossed the magazines on the windowsill. Paris—ugh!

Seija invited the boy. She gave him tea and sandwiches. Saara sulked in the inner room and wouldn't come out on the veranda. The boy kept looking round him. Seija chattered, said she had seen a hawk flying toward the village. The boy ate one sandwich; the chatter died away; the boy went away straight afterwards.

The boy didn't come again. Seija went to the river, to Lehtisaari, the forest, the strawberry place, the bridge, but didn't see the boy. Mother came on Saturday with a big crowd of visitors; some of them were Seija's age and there was one boy a bit older whom everyone was in love with. In the evening they had a party on the veranda by the light of colored paper lanterns and candles, but Seija got bored. The visitors didn't leave till Monday morning.

Seija cycled off to the village as soon as they had gone. She heard a familiar voice in Tommo's yard, stopped, threw her bicycle on the ground, and went into the yard. Tommo's was the slaughterhouse. The boy was there. When Seija went over to him, the boy said he'd been there several days helping. Seija stayed in the yard, though the boy didn't take any notice of her. A truck drove into the yard and three big pigs with their legs tied together were pulled down from it. The pigs were put in the yard; they squealed like mad. There were three sharp reports, and all three rolled over one by one against the wall. They were carried into the shed and the blood was drained. It steamed and reeked of animal, it came from a pig that had just now been alive. Seija felt sick. She was shooed away.

"Do they make soap from the intestines," she asked.

"Sure," someone said, "our Mum does, that's a trick you could learn."

Seija came again the next day. She looked at the garbage heap: there were entrails and bones. Some dogs were trying to get there, but the cats that lived there drove them away. Seija watched how a dead cow was hung up in the shed. Parts of it were cut away; the carcass remained there, sad and pink.

One evening the boy was again by the river. They sat on the boom. The boy said he was going to become a butcher, it was a well-paid job and soon he could start his own meat shop. Seija nodded.

"What are you going to be," the boy asked.

"Nothing," Seija said.

The next day some girls came to the yard to make soap. They all looked at Seija, who was sitting with the boy on a pile of lumber. Soon the boy went to drive back a pig that had got away. Two girls came near Seija and whispered loudly.

"That boy's father's been seen in the village again," one of them said, "every girl wants to look out for herself."

"Is that boy going to be like his father?" the other said. Then they looked at Seija. Seija went over by the boy; he was just tying the squealing little pig up.

"What was your father accused of?" Seija asked, and looked the boy straight in the eye. The boy struggled with the pig, got it tied, and stood up. He looked towards the shed window and said: "He raped some girl." Seija stared at the pig, which kicked feebly and peered at her with its little eyes.

"I've got to go," she said, "it's our lunchtime."

"You coming this afternoon," the boy shouted in a blurred voice after her. Seija quickly made gestures of regret.

Seija didn't go the next day, she was a bit tired. In the evening she went to the boom. The boy was on the landing, but went away immediately. The mosquitoes whined in chorus, otherwise it was quite silent. Seija made a necklace of water lilies and wept.

In the morning Seija went to the lake shore. Now and then she went into the woods to pick wood sorrel, she looked at the reeds and came nearer to the house. It was small and old, heaven knows who had built it. It looked as if they would get plenty of berries and apples, though no one had looked after their garden. The yard was covered in dandelion puffballs, long grass, and plantains. They'd doctored a scratch on the boy's leg once with a plaintain leaf. The house was tarred over. She went up the steps, knocked at the door, and went in.

Seija said good morning. By the door sat a big bearded man reading a news-paper, but he quickly went into the bedroom with his paper. The kitchen was large and dark, because the windows were so low. On one bench sat the boy's brothers, big and little; they were hammering at something. The boy himself was sitting by the table looking through an old magazine. A thin woman moved back and forth between the stove and the table; she wore an old and faded beret, her hair was pressed down inside it, but a few strands hung down on her neck. The woman looked at her and said good morning in an expressionless voice. The woman herself looked expressionless, her features had worn that way, her look was shuttered. She couldn't have been very old, but her legs were already bad. She went over to the table with a baker's peel in her hand, slid a floury, flattened cake of dough on it, went to the oven, and tossed it in. She did this all the time, there were a lot of loaves. There was a certain rhythm to it.

"You have nice-looking loaves," Seija said. There was a giggle from the brothers. They looked in the direction where she was sitting, and stared at her legs. She crossed her legs.

"You'll have a lot of berries and apples," Seija said. Nobody answered. The brothers giggled. She looked toward them; they dropped their eyes to the level of her legs, choking back their laughter. She looked at the boy by the table. He took no notice, but read some article very carefully. The woman went back and forth, wiping her hands from time to time on her skirt. Seija's hands rested in her lap; the brothers had now started to stare at them. Now it was almost impos-sible for them to hold back their laughter. There was nothing to do.

Seija got up and said goodbye; the man peered out of the bedroom. Seija opened the door and went out past the larder, which smelled of mice.

"That girl came here," she heard the smallest one laugh. He'd had stuff from his nose all down one cheek, Seija had noticed.

Seija went back toward home along a path strewn with pine needles. The forest was all dark green, the best part of summer was already over. The boy ran after her. Seija turned to wait for him, but the boy ran on in front. The boy started to throw stones.

"When there was that party at your place I went past your house," the boy said; "There were all sorts of lamps on the veranda and a boy was kissing you, I told them about it."

"Oh, that's why they were laughing so much," Seija said. The boy went on throwing stones.

"I'm not coming to the river tomorrow," the boy said; "I've got to go and weed Hovi's sugar-beet field, I get two marks for that."

"I'm not going to the river tomorrow either," Seija said, "I'm going away very soon, a long way away. I've got to get my things packed."

The boy bent down to look at something on the path, and Seija went past him. She had been walking for a little way right by the water's edge, when she saw a stone graze the surface of the lake right beside her. He made it jump six times again at least, Seija thought; he was a clever boy.

—1962

VEIJO MERI

The Killer

Translated by John R. Pitkin

He lay motionless in the marshland on the river's shore from dawn to dusk and then vanished. He had been there for about a week without his position being discovered.

His bulky, cloth garb was shaggy and shredded. In it he was like an alder shrub rustling in the wind, opening and shutting, but never quite letting you see through.

Now through, now around his telescopic sight, his open eye relentlessly scanned the river's opposite shore, and also the sand bank, thirty yards high. He was particularly interested in the sinuous crest that separated the brilliant sky from the bleak earth. Occasionally he let his wide-eyed gaze slide down the slope for a change of scenery—grey sand and mounds of grey stones of various sizes—until suddenly the log jam that filled the river seemed to be falling over him. Then he slowly raised his wide-eyed gaze, which saw very little but was all the more far-reaching, up to where the earth ended and the sky spread out. So slowly that it didn't seem to move, he raised his weapon, which was dressed in the same kind of shaggy and shredded garb as its master.

So that his body wouldn't grow numb he changed his position every so often— he bent his knees and simultaneously arched his back and then straightened himself while spreading his legs, but so slowly that he didn't seem to move. This movement might consume half an hour, but afterwards he could lie a couple of hours without stirring.

He didn't pay any attention to the rolling fire of the artillery, because the targets were far away from him, to the front and rear. The third day however the enemy had attempted to eradicate him with mortarfire by directing a fierce concentration into the cluster of young spruce right on the shore of the river. The enemy fired supersensitives, which exploded in the air, but he had foreseen this and shifted to the open swamp. He turned over his camouflage and lay there like a yellow swamp pool dappled with blue.

The front was quiet, too quiet. Many times he would stare an enemy soldier straight in the eyes, which seemed to look knowingly through him, but his finger wouldn't press the trigger. He could have been pinpointed on the basis of a shot.

They tried to coax him into firing. They arranged decoys for him: a helmet would creep along the top of the bank like a turtle. When a man moves, his head slightly rises and falls. When his feet are apart he is shorter than when they are near each other. The contrivers of the decoy didn't seem ever to have learned how to arrange even such a simple matter as this. He had been taught all possible tricks. Besides, he wouldn't shoot a man in the helmet, but always in the face, in the center of the face. He aimed at the intersection of the axes of the nose and eyes, the origin of the face. He scarcely ever shot when a head was turned sideways, because the target was diffuse then and it was rather difficult to find a fixed point of aim in a tenth of a second. The only possibility was the ear, but to attain a conclusive result it was best to shoot just behind it. Then, however, the target-area was narrow. Furthermore the helmet had a long neck plate. If a man had a helmet he wouldn't shoot from the side or rear unless the range was very short. Because of its curved structure a helmet would deflect a shot from practically any angle.

A man is considered competent for this profession when he is capable of hitting a head-sized object at a distance of 650 yards with one hundred percent certainty. But that's not enough. You can shoot the face out from under a man's eyes and it's nothing but a squandering of gunpowder. Even in the head there are places were a hit is not fatal. But he knew all the fine points of his field—the structure of the human head through and through. If his bullet didn't immediately prove fatal, he had failed and his whole day was spoiled. A prolonged cry of pain was a blot on his reputation. Nothing less than perfect results were demanded of him. Even a blunderer could disable a man with a shot in a limb or organ. Indisputably instantaneous death is very rare, so rare, that many believe there is no such thing. A man who dies in an instant doesn't even utter a sound; his limbs freeze in midmotion.

The fifth day he didn't get anybody. The enemy had become too cautious. His mission in this sector had been completed. Ahead was the transfer to somewhere else. He was hardly ever in the same sector for longer than a week. He was on tour to wherever he was needed, which might be as far as fifty miles away.

Without firing a shot he left the swamp after nightfall. Mist rose from the river as from a deep ravine and rolled over the opening into the forest. Like a puff of bluish smoke in the white smoke of a straw fire, he drifted there at the same slow speed as the mist.

The soldiers living in foxholes saw him go past. They didn't venture to pose him questions and their conversation broke off as if tacks had been driven into their hard palates. Only a Second Lieutenant in the infantry joined him on the path and offered him a cigarette, but he never smoked. Then the Second Lieutenant began to talk about a machine-gun nest that had inflicted heavy casualties on his unit with enfilade fire. Repeating every sentence, he rattled on the whole time. The enemy was on the other shore on top of a high bank. His men were in a flat swamp below. The western shore of all rivers is high like a mountain, but the eastern shore is swampland. God had intended the nation to be born facing the other direction. . . .

They came to the forest road. The Second Lieutenant's pale face and flickering eyes were discernible in the light. His mouth and eyes were continuously in motion. He explained that at the age of seven he had fallen through the ice. After that his eyes had always fluttered. He didn't know for sure what had caused it, but thought that the icy water had damaged them. He was night blind—couldn't see a thing.

The Second Lieutenant offered him some chocolate when they got to the motorcycle, but the sniper got onto the rear seat with his back towards him and placed the butt of the rifle on his foot. The rifle had no sling. He had found that it caused nothing but trouble, even though it and a tight leather jacket are thought by marksmen to noticeably steady one's aim. But this business was more like shooting on the wing. He couldn't put his rifle on his back but had to carry it in his hand. When the driver started the motorcycle with a kick, the din of a hundred motorcycles reverberated in the forest and drove along beside them in the brush like a huge escort.

The sniper was quartered in a village ten miles away. Every morning before daylight he was taken from there to the front by motorcycle and after dark every evening he was brought back. He had his own room in the officers' club next to the rooms reserved for the regiment's staff. He spent his nights there in a proper bed and the motorcycle driver brought his food there. He was entitled to supplemented officer's rations.

When he telephoned his daily report to the commander of the batallion, the commander began to talk about a machine-gun nest that had inflicted heavy casualties on him. He didn't consider himself able to make it an order, but asked the sniper to destroy it or keep a lookout on it.

The sniper said he had noticed the machine gun. It was right opposite the junction of the river and a small tributary that flowed from the east, and its assignment was apparently to prevent lateral troop movements across the marshy tributary. There was a bridge further up, but it couldn't even be used at night because it was plainly visible against the surface of the water. Even in total darkness the machine gun's fire could be directed towards the bridge. He couldn't shoot at the nest from his own territory because the shore of the tributary was bottomless swamp that wouldn't support his weight. Besides, his rifle couldn't destroy a machine gun and it was not worth the risk of going into no-man's-land with an antitank gun.

He went to his room, ate, and cleaned his rifle carefully, even though he hadn't fired it. Then he put new cartridges into the clip. They had been specially prepared; the grains of powder had been counted exactly. They and the rifle might have absorbed moisture in the swamp. He took just as conscientious care of himself as he did of his weapon. He saw to it that his regimen was consistent. When he thoroughly emptied himself in the morning he could spend his day without having to think about satisfying his appetite or the demands of nature.

When a private woke him before daybreak, he put on his camouflage and dressed his rifle. He had decided to take on the machine-gun nest. The solution seemed self-evident—as if his brain had solved the problem in his sleep, even though it was a difficult equation with many unknowns. Not once did he think of his decision to move to another sector, to which he had already been ordered and where they were heavily counting on him. But he also had a task waiting for him here and he knew just how it was to be accomplished.

He took the map from his map case on the wall and checked that it actually showed the road he needed to skirt the tributary to the Second Regiment's sector. He hadn't known that such a road existed, but it had been a given factor in his calculations.

In passing he noted that the Second Lieutenant had been lying the night before about the menace of the machine gun. If he couldn't shoot into the machine-gun nest from his territory, how was it possible then to shoot from there into the Second Lieutenant's sector! But the Second Lieutenant had to account for his company's losses somehow. The battalion commander had in turn believed the Second Lieutenant's fabrication.

They had to make a detour of over twenty miles before they arrived at their destination. He dispatched the motorcycle driver and ordered him to pick him up at the same place that evening. Then he crawled along parallel to the tributary until he was at its mouth, facing the nest. This shore of the tributary was firmer than the other. In the evening the last thing the Second Lieutenant had mentioned was these "miserable" banks.

He directed his rifle towards the nest and stared at it through the scope. At daybreak the form of a water-cooled machine gun appeared in the black aperture. He couldn't destroy the weapon itself, but its crew, yes. Even at this point he could inflict such casualties on the enemy that its desires and capabilities would be stemmed for a long time. Occasional stray bullets gave off shrill, whining noises.

It seemed that the day would be very quiet. The faint rumbling of artillery could be heard only far off to the north.

The piping yell from beyond the tributary did not draw his attention—nor did the nascent, sporadic rifle fire, which ultimately crescendoed to a deafening crackle, as if an enemy patrol were being repulsed. He noticed the man swimming beneath the surface of the river only when the current had propelled the man almost even with him. The bullets smacked against the water and ricocheted into the opposite bank, where they punched white indentations in the dark logs right in front of him. He saw an arm wrapped around a log, but it disappeared right after he had seen it.

The current was stronger and swifter than might have been inferred from the movements of the logs. Although the Second Lieutenant had dashed into the river at the northern limit of his company's sector, it had carried him almost to the machine gun. With unbelievably long and swift dives he threaded through the water. Between dives he rested behind a log, keeping only his face above the surface. Actually a hand remained in view and divulged his hiding place, but when the bullets began to whistle in his ears he dove out of sight again. Despite the daylight you could distinguish the paths of some tracer bullets. Because of their low trajectory the bullets couldn't penetrate the water's surface, but ricocheted back into the air.

Only when he saw the swimmer dashing to the shore did the sniper recognize the long blond hair—the enlisted men were shaved bald—and the over-all build—the man was naked. The Second Lieutenant hid in the long reeds so quickly that the sniper didn't have time to note the spot where he disappeared. Desultory bullets kicked up small, scarcely visible puffs of dust from the bank.

The Lieutenant seemed to have calculated nicely. Only when the sniper didn't come to his sector did he make his attempt, confidently and at once.

The sniper was the only one to notice the deserter start up the slope. He was only a couple of hundred yards from the man. The nearest infantrymen were three or four hundred yards back and slightly to the side. The Second Lieutenant took long bounds like a mountain goat. He so nearly matched the color of the sand that at times only the steadily advancing wake of white dust betrayed his presence. The sniper reacted quickly. In anticipation he raised his sight straight to the top of the bank. Beyond the sight three enemy soldiers and the machine gun nest were visible in the scope. One of the enemy's faces was cut by the cross hairs. They were all exposed from the waist up! Further along the bank some more men popped up to follow the course of events. The deserter worked himself into a frenzy—when he began to tire, the sniper's ears could pick up his rhythmical wheezing. When the man reached the summit of the steep bank and lunged over the top, it was the sniper's move. In spite of his frantic speed, the deserter froze for a perceptible instant in his tracks and stood out plainly against the sky.

The baffled men instinctively looked along the top of the bank for the source of the bullet. Who shot the deserter? Was the rat one of their own? Judging from its sound, the shot came from someplace nearby. Their impression of the noise prompted them to scrutinize the swamp down in front of them, but it was empty. It was wrong that the man should not be allowed to live the life he had offered for sale in broad daylight. For ten minutes the man had splashed around in the river and scampered along the shores and just when he leaped to shelter, so that he dropped to the bottom of the trench, reached his goal. . . .

Huttunen got hit in the forehead and fell to the bottom of the trench. The others stared at the swamp from which the shot reverberated. There in the vicinity of some clumps of tall grass the stentorian noise still seemed to linger. They dove down headlong as soon as they could. Somebody said, "Sniper." But Huttunen was still alive.

"I'm going to die," he moaned and lay motionless with his eyes open. "Damn it, I'm *not* going to die," he moaned then and probed his forehead. "See if there's a hole in back, buddies."

Even without expressly looking they could all see that there was a hole in the back of his head.

"I can't see any hole," somebody said.

Huttunen sat up. Huttunen stood up.

"I'm going to the dressing station," he said quietly, not believing his own words.

Huttunen went into the connecting trench and was seen to disappear around a bend.

An enemy sniper was right opposite them in the swamp, because, "The bullet got Huttunen right in the middle of the face."

Mäenpää, the machine gunner, already envisioned himself as the destroyer of this abominable creature. Unhesitatingly, so that the others wouldn't have a chance, he seized the grips and began to fire a burst into the swamp. He did this so suddenly and reflexively, that fear, which had been tranquilized by a feeling of security, didn't have time to raise a finger. A bullet snapped into his forehead. Its exit from the neck went unnoticed because of his long hair. Mäenpää lifted himself as if trying to fall upwards and pulled up on the machine gun as the burst continued uninterrupted. The moving parts of the machine rattled as they repeated the same, very monotonous movements. When Mäenpää finished and began to drop, he stooped to see the ground where he fell without uttering a sound or even bending a finger.

When the men dared to look beyond the river after a long time, there had appeared a strangely twisted heap, which there hadn't been a while ago.

No one noticed when Mäenpää started to whimper, but he was still alive and two men took him away.

"I'm not going to die in action," he claimed. He had always made this claim, so it wasn't astonishing in itself, but at the same time he wrenched himself from the arms of his escorters. However, he lost consciousness while stooping through the doorway of the dressing station. A medic verified that he had received a bullet through the head and dragged him behind the tent into a detachment of fallen men. There lay four men, of whom three had received bullets between the eyes: the sniper's prey.

Meanwhile the surgeon examined Huttunen and refused to believe the impossible. Huttunen was dying only because he was not yet dead. Ultimate death could come at any moment, quietly and unobtrusively. Mäenpää crawled back into the tent.

"What are you crawling here for?" asked the surgeon.

"I'm going to die when I bow my head," said Mäenpää, groggy from his lapses into unconsciousness. "If I don't bow my head I'm going to die."

The surgeon left Huttunen and ordered the medic to put some dressing on his head. He set about to examine Mäenpää. He shook his head. Yes, this man, too, was certainly going to die at any moment.

Soon it was afternoon. There were no others in the tent besides Huttunen and Mäenpää. It was the kind of peaceful afternoon that makes you believe there will always be such afternoons. They lay side by side on mattresses. The light of day filtered through the walls of the tent. They waited. Little by little Huttunen's head began to ache and he remarked it to Mäenpää. Soon Mäenpää's head began to ache, too.

Only after a month did Huttunen and Mäenpää rejoin their units. They had been examined by an erudite doctor who knew why they had not died. Occasionally in the past—in the First World War—it had happened that a man had been shot through the head at the most vulnerable point and survived. The brain must have had a passage for the bullets—a zone through which a bullet could pass without doing damage. It had to.

"He was too sharp a shooter. He missed Huttunen and Mäenpää in the head."

—1965

VEIKKO HUOVINEN

Before Beirut

Translated by Philip Binham

Before I began to write this story, I thought it over many, many times; I weighed the matter, searched myself and my motives. The delicacy of the matter appalled me, I struck my brow with my fist and asked myself: Is it right to take up such a subject—what will be gained by it? Is not this one of those matters that should never be broached?

But I felt, nevertheless, that I must write. I knew deep down in my consciousness that I would be right and that the coming generations would not blame me for it.

I had, of course, read of the fate of Marilyn Monroe, a beautiful woman who—even at the peak of her fame—was a terribly lonely person. For the great masses she was only a sex bomb; nobody really understood her as a human being. Yes, and I had seen documentary films of other famous beauties, drifting in a crowd of milling, screaming, shoving admirers like a waterlogged piece of spruce bark in the foaming rapids. And in their faces always dwelt a look of unutterable weariness and boredom.

Whenever I read or saw such things, I swore to write in their support and to show the world that a beauty queen is, in the final analysis, only a human being, with her sorrows, sickness, and fear.

Now that I begin with my deficient pen to tell the tale of a beautiful girl from faraway Northern Karelia, Madeleine Perttunen, I shall try to observe the delicacy that the subject demands. But, on the other hand, it is of course clear that phenomena relating to certain aspects of human life must be called by their proper names. For they are realities that will not change; they are natural but not shameful.

. . . . .

Some have no doubt forgotten that some time ago Madeleine Perttunen was chosen to be Miss Finland. Her limpid skin and unaffectedly sweet smile made a great impression on the judges. All the same, behind the scenes whispers were heard that Madeleine was too girlish, too delicate for the trials of the great world, with her weight at only a hundred fifteen pounds, though her height was five feet eight inches. Those who knew (or claimed to know) something about it, said that two to three inches more round the thighs was what was needed, and a little rounding off in the region of the hips and rump might well prove a step nearer to the crown of Miss Europe. From highly influential quarters came the word that Madeleine should put on twenty pounds before the Beirut contest.

"Help," said Madeleine when she heard this. But she decided to try all the same, for she possessed a good ration of healthy ambition.

Fate put her finger in the game at a ball arranged in Miss Finland's honor, for the hors d'oeuvres included salted lake salmon. Madeleine did not in general like any kind of raw salted fish, but she did not have the heart to refuse when Deputy City Manager Saastamoinen praised the salmon as extremely tasty.

And so, as she put into her cheek a couple of slices of the pink salmon, into her insides at the same time passed eggs of the intestinal tapeworm, which at once began to develop within her stomach. Dear, dear, had Deputy City Manager Saastamoinen only known that, he would hardly have pressed the salmon on Madeleine.

.　.　.　.　.

After the ball was over, everyday work began again. Madeleine made many appearances. She acted as a photographer's model, she was interviewed, she appeared on television and as a mannequin. She was compelled to stay up late and to travel round the country. Hence, she did not at first pay particular attention to a feeling of constant tiredness and dizziness. She ate well and often, but even so her weight went down in a month by almost four pounds. Mrs. Vieno Rustholkarhu, who acted as her companion and manager, noted with concern Madeleine's pallor and dejection. That capable lady had little trouble in making a diagnosis: she had strong suspicions about a certain Canadian salesman who had been laying siege to Madeleine for the past month.

Madeleine went to see a specialist. In this case, it was a false move, for a specialist is often very limited in his scope, and his approach does not extend beyond his own special field. This doctor suspected a disorder of the hormones, and Madeleine had to undergo a series of uncomfortable tests. But the trouble was not located. Then she fell into the hands of a brain specialist. He suspected a growth in the head. There followed a lung specialist and a doctor who specialized in diseases of the blood. And then the hollows of her cheeks and temples and the canals of her ears were examined, but the trouble just could not be located.

Finally she went to see a general practitioner. This man insisted so stubbornly on being allowed to perform a certain examination that Madeleine began to suspect him of all kinds of things. But the examination was performed nonetheless. The mystery was solved. Madeleine had a fat tapeworm.

This was a great shock to Madeleine. She feared that the first and second runners-up might hear of it. How shameful it would be, what malicious glee it would give both of her contestants and those who envied her.

Naturally Madeleine's agent, Mr. A— (B. S. Econ.), did everything in his power to keep the matter a secret known by only two or three persons. It was not, of course, possible to keep Miss Finland's three days' illness a secret, but those interested were informed that it was only a question of a "minor, harmless operation."

The removal of the worm was performed in a well-known private infirmary, and was entirely successful. The doctors and the nurses were very friendly.

And the flowers. They came in masses. The Canadian salesman sent twenty red roses. A certain cotton-fabric firm sent forty carnations, a big department store sent thirty roses, a famous photographer brought freesias, etc. The whole room was full of flowers. Madeleine was radiant with happiness.

Madeleine went to convalesce at the home of her uncle, Vasili Perttunen, near Ilomantsi. A week earlier Vasili had shot a portly bear. So now, every day, they ate bear stew, on the surface of which bubbled a thick layer of fat. Vasili's wife baked pastries and cooked porridge. Madeleine was not afraid to eat well, for there was nobody to keep an eye on her. She spent a quiet month's holiday at her uncle's. During this time her health improved splendidly, and she put on thirteen pounds.

When she returned from Ilomantsi to her mother's, Madeleine was much admired. Her mother said she would not have known her daughter, she had plumped up so well while she was at Ilomantsi. The mother, Mateli Perttunen, was of the famous Teronen clan; the noted "weeping singer" Tatjoi Teronen had once sung to her. And so her mother asked Madeleine in the traditional manner:

"Ah what have you eaten,
and who have you eaten
my daughter, my sexy one?"

And to this Madeleine replied:

"Bear flesh have I eaten,
bear flesh have eaten
mother, my golden one."

. . . .

So dawned the wonderful, unforgettable days of Beirut. Since Madeleine had succeeded in increasing her weight to a hundred thirty-eight pounds, she won the contest. And the prizes came: a rain of money, jewelry, cosmetics; a flood of contracts, propositions and film offers. The Arabs went mad, sheiks and emirs wooed her lustily. But most of all Madeleine was moved by her mother's nostalgic cable of congratulations:

"Here I bide,
a woman grown old,
for she I cherished
to care for me;

Here I bide waiting,
where is the child
of my evening?

Now she has gone,
nothing left
but to plait
my ten fingers."

But the real surprise occurred later at the dinner table in the Beirut City Hall. After the first, Arabian-style hors d'oeuvres, Deputy City Manager Ymar Hanukasvili picked up a large platter from a small serving table, and with his own hand offered it to Madeleine. And on the platter was fresh salted salmon, flown in by special plane direct from Finland, as Hanukasvili proudly explained.

Madeleine had been put in a difficult position. She bit her lip and mused for a moment. Sending a special plane to Finland must have been terribly expensive. And then, what a token of honor to herself and her faraway motherland.

In spite of all this, Madeleine refused with aristocratic coolness, saying: "Raw fish, bad dish!"

Everyone agreed that in so doing Madeleine revealed her true greatness as Miss Europe and proved herself to be "la grande dame." It was as if she instinctively knew that a beautiful woman is a queen, and her word is law. Thus, Madeleine's very modest crack about raw fish, which at least in Finland is a chestnut, aroused admiration at the dinner table. Venerable tribal chiefs and sheiks deliberated on the deeper meaning of the utterance, and held Madeleine to be a wise woman.

And now, in concluding this little tale of the difficulties and the struggle of Madeleine Perttunen, whose prize was the title of Europe's most beautiful woman, I wish still to stress one thing. It is high time that we learned to understand that a beauty queen or a shapely film star is not just a sex bomb, but a deeply feeling and suffering human being.

—1967

HANNU SALAMA

A Girl and a Bottle

Translated by Philip Binham

On the Saturday before Whitsun, Jaakko Lahtinen cleaned and cut up fallen trees till after midday. Work time ended; in the afternoon he lay around on the beach and walked along the shore almost to the limits of the parish and looked at the rocks, and he went into the forest and started to dig up a big tree stump by its roots. When he had started, he dug and broke the roots till he got the stump out, filled the hole up with spruce branches, and only then thought that someone might have seen him.

For a couple of hours he lay on a rock near a little sandy beach; he took off his shirt but put it on again. The mosquitoes were at their most spiteful— they came right down to the beach. He'd bought some mosquito oil but it was at home and he didn't even have a flannel shirt, which they wouldn't bite through.

A couple of days ago Nippe from Sikavaara had promised to bring him a bottle. Nippe was his only friend, a bit old, but he didn't have any others. Don't bring it till Saturday, Lahtinen had said, to save having to hide the bottle. The shops won't be open then, Nippe had told him, but I can let you have it on Saturday if you really want it then. Just give me the money first.

Lahtinen said he'd give fifteen marks from his wages, and wondered how he could stop his father getting to know about it. He agreed to meet Nippe at six o'clock by the kiosk, and Lahtinen thought the time must be between three and four when he left the beach.

He went straight along the side of the hill and the slope that was quarried. Think it over for a day, the farmer had said, and he hadn't yet thought about it. It was a mile longer by the road than through the farm, a shady soft road with pines beside it. As he walked, he planned to have a sauna, change his clothes, meet Nippe, pick up Raija from the kiosk, and go dancing with her. He could do it with some booze inside him.

He'd been working on the road in the early winter, and now he was a hired hand for Pekka Louhivuori. He was a bit annoyed that he hadn't shown more interest in being a driver's mate when the boss had talked about it in the morning. But he hadn't cared for the idea of sitting in a truck all day beside Pekka; a hired hand was on his own a good deal of the time anyway, especially because the boss generally just allocated the jobs in the morning and then drove off himself. And what would it be like to have to handle cattle, when you'd always been afraid of animals and could hardly get a horse between the shafts. But it wasn't so good to be a hired hand, the others looked down on you. A job in the town was what you wanted.

He stopped thinking about things like that when he remembered there were two free days ahead; he snapped off a blade of grass and before long had chewed a dozen stalks to chaff. He decided not to pull up any more stalks, but pulled a long grass and chewed the white part. He started to run and jogged along as far as the main road, walked a hundred meters breathing hard, and ran again for a bit. He felt as if people were staring at him from the cars that passed. Perhaps he was too old to jump around with his face all sweaty when he didn't have a track suit on. And on weekdays he never dreamed of running when he came home from work; he walked heavy and bent, as if he was stiff from work, though a position like that wasn't natural. Now, still warm from running, he started to move more briskly and walked like the city boys from the summer villas. But thinking someone might see him he started to stump along like the other men of his age.

The road went past a pile of wood chips and along the shore, made a turn by the spruce hedge of the post office, and circled the bay. While they'd been working on the roads during the winter, the slope had tipped the big birches by the roadside untidily towards the lake. There among the birches by the bay a man called Joensuu had started a tar factory after the war; he'd been a foundation member of the Party, lived with the Lahtinens at first, got letters, and arranged meetings and spread information, distributed mimeographed sheets, songs, Stalin's speeches, situation reports by Ville Pessi, the communist leader. The man had given Jaakko a book called *Struggles of the Finnish Party* and written in it: "To Jaakko Lahtinen, Son of a Great Communist."

Joensuu was cross-eyed, so it was difficult to read his thoughts from his face, but the tar factory was built in a hurry and Joensuu said he was going to buy up the whole cape and put a gang saw there, just for the use of party members. But after a year there were only three men at the factory, and they were only there because they couldn't do heavier work. The meetings stopped too, but before the party died out completely it dismissed Joensuu, who was already known to have belonged to the military police, and soon the man had sold his land and his factory to the road authorities for a depot, built three houses by the roadside that he sold, and disappeared, to Australia so they said.

Since then this memorial to the foundation member, the main building of the tar factory, had been empty, and so had the crumpled wooden sheds that stood surrounded by the encroaching alder like seed potatoes in autumn with their bumps and protuberances. The barracks for the road workers had been taken away, the red bricks of the factory blackened year after year, and the windows stared as if holes had been pierced in the dark, and as the alders flourished on the cape, Lahtinen noticed that his father and mother became older and drier.

A hundred meters from the factory was an arched bridge. The birch branches over the water darkened the edge of the sandy shore. The wave-wrinkled sand was dotted with pit props and logs sunk in it, sticks smoothed round by the water and black and dark brown bark from the loading place. On the shore was the red-painted cottage where the women from the telephone exchange lived, known as the Cunt House. From the next hill a green wooden building, the savings bank, could be seen; from outside it looked so quiet that one could imagine a couple of old maids and a mongrel living a life of gentle ease there. Opposite the bank was a garage, its front black with oil, and on the left-hand side of the road, the two-story clinic. Farther on, at the crossroads, were a general store and a refreshments kiosk, the only one in the village. It was curious that, since the road had been renovated, buses and trucks had started to use it. A small restaurant there would certainly have paid, for business was brisk at the square box of the kiosk. But Joensuu had been the only businessman, and if the number of people who owned summer homes around there had not increased from year to year, if there had not been the work on the road, the village would have slept its winter sleep the year round, with the local inhabitants becoming fewer all the time.

While the road work was in progress, the kiosk had had to surrender its monopoly on the sale of beer; the workers' barracks had their own beer shop. Chervil and wormwood, long grass and coltsfoot had started to grow over the new road after the second summer, but round the barracks the grass had not grown enough to hide the traces of their habitation. At the side of the hill, heaps of sand and sun-dried clay had remained, and where the barracks had been there were piles of splintered logs that had been used when they were blasting and that had lain along with blocks of stone by the bridge after the visit of the province's governor. In the summer when the road work ran out, the kiosk became the center, the owners of the summer homes came to live in them, and the locals from their work watched the summer visitors lazing around. The barrack life was forgotten; Lahtinen, who was working on the land for Louhivuori, forgot it, too.

Although Lahtinen had been on the wage list for the road work for only three weeks—the local authorities hadn't helped to finance the work and the

horse drivers, except for the local men, had had to leave—he felt part of everything that had changed his home village lately, not directly concerned but still.
. . . The road had been first repaired the winter before last, and it would
provide emergency work for the unemployed again, too—the barracks would be
put up twenty kilometers farther on. There'd be truck drivers on piecework,
driving their trucks into the ground in a single winter, boastful driver's mates,
the big-stomached foreman, the load clerk who spent all his time combing his
fair hair, horse drivers, men with shovels, the driver of the payloader who was
the idol of all the shop assistants, the stoker who always spat after a woman,
the old girls who ran the canteen and all the local girls who never even looked
at boys their own age till the Social Care Board started handing out lectures
and warnings. Lahtinen would have to listen to his mother saying how terrible
it was again, without being able to say it wasn't as bad as all that, just having
a bit of fun if you happened to be part of it, but different if you were just
watching through the window. Lahtinen knew already what the old girl's reply
would be: "And you just keep away from that window." "I haven't been near
it." "And don't you go." "No, I'll go straight inside."

But that was just wishful thinking. And while his father was present he
couldn't say anything, with the old man calling every girl a whore, whatever
sort of woman she was, and warning him against them and giving them kids.
What for? Everyone knew, and could see, that Jaakko Lahtinen had a couple
of half-brothers in the neighborhood. Yes, and they had a sister, too, a mote in
the eye of the Social Care Board and Lahtinen's first. The pleasure had lasted
only a minute, he'd pulled out and hadn't dared put it in again though he
hadn't come yet. But when he saw a dark red frotée jumper like the one that
hid the girl's breasts he still got excited, though he was in love with another
one, had been for a long time.

Turning to the road leading home he looked towards the kiosk; he could
see Raija's thick hair through the window, and that got him excited, too. A
cart track ran up the hill, but Lahtinen's red house was not visible, although it
was no farther away than the main road. The stable could be seen as well as
his mother bending down to get the leaves off her garden rake. Stiffly—the old
woman couldn't do much more now than talk about doing it. Lahtinen had
grinned about that, but his father jumped on him, not for the first time nor the
last for certain. But there wasn't anything else he could do about it, just live
there and pay all his wages for food and board. Up to now he'd felt that if he
moved to Louhivuori's, he'd be tied there like a slave all his life. And he wasn't
prepared to handle cattle, though the farmer's proposal couldn't have come at
a better time. And he'd surely stop being frightened of animals; he'd treat them
so damn rough right away that they'd understand, and he wouldn't have to
shift them by himself, Pekka would be there, too. And then he'd get a heavy-
vehicles license and soon he'd be driving a bus like plenty of former truck
drivers.

"Hello, ma."

"Hello. How long you been hanging around?"

Lahtinen said nothing. He went in and decided to keep his mouth shut, but
when he'd looked round the kitchen he came back to the steps and said concil-
iatingly:

"Nice weather."

"Nothing wrong with the weather," his mother said and went on raking up the dry grass.

"You had anything to eat?"

Lahtinen was going to say he had, but decided to tell the truth. His mother carried a rakeful of grass to her basket, took it on her back, and, bent under her load, went past the steps.

"There's a casserole in the oven, and the milk's in the cellar."

"I'll find it all right."

"Take the casserole out of the oven before it gets dry."

Lahtinen nodded and went in. He ate and looked at the smoke rising from the sauna chimney. The Saturday evening atmosphere made him feel good, but when he'd finished eating he threw himself down on the wooden bed in the living room and pushed a grey-haired and growling dog onto the floor. The bed smelled of dog. One place where there was a knot in the wooden ceiling was like a pinup girl with her legs together showing her arse to the audience, and like a square face looking at the spectators, too. The ceiling should have been varnished two summers ago but it hadn't got done, and the unpainted surface of the boards had darkened, the pinup's backside got less distinct year after year, and over the door the shine of lice poison got more distinct. In the spring Lahtinen had found lice as big as fleas in the living room—they'd come from furniture bought at an auction, and he'd moved upstairs. There were more of them up there, so he moved down again and poisoned them with a DDT solution; he'd stayed awake for hours with real or imagined itches. Anyway, it was true that one twilit spring evening a louse the size of a penny had fallen off the ceiling into his mouth, and he grumbled about it in the morning to his mother, and his father had sneered at him for being so sensitive. In the early summer the lice vanished, and the most nagging memory that remained was the pleasure of his father, an old soldier, that his son had had a taste of what it felt like.

He woke when his father came thumping into the room. The old man cleared his throat a couple of times and farted, and when he saw the boy still lying there he started to sing: pom-pom-rom-pom-pa. Lahtinen turned towards the wall and gritted his teeth.

"Sauna's ready for your lordship."

"I'm going, I'm going," Lahtinen muttered irritably; he turned on his back and tried to suppress his crossness at being wakened. He had good reason to be cross. He stared at the ceiling, shut his eyes for a while, and tried to gather strength by thinking about the warm sauna. His father moved around in the middle of the room, and, unable to think of anything else to do, opened the damper of the stove and bent down breathing heavily to look inside, supporting his stomach with his hands. He hadn't been able to do a proper day's work all those days he'd been up, for more than a month, after the operation, and heating the sauna must have been hard on the wound, carrying the water; Lahtinen couldn't think of any other reason for waking him up or for the old man's sighs.

Lahtinen waited to hear what reason the old man found for peering up the chimney. He turned on his side and watched his father's actions more calmly, his head on his elbow, twisting his tongue into a hole in a back tooth.

"It's about time that was plastered again," the old man said.

268

"How's it got broken?"

"How the hell else but with throwing wood in carelessly," the old man said, bending down again and holding his stomach.

"Who's done that?"

"Not you of course. . . . Those brothers eh?"

By brothers the old man meant his younger brothers who, during the time when there were squabbles over their inheritance, had bossed it in turn, and neither of whom, in the old man's opinion, could do anything. Lahtinen stretched; actually it was a good thing the old man had woken him up, he had plenty of time now to go to the sauna and get dressed, as long as he didn't get sleepy pressing his trousers and putting his clothes on as he often did in the afternoon around five.

"Pekka Louhivuori's buying a new truck."

"Uh-huh."

Lahtinen hesitated to announce the news about becoming a driver's mate. In his mind he wished the cattle transporting would last twenty-four hours a day and Sundays, too, so he wouldn't need to be in the hayfield for two farms on the same day. When haymaking time came, Lahtinen knew he'd have to work long days, well over twelve hours. That was the worst thing, to work at home for nothing after you'd slaved through a nine-hour day in the fields, with all the money going home. And it would be the same thing all summer, the only spare time would be an hour and a half for dinner, an hour of which he'd spend fast asleep, and a few swims on a June night that would mean a corresponding loss of sleep. Summer would slip by quickly, spoiled. Saturday evenings he'd be too tired to go anywhere, and what was the good when you had to get up on Sunday just like any weekday. First cut the hay, then put it to dry, then into the barn, cut the grain and dry it, and thresh it, lift the potatoes, and only then relax a bit, have a rest doing one man's work instead of two.

Lahtinen decided for a moment he wouldn't go anywhere. But what to do then? He hadn't got anything to read, and a few drinks would cheer him up a bit after all, and he could talk a bit with Raija like the last time when he'd got a bit high. He decided to drink only a little at a time, the first one when he offered Nippe a drink for getting the stuff, the second one not till he'd got to the bend where the road turned to the house, the third when he was hiding the bottle among the pines. By then he'd have talked to Raija, he'd be feeling all right anyway, he'd ask Raija to the dance at the village hall and enjoy the last free evening of summer without thinking about getting up in the morning to go haymaking or threshing. Christ, this'll be yours one day, the old man said. But that didn't help much. It had never helped.

Still, he felt a bit ashamed. His father had only just been operated on and was trying hard to get used to light jobs so he'd be fit by haymaking time. And you couldn't say the old man hadn't himself done just as long if not longer working days. But all the same Lahtinen felt bitter. None of the chaps he knew of his own age had to do such a hell of a lot of work, only the old smallholders who borrowed machines from the bigger farmers and used them on Sundays and other times when they weren't paying their debts by working for someone else. But after all, they owned their own land. He didn't, he was the hired man of two farms, taking his wages from one to the other, and he'd go on doing it a long time after his father got better. To avoid work at home he'd gone after it elsewhere, and to get a few marks for himself; his father obviously didn't like it, because his son had gone to work for Louhivuori, whom his father had quarreled with over politics. When he was drunk the old man had gone on about it, and Lahtinen had argued—he wasn't afraid of his father when he'd taken a drop. But against work he never dared to grumble, because the old man himself worked long hours in the summertime. Although Lahtinen felt he had been done wrong ever since he left the folk school, he was ill with a fever that had left him a bit deaf and, in his father's opinion, a bit something else, he didn't dare start an open quarrel, not at least till he saw how things worked out at Louhivuori's. Then he'd just quietly disappear, perhaps before the hay-making began, or preferably in the middle. Driving around with the cattle would take so much time he wouldn't be able to work on Louhivuori's fields even, and as soon as he saw if the job was all right, he'd move to Louhivuori's.

He pulled a half-clean towel from the hook and went off to the sauna, was refreshed by the warmth but hardly felt up to washing himself.

There was nobody indoors; they were probably cleaning up behind the cow-shed. Lahtinen sat on the bench and started to put on his clothes and press his trousers. It was pretty near six o'clock, when Nippe was to be at the kiosk.

He didn't have a summer suit, he'd have to go in his dark suit that was already tight around the shoulders. The breast pocket was worn and stained, though he'd made up his mind when he bought the suit he wouldn't push coins in there. Now pressing the trousers looked like a waste of time; he'd got the crease wrong in the left leg. The suit was striped, not completely black as he'd wanted. Black wasn't right for his father's taste, there had to be stripes in a suit. And when he bought the striped suit Lahtinen also gave up buying one-color shirts, then buying shirts altogether. The one he squeezed into was almost worn through at the left collar point. But the shirt was all right otherwise, the collar fitted and the points stayed under the jacket lapels and didn't curl up like on a newer shirt.

While he was tying his tie, he smelled the cheap washing soap under his nails and sniffed his armpits. He thought of going to the sauna again to rinse himself over, but then he thought it didn't smell much. And he had some Valcream; if you smelled of Valcream and toothpaste, you couldn't notice the smell of washing soap. And if you could, what of it.

"If they won't give it, they can keep their cunt," he said a couple of times to the mirror, looking to see there was no one in the hall. On the mirror there was a brown stain, from a pimple near his lip that wasn't quite ripe and had got inflamed from his squeezing it. He had a narrow chin, his features were ratlike, like an oblong squashed in at the corners, and then he had big eyes. A face like a bloody ghost, one of the chaps on the road work had said, and the longer he stared in the mirror, the more stupid his face looked, till he remembered to smile. His broken front tooth showed. The smile stiffened but spread again as he noticed it suited him: he had quite thick lips.

He dampened his comb in a glass and made a parting and wave. The stiff hairs on the left side had to be stuck down with spit and still they stood up on end. The water darkened his hair. At the temples it looked as dark as his eyebrows, with the flaxen hair higher up in queer contrast. He parted his hair with spit and Valcream and turned a few long hairs that had gone on the left with the wave, pressed it again, and corrected it because it had got too low.

"Where you off to?" his father asked while he was polishing his shoes on the steps.

"Dance," he said. The old man walked a little way, turned towards him and growled:

"Dance huh."

The tone of voice was a sign of good temper. The old man was getting his strength back. His parents seemed to be getting on reasonably well together, and that meant he would be ordered about more. He had to suffer most when they were getting along all right together. When they were fighting they both tried to get him on their side.

Even when he'd polished them his shoes didn't look like much, and they were dusty before he got to the main road. The cart track was hard as iron—well, he didn't have to worry about getting mud up to his knees before he got to the house. And it didn't look like a rainy evening.

At the corner he was still fidgeting with his breast pocket where the ten-mark note was. He'd get the bottle anyway, after an hour of waiting.

2

Lahtinen lighted a cigarette and asked for a bottle of beer. The ice-cream container hummed, the scratch of the shopkeeper's rake sounded from the distance. The kiosk had a service counter and benches on the wall with a cross-legged table in front of them. The board walls were unpainted and warped, the floor with its skirting board had been painted grey and the service counter, table, and benches light green. The front wall and the right-hand side wall had porchlike windows, in the far corner was the ice-cream container, behind the counter were three or four crates of bottles, shelves, and a girl selling. On the back wall there was an ad for Fazer's chocolate and near it a Hellas-chocolate chorus-girl, one and a half meters high, raped with burning cigarette ends and matches, also an ad in which a drunken-looking man with a Tyrolean hat on the back of his head was swigging beer.

Raija gave him the bottle of beer, and said the price in a low voice. Lahtinen paid and sat at the table. Raija was wearing a pink dress, the same one Lahtinen remembered seeing on May Day. They'd come from the town on the last bus and he'd stood behind her and the dress had looked fine and Lahtinen, a bit drunk, had talked a lot and fluently. Raija's legs beneath the dress had looked a bit thin, and she'd had small breasts. After May Day they'd only said hello.

Her breasts seemed to have grown. Nice-looking piece but nose like a powder horn, Lahtinen's mother had said. That didn't matter, but Raija might be unsuitable in another way, she was more than a year older than he. Catch me going with an old bag, Lahtinen said.

"Nice weather," he said aloud. Raija smiled and looked at him under her lashes; she smiled as if someone had turned a key in her back. Lahtinen blushed and poured beer into his glass, put the bottle on the table with the label away from him and watched the bubbles inside gradually disappear and the beer run down on the inside of the bottle. Confirmation national service get married die his father had said and sighed. After the war he had left the church and Lahtinen with him.

"You are smart tonight," Raija said as if the age difference had been ten years.

"That so."

Lahtinen couldn't think of anything else. While he was looking at the bottle, the label side this time, and trying not to look at Raija, a bus stopped in front of the shop.

"Bus from Ruovesi's come," Raija said as if they'd been chatting for a long time. She peered through the glass at the bus, went back behind the counter when the driver came half-running across the road and banged an empty bottle on the counter and said hello in a loud voice. Lahtinen poured beer and emptied his glass. Raija looked under her lashes at the driver.

"One of them," the driver shouted.

"One of what?"

"One of those."

Raija raised her lashes and tossed her head.

"Can't you say what kind?"

"Jaffa and make it snappy," the driver said, and pushed another empty bottle from his pocket along the counter towards Raija as if he were really in a bad temper. He was red faced and straight backed, a little under thirty, a bit bloated looking, and, in Lahtinen's eyes, rather ugly. On his left cheek there was a long reddish scar and under his chin there was more than a suggestion of another chin. His arms were bare to the elbow and the hairs shone light against the sunburned skin. The collar of his light blue shirt was open. On his forefinger he wore a big bloodstone ring.

"Lemon or orange Jaffa?" Raija asked, looking at the driver under her lashes.

"One of each."

"One of each?"

"No, both the same."

"Which for heaven's sake?"

"Orange. Bit of a hurry."

Raija tried to be serious. The driver shifted from one foot to the other, so that his hips seemed to rise outside his belt higher than his waist. His hand was pushed into his back pocket.

"I'm in no hurry," Raija said, lingering.

"But I am. Poor service here."

"Nobody's in any special hurry here in the country."

"Get moving girl," the driver grumbled.

"No hurry."

Raija had taken two bottles of orange Jaffa from a crate and put them on the counter. The driver pulled out his wallet, yawned and pushed his driver's cap back, and pushed his fingers through the black and greasy-looking curls on his forehead. Raija put the five-mark note the driver had given in the dark green metal money box, poured coins through her fingers into the driver's fist and said softly:

"There you are sir."

"Mercy bien."

They smiled. Lahtinen quivered at the intimacy in their tone. The driver stopped scratching his head and put the money in his wallet, in which a couple of photos showed under a celluloid plate on one side, and an Automobile Club badge on the other, pulled his cap over his eyes again, and said as if he were talking to a man:

"Damn good thing when this Whitsun business is over."

"Hasn't really started yet."

The driver shook his head and blew out his lips like a horse.

"You driving anyone to the dance?"

"To Huviniemi. I'm going there as soon as I leave here. Coming?"

"To Huviniemi?"

"Yeh. Or you could get to the town if you left right away."

"I don't get away from here before ten."

"I'll fetch you."

"Ha, ha, one woman in a bus, that'd be something for people to stare at."

"What's that got to do with anyone? That's my business."

"And I've got to have a sauna first and do my hair and sew some buttons on my dress."

"There's buttons there already. Put a few safety pins there."

"That's right, I'll put this beer barrel cover round me with safety pins."

"Well, you'd look nice in that too. Just make sure the pins don't stick into a chap in the wrong place. When you're doing a cheek-to-cheek I mean."

"Anyway and I'd get there after ten looking like a washerwoman. And the others been dolling themselves up since morning. Go on now, people are looking."

"That's because I said half a minute and now we been here nearly five. They'd all been pushing over here otherwise."

"And I'd have sold some ice cream."

"Give it to the boys. Tell them no beer without ice cream. You'll take a couple, won't you?" the driver asked Lahtinen.

"All right," Lahtinen said and blushed.

"When'll you be ready?" the driver asked Raija softly, as if he were begging something.

"What for?"

"I'll fetch you after ten, like I said."

"If you come in a car, all right."

The driver looked at Raija silently. She looked back at him seriously.

"I'll come at eleven."

"I'm not going in a bus, and that's for sure."

"Who's been talking about a bus?"

"Where you going to get a car from?"

"I can get what I like. Eleven o'clock?"

Raija nodded slowly and closed her eyes and pushed her lips forward. The driver smacked his lips and spread his hands behind his ears, and ran off. Raija smiled but, noticing Lahtinen, changed her expression. She ran to the door behind the counter.

"Lasse, come back here a minute."

Raija closed the door. But Lahtinen heard her whisper:

"Don't come."

"But hell, we agreed."

"I can't."

"Course you can. I'll come in a taxi."

"Don't come, please don't come. We'll see each other later, at the hall. It's only, well they'll think anything in this village."

"What'll they think now?" Lasse asked loudly. Raija didn't answer for a bit, then said quietly in a low voice:

"If you start shouting about like that I won't go anywhere."

"Don't then."

"I won't either."

"Oh come on now," the driver said. Lahtinen didn't hear Raija reply. The driver went briskly to the bus, pulled his cap over his eyes again though the sun was shining from behind. Raija came back into the kiosk and looked questioningly at Lahtinen who, trying to explain his smile, said:

"That Lasse's a tough nut."

It came like the continuation of a sigh. Raija stared, Lahtinen didn't have time to creep back into his shyness before he breathed:

"Or d' you say he ain't?"

Raija allowed a tiny ghost of a smile in the corner of her lip as she said: "No."

"So Lasse's a tough boy."

Sure. Bloody tough."

Raija went to the steps again. Lahtinen would have gone, too, if he could have been sure to pass Raija naturally. In his nervousness he tapped the table top and watched the match box jump towards the edge of the table.

He knocked over the beer bottle but managed to stand it up again before the table got wet. He drank his beer, got up, and went to the door. Raija turned to get into the kiosk, both of them stopped, and Lahtinen tried to get to the door but Raija had already got there. In Raija's armpit there was a big, hairy mole.

"Nice weather," Lahtinen said when he got to the steps, and remembered he had already said it. He did not turn towards Raija and did not see how the girl looked as she said:

"Looks like it."

"Funny, I was thinking about your dress, too," Lahtinen heard himself saying.

"How did you come to think of that?"

"Just happened to."

"Really? That's nice."

"You seen Nippe?"

"Who's that?"

"You know Nippe, surely Raija," Lahtinen said more boldly.

"I haven't seen any Nippe."

The bus went down the hill by the shop, and its sound was lost in the hollow. Lahtinen wanted to say something more about May Day but said so long over his shoulder and looked hurriedly at Raija, who nodded, he thought. After he had walked ten meters Lahtinen glanced back. Raija was leaning in the doorway and had lifted her face towards the sun.

Cars were pouring out from the town. The bald optician, who had a summer place where Lahtinen had been working for a week with his father, sat there small and round behind the steering wheel and drove fast, always. On the front seat he could see the snout of a grey, wirehaired terrier. In the back were the

optician's old woman and son, Pauli. The optician didn't give any greeting, nor
did the boy, to Lahtinen standing there in front of a cinema advertisement.
Naked Model on the Run. Lahtinen had seen the film but couldn't help wondering what the others were laughing at because he couldn't make out what
they were saying on the screen.

It wasn't dusty on the main road, but the road leading off by the kiosk hadn't
been watered although there were dozens of summer places beside the road and
most of the owners had cars. When the optician's car had dived down past the
shop and vanished into the forest half a kilometer away, a thick cloud of dust
showed where the road went. The fields and narrow grass banks on either side
of the road were grey.

Lahtinen walked along the main road. He didn't take any notice of the
shopkeeper, afraid that he would make some remark he couldn't find an answer
to. The shopkeeper was a nasty character.

A Moskvitch passing in front of the shop quivered like an old man rocking
his shoulders. In front of the kiosk a wide, American "dollar grin" overtook and
passed it. Raija, standing on the steps, waved languidly. The Moskvitch went
round the shop corner as if it were limping.

Between the pond opposite the shop and the road, five meters from the roadside, were a couple of rusty and beaten-up fish traps, and if the shopkeeper and
Raija hadn't been in sight, Lahtinen would have jumped down the slope and
lifted the traps to hear the grass that had grown through the netting squeak. He
sat down at the top of the hill on the steps of a milk stand and tried his muscles.

He could see down the road for a couple of hundred meters, and when Nippe
came he would walk to meet him: they'd go into the cover of the woods where
they reached out to the road and then to the cart track that went to the village
hall, and probably Nippe would go through the back door onto the stage because
he looked after the scenery at the hall, had been doing so for twelve years to
Lahtinen's admiration: walked with an unlit, half-eaten fag end through a full
house to the stage to turn the lights on and off; appeared at every occasion many
times until the benches were pushed back against the wall and the dancing started.

"The next item on the programme is sticking one foot in front of the
other. . . ." The announcer's voice was drowned in the scraping of benches and
Nippe came forward for the last time from the stage door, glowering at his
turnip watch as if he'd known at least three minutes ago that after Mimmi
Kutanen's recitation number the hop would start.

Above the field a hawk circled, hung motionless and dived, but rose again
half-way down and continued its watch. A big diesel truck pounded past and
the hawk glided slantwise to the edge of the forest and disappeared in the direction where the highest chimneys of the town could be distinguished and above
them a motionless mass of smoke.

3

Nippe had a black suit on. You couldn't see any sign of a bottle under it.
But Nippe was thin, sometimes he had a bottle hanging on a bit of string inside
his trousers. Lahtinen didn't dare ask, and Nippe wouldn't have answered even
if he had asked; he had to be self-important and keep you in suspense.

He nodded his head towards the side road. Lahtinen looked to see there was nobody watching and walked back along the forest path without looking behind him. Nippe followed.

"Got it?" Lahtinen had to ask. Nippe didn't answer. He walked farther along the forest path and offered Lahtinen a cigarette. Lahtinen gave him a light and lit his own. He inhaled deeply.

"Get it?"

"What?"

"Get it?"

"What you mean?"

"Bottle."

"What you think my hand is, a bloody pine branch?"

The bottle was in Nippe's left hand under his jacket.

"Take it and start walking."

Lahtinen went so near Nippe he could smell the odor of sweat and tobacco, took the bottle and put it under his jacket. Nippe smiled, and so did Lahtinen though he wasn't feeling so good.

"Give us a drop for getting it. Let's go over there a bit."

Lahtinen twisted the cork open and gave the bottle to Nippe. He took a long swig. Lahtinen did, too; the spirit burned his mouth and throat.

"I'll pay," he said gasping.

"Pay from your pay-packet."

Nippe looked at his pocket watch.

"No good, I gotta go," he said, like to a pal.

"Going to the hall?"

"Yep. I gotta shift the tables and benches from the stage."

Lahtinen would have liked to go with him, but didn't care to ask.

4

After four hours he had seen Raija in Lasse's bus, drunk the bottle empty, the men at the door had driven him farther away from the hall and ordered him to stay there or else, he'd woken up shivering in the bushes and found he'd been sick on his jacket. The last cars rumbled along the road. He searched for cigarettes but there weren't any. He stood up, thought he'd be in time for the bus from the hall, but realized he hadn't any money. He decided to walk home by the short cut.

There was mist in the meadow. The road from the house was dusty. The last cars had gone, the bus at the tail end, and on the main road a couple of kilometers away a car threw its wedge of light from the top of the hill down to the hollow then up to the sky.

By the stream he tried to wash the vomit from his jacket, and drank. The stream tasted of surface water, and he didn't feel much better when he got up from the stream, where he'd got his shoes wet. He had two and a half kilometers to go by the forest path, which was wet all through the summer—there was a spring there. At first he tried to save his shoes, but then he went straight through it. He came to drier heathland, then where his father had sown grass for hay, walked along the edge of the main ditch, and went round the field where the horse was kept, because he was afraid of it: he'd shot peas at it through a hole in the stable door once, and the horse had pushed its muzzle through the crack in the door so far that it had got its eye to the same hole to see who it was. Since then it had hated him.

At the corner of the cowshed he stopped to piss. He tried to walk without staggering across the yard, but when he reached the steps he felt more drunk than when he'd started. The outer door was locked; usually it was open till he came home.

He went to the barn and tried to get to the upper floor of the cowshed, but couldn't manage to climb up, and threw himself on the remnants of hay strewed across the floor of the barn. He couldn't sleep; he was cold. He went again and knocked to wake someone up.

He rapped at the bedroom windowpane with his nails, heard someone get up and come to the door. His father. He looked him in the eyes.

"Long dance that was . . . and red eyes. . . . And stinking like a sewer."

Lahtinen did not reply. He stood straight.

"Who were you drinking with?"

"No one."

"Where d'you get it from?"

"Some chaps."

"What chaps?"

"I dunno. From the town."

"Get to bed, there's no food here for drunks," his father said to him when he started towards the kitchen. He turned back, went to the living room and, with his father watching, quickly pulled off his coat and trousers and put them on the chair back, tottered a little, but managed to get into bed and pulled the covers over his head.

"Get to sleep now. We'll talk about this in the morning."

He didn't answer. His father went to the bedroom. He could hear them talking softly. Lahtinen wasn't worried about anything as long as he could sleep. He heard a bus go by. He was thirsty but he didn't dare get up and go to the kitchen. He looked at the revue girl on the ceiling, turned on his stomach, and tried to think of being a driver's mate, then later of being a bus driver. He didn't think about Raija any more. When he was a driver there'd be plenty of others.

—1969

TIMO K. MUKKA

The Wolf

Translated by Diana Tullberg

A big grey wolf that had come across the eastern border, from the Soviet Union, was shot here a few days ago. It had run all day. Its muscles felt weak and painful, and now, in the afternoon, its breathing was harsh and labored. As it ran along the ice-covered river, it had often glimpsed the man pursuing it, and realized that however hard it tried, it could not increase its lead; quite the reverse . . . the distance between them was shorter than a while ago.

The sinews of its legs and back hurt. It ran with its mouth open, and flicked at the snow with its tongue, not daring to stop, even for a second. Could anything be better than a chance to sleep? No, nothing.

It had only a few minutes left now. It was approaching death and the longing for sleep had conquered the will to live. It glanced constantly at the foot of the trees it passed, and had stopped thinking of the man skiing after it with a hunting rifle on his back, three hundred yards away. The man who was just climbing the slope, panting like the wolf, fast, and with flecks of foam at the corners of his mouth. But the man's panting was different from the wolf's: the man was gripped by the lust of the hunt. He had been skiing all day yet felt no fatigue: the man was determined to kill the wolf and now his goal was in sight, there on the edge of a forest clearing.

The wolf ran on. It moved its legs automatically, without the thought of escape to lend wings to its feet. The longing for sleep weighed heavily on its mind and was painful. Was that another wolf howling somewhere? What was it? The wolf thought it heard the heartwarming call of a member of its own tribe: a tear rose to its eye. It would have liked to sit down in the snow and howl in reply: I can't go on . . . I'd like to sleep. . . . I know the man's getting closer, but I can't think about that . . . I want to sleep. . . .

All the time it was casting wistful glances at the foot of the trees—there . . . or there would be a good place . . . to sleep and lie at peace.

The man skiing after the wolf summoned up all his strength—he had enough left for this moment. Five minutes more, perhaps, and you're mine!

He saw the wolf in his mind's eye and observed that it was running laboriously and unwillingly, that it was tired. Good, thought the man, I'll soon get it now. He saw how the wolf began to stagger and how its legs trembled . . . now he was catching up with it quickly. The wolf was trembling all over, and sank down on its side in the snow and waited. The man saw all this.

But the man did not know that the wolf was asleep. Sleep came the moment its tangled coat sank into the crisp snow. The wolf had a dream. It dreamed it was lying near its home district in the Don valley, near the river, close to the broad fields. It was late summer and the scent of the corn filled its nostrils from all around. It was full. Its bowels were warmed by the corn it had just eaten in huge quantities—there was no lack of food. Dusk was just gathering. The smell of the river mingled with the smell of corn and earth after rain. The land was good in those parts, good black earth: reddish black like blood. With a strong fragrance. Perhaps somewhere nearby there were nets drying—this smell, too, reached the wolf's nostrils. It lay flat on its stomach, its tail quite slack, contented and sleepy. The village was just nearby, and at six o'clock quite an uproar started up: the children, laughing and shouting, were off to the sports field of the collective to play and kick a ball about. Children. The wolf would have liked to join them, yet it felt shy of such boisterous children. They were still so young and didn't know how to behave properly. That was it. But it was good here, too. The secretary of the collective went along the main road on a motorbike. His wife was sitting on the pillion and holding onto her husband with both hands. There were a lot of evil rumors about them on the collective. Folk said that they had stolen a lot of the cabbage crop and sold it far away in Odessa so as not to arouse suspicion. But there was no proof. Perhaps they would improve their ways. . . . Ah, that feels good, warm and contented; so thought the wolf in its dream.

It lay in the snow with its mouth open, and did not stir when the man skied up to it, tense and excited, and thrust one of his ski poles into its mouth and cried, "Bite it, you old wolf . . . damn, you, bite the ring, go on. . . !"

The wolf was sleeping so deeply and contentedly that it was completely unaware of the man. The steel tip of the ski pole lay on its tongue, but it did not feel it. It imagined it had a spear of corn in its mouth, that the snow it was lying on was good warm earth. The strange smell that came from the man's clothing was the smell of cigarettes, sweat, and dirt, but deep in its death-sleep the wolf felt it was the smell of the slow-flowing waters of the Don. It thought that somewhere nearby—perhaps over there, in tractor-driver Ivannikov's house— somebody had been frying cabbage. In some way, a warm evening like this and strong, pungent smells like these easily gave you a rather melancholy, yet happy, feeling. . . . The wolf knew these regions, many hundred miles of this tributary of the Don. It was born close to this village, felt this was its home. Everything was familiar and safe: the river, the bank leading down to it, the cornfields, the village. . . . It had no idea it was lying in the snow, close to its end. It didn't sense the man standing at its side at all.

"Go on, damn you, bite the pole!" said the man, but when the wolf didn't stir, he withdrew the ski pole, moved a little way off, and took his rifle from his back. He drew back the bolt, raised the gun to his cheek, smiled to himself, then pressed the trigger with his first finger. CRACK!! The wolf's hide shuddered as the bullet crashed through it.

The man wiped the sweat from his brow; now, at last, he felt tired, but so what! He was a wolf killer, a happy man. He took off his skis and sat down on the wolf. It still felt warm, and now, through his trousers, on the skin of his behind, the wolf killer felt the warmth. He looked at the wolf's mouth and open eyes, turned its head with his hand: yes, the wolf's eyes were really open.

"Well, all the better when I get it stuffed and put it in the bank window or some school natural history room. Really, it's quite beautiful, a handsome-looking wolf!" thought the man. He dug his watch out of his pocket, looked at it and thought, "I still have time to get it to the village today. Or then get some others to fetch it. But no, after all, I'll come and fetch it myself. I usually see things through. That way there's no grumbling."

In the evening he skied to the Border Guard barracks and asked for the loan of a sledge, then set off into the forest with two men to fetch back the wolf.

"It took some skiing, you know!" he told the sergeant, one of the two NCOs sent with him. "But I got him in the end. Everybody's after something or other like this . . . some are satisfied with something not so big, others get a wolf. Ever since I was a boy I've had one thought . . . to get a wolf."

"Yes, I've been hoping to get onto the track of a wolf myself for years, but every time the others get there first," said the sergeant. "Oh yes, you need a bit of luck. . . ."

"And not just luck, of course . . . I'd say pure grit, too," the man said to the sergeant, "just like truck driving. . . ."

They lifted the wolf onto the sledge and dragged it behind them in the darkness of the forest. The sergeant and a border infantryman helped to pull the sledge, but for most of the way the man pulled it alone: that was the way he wanted it. A man doesn't shoot a wolf every day! That's obvious. He was thinking, "What will my wife say? And there's my son, too. A little boy whose father's killed a wolf. Oh, there'll be talk enough about it in the next few days." He was a truck driver by trade, and everybody knew him.

They left the wolf in the barracks yard for the night and went inside to sleep. The wolf killer, too, was given a bed in the barracks for the night, though there was a sign by the door reading: *No entry to civilian personnel,* in large letters.

The wolf lolled in the sledge in the deserted yard. Its front legs were in the sledge, but its tail and back legs hung over the edge: its mouth and eyes were open, yellowish eyes and completely yellow teeth. It was slack and seedy looking; there was blood on its coat over the heart and the fur had frozen solid. It hadn't woken at all when the bullet went through its heart, and death had not been in the least painful. All that happened was that its dream had ended suddenly, the image built up by its tired wolf's brain of a warm homeland, which the wolf had in fact never visited since its youth, suddenly shattered, and life had flowed out of its limbs without the wolf itself knowing anything of what was going on. At the same time, without noticing it, the wolf had passed on to join the brothers of his tribe across the bitter frontier from life into death; from summer into winter; from the warm bed of snow that made a fine resting and dreaming place for the weary, into a coffinlike sledge in the barracks yard of the Border Guard.

. . .   . . .

Those moments in the middle of the night were strange indeed. The wolf, which had seen so many different scenes in its lifetime, now lolled in a Border Guard sledge in the middle of the yard! The sky was hidden by a thin veil of cloud, and there was a light frost. Every now and then the full moon came out from behind the hazy cloud. In a way, it was light, with the white snow glimmering ghostlike in the moonlight. And quiet. All the eighty national servicemen in the barracks were deep in sleep, with only one drowsy duty guard awake at the desk in the corridor on the first floor. But not even he knew there was a wolf in a sledge in the yard. Otherwise he would have been curious enough to go and have a look!

And the wolf, which had died in the middle of a deep sleep completely unaware of what had happened, now assumed it was in the courtyard of Death, and had no idea that the building behind it was just the Border Guards' barracks. It was so strange and quiet and the barracks looked so big and gloomy—frightening! With its rows of black windows it watched over its own courtyard, which was large and had a white flagpole in the middle. The wolf's lifeless eyes, which had remained open quite by chance, now saw many things it had never imagined possible while it lived, and that it would never have had a chance to see.

All night it lolled in the sledge. There was no warmth left in its body: by morning it had frozen quite stiff and the eyes that had still been bright in the evening were faintly rimed with frost.

Early in the morning the sound of footsteps from inside the barracks rang in the wolf's dead ears. And then came the shout: RISE AND SHINE! RISE AND SHINE! The voice echoed against the walls of the stone-built barracks and could be heard as far away as the yard. In a mere minute the whole barracks began to come to life: there was the sound of footsteps, of dozens of boots running down the stairs, the sound of steps and commands came from all around, while the rank and file ran here and there, shying like colts at the corporals' and NCOs' orders. Going about their morning business, pouring into the canteen and bolting down the poor food, then rushing into the yard and forming up into three lines. Each sleepy-faced serviceman merely looked to make sure he was in line, and none of them dared glance in the direction of the wolf. But the squad leaders strolling in front of the detachment with their hands in their pockets noticed the sledge and the wolf lying in it.

They gathered round, all ten NCOs, and talked it over together. Whoever had shot a wolf? It had been brought there during the night. Yes, it would seem so. One of the NCOs shouted: DETACHMENT, AT EASE! Then the infantrymen, too, turned their heads and whispered among themselves. Every eye was turned curiously on the wolf, but there was not a man in the whole detachment who dared express an opinion about it.

A few minutes went by. Then the company commander strode out of the officers' mess, accompanied by a lieutenant and two sergeant majors. DETACHMENT, ATTENTION! EYES RIGHT! yelled a tall, gangling 18-year-old sergeant.

"All right, men—at ease," muttered the company commander, and happened to glance into the sledge where the NCOs were gathered. "What's this then?"

"A WOLF, CAPTAIN!"

"Oh, a wolf . . . how did it get here? It's certainly . . . good heavens," the company commander exclaimed.

As the day went on, all kinds of things happened. Sergeants, sergeant majors, corporals, and lance-corporals, and dozens of infantrymen who were doing their national service in the Border Guard passed by the wolf. After the morning parade the men went back into the barracks and came out again wearing their white snow suits, with axes at their belts and assault rifles on their backs. They formed up in the yard, again no one daring to look at the wolf, then marched off to the ski racks, strapped on their skis, formed up again and set off in a long line for exercises in the forest. Some of the NCOs skied at the head of the line, others at the rear. The poles bit into the snow, the leather thongs of the ski bindings creaked, hardened by the cold, but otherwise the troop moved silently, for the sergeant had told them, NOT A SOUND! And the ski line disappeared into the trees.

A bit later the sound of shooting came from the forest: they couldn't be far away. The assault rifles cracked or shot in bursts. BANG BANG BANG BANG . . . and machine guns clattered in the hands of the squad leaders. The wolf lying dead in the sledge in the barrack yard had never heard such things in life. The shooting sounded frightening.

Just before dinner time the detachment came back from the forest. The perspiring infantrymen skied with a greedy look on their faces. They were all impatient to get at the food: the guerrilla exercises had made the youngsters hungry. The stairs thundered and the walls rang again as the detachment poured into their quarters on the first floor. Then straight after the meal, the infantrymen started gathering round the wolf in the yard. They came singly and in groups. They all discussed the wolf and stared at it, round-eyed.

"Look what a red tongue it's got!"

"And look at its eyes!"

"How much d'you think it weighs. . . ?"

"A hundred pounds . . . or more. . . ."

"Aw, that's crap . . . you'll be lucky if it's eighty!"

The boys smoked and stamped the butts into the snow, though this was forbidden. Then the wolf hunter came into the yard, too, with the company commander, who was carrying a camera.

"Let's take a picture!"

"Right you are . . . let's take a picture," spluttered the wolf hunter.

He was drunk, after downing half a bottle of brandy in honor of the successful wolf hunt. He lifted the wolf out of the sledge and sat down with it in his arms on the edge of a pile of snow.

"Whee . . . let's give him a kiss then . . . now then," he said and forced the wolf's mouth open with his hand.

The servicemen burst out laughing, but the company commander threw them an angry look, "Quiet! None of you could have done that!"

The company commander knelt down on one knee, focused, and pressed the shutter: click! A picture showing the wolf killer kissing the wolf he had shot was safe in the camera.

. . .   . . .

The day was short and it was soon evening. The barracks yard grew quiet and minute by minute the dusk thickened. The manageress of the soldiers' home stopped for a moment by the sledge and stared at the wolf. There was no other movement in the yard. But inside the barracks there was plenty of life. Light poured out of the dozens of windows, words of command rang out, the whole barracks shuddered and trembled as the servicemen rushed up and down the stairs. The wolf killer was there, too, somewhere, celebrating his bag. He did not dare go home as long as he was drunk, and the company commander and lieutenant went on refilling his glass every time he drained it. "Let's sing *Rise, Finnish Lads, On with the Skis* . . . what d'you say?" said the company commander to the wolf killer.

"OK," he replied.

"RISE, FINNISH LADS!!"

And they sang.

But in the infantrymen's quarters, other Finnish lads were writing home. Dear mother . . . or *Dear Sister, Do you think you could send me a parcel soon. . . .* One infantryman, on a small piece of paper, wrote: *Wolf, over there in Russia, I'm writing to you. Come and make me some sign. But don't mention me by name. I'll be put in jail if they notice I'm soft and a coward. I'd blaspheme if I dared, but there's been such a lot of talk and fuss about that recently. . . . But make me some sign. All these here, they're sheep, they don't know how to defend their own interests, they'll do anything if they're ordered to, even if it's against the law. And as for morals, I don't want to talk about it. Come and fetch me. I feel as though I had to leave life behind too soon, too young, and I want to go back to it.*

After his evening fatigues, after going out into the corridor for a smoke, this infantryman went to bed like the others, pulling the blanket over him, no one saw him moving around after that. The deputy duty guard was more alert than usual, as was the duty officer, who otherwise usually just slept in the duty room. They both glanced out into the yard every now and then, and at the sledge drawn up against the wall of the barracks. "Have you ever heard anything like that? A shot wolf just lying around for days in the barracks yard—just think of it!"

But in the morning when the duty officer went to open the front door, he noticed something even more incredible—the wolf had disappeared, sledge and all! When, nobody knows, for the deputy duty guard and duty officer had both really looked out into the yard every now and then all night, and the wolf had been there then.

The detachment was ordered out and morning fatigues could wait, while they numbered off. The infantrymen shouted out their numbers, their faces blue with cold. "Seventy nine. That's the lot, Lieutenant," shouted the last infantry-man.

"One missing, Lieutenant!"

"WHAT THE HELL!" shouted the lieutenant.

The detachment were left standing in the yard while the lieutenant and sergeant majors and sergeants dashed inside to check through the men's quarters. They were all in a mess, with the beds tousled, and clothes all over the floor. The lieutenant rushed from one room to the next, and in the last one discovered what he was looking for.

In one of the beds, under the blanket, lay the wolf: it had thawed in the warmth, the stiffened muscles had relaxed, and the melted blood had stained the whole bed. It lay there in bed as dead as it had lain in the sledge in the barracks yard. Its mouth and eyes were open, just as before.

"Well, damn and blast it all!" exclaimed the lieutenant. "HERE'S THE WOLF! BUT WHERE'S THE INFANTRYMAN?"

The sergeants and sergeant majors looked at each other and glanced cautiously at the lieutenant.

"Yes, where is he?"

The infantryman had disappeared without trace.

The search was hampered by the infantrymen's superstitious attitude. They only dared move around in the nearby forest during daylight. No one ever picked up the infantryman's trail. Missing, lost: they had to rest content with that.

—1970

Swedish-Language Prose

CHRISTER KIHLMAN

Alcoholic

Translated by Bobby Calonius

Sometimes I believe that my brain displays some trivial but important deviation, a slight fault in construction, just a mishap, and that is why it doesn't really function like other brains. Its receptivity is clearly dwarfed or inhibited, it has bestowed me with an incomparably low and underdeveloped learning capacity. But this handicap, this shortcoming is on the other hand counterbalanced by an immeasurable need, an invincible desire, at all times and in the most impenetrable contexts, to myself find out, myself discover, myself explain, and myself create something from absolutely nothing. My brain consistently forces me to distrust the conventional but on the other hand constantly surrenders in the face of the dissentients and eccentrics. It deters me from keeping agreements or from being prepared to take orders from others but sometimes gives me its wholehearted support when I am in the mood. Without a doubt I didn't succeed with my studies in the early fifties, largely just because of this poor receptivity, this deviant construction of my brain. My years of study—a nightmare of compulsory learning. And all fruitless. Absorbed in the history of philosophy and literature, but without comprehending a word or in any case without comprehending the sense of this theoretical material to be memorized. Perhaps it meant something to somebody, but it meant nothing to my brain. Books, books, darn it, I have read a lot of books in my life, but when I *had* to learn I didn't. I could learn only when the reading, when the studies gave me *pleasure,* when the fruit of knowledge tasted strong, meaningful, fertile. For the Puritan the brain is a duty center, for me it is a center of pleasure. It harshly rejects knowledge that does not fertilize or stimulate its creative needs and ability. It wants to mate with the material of knowledge, the damned libertine. Or put it this way: it has learned infinitely more in the brothels of knowledge than in her cathedrals.

My work is at the mercy of this lax brain and I don't even need, like politicians or business managers or professors, to call on the vocal cords for help. Nobody listens or takes orders, nothing like that may be around during working hours. The brain is at work quite alone and what else could I, with my slight powers of contact, prevail on it to do? The story of my work is an undramatic, static, uninteresting recapitulation of a series of silent lonely rooms, commonplace interiors, where the brain hums alone and, in the summer, in time with the flies. When my daughter was little we noticed her sitting for minutes in succession at my desk, without speaking and without moving. "What are you doing?" we asked. "I'm working," she of course answered. How I loved her then.

The classical blacksmith works with his hands and is dependent on the strength of his muscles. I work with my brain and am dependent on the strength of its ability to combine, summarize, penetrate. For the blacksmith fire is a tool; alcohol is a tool for my brain. It became a habit and a necessity many years ago, when I was writing my first novel. (But habits become vices if one allows oneself to be fettered by them, and so it was with this habit, which at the time this is written was broken or defeated some time ago.)

In *A Book about Intoxication and Inspiration,* 1948, Marika Stiernstedt wrote an article, with the bitter aggressivity of temperance and denial, in which she rather challengingly says that to be sure, she once tried taking a couple of drinks while she wrote, but it didn't help; on the contrary, things grew worse, worse. So alcohol has no good influence on inspiration and the ability to write; no, don't tell her that, because she knew from personal experience. That's easy to believe. Because that isn't the way it happens. You can't write while you're drinking. You can't write with a hangover either, then the brain *really* doesn't tick.

My second book in some places bordered very closely on my personal biography and included pages with tangible renderings of latent and displayed sexual sadism. From the beginning it was clear and unavoidable that the book should and must include just this. But at the moment of writing I was again and again struck by such strong inhibitions against the material that all work ceased. On certain days I could not write a line and depression and doubts of my ability to accomplish the task I had set myself grew and became a new, equally effective inhibition. The brain cools at such moments, like an engine that has stopped and refuses to do its duty. It refuses to put words together, refuses to formulate, refuses to find words and understand their implication. And the material withdraws, contracts to a dead or hard lump that absolutely refuses to allow itself to be shaped. One glimpses it all right, or suspects it, but it is sterile and unattainable and impossible to treat.

I perceived that I needed a tool to help me break open my locked and reluctant subconscious again and I even perceived that this tool could be found neither in my own will nor on the psychiatrist's couch. Since the distance between me and the bottle has never been great, the problem almost solved itself. I bought a bottle of wine or, in a bad case, two, and while I sat at the typewriter drinking or walked back and forth in the room (particularly in the early stages of intoxication when the brain is activated by the blood, which runs faster at the same time as the blockages are taken by surprise), disarmed and the inhibitions cease, before paralysis takes over and the intoxication becomes compact, the brain waves began

—so joyous—to come back at ever closer intervals, the knots loosen, the material slides up to the surface of consciousness and is available, moldable. The next day, when the last of yesterday's intoxication had fled the body, it was once more possible to continue on the grounds of the insights and discoveries the wine's expedition had brought through the brain to the memory and consciousness.

Afterwards, it was for many years a rule, in any case during the critical stage of the work, that after a completed daily assignment I drank one or one and a half liters of wine or whatever happened to be available, while I relaxedly reflected over what had already been written, allowed the associations to come and go as they liked, prepared for the next day's work through linking up the general picture, *the vision,* and imprinted in the memory or in a note the adequate and usable.

Thomas Mann and Eyvind Johnson state that they went through the same preparatory process during daily solitary walks. And certainly walking is good, perhaps even more wholesome and healthy. But for me, not nearly as enjoyable. Alcohol is the pleasure of the brain. It is nice to drink. It's nice that something that's nice also serves an important purpose, is a dynamic and indispensable part of the working picture.

DRAMA

Finnish-Language Drama

EEVA-LIISA MANNER

Snow in May

A Play in Three Acts

Translated by Philip Binham

Dramatis personae:

> *Paavo,* a civil servant
> *Helena,* his wife
> *Maija,* their daughter
> *Lassi,* a schoolboy

I am gradually beginning to get used to the idea that all sexual activity is between four people. We shall have much to say about this later.

S. Freud

ACT ONE

Scene 1

A middle-class living room, with a big window in the far wall, furnished with a desk, a sofa with a low table, and a tall mirror near the door. In the middle of the room stands a tall, helpless-looking boy of eighteen–nineteen. Maija, Paavo and Helena's daughter, comes flying into the room. She stops, gives the boy a long, careful look, and then bursts into a gay flood of speech.

MAIJA. Hi—aren't you from our school? Eighth grade? Aren't you Lassi? I know 'cause the boys call you "Little Lassi"—it's so silly when you're so terrifically tall. Did my father let you in? Yes, of course, Mother hasn't come in yet. You waiting for Mother? D'you take lessons with Mother? What sort of lessons? Italian or Spanish? You been taking them for long?

LASSI. Spanish. Couple of months.

MAIJA. Why Spanish? You going to Spain?

LASSI. Maybe . . . some day. But I'm interested in . . . (*shamefacedly*) Spanish poetry.

MAIJA. (*Laughs gaily.*) Really? How exciting to meet a boy who's interested in poems. Nobody much reads them nowadays, and those who do usually read them in secret. Here, let me look—what kind of a creature are you? (*Walks round Lassi with her head on one side.*) Tall, about six foot—like Greta Garbo. Head in the clouds . . . what a man.

LASSI. A cloud in trousers.

MAIJA. What did you say?

LASSI. I said I wasn't a man but a cloud in trousers. Or actually I didn't say that, it was Mayakovsky.

MAIJA. Who? Oh yes. That Bolshevik poet, the trumpet of the revolution. Yes, I know. He was the one that drew designs on sweet papers and advertisements and wrote awful poems on them wasn't he? Are you a poet too? And a communist?

LASSI. I'm not . . . anything.

MAIJA. Don't try and pretend. All intelligent people are communists nowadays.

LASSI. I'm not. Politics is for the masses, though they don't understand it.

MAIJA. But you write poems anyway. I know—you look like a poet—so awkward. Poor you. Do you write poems on sweet papers, too—like Mayakovsky?

LASSI. No, but it might be a good idea. Step up the circulation.

MAIJA. Then you must give sweet-poems to us, too—one for me, one for my mother. Really . . . sweet ones. D'you know something? You're going to fall in love with Mother. Everyone loves Mother. (*The boy blushes and hangs his head in shame.*)

MAIJA. (*laughs.*) Mother's wonderful—like a lilac. Evergreen. I love Mother, too, till. . . .

LASSI. Till what?

MAIJA. Till I become her rival. Mother's a femme fatale, but I'm even more fatale! Nobody's noticed me yet, but when (*pushes her chest out*) I grow a bit here . . . and . . . and wear high heels (*stands on tiptoe*), then I'll show.

LASSI. What'll you show?

MAIJA. That Mother's just a dim reflection beside me!

LASSI. You're quite bright already.

MAIJA. I'll—I'll show Mother and—and everybody.

LASSI. You're like your mother—to the power of six. Your mother is much—

MAIJA. What?

LASSI. More reserved.

MAIJA. D'you think that I'm not able to be reserved? (*Looks down her nose at the boy.*) And even aristocratic. (*Throws back her head, sways her hips.*) I can be what I wish. But—I haven't Mother's other tricks.

LASSI. What tricks?

MAIJA. Artfulness. Resources. Artfulness is a kind of capital. Mother's artfulness looks like childishness and . . . sweetness, but it's really something different. When Mother wants to clean her wings, she pretends she understands nothing. But Mother doesn't have her resources any more, we're poor. Mother's poor, too, though she doesn't always remember. But before she got married, she was rich. Mother had everything she wanted . . . or that Grandfather wanted for her . . . fine manners . . . culture . . . travel . . . music lessons . . . painting . . . all that nonsense. Then the war came and inflation . . . and Father. Father took the rest.

LASSI. What d'you mean, Father?

MAIJA. (*The girl is silent. After a while, hesitantly at first, then without restraint.*) Father is like that . . . bottomless. Mother said once Father's like Midas: everything he touches turns . . . not to gold, but drink that goes down his throat. She says Father has done magic: he changed a whole furniture factory into whiskey. And Father said, wasn't that a good thing. 'Cause you can't drink furniture. (*Laughs.*) But I like Father . . . he's good and wise . . . and Mother . . . she's refined. Though I can tell you that—

LASSI. That what?

MAIJA. The she's not really so cultured as she makes out to be. Oh yes, she can teach you the first steps of Spanish, but when you get to conjugating verbs, you might as well ask the table leg for help. Once when Father was angry with Mother, he said that her Italian was like Russian and she spoke Spanish like a laundress. Like an old washerwoman.

LASSI. A laundress may speak very beautiful Spanish.

MAIJA. Yes, of course. I think Mother speaks beautiful Italian, and beautiful Spanish, and beautiful Finnish, and Mother is beautiful, too. When she's sat for an hour in front of the mirror and done all her tricks, she's really beautiful. But it takes such a time! Then she has *such* long eyelashes, (*shows*) and *such* long nails, and *such* a tight corset (*wriggles in agony*) and . . . (*the outside door is heard*). Now she's coming. On your knees, drone, the Queen Bee is coming. (*Laughs.*) I'm off. 'Bye.

(*Helena enters; quiet and at the same time radiant; the boy bows politely and shyly.*)

HELENA. Buenos dias.
LASSI. Buenos dias.

(*Helena goes to the desk and remains standing there, with her back to the boy, playing with a pen.*)

HELENA. We will take last week's lesson again. The little folk song, *Una Copla*. Translate please: *Las palabras amorosas* . . .
LASSI. The words of love . . .
HELENA. *son las cuentas de un collar.*
LASSI. are the pearls of a necklace.

HELENA. *Que en saliendo la primera,*
LASSI. When the first one comes,
HELENA. *salen todas las demás.*
LASSI. the others come, too.

(A brief knock at the door, and the husband comes in. Helena turns quickly and continues the lesson without taking any notice of him.)

HELENA. *La casa es grande.* Please translate.
LASSI. The house is large.
HELENA. *El muro es blanco.*
LASSI. The wall is white.
HELENA. *El jardin es verde.*
LASSI. The garden is green.
PAAVO. Oh, you're having a Spanish lesson here, excuse me. Did I leave my glasses here? Can't read my paper without them. *(Goes to the desk, searches.)* Not here. Well, I'll take the magnifying glass. *(Turns, gives Lassi a long look.)* Such a big lout, but still only a child . . . *(raises the magnifying glass to his eye like a monocle and looks at the boy through it)*—whose thoughts are written as clear as daylight in his eyes.

(He slaps his hands together as if he wishes to brush away his critical words, and goes out. He shuts the door gently behind him.)

LASSI. What did he mean?
HELENA. Nothing. Looking for his glasses and talking to himself. Let us continue —we will take the same song the other way round. The words of love . . .
LASSI. *Las palabras amorosas . . .*
HELENA. are the pearls of a necklace.
LASSI. *son las cuentas de un collar.*
HELENA. When the first one comes,
LASSI. *Que en saliendo la primera,*
HELENA. the others come, too.
LASSI. *salen todas las demás.*
HELENA. And now once more without translating. *Las palabras amorosas . . .*
LASSI. *son las cuentas de un collar.*
HELENA. *Que en saliendo la primera,*
LASSI. *salen todas las demás.*

(The boy is stiff and restrained all the time. When Helena moves from the desk to sit on the sofa, she absentmindedly puts her hand on the boy's hand.)

HELENA. *Muy señor mio,* you are a very good pupil, you learn very quickly. So young and so . . . *(looks at him searchingly)*. Do you even shave yet?
LASSI. *(Shyly.)* Twice a week. As often as . . . I come to you.
HELENA. Twice a week! You're hardly a man yet.
LASSI. What's *"Muy señor mio"*?
HELENA. Dear Sir. Literally "much sir mine".
LASSI. And Dear Madam?

HELENA. *Muy señora mia.*
LASSI. "Much madam mine."
HELENA. What's this in Spanish? (*Shows a book.*)
LASSI. *El libro.*

(*Helena shows a vase, flowers, a pen, a pencil, a clock, paper, a calendar: the boy touches each object and says: El vaso—la flor—la pluma—el lápiz—el reloj—el papel —el calendario.*)

HELENA. (*Deliberately.*) You are a toucher.
LASSI. A toucher?
HELENA. Yes. You touch things all the time. (*The boy hangs his head.*)
HELENA. (*Suddenly becomes more formal.*) On page twenty-one of our book are some verses of Calderon that it would be a good idea to learn by heart.

> *Qué es la vida? Una ilusión,*
> *una sombra, una ficción,*
> *y el mayor bien es pequeño;*
> *que toda la vida es sueño,*
> *y los sueños sueños son.*

> —What is life? An illusion,
> a shadow, a fantasy,
> and its greatest good is small;
> for all life is a dream,
> and dreams are dreams.

LASSI. (*In a tone of conviction.*) Life is not a dream.
HELENA. Really? (*Laugh.*) Do you think *you* know that, so young—
LASSI. (*Sarcastically.*) Don't even shave yet. Don't despise me for my youth. I knew when I was a child that life isn't a dream.
HELENA. Really? Wiser than the wise. You aren't very modest.
LASSI. (*Modestly.*) No, I am not modest.
HELENA. (*Disconcerted.*) Well. Our half hour is finished . . . *muy señor mio!* (*Laughs.*) Come again on Friday at the same time.

(*Before leaving, the boy puts a folded piece of paper on the table, bows awkwardly, and almost runs out of the room. Helena opens the piece of paper.*)

HELENA. A poem . . . again. So young and childish . . . *sin barba* . . . but poems come all the same. (*Tenderly.*) Young puppy. (*Reads lingeringly.*)

> Turn your back on me, if you wish,
> and from the sweat of my heart will burst a rose of stone.

> Come to me, if you wish,
> and the street will vanish beneath my feet like a carpet,
> and I shall fly.

(Paavo has meanwhile come in quietly; he sits beside Helena and reads the poem over her shoulder. Helena shifts away from him.)

HELENA. Paavo . . . how tactless you are!

PAAVO. I only want to see what the baby has written to you.

HELENA. Really. Surely you're not jealous . . . of that boy.

PAAVO. No. I should be jealous of the poem if it were a good one, but it's only a poor imitation, a mixture of the English Romantics and Hafiz. "Remember if you wish, if you wish forget," and Hafiz says—oh yes, I know my Hafiz, when I was a youngster of that Lassi's age I was lying on my bed with a copy of Hafiz while the other boys were lying with girls. . . .

HELENA. How coarse you are. Well, what does Hafiz say?

PAAVO. "The streets vanish beneath me, and I dance."

HELENA. *(Annoyed.)* Why do you spy on me? On my lessons?

PAAVO. Your lessons or your feelings? I don't care about your feelings, I just want to protect the boy.

HELENA. No you don't. Let everyone learn his lesson where he can. I'm not doing anything to him. He's safe *here.*

PAAVO. Is he? Flirting can be dangerous, too!

HELENA. Well, in that case it's dangerous to walk along the street. It's best just to crawl into one's cell and die.

PAAVO. Quite. All misfortunes start from our not being happy in our own room and going out. Somebody said so . . . Pascal—and Pascal smelled a bit of the study. In any case, flirting can be very dangerous.

HELENA. For the boy?

PAAVO. Don't pretend to be stupid. For the boy, of course. Not for you certainly. Flirting's a charming adventure for you—you're just that little bit adventurous.

HELENA. What do you know about me?

PAAVO. I know your life is dull and empty—

HELENA. Really!

PAAVO. Your life is dull and empty beside mine.

HELENA. Is that my fault?

PAAVO. Your fault, and my fault. You should only have boys like that round you, you're that sort. You want to bewilder them, hold their hands, get little bits of paper from them as mementos.

HELENA. What do you mean? You're insulting.

PAAVO. But it's true and truth is insulting. A thief is hurt if you call him a thief. You're like that, you enjoy just playing. You want—and you don't want. You want to have your cake and eat it. It's your way to play with people, to stir them up. You handle them, finger their nerves, but *you* mustn't be touched, you don't give yourself. We've been married for sixteen years, but you've never yet really given yourself. Always you're in your own world, your own love dream.

(Helena shakes her head as if she wished to shake away Paavo's words.)

MAIJA. *(Enters the room with a cat in her arms.)* Mother, Mother, Father's hat's fallen down from the shelf, and Diana's made a mess in it.

HELENA. Ugh, what d'you want to come and tell that for? You could have cleaned it up.

PAAVO. The cat's social protest! The first female that's dared to desecrate my hat. But why does the cat wish to revenge itself on me, why not on the women-folk? On me of course, because she's a lady herself. That's just typical of the social and sexual emancipation of women: men must pay for it. First the wife's fanciful revolt, and then the cat's anal—

HELENA. Go and clean it up, Maija! (*To Paavo.*) And you—you think you are very witty I suppose. How could you—talking like that in the girl's presence. You have no taste. You're drunk when you talk in that way. I'm afraid of you when you talk like that.

PAAVO. Afraid of me? Everyone's afraid of me. D'you know why? I'll tell you. Because I stink . . . like Philoctetes* . . . I stink of intelligence.

HELENA. You stink of alcohol.

PAAVO. Oh no, I've only drunk beer today. Now there's a bar on both sides of the falls, it's impossible to cross the bridge without dropping in on one side or the other.

HELENA. You must have dropped in on both sides.

PAAVO. No, only one. They wouldn't even let me in on the other.

HELENA. Poor thing. And I have to put up with a man who talks and talks and on top of that stinks.

PAAVO. Stinks of intelligence. The Greeks on their way to Troy left Philoctetes on a deserted island, because he was poisoned and he stank. But when the war went on and on, they had to go back for him . . . they needed his intelligence.

HELENA. Oh don't. I can't stand it. Always your mythology.

PAAVO. No, my dear, it was an allegory. If you drive me away . . . leave me . . . you will find, like the Greeks, . . . you can't manage without me. Sooner or later you'll have to come back for me.

HELENA. For your intelligence?

PAAVO. Intelligence, and habit. Because I love you and you avoid me. Hate binds, too. But most of all because you need my intelligence—my scepter. Although you haven't given yourself to me. I have yielded to you my scepter, the mark of a king. My sword—

HELENA. A wooden sword, as long as you go on drinking.

PAAVO. (*Embraces her quickly and violently.*) Do you want to see—it isn't a wooden sword. Now it isn't a wooden sword.

HELENA. Stop it! You frighten me to death when you talk like that. You get so violent.

PAAVO. Frightened to death! Frightened, death. Do you know why you are frightened of death? Because one must give oneself to death. You don't want to give yourself, you are . . . aristocratic. But one must give oneself to death, because death is even more aristocratic. Death takes you . . . lightly, chivalrously, casually, but completely.

HELENA. You go on too long about the same thing. Haven't I given myself . . . to you . . . a thousand and one times?

PAAVO. You've given your body—what then? What does that mean? Bodies are

---

*Son of Poenas; possessed Heracles' arrows, which were necessary to take Troy; bitten by snake on journey to Troy, he was put ashore at Lemnos; when Trojan seer said that the Greeks could only take Troy with Heracles' arrows, Philoctetes was fetched from Lemnos; he slew Paris.

always available. You yourself are always on another star. When I talk about love, you're silent as a wild animal at bay. I can't stand your wild-deer look, it makes me feel barbarian, and then I am barbarous. You've never even said one banal phrase: I love you.

HELENA. That's not true. In the morning, when you go to work, I ask you: "Are you dressed warmly enough? Did you remember your scarf? Have you got a clean shirt?" At dinner I say: "Don't eat so fast, dear. Don't drink any more white wine, it upsets your stomach. I'll bring you a bottle of beer if you like." In the evening: "Give me those socks, I'll wash them. Wait a minute, I'll bring you a clean pair of pajamas. What book would you like? I'll bring you your cigarettes and an ashtray." All this means: I love you.

PAAVO. But why can't you say it then, sometimes at least. Modesty makes women insincere. Besides, that isn't what love means. It's cherishing, not loving. Someone else could do, or not do, all that. I don't want a servant, I want a lover. But women are so odd, it makes them ashamed to show love. They're not ashamed to nag, though.

HELENA. Now you're nagging yourself.

PAAVO. (*Not listening, goes on.*) I don't believe you know what the expression "to give oneself" means. You don't know what this world demands of you—what love demands of you. You must give yourself away to another, so that you no longer know which you are, the other or yourself.

HELENA. Don't preach.

PAAVO. I'm not preaching. I'm philosophizing. . . . For what is self? What are you yourself? You are beautiful . . . let me look . . . (*lifts her hair tenderly*) your face brightens the darkness. But your beauty is hermetic, turned in on itself, selfish, purposeless, as long as you do not. . . .

HELENA. What do you want of me? One can only give oneself to God.

PAAVO. To God? What do you know about God?

HELENA. I don't know anything. But I have a dream.

PAAVO. You have a dream of God and another dream of life. You live a life between two dreams.

HELENA. And you live a strong and animal life between two glasses of whiskey. You are coarse.

PAAVO. And you are miserly. But the miser is miserly to himself. In the Middle Ages maidens saved for Christ what they should have given to men, and knights gave their best strength to God. I've never understood that kind of fanaticism and I don't believe God cares a damn for such gifts. . . . You're medieval—your chastity is in a belt.

HELENA. What nonsense you talk!

PAAVO. Why do I talk? Why do I talk? I talk to myself, the words of a fallible human being. I don't know anything about you, and not much about myself, either. I've thought of you as a garden, closed, perhaps enchanted, but you're only a rosebush with a fence round it—you're nothing at all, the roses are small, always in bud, although the bush is old; the bush is old and doesn't grow— you're mediocre, insignificant, why should I try to subjugate you? You don't even have a heart, my heart is a flood, your heart's only a little flint, but still it sets the flood on fire. . . . And the light that shines from you is only a borrowed light, perhaps my light, perhaps it's reflected from my own self—

HELENA. From you, from your drunken face! Look at yourself in the mirror!

(Shoves him in front of the mirror.) You become eloquent and mad when you drink. Stop it!

PAAVO. Eloquent and mad. Yes. Yes! I suppose so. Perhaps they're just the same thing.

HELENA. Yes they are. Yes they are the same. You blame me because I don't give myself. Haven't I given myself? *(She stops to think.)* Haven't I? Perhaps I haven't given myself. . . . *(Whispers.)* Still . . . there's no foolishness I haven't done.

PAAVO. Just so. *(Leaves the room and Helena to herself.)*

HELENA. *(Goes in front of the big mirror and holds out a hand.)* How he talks. Can't he see how he embarrasses me . . . how his coarse directness upsets me . . . wouldn't a hint be better? Doesn't he see how I shrink away from every touch? What is self?, he said. Maybe I am not myself, maybe I am someone else . . . maybe I have got into the wrong body by mistake. I have been created . . . and then left . . . to myself, although I don't even know what I am. My senses need a veil, otherwise I dissolve. He is solid, or anyway robust, alcohol keeps him together and makes him tough, and coarse. I dissolve every moment. And then he demands that I give myself, when I don't even know who I am and where . . . I dissolve *(loosens her hair)* like Berenice's hair across the firmament. . . .* How gladly I would give myself away . . . to a man or to God . . . but that's just what I can't do . . . I can't give myself away. Oh God, I haven't anything to give away!

(She covers her face with her hands; the stage darkens slowly. The noise of the street rises and fades; silence.)

Darkness.

Scene 2

The same room, the next Friday. Lassi is standing, lanky and awkward, in the middle of the room with his cap under his arm. Maija is chatting with him.

MAIJA. Mother will be late today, she's gone out; she'll be coming about nine, you can wait if you like. I'll keep you company.

LASSI. Will you? Oh. Well, I can wait. Let's look at the moon. It's a full moon now, like cheese. *(Goes to the window.)* Hey, there it is on the roof of the factory. *(Takes opera glasses from the desk.)*

MAIJA. You can't see anything with those. Father's got proper ones, terrifically big, I'll fetch them, they're in the hall. Father watches birds with them. *(She fetches field glasses and hands them to Lassi. He twists the lenses, looks through them, and passes them to Maija.)*

LASSI. Look, I'll show you something. There—that dark shadow *(points and presses his head against Maija's)* is Mare Humorum.

*Coma Berenices, constellation.

MAIJA. Is that the Sea of Humor?

LASSI. No, it's the Sea of Liquids. And then there's the Sea of Clouds and the Sea of Rains, and the Sea of Fruitfulness, and the Sea of Nectar.

MAIJA. Are they really seas?

LASSI. No. They're probably solidified splotches of ore. The people who discovered them just thought they were seas.

MAIJA. Hoped. Sea is more poetic than . . . splotch. Astronomers are poetic people.

LASSI. (*Laughs.*) And then there's *Mare Serenitatis,* the Sea of Tranquillity, and *Mare Crisium,* the Sea of Crises.

MAIJA. Gosh, the moon is poetic. I'd like to live in a moon village and swim in the Sea of Love. And become clean in the Sea of Coldness.

LASSI. Why become clean?

MAIJA. I don't know. Just because. Everything's so romantic on the moon. I feel dizzy when I think of all the seas on the moon. The moon ought to be more matter-of-fact. I suppose there's a Sea of Mists?

LASSI. Yes. How did you know?

MAIJA. I didn't know. I made it up.

LASSI. It's there. *Mare Vaporum.* The Sea of Mists. . . . Women are awful—they know everything, though they don't understand anything.

MAIJA. Silly, it's just the other way round. (*Laughs brightly and pulls his sleeve.*) Hey listen, let's dance a bit. There's a record player on the bookshelf. What shall I put on? The Moonlight Sonata? (*Laughs.*) There ought to be a jazz arrangement of the Moonlight. This way it's like soup. When I get bigger, I'm going to make jazz arrangements of all Bach and Beethoven.

LASSI. What d'you want to get bigger for? D'you think you're still going to grow? Start doing your arranging now, right away. Don't make excuses.

MAIJA. Do you think Father and Mother would let me? It would be sacrilege.

LASSI. Do you think jazz is so wonderful?

MAIJA. Yes it is. I'm so fed up with screeching violins, and especially the piano— Mother's always playing it—and what does she play? Not Bach or Beethoven even, but Tchaikovsky and Grieg—they're really awful, they both ought to be killed.

LASSI. They can't be killed any more, it's too late.

MAIJA. Oh yes they can. They can be hotted up. . . . Though I don't know if they're competent enough, whether you could get anything out of them. If you could, I'd hot up that old crybaby Grieg.

LASSI. Could you?

MAIJA. I can do anything I want. (*Spins round trolling a highly syncopated version of "Jag elsker dig."*) Hey listen, we've got some jazzed-up Bach, Juan Sebastian Bach! (*She goes to the bookshelf and looks for Jacques Loussier's record: "Play Bach No. 1, Fugue No. 1" (Decca BLK 16167 p) and puts it on. When the syncopated fugue begins, Maija and Lassi do an improvised dance together. Maija shouts from time to time: "Isn't it nice!" and at some point sings the words of some well-known song that easily fits in. Suddenly she moves away from Lassi and begins to dance a solo. She dances intensely yet dreamily.*)

LASSI. Hey, you forgot me. Maija!

(*Maija still spins round, without answering.*)

LASSI. Who are you dancing for—me?
MAIJA. No. Don't disturb me.
LASSI. What are you dancing for then?
MAIJA. I'm dancing for the dance.
LASSI. Dance for me a bit.

(*Intoxicated by the dance, Maija slips into Lassi's arms. The moon rises slowly above the windowsill, the intertwined shadow of the young pair can be seen against it. They kiss. When the outer door is heard, Maija pulls herself away and whispers breathlessly:*)

MAIJA. Now she's coming.
LASSI. Who?
MAIJA. My rival. Mother. (*Maija runs out through the doorway. Helena enters a moment later. Lassi, who is now quite off the rails, makes a bold movement, grasps her hand and says:*)
LASSI. *Muy señora mia!*
HELENA. What do you mean?
LASSI. Much madam mine . . . I love you!
HELENA. How can you dare?
LASSI. Each one dares according to his chance. I have nothing to lose.
HELENA. I don't understand you.
LASSI. Oh yes you do. I don't hint. I don't flirt. I speak straight out when I have something to say.
HELENA. You do, do you? But when you get older, you will find that it is better after all to hint and flirt . . . your passion is youth. . . . When you are older you will understand that the best thing you can hope for is perhaps that you can be alone with the one you love for half an hour . . . not everyone is allowed even that.
LASSI. I don't measure my feelings against those who are not allowed . . . (*proudly*). Flirt if you want, but I tell you that you have wounded me . . . mortally.
HELENA. (*Pityingly.*) Mortally? (*Laughs.*) When one is young, one dies so easily. Incidentally—are you so sure that I have flirted . . . with you? Supposing you have misunderstood? Perhaps it is all a mistake? The imagining of a half-grown boy? A mirage? (*Sits and crosses one leg over the other.*)
LASSI. If it's all been a mirage, I hope the visions will begin again.
HELENA. What do you mean?
LASSI. I want . . . to make you . . . favorable towards me . . . by every means available.
HELENA. (*Astonished.*) Every . . . means available?
LASSI. Yes. But I do not have *every* means available.
HELENA. Well, and what are your means?
(*Lassi kneels and begins clumsily to kiss her hands.*)
HELENA. Get up, you impudent boy. How dare you!
LASSI. You asked yourself what my means are.
HELENA. I didn't think . . . I didn't believe that you . . . a young man, hardly even a man yet. . . . (*Tenderly.*) Almost a child. (*More severely.*) Oh don't, stop this comedy, you're pathetic and laughable.

300

LASSI. Of course, because I worship you.

HELENA. You do not worship me. You only want to put your young and insufferable self-importance at my service. In reality you worship yourself.

LASSI. I idolize you.

HELENA. (*Coldly.*) And supposing you do idolize me. What then? One doesn't need anything more than good corsets to make kids like you idolize one. But don't start thinking that that is love!

LASSI. It's not enough for you that I idolize you. Let me love you then.

HELENA. Listen now, young man. You think you are in love, but you are only impudent. You love yourself and idolize your own idolization. Please spare me these outbursts.

LASSI. I must spare you, but have you spared me? Have you? I loved you . . . very much . . . tenderly . . . tragically, and you led me on. Why did you encourage me with your looks? You smiled charmingly when I trembled. You enjoyed my foolishness and fear, you were amused by the hopelessness, the signals of distress, and the crazy peace offerings of a trapped animal, you are cruel!

HELENA. What hurtful words you speak! I realize you can't mean all you say, you are only bitter.

LASSI. Only you have the right to hurt. . . . You have wounded me . . . and yet so politely and formally . . . it makes me twice as furious.

HELENA. (*Sighs.*) First so gentle and good, and then so cruel and gloomy. We used to hide our innermost feelings. The world has changed. How much it has changed. When I was young, people had manners, dreamed in solitude, exchanged glances behind a curtain . . .

LASSI. (*Mutters gloomily.*) A lace curtain perhaps?

HELENA. (*Continues unperturbed.*) . . . directed their energies to other matters, ideals, politics, religion. Now . . . how mad.

LASSI. And then, on top of everything, after you have driven me out of my mind, you start moralizing. Why can't you just be honest and say: Go to hell.

HELENA. (*Coldly.*) It seems to me a little more moralizing is called for. I have not yet met a young man who was improved by his youth—why should you be an exception? Men do not carry their youth discreetly, nobly.

LASSI. I am not discreet nor noble. I am mad, and *you* have made me mad. But your cruelty gives me the right to speak straight out. You are dishonest, and I am straight. (*Weeping.*) I love you, and I despise you.

HELENA. Stop it. Stop it. You must not. I can't stand it.

LASSI. You started this crying yourself, and now you can't stand it. You can't stand *anything*. (*Thinks and concentrates.*) Are you so afraid of my arms?

HELENA. (*Thinks for a moment, then answers quickly.*) No, I am not afraid of your arms. I am afraid of your opinion.

LASSI. Why?

HELENA. I am afraid that you will despise me afterwards.

LASSI. What do you mean? Or rather—of course. Women love nothing so much as respectability.

HELENA. Perhaps. If you love just what you wish, everything gets mixed up.

LASSI. So what? Let things get mixed up. There are always others who follow behind to pick up the pieces.

HELENA. So that's what you think—you must be mad. I don't want to hear any more, stop it, take your proposition elsewhere. (*Suddenly bursts into laughter.*)

Ah youth! You are so young . . . and so emotional. Silly boy! (*She turns and goes over to the window.*)

LASSI. Who made me emotional? You. You treat me like Pavlov's dog. Do you know how it was treated?

HELENA. I don't remember.

LASSI. It was given contradictory impulses, electric shocks and food in turn, till it got so upset it became a drunkard—it chose a bowl of wine instead of a bowl of milk. In the end it got fed up with the game, went to the electric grid, and just lay down there. It meant: "I can't stand any more. Kill me." . . . I am Pavlov's dog.

HELENA. (*Pityingly.*) *El perro soltero!* Poor dog—lonely dog. Unmarried dog. But now we've talked enough psychology. From now on I am going to give you very quiet impulses: Spanish, correct Spanish. For next time please prepare the lesson on page twenty-three. Goodbye.

LASSI. Perhaps there won't be a next time.

HELENA. (*Hiding her fear.*) What do you mean?

LASSI. I am your pupil voluntarily. I take lessons of my own free will. I can pay and leave. But I can't pay just now . . . I mean I haven't got the money with me.

HELENA. Don't insult me with money, you've done enough with words already. We'll talk about it another time. *Buenas noches.* (*The boy takes his book and leaves, closing the door silently behind him. Helena leans on the windowsill, fingers the window frame and weeps bitterly.*)

HELENA. Isn't it me that is Pavlov's dog? Isn't it me that is Pavlov's dog?

Darkness.

ACT TWO

Scene 1

The boy's bed-sitter about three months later. The room is quite bare, empty, and white; the only furniture a truckle bed. On the wall some glaring poster for a jazz festival or a film week, a picture of Lenin or Mao. Maija and Lassi are lying on the bed and smoking, that is Maija from time to time takes a puff at Lassi's cigarette. Maija is covered by Lassi's overcoat; her arms and legs show from under it. She is wearing black knitted underwear—tights and black cotton vest, for instance.

MAIJA. Just think, you're the first man that's touched me. Before I couldn't stand the idea of . . . but I didn't know it was like this. Even if you left me, I'd remember you always. My mouth and my eyes would remember you, my hands would remember you. (*Caresses the boy in her thoughts.*) But you won't leave me, I was made for you. I exist for you. (*Lassi does not answer.*) You don't say anything. Don't you realize, I don't want to be alone any more. I don't want to read botany and geometry and cram my head full of German irregular verbs. I think it's idiotic to learn useless things when people are fighting wars, dying of starvation, and being driven from their homes. Now we have shared experiences, we can remember them. We can hold our own against the others, the bad men. Against the whole world if we want.

LASSI. (*Gloomily.*) I'm the bad man of this story.

MAIJA. You are funny. You don't listen to me at all. All right, you can be a "bad man" if you want, I have chosen you and I love you. I want to forget . . . with you I want to forget . . . that the world is bad, that there is no God and that heaven is empty and black.

LASSI. Black world, black heaven, black God, black universe. And then romantic little girls want to love . . . yes, of course.

MAIJA. Don't you want to as well? I'm not the only one who does the loving. When I'm with you, I feel as if we were alone together in the world.

LASSI. (*Sadly.*) I feel as if I were alone in the world.

MAIJA. (*Hurt.*) When you make love to me?

LASSI. Yes. No. Afterwards.

MAIJA. No! You can't mean what you say.

LASSI. Why shouldn't I mean what I say? Love makes one depressed.

MAIJA. Do I make you depressed?

LASSI. No, love does. It makes one bored, too. But all the same it's important . . . how shall I say . . . for the peace of the scorpion.

MAIJA. What did you say?

LASSI. I said: for the peace of the lower organs.

MAIJA. You're horrible. Why should they be the . . . lower organs?

LASSI. They don't have to be. For *women* they're the higher organs of course. Women don't have anything higher.

MAIJA. (*Very hurt.*) Really.

LASSI. Yes. Love makes *intelligent* beings depressed and flat. Only women, ostriches, and monkeys are made happy by love. Oh yes, and parrots.

MAIJA. Now you're talking rubbish. You know perfectly well I'm just as intelligent as you are.

LASSI. Your intelligence is all in your stomach.

MAIJA. Why do you want to hurt me? How have I annoyed you? (*Tries to conciliate him.*) Show me your poems, will you?

(*Lassi carelessly pulls out of his pocket a bunch of papers, crumpled money, and poems. Maija wriggles into the overcoat, buttons it up in front, half sits up, and starts straightening out Lassi's bits of paper.*)

LASSI. (*Tries to be conciliatory.*) Now you're like a Picasso guitar.

MAIJA. (*Does not understand.*) Whad d'you mean, a guitar?

LASSI. That big overcoat on you. It's like a case.

MAIJA. (*Nods and read aloud.*)

> Fear not pain,
> pain has washed your face
> fragrant with snow.
> I love you
> more than the mother
> who bore me.

LASSI. (*Is embarrassed and whistles in an offhand manner.*)

MAIJA. It's queer.

LASSI. What d'you mean, queer. Are you jealous?

MAIJA. I didn't think of it like that. I didn't even remember you—it's like a folk song. Like the Spanish gypsy songs my mother sings sometimes. Primitive and—

LASSI. What?

MAIJA. I don't know. Tragic. The feeling is tragic.

LASSI. I suppose you mean the feeling is inseparable. That's because it's written to a woman who combines all the basic types of woman; sister, mother, daughter . . . the complete woman.

MAIJA. Who is it?

LASSI. No one. Just imagination. A whim. Or an obsession.

MAIJA. Show me some more poems. (*She straightens out another piece of paper and reads; Lassi whistles all the time, softly between his teeth.*)

> Love is like sierra snow.
> How long is there snow in May?
>
> Love is like distant rain.
> There has long been rain in my heart.
>
> Rain is falling in the woods.
> Flowers have gone on falling from the trees.
>
> The parks are empty. The woods are empty.
> There is snow in the alleys and roads.
>
> My heart streams away like a river.
> The stream is full of flowers, of snow.

MAIJA. It's beautiful. "Snow in May" would be a good name for it. Shall we call it "Snow in May"?

LASSI. Call it what you like, I don't give a damn.

MAIJA. (*Repeats.*) Love is like sierra snow. How long is there snow in May? . . . Who did you write it for?

LASSI. I don't know. No one. The poem. Or love. I write for the poem, as you dance for the dance, that's all.

MAIJA. Love is like distant rain. There has long been rain in my heart . . . who for?

LASSI. Stop it. I don't want to hear it. It's stupid. Neoromanticism. Laughable— horrible. It's like a bloody pop song. (*He snatches the poems from her, puts them in an ashtray and sets fire to them.*)

MAIJA. Go on and burn it. I know it by heart already. I'll always remember it.

LASSI. Remember as much as you want. I couldn't care less.

MAIJA. (*Timidly.*) Have you got any others?

LASSI. What others?

MAIJA. More poems?

LASSI. More and more. You always want more. You never have enough. (*In a strained voice.*) I've got enough for a whole book. I'm going to have a collection published in the autumn. It'll be called *Screams of a Madman*.

MAIJA. Ugh. They're not mad at all.

LASSI. Not these, but the others. These are all right to show to little girls, not the others.

MAIJA. Keep your poems! What are you so cross about?

LASSI. (*More amicably.*) Because those poems you saw are really lousy. No one with any intelligence writes things like that any more. A proper poem ought not to have any meaning. Only rhythm! like the ripple of waves or syncopated music. Like this: (*Taps his fingers in time with the rhythm of the poem.*)

> I walk
> in the street
> on the shady
> side
> On the shady side
> of the shady street
> I walk
> in the shade
> in the shade
> I walk
> on the side
> of the street
> On the shady side
> I walk
> of the street.

—But you wouldn't understand that sort of thing!

MAIJA. I do understand! (*Suddenly inspired.*) I walk/in the street/on the shady/side. . . . (*She gets up and starts to walk rhythmically, "syncopating," then dances dreamily. In her black underwear she is like a Pierrette. Lassi puts some quiet jazz on the record player. Hodges "Shady Side" (Gerry Mulligan meets Johnny Hodges, Verve, LCLP 202), which imitates walking. They dance slowly together, from time to time walking past each other and in turn monotonously reciting the poem. During the poem and the jazz a contact is felt between them, the jazz stimulates both of them. After "Shady Side" they fall on to the bed, but so that one's head is at the other's feet.*)

LASSI. (*Irritably.*) Don't push your feet in my mouth.

MAIJA. (*Pulls her feet up. Silence. Then hesitantly:*) You're in an awful bad temper. What other hobbies do you have besides writing poems?

LASSI. Nature.

MAIJA. Nature? How can that be a hobby?

LASSI. In all kinds of ways. When I was small I collected stones, then insects and birds' eggs. Nowadays I collect women.

MAIJA. Pooh! (*Laughs.*) And is your collection a big one?

LASSI. Not specially. Including back numbers about the same size as my collection of birds' eggs. About twenty specimens. A good score.

MAIJA. (*Not believing him, laughs brightly.*) All smooth and round like birds' eggs.

LASSI. Not quite. They have a hole underneath, that's important.

MAIJA. (*Embarrassed.*) Really. Well, tell me more about women. Though I shan't believe anything, you tell lies all the time. Boastful!

LASSI. Women are like starfish—they belong to the echinoderm family anyway. D'you know what starfish are like? How they behave?

MAIJA. No.

LASSI. Oysters are their special delicacy.

MAIJA. Oh? Pearl oysters you mean? Like you?

LASSI. (*Goes on cold-bloodedly.*) I suppose you know how an oyster closes its house? It's as strong as hell, the shell is tight as if it was screwed together. But the starfish is stronger, and it has a strong stomach, too. First it twists and twists, till it's pried the shell open. Then it pushes its stomach out of its mouth and pours its digestive juices into the victim. When the oyster has dissolved sufficiently, the starfish sucks it in as food.

MAIJA. (*Reluctantly.*) What does all that symbolism mean?

LASSI. Don't pretend to be stupid. Women, at least the most feminine ones, operate in the same way. The female is designed on the same principle as the starfish. Those creatures that the woman doesn't swallow she melts outside her body until the soft parts dissolve and only the shell remains.

MAIJA. You're horrible. Do you mean that I am one of those . . . females?

LASSI. No, I don't. You may be, but it doesn't worry me. You can't eat me, there's nothing left of me except the shell. I mean real women, not half-grown bunnies. It's easier to give the Venus de Milo an anal injection than make a crack in a real seafish woman. . . . Though I don't know, that's not what I really want, not any more. Do you want to hear the truth about love—do you?

MAIJA. If it's something disgusting again, no I don't.

LASSI. Truth is often shameless, truth is not shy. Truth can be murderously horrible.

MAIJA. (*Reluctantly.*) Go on then. It'll take more than that to kill me.

LASSI. (*Bitterly.*) Erotic love works on three levels: head, heart, and bed. In the head it's sweet, in the heart it's cruel, and in bed it's hateful. Fitting the excretive organs into each other—laughable. Disgusting. To hell with all love. To hell with the starfish.

MAIJA. You're brutal. How you've changed. At first you were so nice and polite, and now you're just a . . . brute. Besides, if women are starfish, then men are octopuses, (*imitates him*) "designed on the same principle." You're stupid to imagine yourself to be an oyster.

LASSI. I don't. I'm just the pearl.

MAIJA. You're a pig. An octopus. Pig. Octopig.

(*Lassi laughs and blows smoke in Maija's face, until she starts to cough.*)

MAIJA. Don't. Stop it. . . . Letting it all come like that! Do you want to hear what you are? I had a dream about you. You were a little pig, a little rose pink baby pig, a real piglet. We were in some hut, it was a bamboo hut, and I was almost naked, only in a topless, and I had terrifically big breasts, like hunting horns. It was very cold, there were only a few twigs in the hut, and there wasn't any fireplace. Then Mother came there or someone, and asked where I was going to put the pig when it grew bigger. I said that it wouldn't grow, it was that sort of a pig. Then I started to make a fire, though there wasn't a stove, and the walls caught fire and a moment later the whole hut was on fire. Then I woke up.

LASSI. (*Hurt.*) It's insulting to see me as a pig, or even just a piglet. It's insulting.
MAIJA. But you *are* a pig. I saw you as you are. You were a very pretty piglet mind you, you pushed yourself against me and squeaked. And why should I be sorry for you, why? I didn't mean to tell you, but I'm going to anyway, because you're brutal and stupid, too, and you don't realize how stupid you really are at all. I'm going to have a baby.
LASSI. For Christ's sake!
MAIJA. You don't know anything. You go on about women and you yourself are as stupid as an ox. You great stupid thing.
LASSI. For Christ's sake!
MAIJA. When I was five years old, I knew everything already. I found out about things—I read about them. You're nearly a grown up man and you seem to think kids come from cabbages.
LASSI. For Christ's sake.
MAIJA. Stop swearing and help me. You must help me. I'm asking you.
LASSI. (*Miserably.*) What are you asking me?
MAIJA. For signs of genius. Use your brains, you . . . poet. Think of something.
LASSI. (*Shyly and awkwardly.*) Maija . . . poor Maija. I can't think of anything . . . sensible. I don't dare to start thinking, this is so serious. You must tell your parents everything, and quickly. You mustn't waste any time, d'you understand?
MAIJA. Do you mean it can be taken away?
LASSI. Yes, right at the beginning it can be taken away. But no mumbo jumbo. Some people try to do it themselves, but it never comes off properly. D'you realize? It's firmly there . . . like in a can. Taking quinine or jumping off tables or poking about won't help. You must tell your mother.
MAIJA. Mother . . . never.
LASSI. Would she be very angry with you?
MAIJA. I don't know . . . and even if she was. . . . That's not why, but . . . Mother has lived like a Sleeping Beauty—d'you understand? She's lived in her room of roses too long. She doesn't understand ordinary brutal facts.
LASSI. Well, if she's a Sleeping Beauty, it's time she woke up isn't it?
MAIJA. I don't think . . . she'll ever wake up. She's rather die than wake up to harsh reality, the way ordinary people live.
LASSI. Try anyway. Tell your father—tell both of them. They can't be complete idiots, surely.
MAIJA. No . . . I suppose not. But they don't live, or they live in their own worlds. Father in his books. Mother in the past, or in the future, how should I know, somewhere far away. Father's a bookworm and they're always a bit silly . . . and Mother . . . Mother is a super doll that sleeps.
LASSI. Haven't you ever talked to your mother seriously about . . . trivial things?
MAIJA. No . . . I can't get near her. I can't make her out . . . she's always on guard and terribly sensitive, calm and wild at the same time . . . I mean, she never shows her storms. But she's unpredictable all the same.
LASSI. Capricious and free?
MAIJA. She's as patient as an angel, and that's what makes me think she's terribly dissatisfied. She pretends to be gentle but she's terrifically demanding—that's why she makes people her slaves.
LASSI. What people?
MAIJA. I don't . . . know.
LASSI. You must know, when you said it.

MAIJA. No, I don't. Father says she makes everyone lose their senses, but how should I know? She's a mother. She's like mothers are—usually she doesn't notice me, only when I'm all to pieces for some reason, really unhappy and tired out, she's very nice and just like she was secretly content. Her supremacy is complete then, you see.

LASSI. Hmm . . . do you love her?

MAIJA. You just have to love Mother . . . perhaps just because she's so changeable. If you ask her for something, she's cross and cold. But then all of a sudden she's so good and tender it touches your heart . . . she's always different.

LASSI. What d'you mean, "different"?

MAIJA. She's always different from what you expected. When she's cold and polite so it hurts you, she can seem quite unbearable, but when she starts to get interested and listens with shining eyes, you have to forgive her and start feeling ashamed you ever felt angry with her. You can never be really angry with her. And she knows it, and that's why it's easy for her to keep people under her spell. . . . She only needs to look at you and your legs stop in the middle of the street and you can't move an inch . . . she seems to control people with looks . . . hard, gentle, mocking, disapproving . . . she has terrible power over people.

LASSI. Would you like to be the same kind as your mother?

MAIJA. I don't know. Maybe. But I'm not the same kind, I'm much more humdrum. Father . . . Father is melancholy and he made me when he was in his most melancholy mood. I can imitate Mother, but inside I'm like Father—I think so anyway.

LASSI. And you love your father too?

MAIJA. Of course. Father is reliable.

LASSI. (Alert.) Isn't your mother reliable? Isn't she . . . faithful?

MAIJA. Mother doesn't need to be faithful, everyone loves her without. Only the ugly and stupid are faithful. D'you know, Father once said when he was very sad that he was unhappily in love with Mother. Wasn't that funny? "How can you be unhappily in love when you're already married?" I asked. Father answered that it's marriage that makes you unhappy—all other unhappiness goes by.

LASSI. Perhaps that's true. If one's married to a really hermetic being, it's like being married to a bottle. Hm. Only the ugly and the stupid, you say. D'you think faithfulness is stupid?

MAIJA. It's unpractical. But I . . . (adds quickly) I'm unpractical . . . like Father. Father is so clear-cut and reliable.

LASSI. What do you mean by clear-cut?

MAIJA. Why are you examining me? I mean that I always know what Father is thinking, when I can snuggle up close to him and when he wants to be left alone. I know when he's going to be angry, too, but with Mother I never know. Mother is like your "Snow in May" poem.

LASSI. (Watching her.) What d'you mean by that?

MAIJA. Cold when you expect warm, at the wrong time in the wrong place, full of unstable emotions, unexpected, always a bit late or somehow surprising.

LASSI. Yes, and that's what makes her so attractive.

MAIJA. Is that what you think, too? Why?

LASSI. I love uncertain things . . . things that are certain bore me, make me depressed, like everlasting rain. And reliable and safe people are as boring as textbooks. Incalculable people are lovable, although they cause suffering, too.

MAIJA. Lovable?

LASSI. Exciting.

MAIJA. Then Mother suits you all right. Mother is . . . ethereal.

LASSI. (*Suspicious.*) Suits you—what d'you mean by that?

MAIJA. Nothing, silly. I only thought you liked Mother. You got into a good temper as soon as I started to talk about Mother. (*She adds, laughing.*) Now I know how to get round you.

(*Lassi touches her gently. Maija slips down to his knees. They lie down side by side, and embrace. The light fades; darkness.*)

Scene 2

(*Maija's home a day later; the same room as at the beginning. Helena and Paavo are sitting apart from each other. Paavo is reading, Helena is resting her head on the back of the sofa and resting her eyes, her knitting in her lap. The sound of the outer door; Maija runs in.*)

MAIJA. Mother! Father! Something's happened to me, something . . . terrible! (*Comes besides her mother on the sofa and embraces her.*) Mother . . . (*sobs*).

HELENA. My little one, what is it? (*Tries to look her in the eye. Maija shuts her eyes and weeps silently but unrestrainedly.*)

HELENA. But Maikki, my little Maikki, calm down, control yourself. Don't cry . . . or cry my darling if it helps. What is it? Tell me your worries.

MAIJA. I don't have worries, I have sorrows. I. . . .

PAAVO. Do you want to talk to your mother alone, Maija?

MAIJA. No Father. Don't go. I want . . . (*she cannot speak for crying*).

HELENA. Maija dear, tell me now. Tell me like a good girl. Well—

MAIJA. My . . . (*sobs*) periods stopped two months ago.

HELENA. Really? And that's what's worrying you. Don't upset yourself about that dear girl. They'll start again all right, just be patient and wait. That's no sorrow, that's just a worry, it doesn't even need to be that.

MAIJA. But Mother . . . (*weeps*).

HELENA. Now Maija, dear child, don't be hysterical.

MAIJA. But I've been as regular as a clock.

HELENA. Even a clock can go wrong. And a woman . . . a young girl . . . is usually such a delicate and sensitive clock that she will get well by herself. You are only at the beginning of puberty, of course there can be upsets, that's nothing to cry about. I think you are overtired, you have been reading too much. My periods used not to come when there were some special exams I was afraid of. Then they just started again by themselves; it will be the same with you, you'll see, you have inherited my sensitiveness. But if it hasn't come next month, you can go to the doctor. You can go to Uncle George, but you mustn't bother him unnecessarily.

MAIJA. Uncle George is an old fool. I'm not going to let him look at me.

HELENA. Uncle George is a good doctor. Now don't start getting upset for nothing.

The bodily functions of a sensitive young girl easily go wrong. Quiet now, dear. You know, I have worries too, do you think I don't? Every day, from morning to night.

MAIJA. No Mother, you don't have any worries, your skin is quite smooth. You haven't any wrinkles at all.

HELENA. Wrinkles don't come from worry, they come from lack of moisture.

MAIJA. Then you are very moist, Mother. (*Caresses her Mother's cheek with her forefinger.*) Listen Mother. . . .

HELENA. (*Moves the bowl of sweets on the table in front of Maija.*) Take a sweet, Maikki. Fazer's best. I haven't eaten them for years, and suddenly I got a craving for them and wanted to refresh the memories of youth. Tosca, Island, Lacta, Regina. . . . But they are not the same at all, they have lost their subtle individuality, even the wrappings are not the same as before. Oh dear, how disappointed I was. I hoped at least Fazer's best had stayed the same.

PAAVO. (*With weary irony.*) Of course, yes. At least Fazer, when even the church isn't. . . .

MAIJA. (*Shyly.*) Mother. . . .

(*The telephone rings in the hall and Helena rises hastily and goes out, looking relieved, to answer it.*)

MAIJA. (*Dejectedly.*) Now she'll talk for ages . . . at least half an hour.

PAAVO. What's the matter, Maija?

MAIJA. (*Hesitates, draws back.*) I . . . don't know. I'm burning.

PAAVO. If you're burning, you're only burning with purity. So you should be. Life is fire.

MAIJA. Now you don't understand.

PAAVO. Don't I? Don't I understand my little girl ?

MAIJA. No. You start philosophizing. But I'm really on fire. (*She gets up and goes to the window, pushing her cheek against the cool glass.*) Mother . . . doesn't understand of course . . . she's never understood. She's so . . . inside herself. But you . . . why are you so far away? Nobody understands.

PAAVO. That's true, Maija. Perhaps it's a good thing to know that right from the beginning, then there won't be so many disappointments. Man is alone. Nobody understands.

MAIJA. (*Tries again.*) Father. I. . . .

(*Then Helena comes into the room and puts her arm round Maija.*)

HELENA. What is it my little girl is dreaming about?

(*Maija pulls herself away and rushes out of the room, crying.*)

PAAVO. (*To Helena.*) It seems to me the girl is really suffering.

HELENA. (*Sits languidly.*) Really? Oh dear, how tired I am, my head aches. How can she be suffering? I won't think about it today, I'll think about it tomorrow.

PAAVO. Yes, you have other thoughts now.

HELENA. What thoughts? What do you mean?

PAAVO. Shall I tell you? It seems to me that youngster, that great lump, is bringing unhappiness into this house. Do you think I am blind? You are in love—

HELENA. (*Painfully*) And do you think I haven't reproached myself for it? Don't reproach me any more . . . Love is a monster. . . . When I was young, I fell in love with old men, and now . . . I don't understand. . . .

PAAVO. All middle-aged women fall in love with young boys, but usually they are their own sons. Therefore it's permitted to some degree and it's not noticed—

its quality is not noticed. But you . . . you're only to be pitied. And I, who see and understand everything, I am to be pitied, too.

HELENA. This is horrible. I hate my heart. If I were hard, this kind of thing wouldn't happen to me.

PAAVO. No, you don't hate your heart. When you say: I hate my heart, you mean, I hate the goodness of my heart. But you are not good, you are soft. Illusions! Illusions. Illusion of innocent love, illusion of the heart's goodness, illusion of the sacredness of the pure life. But your virtuousness is only love of comfort, bourgeois self-satisfaction. Give up what you hold so dear: your illusions, and you can return to reality and become your real self.

HELENA. And your wife—that's what you really mean, isn't it?

PAAVO. That too, perhaps. When this foolishness goes over, you'll come back nicely into my arms. When the great emotions collapse they can be nicely patched up with the smaller old ones.

HELENA. Don't be unkind, Paavo. When I confessed everything to you, I threw myself on your mercy. That's why I hoped you wouldn't reproach me. Just now I can't stand it.

PAAVO. I don't reproach you because your love is foolish and unsuitable! I reproach your lack of taste and sentimentality. I've heard you playing lately all the worst Russian romantic trash.

HELENA. Why should they be worse than say French pieces?

PAAVO. Because they are fleshy, and because they have no irony. You can't stand irony in your present state, and it's irony that could cure you of your madness. You want it to go on, and so you play "White Acacias," or whatever it is, and "Black Eyes".

HELENA. You don't understand anything, you have never understood anything!

PAAVO. Oh yes, I do. You're hurt just because I do understand.

HELENA. (*She is wounded. She gets up and begins to sing, in a powerful and sad, deep voice, some popular arrangement of a melancholy (Russian?) romantic song. She sings part of a verse, then breaks off, and remains as if listening.*)

PAAVO. Go on, sing. You think you are singing sadness, but your sadness is joy, it's a kind of joy, and you don't want to lose it. You rejoice over your foolish love like a saint rejoicing over his sores.

HELENA. Don't explain. Stop explaining. Why do you explain me all the time?

PAAVO. (*Gets up, and speaks in a bored yet strained voice.*) Explain yourself to yourself, be your own physician. (*He goes out of the room and slams the door shut behind him.*)

HELENA. (*Rises, and walks back and forth, clenching her hands in her suffering.*) If I were my own physician, I should say to myself: Go with him, make that little, terrible mistake!—Such an absurd little thing, and yet it would give me back my health and peace of mind. Or would it? Supposing it took the rest away, too? Where does this sorrow come from, this pain that is wider than an ocean and sharper than the point of a needle? O all-conquering sorrow! Why do I love him? Because he is young? But that is no reason, the world is full of young people—each one more demanding and more arrogant than the last. He is not especially handsome, nor especially wise, and he is selfish like all young people. I love him in fact for no reason at all, and therefore my sickness cannot be cured. But that's insane. If hope shows the depth of sorrow, then hopelessness must cure sorrow. From this moment on my curing begins, I shall change. I have made up my mind, I shall change!

Darkness.

Scene 3

(*The same room. Paavo is alone, looking at himself in the mirror, a drink in his hand. He talks to himself, drinks a toast with himself in the mirror so that the glasses clink against each other.*)

PAAVO. Paavo, Paavo hard-luck bum, why are you chained to this dreadful city, stupid job, cramped marriage, dull apartment, shabby suit, eh? Drink Paavo, drink doesn't cure your cares, but it makes them more enjoyable. (*He clinks his glass against the mirror.*) Though it's always the same, whether it's the driver or the driven—the same old slavery, just the same. (*He sits.*) What was it that fellow said on the Kotka train . . . "Life's a bloody dear drink. I got two accordions at home, but I don't play neither of 'em". It's on a train that you see what a sad place this Finland is. Like going across Siberia, so monotonous and dull. . . . Going incredibly slow, standing and standing . . . water all gone from the tender, melt some snow. . . . Station like a nineteenth-century prison, windows frozen up, ornamental door frames . . . some lantern glimmering through the snow. A poor idle lantern in the snow, isn't that what I am? But if I lived in Heidelberg . . . Königsberg . . . Heilbronn . . . Frankfurt on Main . . . alone . . . I'd create a philosophy . . . a new metaphysic . . . a new mathematical explanation of the world. . . . I'd turn all the old theories upside down and make a system with imagination and movement. I'd make the Great Synthesis; everyone spends their time just analyzing, man and the world are already disintegrated enough, but noone knows how to make a synthesis. I'd be the one to do it. I'd live in a garret surrounded by old folios. I'd read, study, organize. In the evenings I'd walk through the streets of Heilbronn with a shaggy dog on a lead and at night I'd write, while the city slept. A new mathematical explanation of the world . . . mathematics is the most beautiful and the purest of all the sciences, it doesn't have the smell of people about it, not the least smell of people. The tower of my intellect would be the fulcrum from which I'd lever the world from its place. Or I would write a total novel, none of your random fragments from life, beautifully polished pebbles, but a real book. (*Pause.*) A book, a novel, too, must be a system, and then there must be one more unknown dimension, the book mustn't be a speech—I hear enough speeches without that. And for the reader the book must be a kick in the stomach, it must lay open the intestines, refurnish the head completely. A book must wound, tear in two, punch the diaphragm. (*Pause.*) But there's one group of people who have to be protected from everything, and yet they're hurt in by everything: science, art, literature. They're religious. They've given up rebelling and defying, which was the birthright of the early Christians, they've given up the anarchic truth of Christianity, which despises work and money and bourgeois comforts, and exchanged it for a vague and mysterious consolation, manna from heaven. With their forget-me-not eyes, innocent and young, eternally rich young people, they want to live in a house of pleasure, so they live their serene, beautiful, and peaceful lives for ever, but Christianity, accommodated to their purposes, dies. (*He goes to his mother's photograph, which is on the bookshelf, and addresses his words to it: in his voice there is both tenderness and censure:*) Mother . . . so young and beautiful and good, eternally young and faithful . . . O Tannenbaum, Wie treu sind deine . . . Why were you so good, you discouraged me with your goodness. You forgave everything, you always said yes, never no, you were perpetual consent. You didn't raise impossible barriers for me, too-high thresholds, you were never severe, always so soft, understanding and trusting. It made me doubt myself . . . that's why now I have no will . . . wings . . . that's why my splendid talents are going to waste. (*Sits.*) When God wants to make a man great, he gives him plenty of suitable obstacles and little love. Great men are born in stable straw and they are put in a basket of reeds for the river to carry away. They are allowed to form their own souls—God looks after their bodies. They're not fed with warm milk, they must drink from the streams of the world, they do dirty work; the polisher of the mirror has dirty hands. Mother, I am bitter towards you because of your goodness.

HELENA. (*Comes in with a duster in her hand, and says in a quarrelsome voice.*) Drinking and talking to yourself again? Oh yes, I heard your little speech to your mother's picture. Always you men have to put the blame on women! The mother or the wife always gets the blame if the man fails. You criticize your mother for love, me for lack of love. That young hooligan, Lassi, for whom I am some kind of a combination of mother, sister, and mysterious blonde, attacked me yesterday and criticized me for both, for love and for lack of love.

PAAVO. What do you care about a young calf like that, he hasn't even got any occiput, any thalamus—no emotional life at all. Only hormones, no feelings.

HELENA. No feelings do you say! Do you want to hear? He came here yesterday in the middle of the day, beastly drunk, when you were at work, and the only way I could get rid of him was by leaving the house. I took a taxi, but the boy forced his way into it and started to give instructions to the driver. When we came to the bridge, he opened the window, threw his cap into the falls, and said he was going to jump in after it if I didn't do what he wanted. I said, "Please do, it would be very considerate." Then he calmed down, but started to be violent again when I drove back home. I only managed to get away from him when I threatened to call the police.

PAAVO. But supposing he does jump in after all, this young Werther?

HELENA. He can't, he can't do that to me. He can't do it—not to me.

PAAVO. Surely it wouldn't be to you, it would be to himself.

HELENA. Yes, to me. From pride, for revenge.

PAAVO. Well, let him do it then. If it's not you that incites him, there'll always be someone else. The Werthers always seek their own impossible objects. And you for your part will find a new Werther to tempt, a new Werther all for your very own.

HELENA. (*Agonizedly.*) What did you say?

PAAVO. I mean that you are a kind of temptress, who appears as a guardian of morals. Bourgeois ladies think they are moral, because they dream of life's purity—

HELENA. (*Very angry.*) And do not surrender themselves, yes. And supposing I did surrender, what would happen then? Oh yes. I know the way men speak. "So you've got nothing better to do than jump into bed." It's always wrong, whatever one does. How can you!

PAAVO. I didn't quite mean that. You see—this is part of a great common theme. I criticized my mother for the same weakness—she too was so soft and vulnerable that she just wanted to be good. I remember her as always smiling, looking up to heaven—there's something of the same in you. And as I longed for discipline from my mother, a stricter love, so I need from you the whole spectrum of personality—deeper colors, from the dark side, too. You are like a summer sky, almost colorless. A little courage, Helena!

HELENA. I think self-control requires the greatest courage—at least you cannot accuse me of lack of control. But you? You are always undoing Gordian knots, you sever them with a sword, by force. No patience at all. But I don't believe in you any more, you just talk and talk. You're just a dreamer.

PAAVO. I'm not a dreamer, I'm a genius. There's a big difference. A genius is an expansive spirit, a dreamer is only restless. A dreamer seeks and does not find, a genius finds even if he does not seek.

HELENA. Indeed. And in what way does your genius appear?

PAAVO. I know that I am not brilliantly talented, I am not a specially good prophet nor a very good organizer. But I love more than others, that is why I am a genius.

HELENA. What is it you love so much then?

PAAVO. Everything. I love trees, and trees don't understand it. I love stones, and stones don't understand it. I love you, and you don't understand it. That's how it is.

HELENA. Oh, how you talk! Surely you're not seriously suggesting you love me—after all these years?

PAAVO. I do love you—what mortifying fidelity. Those who have loved too well are punished by having to go on loving.

HELENA. You should love yourself, then everything would be all right.

PAAVO. No Helena. That is just the difference between the dreamer and the genius—the dreamer loves only himself, the genius only loves something else.

HELENA. Oh my God, do you think I don't love? That doesn't make me feel like a genius though, but the most miserable creature on earth.

PAAVO. Hm. Do you still feel like that? I thought you'd got over it. You seem to me to have changed in some way. You're sharper, harder than before.

HELENA. Yes, I am sharper and harder. But not happier. (*She covers her face and bursts into tears.*)

PAAVO. (*Raises his hand, intending to soothe her. Helena wrongly interprets the gesture.*)

HELENA. That boy has humiliated me with his feelings, and I have humiliated myself by showing my heart to you. Hit me now, if you want. Hit me!

PAAVO. No. But I would like to beat that miserable admirer of yours. I believe the despicable should be despised and rascals should be beaten. Somehow I feel that misery has come to this house. That hooligan. Pup! When I was defending the frontiers of this country, that wretch was still wetting his diapers. (*Helena slips away, and leaves Paavo talking to himself.*) I'd like to kill the dog. Not from jealousy or even from anger, but from pure disgust. That young devil is a sort of refined teddy-boy. If he was just an ordinary hooligan, I wouldn't mind so much him bringing his filth into this house. But he's an aesthete, soft and flabby— I ought to challenge him to a duel. I'll take him to the country and shoot him like a duck. (*He goes to the cupboard, takes out a shotgun, and examines it.*) Funny, I've never killed an animal, my father used to shoot birds with this, I only shoot birds with my camera. But now at any rate I want to pour shot into that lyrical mail bag. Lassi! A dog's name, and that long-haired cur lives up to his name. What is he anyway? A whimpering animal. Oh, yes, I've read his scribblings in the papers, yes, and the ones my wife has hidden. Always sorry for himself, but never sorry for anyone else. Self! Self! I my me mine. Christ, I'll take him by the neck, I'll take him to our cottage. I'll put the weapons in front of him, there you are, I'll say, choose your weapon, there are two good shotguns, try which of them suits you better. I'll be chivalrous and let him shoot first, he'll tremble like an aspen, of course, and miss, and then I'll make sure of that chevalier of the pen, I'll make sure of him like. . . . that! (*He lifts the shotgun, aims at the table lamp, and fires. The charge explodes, there is a tinkling of broken glass, then darkness. From the back room can be heard Helena's shocked cry.*)

HELENA. Paavo. Paavo, what happened?

PAAVO. Nothing. Nothing at all.

HELENA. What was that shot? Paavo. Are you all right?

PAAVO. Yes, yes. I am all right, you are all right, he is all right. We are all right, right as bloody rain. Everything's all right. It's just the acoustics here are so damned bad.

Curtain.

ACT THREE

Scene 1

(*The same room, a week later. Maija and Lassi are sitting on the sofa.*)

LASSI. Why haven't you been round to my place?

MAIJA. I couldn't. I've been thinking about things.

LASSI. Did you tell your mother? What'd she say?

MAIJA. I tried, but it wasn't any good. They didn't understand anything.

LASSI. What d'you mean, "didn't understand"? You could have told them so they did understand.

MAIJA. I tried a dozen times, but it didn't do any good even then. They thought I had too much homework and nervous tension. They just patted me and hushed me, and in the end I got so angry I had to cry and get away from them. I don't think they would've understood if I'd got a big stomach already. They don't realize I'm becoming a woman you see. For them I'm always and for ever just a little girl—they *want* to think like that.

LASSI. Bloody, bloody hell. They ought to put chastity belts on girls as soon as they get to the age.

MAIJA. What . . . chastity belt?

LASSI. Sort of iron band, with a lock. In the Middle Ages they used them. When the knights went to war, they locked their wives' treasure up. Then it was safe till they came back.

MAIJA. Horrible. Ugh. How messy. . . . And why was it the girls they had to lock up?

LASSI. (*Shrugs his shoulders.*) Well, after all girls suffer more if anything happens.

MAIJA. Really. (*Coldly.*) Yes, of course.

LASSI. I mean the girls had to be locked up for practical reasons, not moral ones. That's what I think, of course.

MAIJA. And I think boys should be locked up for moral reasons. . . . Oh, you're hateful.

LASSI. (*Suddenly.*) Am I? Why did you ask me here anyway? And where's your family?

MAIJA. I asked you because I want to talk this thing out. Father and Mother flew to Stockholm this morning; Father has some business there, and Mother went with him just for pleasure. They're not coming back for three days. We can be here without being disturbed tonight and do what we like.

LASSI. Uhuh. And what would you like us to do?

MAIJA. Anything. We're a married couple now. You must marry me.

LASSI. Marry? Did you say *marry*? But I'm not even in love with you. I'm in love with your *mother,* not with you.

MAIJA. (*Shouts.*) What?

LASSI. I'm in love with your mother. D'you understand. Your mother!

MAIJA. Mother . . . my God . . . I should have guessed. My God.

LASSI. You . . . a kid like you with your arse still dragging on the ground. Your mother's from a different race, she's a long-legged thoroughbred.

MAIJA. (*Hitting him.*) Shut up! What do you know about Mother?

LASSI. And her neck is like a young colt's. I know . . . instinctively. Women are stuck-up about their instinct and think that men don't have any. But men have much more of it, they just don't make a fuss about what they see and know, women sing out everything in public and so they think they know more. . . . Now I'm talking like a woman, I've never talked so much before. On top of everything else you make me like an old woman. And I ought to get married to you!

MAIJA. You are an old woman if you don't marry me. It's not fair to leave the other one in a fix and run away from what you've done.

LASSI. What have I done? I wouldn't run away if I'd been laying siege to you for six months, or I'd seduced you, or talked you into it, or raped you. But the fact is I didn't want you at all. You wanted me, you made a beeline straight for me.

MAIJA. What then? I want to choose for myself. I don't want to be like a flower that waits to be plucked—if it is plucked.

LASSI. Well. Then you got what you wanted.

MAIJA. I wanted you, and I don't regret it. But did you have to give me a baby?

That's something you're responsible for. You should have been careful. You made a mess of things.

LASSI. I didn't know kids had kids. Even if you're sharper than your mother, you've got a kid's body—hardly any breasts even, you're like a rag doll. Pah! You're no woman. You're just a fat little honey bunny, an under-aged hag. (*Maija covers her ears.*) Listen, you're just a little cow, that's all you are. And yet you're maddeningly complex, you're as full of nooks and crannies and compartments and corners as an old chest of drawers. You have all the bad sides of a woman, but none of a woman's charm. I can't stand you, I can't stand little girls as a whole. Beside you, your mother is the Praxiteles *Venus*. I'd rather die than marry you.

MAIJA. (*She is numb with suffering and fear. When she speaks her voice is thick, stiff with shock.*) If you don't want to marry me, do you want to die with me?

(*Lassi looks at her with surprise and strained attention; he does not answer.*)

MAIJA. (*Cold-bloodedly.*) You can't marry my mother either. You might just as well marry the Praxiteles *Venus*.

LASSI. All right. I'll marry the Praxiteles *Venus*. I'll write my name on Venus' arse, bow and say: Dear Madam, I have written my name on your hypotenuse, you are mine now!

MAIJA. (*Scratching his nose with a pencil.*) And I'll write my name on your hypotenuse, like that. Then I'll go away. I want to die before I get old and fat and ugly and stupid. It's wonderful to die when life has taken back its gift and yet you love someone all the same . . . I love you, you love Mother, Mother doesn't love anyone . . . isn't that enough reason to die? And on top of everything I'm going to have a baby.

LASSI. You said your mother doesn't love anyone. That's not true. She loves me, I know. I can't prove it, but I know it.

MAIJA. What good can that sort of love do you? But if you died, then—

LASSI. I could have my revenge. Before I died I would send her a telegram or a letter: "I have gone to Pavlov's electric grid. Your dog, Lassi." (*Considers.*) But revenge is only of some value as long as she loves me. When she stops loving, she'll only be pleased to get rid of me.

MAIJA. Then we must die now. Wait. I'll fetch something (*She goes out of the room.*)

(*Lassi smokes nervously. He gets up, crushes his cigarette in an ashtray, and walks restlessly back and forth. Maija comes back and pushes a bottle of sleeping pills into his hand.*)

MAIJA. Father says they're so strong that one makes you sleep for seventeen hours. There's nearly a hundred here.

LASSI. (*Reads the label, smiles, and puts the bottle in his pocket.*) Metronox. Forte. Gosh. Underground Darkness. Why not Styxnox? Or Noxstyx?

MAIJA. But let's not do it here, let's do it in your place. No corpses for Father and Mother.

(*They embrace each other, Lassi absentmindedly, Maija passionately.*)

LASSI. Look, now the dawn is breaking . . . the window's like a Japanese screen. The light draws a tree on the window. . . . Now a bird flies there and whistles. . . .

(A distant trill, repeated and repeated.)

MAIJA. *(Sadly.)* It's spring outside, and we must die. . . . Why not? Let's break the mirror before it becomes dirty and shows the world all splotchy.

LASSI. My mirror was broken ages ago. I saw the world ages ago for what it is: a dung heap. Only dreams are beautiful . . . an unopened bud against a cold screen . . . and a bird that whistles and cheeps . . . *(He goes to the window and whistles and cheeps.)*

MAIJA. You criticize everything and then you have nothing left. Criticize yourself as well. You are a . . . what was it? *Mare Crisium?* The Sea of Crises. Or the Critical Sea?

LASSI. The proper translation is the Dangerous Sea.

MAIJA. Yes, you are the Dangerous Sea, because you think everything out in your head, and then nothing has any value for you any more. But I don't blame you. You know, I think it's good to be able to die. I didn't ask to come here, I didn't come voluntarily, so I suppose I can at least leave voluntarily—

LASSI. Nothing is ever voluntary. Even when a person thinks he's doing something of his own free will, he's being compelled to do it. Only the dead are free, the chain is broken . . . but perhaps they miss their chains? *(He starts to walk.)* And the girl lived for fifteen years, and her book was filled with dreams and disappointments, and then she decided to die. . . . But what if death is a disappointment?

MAIJA. Really I've wanted to die many times before, once I did throw myself in front of a tram, because I was so full of causeless suffering and thought it would be easier if I could feel it bodily. But I didn't do it, because I didn't have any reason for it. Now I have. They'll say it was temporary insanity, but isn't it the moment of clarity? We're doing it in a fit of clear-sighted common sense, aren't we?

LASSI. You're a rationalist as always. Women are like that, they want reasons, whether it's a matter of life or death. Women, nest-builders, want sensible reasons, and if there aren't any, they make them up. I start from an impulse, a whim, I don't ask for reasons—you can always find them. I die because it amuses me to do so. One feels light and bright, as if one had thrown one's burden away and refused common slavery. . . . In a couple of weeks' time the other chaps will be writing their exams, but I'll turn in empty papers. . . . I am free, I walk with my hands in my pockets, I render nothing unto Ceasar. . . . I just walk and whistle. *(He walks back and forth, whistling Jerome Kern's "Yesterdays.")*

MAIJA. Farewell lovely life! Death is lovely, also.

LASSI. *(Suddenly angry.)* Shut up Maija! Rubbish. Women! *(Bitterly.)* There isn't anything so bad that they don't soon start to enjoy it. Even if they lived in a barrel of shit they'd start making a home out of it, with everything nice and cozy. And they wouldn't think it was crazy or illogical, but only decent. "Death is lovely." Disgusting. Laughable. First you dream of love, then of death, and always just as fascinated. You're stupid!

MAIJA. *(Strainedly.)* You're not thinking of running away, are you? You can't leave me like this. Betray me a second time! Aren't you thinking of leaving me? Why do you keep changing your mind?

LASSI. *(Comes slowly to her and shouts into her mouth.)*

> I went to pick roses,
> found death in the garden.
> I went to pick roses,
> found death in the rose bush.
> I die in the garden
> Hanged on the rose bush.

(*He turns on his heels abruptly and adds shamefacedly.*) I'm so confused. I'm split and confused like an Indian who sacrifices maize to his big toe. (*Weeps.*)

MAIJA. Was that poem your maize then? I know, don't say anything. You write your poems for Mother. You don't want to die. You want to live and suffer, to be tortured in my mother's web. Go on, whine! Oh yes, I know you now, you're nothing, nothing at all. You haven't got any will of your own, all your will is in Mother, and your heart is mad. You're in the power of an obsession, a tornado called Helena.

LASSI. (*Bitterly.*) Ah, you've noticed that tornadoes have women's names. They always do. And you're one of them, a storm called Maija. I've hardly got out of the eyes of the Amazon typhoon before I'm torn away by the daughter-storm, Maija.

MAIJA. (*Coldly.*) Don't be afraid, I don't intend to tear you away. Just stay if you want to, wriggle away there, since you love it so much. I can go alone. I don't need company. There's no need for you to hold my hand. I want to go with a clear head. *I* don't intend to suffer from softening of the brain for anyone.

LASSI. You're damned stubborn. Are all little girls so stubborn—when they get this idea of dying?

MAIJA. I don't know—I am not all girls. But I shall die—I shall be dead to you altogether. Even if I don't kill myself, I shall be dead to you. Because I love more, I shall die more than you.

LASSI. Of course you'll die more, because, in fact, I am already dead. The cold is rising slowly upwards—if I go on, I shall only live inside my head; my body is really dead already. What an ugly life—it's not because of its dirtiness that life is ugly, but a cold life is ugly. My mother used to say that the art of living is the art of suffering. My father drank, beat Mother, and was snotty-nosed. Mother meant by the art of living that she had to stand Father's foulness, although she no longer loved him at all. I don't see any sense in having to learn to stand something you can't bear. I don't see any value in that kind of art. I'd rather run head first into a well. I don't want to submit, I want to choose.

MAIJA. How are you going to choose? You said just now that nothing can be done voluntarily, and yet you're going to choose. Go ahead and choose! Are you coming or not? You don't know. Of course you don't know. You're completely lacking in character. A poodle pup has more character than you have.

LASSI. Oh yes. You think I lack character because I'm not *your* poodle. (*Fit of weeping.*) Don't think I'm crying from fear, or disappointment, or bad luck. I'm not even crying from shame. I'm crying from sheer anger. Christ almighty! I hate life, and I love it, I want to get away, and I'm tied to it, like an animal in a trap. I don't want to die! I don't want to die! (*Drums on the window pane.*) D'you know something, life is a hunter. Death is nothing, death is only an empty sack. (*A strong light spreads through the rooms. Lassi imitates Ginsberg.*)

Lost market youth
fainted in the office
wept in the typewriter

Dawn rises. The sun
smokes in the east. O bedroom
I am damned eternally
what alarm clock rings now?

Darkness.

Scene 2

(*Morning three days later. The same room. Helena and Paavo have returned from their trip.*)

PAAVO. (*Yawns.*) Hoo-o-ohh. I feel so damned tired.

HELENA. Go to bed dear.

PAAVO. I thought I'd wait for the morning post.

HELENA. (*By the desk.*) Here's a note from Maija that's she's gone to Kaarina's place for the night. She didn't want to be here alone.

PAAVO. Who's Kaarina?

HELENA. The Sauri's daughter. A classmate. . . . But where's Diana? Puss-puss-puss. (*She fetches the cat from the kitchen, and sits on the sofa with the cat in her lap.*) Mother's little darling. Didn't Maija leave you any food then?

CAT. Meow.

HELENA. Have you been here all alone the whole time?

CAT. Meow?

HELENA. (*Kisses the cat's head.*) Do you hear, Paavo, how she answers?

PAAVO. Understanding words from the mouth of an uncomprehending piece of nature.

HELENA. What do you mean, uncomprehending? Don't you believe that animals have understanding?

PAAVO. Oh, of course—instinct's a kind of understanding, more refined than intellect perhaps. But that creature hasn't got any understanding, the breed has deteriorated, she thinks she's human.

HELENA. What do you mean, deteriorated; how do you know?

PAAVO. Wild animals have an expressive language—that fine lady has only six notes and two verses. Wild animals have a social pact, laws, culture of a certain level, skill in civil engineering, architecture—quite complex, too—Diana doesn't have any of those. But she may possibly have a religion—I'm very much afraid she has a religion. And you are her god.

HELENA. What do you mean, you are very much afraid?

PAAVO. Even man started to mold religions when genuine and living magic forsook him and and he no longer knew where the tree of life grew.

HELENA. You always try to be clever when you are drunk or even when you are just tired.

PAAVO. I'm not trying to be clever, I'm serious. People's instincts got confused when they started to live together and no longer found the way to the source of life. . . . But I certainly am tired. Oooh-hoohh. I don't like flying, my ears are still popping.

HELENA. Would you like something, shall I make you some coffee?

PAAVO. Thank you. A cup of coffee wouldn't be a bad idea. (*Helena goes to the kitchen with the cat, Paavo glances through the newspaper, reads the headlines.*) PEACE FEELERS CONTINUE . . . INTENSIFIED BOMBING. COMMUNISM IN CHINA—WHAT IS IT? What is it—what is it—a handful of rice a day, of course. ELK RESCUED FROM THE ICE, BUT STRANGLED BY THE ROPE . . . yes, elk are stupid, we all know that. Good God, what's this: DOG KILLS DOG . . . strange news, have even dogs gone that far? (*He goes on reading the paper.*) I say, here's a nice little verse in the obituaries: "Life is woven wind/ but death is tall, tall grass./ We are half-part grass, half-part wind." Grass, wind, yes, and grass. (*He gets up and switches on the radio, the news, the weather forecast. He listens for a minute, turns it down to a murmur. He begins to leaf through the paper again, dozes off intermittently, and reads on again. Helena brings him a cup of coffee, and puts it in front of him on the table.*)

HELENA. It will wake you up. (*Caresses him briefly.*) Paavo, Pablo, Paul, Porphyrio, Polykarpo.

PAAVO. (*Rouses himself.*) What did you say?

HELENA. Drink darling, so you can wait up for the post. (*She arranges something near the bookshelf. She turns up the radio: Scarlatti Sonata in G-major.*)

(*A déjà-vu scene follows, which Paavo experiences and which is shown as a concrete event to the audience: The door opens by itself; the doorway is flooded with dazzling light. Maija rushes into the room dressed as a little girl, her short skirt flying, her hair in tight plaits on either side of her head. She runs to Paavo, shouts "Father, Father," embraces him quickly and vanishes. The whole scene is very short*)

PAAVO. Maija, my child, my little sweetheart. . . . Where did she go?

HELENA. Who?

PAAVO. Maija!

HELENA. But you know she's not at home. She's at the Sauris's.

PAAVO. But—she was here just now.

HELENA. What are you talking about? You are tired, you are seeing things.

PAAVO. But good God, I *felt* her. She was in my lap.

HELENA. Paavo dear, go to bed now. You can read the post in the afternoon. (*Paavo looks at her closely, but does not answer.*)

HELENA. The morning hours are horrible, when one has not slept all night. I should not be surprised if—

(*Sound of letters being delivered. Helena goes out to the hall and brings in a pile of letters. She puts them on the table in front of Paavo.*

From here on everything begins to slow down. The music from the radio continues: it is now Scarlatti's Sonata in D Major, which suddenly slows down to half speed. The effect can be obtained by playing a 33 r.p.m. record at 16 r.p.m.

(*or a 78 r.p.m. at 33 r.p.m.*). *Helena remains rooted in her place, all of Paavo's movements become excessively slow. Paavo stirs his coffee very, very slowly. Clink. Clink. His wrist describes a circle. He lifts the cup to his lips as if it were very heavy and slowly puts it down again. Everything about him seems heavy and difficult to control as if not only time had slowed down, but the magnetism of the earth had increased. Then he takes a big pair of scissors, opens them inch by inch, and begins to cut open one of the envelopes. He takes out the letter, slowly, with a delayed movement. The strange atmosphere is broken by the sharp ringing of the telephone. When the following Scarlatti Sonata, the A Minor, begins, the speed is normal and the room darkens.*)

The End

PAAVO HAAVIKKO

The Superintendent

A play in 15 Scenes

Translated by Philip Binham

Dramatis personae:

The Superintendent, himself, 62
Hildur, his wife, just 60
Rolf and Rudolf, Hildur's two brothers, minor officials in the Customs
Arina, daughter of Hildur's sister, 30, married
Grönqvist, doctor, her husband, 34
Adler, Assistant Superintendent, present for some unaccountable reason, no relation, 40
Kyllikki, unmarried, Arina's youngest sister
Aili, housemaid
and others

The play takes place in 1906 at the official residence of the Superintendent of a mental hospital.

Scene 1

(*The Superintendent enters by a door behind a long table already laid.*)

SUPERINTENDENT. Aili, why have those candles been placed here?

AILI. Your wife ordered that they should be put there.

SUPERINTENDENT. Ordered. I told her that the candles I was given for Christmas should be placed here.

AILI. Yes, of course, but when they're so very—a bit unusual.

SUPERINTENDENT. H'm. The patient who made them, later made a complete recovery.

AILI. If I change them right away.

SUPERINTENDENT. If you please, Aili. Now, is this seating arrangement really a sensible one? What would you say, Aili, would it not be sensible to put my wife's brothers to sit here beneath the chandelier? They suffer from poor sight. There. Then let us take this candelabrum and put it between them. They have a bad habit of whispering to one another while at table.

AILI. Should the candles be changed?

SUPERINTENDENT. Of course, there are seven dozen of them.

AILI. Shall I change them in the chandelier too?

SUPERINTENDENT. Yes, I am almost inclined to say it would be wisest to change them at the same time.

AILI. Very good, I'll change them all then.

Scene 2

(*The Superintendent comes into the kitchen, where there is a flurry of preparations. Three women and Aili.*)

SUPERINTENDENT. I want everything to go as smoothly as possible. After all, this is my wife's birthday. I expect much from this. I have done all I can to ensure that nothing is lacking from this great day, and that my wife's relations, these brothers cannot say that I am a tyrant. They are in the Customs. There is nothing to be ashamed of in that. Is there?

AILI. No. I suppose not.

SUPERINTENDENT. They are great gourmands, these brothers; they are only small men and eat little, but especially if one considers that, they are great gourmands. Is there enough cold fish—the brothers are great ones for eating fish. Roes are their favorite. Quite in character. Two cold fish in jelly.

AILI. Yes. That's right. Or . . . yes, after all. Of course. There they are.

SUPERINTENDENT. Now you have made a mistake, Aili. There is no need to take the fish molds away. Bring them here.

AILI. Here they are.

SUPERINTENDENT. Decorative. Now, let us—do you still have some of the jelly stuff, the liquid, or whatever it is the jelly on the fish is made of? Good. Now Aili, put this smaller mold back here and put the jelly with the big mold on top of the small one. This will make a fish such as has never been seen before. I shall call it the copper fish.

AILI. But the jelly won't keep like that when the mold is taken away. Oh, but it won't be taken away. Yes. No.

Aili looks at the Superintendent for a little while; he watches her without moving, expecting her to understand.

AILI. (*In a colorless voice.*) Very well, I'll do it. I'll do it myself.

Scene 3

(*The visitors begin to arrive: Rolf, Rudolf, Arina, her husband, the doctor and others. The Superintendent and Hildur shake hands with the visitors.*)

SUPERINTENDENT. And it is very nice to see you again, after such a long time, hello, Rolf. How are you keeping now? How's the heart?

(*Rudolf raises his hand to his heart.*)

ROLF. Very well, except that I am Rolf. This is my brother Rudolf here, but you have met before, haven't you?

SUPERINTENDENT. Oh yes, of course, it's you Rudolf. It really is most strange that I do not learn to distinguish between you, although I have met you exactly the same number of times. But let us go in. How did the journey go? And so on. Very nice to see you. Hildur, have I shown sufficient pleasure that your guests have arrived?

HILDUR. And that they all managed to come, how nice it is.

SUPERINTENDENT. And Arina, our young wife, have I now been sufficiently attentive?

ARINA. But uncle, it really isn't for me to say.

SUPERINTENDENT. Arina is so terribly afraid that she is not being noticed all the time.

HILDUR. Don't please. Remember it's my birthday.

SUPERINTENDENT. Yours, and many others'.

ROLF. Yes, many others'.

RUDOLF. There is no one among the people I know at least whose birthday happens to be today.

Scene 4

(*The visitors are in the dining room, waiting to be asked to the table. They talk; the conversation dries up. Rolf tries to think of a subject for conversation. He says sadly:*)

ROLF. I saw a male chaffinch yesterday. Or perhaps it was a curlew.

HILDUR. Well, that was nice, wasn't it?

ROLF. I don't know. I just happened to think of it. I'm no expert about birds. But I like birds.

ADLER. Do you like birds, Miss Kyllikki?

KYLLIKKI. Yes. Yes I like them, I like them very much. I like them.

SUPERINTENDENT. I would say that my most powerful experience with birds was in connection with the bittern. You would not perhaps believe that I have heard it here with my own ears. My wife does not believe it, this lady here, not even so much as to bother to tell me she does not believe it; she is always willing to grant that I have heard the cry of the bittern. It is a powerful sound. Like a ship's foghorn. The origin of the sound is that the bird blows out its breath heavily; huuuh huuuhhhuuuuuuh, like a foghorn; it can be heard for miles over the water, and again huuuhhuuuh; then, sometimes a more muffled hup hup hup when it draws in its breath. It bellowed, no, that is not the right word—and it is no owl hooting in the depths of the forest, this is different, it is meant to be heard, it is like a ship's foghorn. It is as rare a voice as that of a civilized being. Where are they? To whom does it cry? I do not know. They have not been seen except for a single one here and there, and only in quite recent years. I heard it last spring.

HILDUR. If you please. If you please, come to the table.

Scene 5

(*They eat. Hildur has a tray of cheeses in her hand; she passes it along the table over the brothers sitting opposite her halfway down the table.*)

HILDUR. Would you like some cheese, Rolf?

ROLF. No, thank you.

HILDUR. But you used to be so fond of cheese. Do you remember what Mother used to say? Rudolf, will you have some?

RUDOLF. Thank you, no.

HILDUR. Dear, dear, and I bought so much cheese. Who is going to eat it now?

ROLF. Perhaps I will take a little.

HILDUR. Yes, do take some, do please.

ROLF. Thank you. Dr. Grönqvist, won't you take some?

GRÖNQVIST. It's a little cramped here, thank you.

ROLF. Let me hold it for you.

GRÖNQVIST. Thank you.

(*Grönqvist cuts a piece from a cube-shaped pat of butter, which stands separately on the cheese plate. He puts it with his fingers in his mouth.*)

HILDUR. Doctor, good God, Dr. Grönqvist, but that's butter. Oh dear oh dear. It was my fault.

(But without turning his head, with careful slow movements of the mouth, Dr. Grönqvist eats the piece of butter, though his eyes bulge, and only afterwards turns towards Hildur.)

HILDUR. Take a piece of sour bread, please, doctor, this is specially sour. It is just what you need.
GRÖNQVIST. Thank you, but I have already had some bread.

Miss Kyllikki swallows the piece of food in her mouth like an ostrich, then straight-backed, with fine bearing, she puts a hand in front of her mouth. And Dr. Grönqvist continues to eat, with slow, precise hand movements, which nothing can upset. He knows that everybody, impolitely enough, stopped eating, and saw what happened. Only the Superintendent, looking up and seeing, went on eating at once. He nodded briefly, approvingly on seeing Dr. Grönqvist's reaction. The Superintendent notices everything that goes on at the table all the time, his eyes are alive.

GRÖNQVIST. I hope nothing has stung you, Miss Kyllikki, some insect, for example.
KYLLIKKI. Oh no, hiihhhi.
GRÖNQVIST. An experience—for example, if you, Miss Kyllikki, had been suddenly stung by some insect—is special in that according to new experimental research by the Austrian Doctor Swaboda it comes back to mind after regular intervals, for example that you . . . you remember this after forty-eight hours, whether you wish to or not. And that is not all.

Dr. Grönqvist speaks loudly, watching to see how the Superintendent reacts; although he addresses his remarks to Miss Kyllikki, he is really speaking to the Superintendent, who clearly underestimates this Dr. Grönqvist, pretending to take no notice of him. Now the Superintendent stops eating, and listens for a little to what Dr. Grönqvist is saying. Dr. Grönqvist pauses for a while, waiting for a chance to ensure that the Superintendent hears what he has to say. Miss Kyllikki clearly does not understand a word of what Dr. Grönqvist has to say, as can be both seen and heard.

KYLLIKKI. I have often noticed it. It's true.
GRÖNQVIST. I should say that you imagine that you have experienced this phenomenon which I just mentioned to you, but you have not noticed it.
KYLLIKKI. Oh yes I have. Was it me it stung, or you?
GRÖNQVIST. It did not sting. You imagined that immediately. You are probably susceptible to hypnosis.
KYLLIKKI. Hypnotize me a bit.
GRÖNQVIST. This whole theory has only just recently been revealed to the scientific world. You would hardly have heard of it. I should not have thought so, at any rate.
ROLF. And that puts *you* in your place.
KYLLIKKI. I haven't been put in my place.
GRÖNQVIST. The question is not who is right, the only question that interests me is what is right. I should say that this theory as theory is both absolute, logical, and always true. Doctor Swaboda examined a female person, a young female

person, who had been stung by an insect, and discovered that the pain caused by the sting was renewed after exactly twenty-three hours just as severely as at the moment when she was stung twenty-three hours earlier.

HILDUR. That's really absolutely terrible.

ADLER. Fortunately it is not true.

GRÖNQVIST. I should like to say that I have tested it myself and it is . . .

ADLER. I should like to say that this theory, if it is a theory, is unpleasant, absurd, and narrow-minded.

GRÖNQVIST. . . . inasmuch as other matters do not come back to mind at such short intervals, and the theory holds good in these matters, also. Doctor Swaboda has remarked that these long intervals are of different lengths for the different sexes, I mean for men and for women, for men twenty-three days, for women twenty-eight days. And this theory that is based on the fact that matters return to mind independently of the will when a certain time has passed, would explain rather ingeniously the fluctuations of good and bad temper for which it is otherwise very difficult to discover any sensible reason.

ADLER. I should like to say that this theory, besides being unpleasant, absurd, and narrow-minded, is also unscientific.

GRÖNQVIST. I should like to say that we are not perhaps competent to judge the scientific integrity of Doctor Swaboda.

SUPERINTENDENT. Young friends. I should like to say that this profession demands above all complete self-control. One must first learn to control oneself. Many are afraid of appearing ridiculous; the young nerve specialist is particularly prone to this fear. The fear must be admitted. One should learn to control oneself in every situation. I should no doubt criticize this young relation of mine, or rather he is not my relation, he is the husband of my wife's sister's daughter, as you all know very well, quite, but in any case his complete ability to control himself just now when he cut with a knife from the cheese plate a piece of cold hard butter that looked like cheese, and although he was told that good God, doctor, that's butter, before he had time to push it in his mouth, without interrupting the movement of his hand, without a flicker of expression, he put the piece of butter, which had just turned from cheese to butter in his hand, into his mouth, ate it for what it was—perhaps it was cheese according to his theory of sensory physiology, I don't know, since he had first apprehended it as cheese. Admirable. But I do not believe that anyone other than a specialist would in fact be able to appreciate how admirable, and why.

Scene 6

(*The candles are burning. From the chandelier above drips tallow on the shoulders and hair of the brothers, Rolf and Rudolf. They try to move, but only manage to get closer to one another, and on the table in front of them is the candelabrum, from which tallow begins to drip on their hands and plates. They scrape and push it away with knives. Hildur tries to give signs, and coughs, to tell them to move, but glances then at her husband, and after that gives no more signs. The Superintendent and Hildur are sitting side by side almost opposite the brothers.*)

Scene 7

SUPERINTENDENT. You always tell of me that I ordered my wife, this relation of yours, this sister or aunt of yours, or the aunt of the wife of this young man, my colleague, to get up on top of a clothes cupboard. As far as I have heard, the story is that the cupboard wobbled here and there, with my wife up there in mortal agony. This is not true. It is an example of the uncritical attitude that is so characteristic of you. Naiveté, which in itself is, of course, sympathetic, childlike. The truth is that when I had heard for a sufficiently long time the person already described, my wife, your relative, talk about mice and shrews, I said that if a person finds something so frightening, something must be done, some action must be taken. Otherwise it is only hysteria, and incurable. I do not blame her for it. But a person must have some sense. This is the background of the matter. And that cupboard was not a linen cupboard, it was a sideboard, that sideboard which you can see there—try it, does it wobble even when I climb on top of it myself? It was in no danger of falling at all. I am afraid of confined places. She is afraid of little mice. That's how it is. They are definite facts.

Scene 8

(They eat. The Superintendent has watched while the fish is passed round the table. He passes the metal fish across the table between the brothers.)

SUPERINTENDENT. And now, good friends, do not let the fish swim past you.
ROLF. Fish is really my favorite.
SUPERINTENDENT. I know that. I know it is your favorite.
RUDOLF. So it is.

(The handling of the fish follows. The brothers, first watching for the other to take first, try to take a piece of the fish, but it is of metal. They stop trying for a moment, glance round to make sure no one has noticed, look at their empty hands, move their fingers to make sure there is nothing wrong with them. Then they try the knife, to see if it is sharp, the fork, all the cutlery they have before them. In the end it is no longer a question of manners, it is a question of a struggle against an overwhelmingly unpropitious fate that has come before them in the shape of the unlucky fish.)

ROLF. . . . I . . . don't somehow . . . feel quite well . . . what about you?
RUDOLF. I don't know.

(They give up. Neurosis: they no longer eat anything, they let the roast go by. They dare not try anything any more, although the meal goes on. Foods come and go.)

Scene 9

(This is Dr. Adler, the Assistant Superintendent's scene.)

ADLER. He is the devil himself. I am his assistant, although, as he says, it is the other way round, I am not his assistant, because he gets no help from me—on the contrary, he is my assistant, he says. Well, in any case, once when he left the hospital, he told me to get into his sledge. I refused, I do not want to continue my working time at the cost of my private life. He became angry, as it appeared, when I had walked a short distance. At the last moment I managed to jump out of the way, still in sight of my patients, and found myself up to my navel in snow in the ditch, and all this only because, as he said, he had decided to test my speed of reaction, and therefore ordered the driver to drive along the road where I was walking straight towards me. When I demanded an explanation, he said that if I had not reacted quickly enough, I would certainly not be suitable for this work. Someone else might indeed have reacted at once when I told him to come with me in the sledge, he said then. But I wanted to get some fresh air, I said. I meant a great deal by that. He's the devil himself. Listen. But he's a damned good doctor.

Scene 10

SUPERINTENDENT. My wife, she is afraid of mice; I, I am afraid of confined spaces. Her family has weak nerves on her mother's side. I remember clearly how my wife's mother on my wife's birthday ten years ago sat there; there where brother Rudolf, my wife's brother, is sitting now, their mother sat and began to be paralyzed while she was eating. She behaved foolishly. Instead of telling me that she was beginning to be paralyzed, she began to beat her knees with her hands and shout. She behaved as if she were out of her mind, I mean inappropriately. Since I was sitting here at the same table, she could very well have told me about it without raising her voice. Although she had here someone, myself, to whom she would have gone as far as Wurttemberg, if there had been anyone there as famous, and although it would have been sufficient for her to speak in a normal voice—even a whisper would have been sufficient, she shouted. I therefore had to give first the kind of treatment for one who cannot control himself, a piece of sugar and a severe, loud voice, authority. Only then can one make a diagnosis. And that was clear immediately. Things soon quieted down after that.

Scene 11

SUPERINTENDENT. And you who consider yourselves such nice people, you brothers and sisters who when you were young thought you could converse, in other words, jump from one subject to another like little girls with their skirts around their ears—you sit there now as quiet as mice. The young ones cannot even sound as if they enjoyed life. I believe it is inherited through my wife's mother, and yours, dear brothers, your mother and your grandmother, young Mrs. Grönqvist, from her father, who was, as I suppose you know, a senator, whereas my wife's father, your father, dear brothers, was only a clergyman. The most important thing is the diagnosis, and choice of treatment. For you, dear brothers, I would prescribe for a weakness of power of observation, which has, I presume, become sufficiently apparent; yes, for that I prescribe for you butter. Butter, and sugar. In the form of pastries. Two pastries every day before meals. We had here a patient, a girl, who thought she could not move. I let my assistant, or rather it is wrong to say that he is my assistant—I get no help from him, he gets help from me, it is I who am his assistant—yes, he got this girl with his treatment into a pretty bad state. Then in November I said one day now we will take her, this girl, for a walk, every day, out-of-doors for twenty minutes or so. This assistant of mine stared at me as if I were crazy, and started to read all the pages he had concocted about the girl. I had the girl carried outside, in her nightgown, and ordered them to raise her to a standing position in the courtyard. When she felt—it was November, you see—the hard cold frozen ground under her feet, she lifted first one foot, then the other, there was a need to move, well, you could in fact call it walking. At first she had to be supported, but after a week she was already asking for some more clothes to put on when they started to take her out; first she wanted stockings and shoes, although up to then she had behaved as if such things had not been even invented yet, and in December she asked for a coat, too. In spring she left, completely recovered. In autumn she came back here again, of course.

Scene 12

(*They have finished eating, and have started to drink coffee. Dr. Grönqvist, his wife Arina, Kyllikki, Rolf, and Rudolf in one group, looking round furtively.*)

GRÖNQVIST. Let us talk about the matter casually, so that we do not ourselves unnecessarily make him feel the matter is awkward.
ROLF. It's been tried.
RUDOLPH. Twenty years.
ROLF. That's not enough.
GRÖNQVIST. And you can say that as though it were nothing.
ARINA. I say we should go straight to the point, appeal to sense.
GRÖNQVIST. One could just as well appeal to good manners. He has neither. We saw that just now.
ROLF. Quieter, quieter.
ARINA. Do something now, you men.
GRÖNQVIST. I, as your husband, say that either you let me look after this matter alone or you look after it yourself.

KYLLIKKI. Supposing I try to talk to him first—just something silly.

ARINA. You keep out of this.

KYLLIKKI. It's just as much my business as yours. Half mine.

GRÖNQVIST. If your grandfather's estate had been divided in time, there would be none of these difficulties.

ARINA. Would be, would be, if and if, all you men are the same. You and your theory!

ROLF. Now, now, dear girl, it might be worse you know.

ARINA. What do you mean, worse?

ROLF. For example, we might all be dead already.

ARINA. What are you talking about again, Uncle?

(Kyllikki has separated from the rest of the group; she goes to the Superintendent, who is talking to Dr. Adler.)

KYLLIKKI. You are very lively, Uncle, for someone who looks so tired. I'm sure we've been an awful lot of trouble.

SUPERINTENDENT. Trouble did you say?—on the contrary. But what kind of uncle am I?—Hildur, my wife is your aunt it is true, but I am no uncle.

KYLLIKKI. But Uncle, I can call you Uncle can't I?

SUPERINTENDENT. Oh, very good, you may.

KYLLIKKI. When are you going to have your holiday this year, Uncle?

SUPERINTENDENT. Holiday, I, how could I have a holiday in a world that is full of madmen?

KYLLIKKI. Oh, what a shame.

(Dr. Grönqvist and his wife have together, side by side, come in front of the Superintendent while he is talking to Kyllikki. Miss Kyllikki goes away. The Superintendent signals to Dr. Adler, who is the outsider, tactful, always ready to stand aside. Dr. Adler comes closer.)

SUPERINTENDENT. I invited her here for your sake. She is still a quite unmarried young girl.

ADLER. I will try to be interested.

ARINA. Now what are you trying to arrange, Uncle—now, now, Uncle.

SUPERINTENDENT. Uncle. Uncle. Who? I?

ARINA. But Uncle dear.

SUPERINTENDENT. I understand that you wish to speak to me about some matter. All of you, including my wife, have the habit of circumlocution, which is not always healthy. It hurts me that you consider me so difficult a person that you have to invent opening phrases and explications like a schoolgirl writing an essay on "My country 'tis of thee. . . ." Say what you have to say. You start hemming and humming—no, one should say hemming and hawing—I remember well my wife's father, who was only a clergyman, though my wife's mother's father was a senator, as no doubt you know.

ARINA. Yes, but. . . .

GRÖNQVIST. If only you would listen for a moment.

SUPERINTENDENT. Hildur's father said to me, this clergyman, when I spoke to him about my career, Hildur's and my future life, that trees do not grow to the sky. That is a proverb. Your family has a penchant for proverbs, which indicates a certain stereotyped quality. You speak in clichés. When I say something it is always to the point. But I decided, let us see whether they grow or not. That forest has now been growing for nearly one hundred twenty years. He was afraid that I would waste that forest on my studies, that part of it which would come to Hildur after her father's death. Which in fact occurred quite soon. As you perhaps know.

GRÖNQVIST. I have heard about it.

SUPERINTENDENT. Ah, good. I was thinking, in so far as it depends on me, I want to see whether the trees will not grow to the sky after all if only they are allowed to grow.

GRÖNQVIST. But as far as I can understand, even from the silvicultural point of view alone. . . . There is such a lot of talk about that nowadays, is there not?

SUPERINTENDENT. This is not a question of silviculture but of proverbs. When they have grown a couple of hundred years, let us take up the matter again. You are all characterized by this terrible hurry.

GRÖNQVIST. But in sixty years time it's unlikely that. . . .

SUPERINTENDENT. At least I shall no longer exist, and you will be about a hundred years old.

ARINA. But then everything is quite clear.

GRÖNQVIST. What do you mean, my dear?

ARINA. He will agree to sell the forest, or the trees. We shall get the money, it's wonderful.

GRÖNQVIST. On the contrary. He will never sell, nor let his wife put her name to anything. That forest will always just grow.

ARINA. I . . . I. . . .

(Dr. Grönqvist helps his fainting wife Arina out.
The brothers come behind the Superintendent, whispering together. Rolf puts his hand cautiously on the shoulder of the Superintendent, who turns a little and sees him; at the same time Rudolf plucks his coat sleeve from the other side, and the Superintendent turns that way, too, and sees him. The Superintendent's face during this scene begins to take on the expression of a hunted animal. The brothers act almost soundlessly, making clear their intentions by signs. The scene is extremely slow, like a struggle taking place in the dark. First Rolf puts the candelabra he is carrying on the table. One of the candles is alight.)

RUDOLPH. I tried to blow it out but I couldn't. What's wrong with my lips, or is it in my lungs?

ROLF. I tried too.

RUDOLF. Or perhaps it's the heart. That's what it is of course.

SUPERINTENDENT. But my dear friend. . . .

ROLF & RUDOLF. Don't get upset, dear brother, don't get upset . . . how about . . . you . . . you . . . how about you trying to blow out this candle?

SUPERINTENDENT. Blow it out . . . why?

RUDOLF. Don't go.

SUPERINTENDENT. Let me go.

ROLF. . . . try. . . .

SUPERINTENDENT. Don't bring it so near. You're burning me.

RUDOLF. This is a test, a test that shows whether a person is able in any situation to control the movements of his lips, a test that I have invented myself, and though this may seem amateurish, you cannot deny, dear brother, that it has a certain effect. Now, try to concentrate, don't take any notice of us, you won't fall, we will hold you up; tallow, it's tallow, this candle, it won't drip on you, I'll see to that. Now, now, when I say now, then you blow, and it will go out, if your lips are a proper pair. This is a clinical test.

SUPERINTENDENT. Phuhuuuhhuuuu! . . . The candle does not go out, its flame bends, flickers, but does not go out.

(Adler and Grönqvist have come there in time to see this. They watch.)

ADLER. Is this some game?
ROLF. Yes, we often played it as children.

Scene 13

(Dr. Adler, speaking to himself, looking forward as if seeing something. Kyllikki is playing the piano; Dr. Adler speaks at long intervals.)

ADLER. Music. Love. Love. It is associated inevitably with winter. Winter, autumn, the end of October when the trees are bare, and especially the hedges, the grass lying on the ground, from the end of September until the beginning of December, if it's a December without snow, cold enough to make the ground hard—that is the time of my feelings. It is because everything at that time is done by oneself, discovered by oneself, they are not the trees' feelings or the moon's feelings but my own. I am sure of that. When the ground has become hard, one can walk where one wishes, and in some place, even if one has lived there a long time, everything is surprising, the landscape is quite other, it acts in another way, and even if one has lived all one's life somewhere, one may walk at this time of autumn past some hedge, and see through it. I can't find words. The frozen ground, and the hedges, autumn makes everything open. One does not love one woman, if one does not love two women at the same time. It does not depend on the person. It is for the same reason that all the women I have known best have been of the same type, like sisters. Some side of them has always been the same. It is as if they had had the same father, or, just as well, mother—no, the same father but different mother; if two women really exist, which I strongly doubt. I was going to speak about Dostoievsky. Once, it was years ago, and it was autumn, I was younger, there was a nice girl at the hospital, a nurse, and I wanted to make an end of what had been between us. Or did I? She knew that I had another girl, a woman in the town, and this nurse knew that I was going there. I told her to go out to meet the sledge, for I had ordered it for seven o'clock. It was the end of December. It was snowing. She went out in low shoes, without a coat, waited so long that she fell ill. I remembered all the time that novel of Dostoievsky's where something equally wild happens in a wild storm. I believe it was right that she stood there. I went back and forth that autumn between those two women. Memories like these are like some kind of food that belongs to that time of year.

Scene 14

(Hildur points to sweets. There are many kinds. She goes to Rolf.)

HILDUR. Rolf dear, are you tired? You have to work hard there in the Board of Customs. Oh yes, I know. You don't need to tell me. I bought so many kinds of sweets. You always used to like chocolate so much as a child. Do you remember? Always when we were given some chocolate, you didn't just eat it at once, you saved it. He who saves today, has tomorrow, that's quite true. I've always tried to save in many things, too. And then you ate all the chocolate, there must have been a kilo of it, all at once. And how ill you were then.

ROLF. Thank you, but I don't suppose I've put a piece of chocolate in my mouth for twenty years or more.

HILDUR. No, but Rolf, you've always liked chocolate.

ROLF. As a child, I dare say I ate it like all the others.

HILDUR. More than others, really you did; I remember it just as if it were yesterday. Yes, when we were children. Rudolf, *you'll* have some won't you?

RUDOLF. But Hildur dear, I've already had some.

HILDUR. You are tired too, when you yawn like that. You have to work very hard too, and you have so much work—oh yes, I know.

RUDOLF. It's not that so much, but it's as if one can't say anything any more, as if everything had been said already.

HILDUR. Quite, quite. But now we must play something, just like in the old days.

Scene 15

(The Superintendent is alone. It is late in the evening. The remains of the birthday have almost all been cleared away. Aili is moving about in the room. She begins to put out the candles.)

SUPERINTENDENT. I shall go to bed soon, too. That's right, Aili, you can put them out. I have met in my lifetime only very few, perhaps a dozen, perhaps not even that, cultured people. Good that that does not happen more often. Sometimes it may be years. It always makes one feel gloomy, sad. Luckily it does not happen often, with cultured people one does not feel like saying much, what is the good of telling someone what he knows everything about already. After all, it is very simple, this life. Birth and death. The same feeling comes when one sees after several years a nice animal, as I saw a couple of days ago a hedgehog. I had thought they had completely rejected this hospital area. A cultured person resembles in some ways a dumb animal. It is difficult for him to say anything. Perhaps, after all, that is hardly a sign of mental disorder. Good night.

(The lights are dimmed.)

Swedish-Language Drama

WALENTIN CHORELL

Cats

A Play in Three Acts

Translated by Philip Binham

Dramatis personae:

> *Anna*
> *Ingrid*
> *Magda*
> *Martha*
> *Flora*
> *Greta*
> *Irma*
> *Xenia*

Place: Women's Room
Time: Present; Fall

STAGE SETTING *The women's room, the dressing room for the women workers in Department Three of a factory, the room where they also eat at mealtimes. In*

335

the background are tall cupboards, where they hang their clothes when they put on their factory overalls in the morning. To the right, a small glass booth for the cleaner-cum-caretaker (Anna), and a time clock by the door opening onto the yard. The walls are tiled; there are two white doors, behind which are the shower room and the toilet. Between the doors is a tall mirror. To the left, a steel door, through which the women go to the factory hall. Near it, an old iron bedstead, some stools, a round table. The women usually gather near the bed and table, when they have time. Over the door to the factory hall is a big white clock. When the play begins, the time is 6:30 A.M.

Everything is worn and ugly—the working overalls, too. They are like a uniform—and there's nothing the women can do about it. They are like a brand—and thus humiliating. On the other hand, they help the women to forget the cares awaiting them outside the door. The women wait till the last minute before they change into the overalls; they run about half-dressed—they want to avoid putting on these ugly clothes for as long as possible.

ACT I

Scene 1

(*Just before the curtain rises, a shrill whistle announces that a new work day has begun.*

The curtain rises, and before us is the empty women's room. Nobody has arrived yet except Anna, who is sitting in her place—an old, cynical worker who looks after the women's room and is the doorkeeper. She is sitting on a stool in front of her booth, reading the newspaper, her spectacles perched on her nose. Her jaws chew up and down all the time—she can't help it, she likes chewing gum.

After a moment, Ingrid enters. She is in a factory and a city for the first time; you can see it clearly from her dress. Everything she does in the first hour expresses a touching sense of insecurity.)

INGRID. (*Enters cautiously, hesitates, stops by the time clock, which she doesn't know how to use, looks at Anna. Speaks to Anna, who does not hear at first.*) Good morning. . . . Good morning.
ANNA. Eh? Oh yeah. The new girl. Hi. What's your name?
INGRID. Larsson. Ingrid Larsson. I seem to have come too early.
ANNA. That don't matter. Got yourself a card? Lemme show you. Push it in here and pull it out there. Ain't no more difficult than that.
INGRID. Thank you.
ANNA. 'N' you can call me Anna. Some of them call me Grannie. Not that I care. . . . When you come up from the country?
INGRID. I've been here for a month. My sister is here. Not here in the factory—in the town. Is—is it difficult here? I mean, does it take long to get used to it?
ANNA. Nothing much here to get used to. Just remember that when Mrs. Porsche comes, you'd best behave yourself. She can be dam' difficult sometimes. (*Looks*

carefully at the girl.) And you're young and pretty. Well, you'll learn, in time. Come here, I'll give you your overalls and the key to your cupboard. (*Anna goes into her booth, and brings out overalls and a key, then shows the newcomer her very own cupboard.*) You better change your clothes now. (*Ingrid wants to change in some secluded corner, but is in two minds about it. She glances round shyly.*)

ANNA. (*Looks at Ingrid.*) Oh yes—and there's the shower and the john. But don't you go throwing nothing in the john, 'cause the pipes'll get blocked up. And then you'll have Frieda after you. (*Points inside the door—the boxes aren't visible.*) Them boxes is for that.

INGRID. Is that where we change our clothes?

ANNA. What you want to change them there for? There's nobody here but girls— well, nearly nobody. Well, go on, take your clothes off. Got any gum?

INGRID. (*Shyly does as she's told: she's not used to anyone looking while she's undressing.*) Chewing gum? No, I'm afraid. . . .

ANNA. You can buy me a packet tomorrow then. And at half after eleven you have to treat the whole gang to coffee—all them as works on machines in the same row as yours. That's one of the rules here . . . (*looks at Ingrid's clothes*). You bought them in the town, didn't you? Can't get them in the country, not even nowadays. But ain't you got no rubber boots? Didn't they tell you at the office? Can't go walking around here in them high heels. Just you remember that. Well, I'll lend you a pair.

INGRID. These overalls smell—a bit. . . .

ANNA. Don't you worry about that. They cleans 'em chemically. Here, you're all sweaty. Nervous, ain't you? Well, people is always getting nervous sometimes. You got a man? I mean, you going steady with someone?

INGRID. No . . . well, yes. . . .

ANNA. What, ain't you got no towel neither? They must have gone clean crazy.

INGRID. Should I go in there now—or do I wait here?

ANNA. You just wait till Mrs. Porsche and Frieda comes. They'll tell you what you gotta do. Just you wait here. There'll be a whole bunch of them here soon.

INGRID. I—I have to. . . .

ANNA. You'd ought to do that before you puts them overalls on. Otherwise it's helluva difficult. Well, go on then for God's sake—before anything happens (*Anna laughs at the girl's naivete, but her laugh is sympathetic. Anna sits down in her former place, the newcomer goes to the "shower" and locks the door.*)

ANNA. No (*loudly*). No, No. Don't you lock it. There'll be twenty women wanting to get in there. D'you hear what I say, girl? No need to be shy here. Nobody here but girls. We're all like sisters here. You gotta beat that shyness of yours, or they'll tease you about it. Well, do your business now.

(*There is a short pause, during which the "girls" begin to come into the room. Within a few minutes it is full of workers. They are all individuals even as they enter and wait their turn at the time clock. They still remember everything their leisure time has had to offer them: a movie, a walk with a friend, an experience, a sorrow. Their chatter fills the air. But they are still individuals, and the way they undress and pull their overalls on reflects the type to which each belongs. Some move gracefully, coquettishly, even in this room. Others are tired and stare bitterly ahead. Some talk shrilly, other whisper together. Some greet Anna. One of them has a packet of gum that she throws in the old woman's lap. Others don't even glance at her.*

These women talk dynamically, restlessly: ". . . . I said that four yards would be quite enough, but the fool said I ought to take five. . . . Isaacsons had a birthday party and the neighbors broke all the windows, so they had to call the patrol car there. . . . But I said I wasn't coming out no more, 'cause he got fired again. . . . That man'll never come to anything, mark my word. . . . But anyway, it took four hours, and by then the kid was dead. . . . Morning, Anna. . . . Hi, Grannie. . . .")

XENIA. Anna dear, will you sew this for me. I am always forgetting it.

(One of them—Flora—is obviously pregnant. She won't be coming to work much longer. She enters with conscious deliberation, as if triumphantly.)

FLORA. *(To Anna.)* I was at the clinic yesterday and they listened. Everything's just as it should be. Won't be twins, anyway. Though in my husband's family there's lots of twins.

IRMA. *(Mimics.)* In my husband's family there's lots of drunks. Everything's just as it should be. The cops picked six of 'em up yesterday. Huh—rubbish. . . .

FLORA. Some get children, some don't. Don't you get picking at me, before you get married.

MAGDA. Anna, could you tell Frieda. . . . No, I'll do it myself. *(Magda looks worn, older than the other workers. She has already put her overalls on, and sits down heavily on a stool. She has difficulty in holding back her tears.)*

XENIA. *(Xenia is not Finnish; she has come to the country as a refugee. Her language and pronunciation reveal that she has not been long in the country. She is combing her hair, but stops in the middle to yawn audibly.)* I see a dream last night that I am flying. We stand in an airplane and look down and I say: "Look, there is the church. . . ."

IRMA. Do you know what little Marklund said to the minister? One day they were having one of those evenings, and Marklund went there in a bad mood. They were talking about whores. "Poor suffering women," Marklund said. He said: "Listen, Minister. Don't you know that the number of *professional* prostitutes is going down every year in this city?" The minister said: "Well, that certainly is good news. Has the moral standard really risen so much?"—"No," said Marklund. "The opposite, Minister. Just the opposite, Mr. Minister."

(Some girls go across the stage to the lavatory or the shower room half-dressed. After a minute there is some commotion, as two of them—Flora and someone else—come back bringing Ingrid with them).

IRMA. Flora—have you given birth already? To a full-grown baby?

INGRID. Let me go—please, please let me go.

FLORA. She's new here. Sitting there on the throne crying her heart out. She's scared. Don't be frightened. Oh my God, these kids.

XENIA. Good morning. I am Xenia. We are not at all dangerous. We only speak much so we do not explode. You need a handkerchief. If you have not one, you get mine.

FLORA. The girls in this room are all nice and kind. Their mouths want washing out a bit, that's all. Now, those women in Five are a lot of roughnecks. There was a knife fight there once even.

INGRID. I'm not afraid—it's just I'm not used to it. I expect you understand. (*Indicates Anna.*) She said I ought to wait here—for someone called Frieda and for Mrs. Porsche. Who is—Mrs. Porsche?

(*Her question is followed by a short silence; for some reason no one speaks*).

INGRID. (*Uneasy.*) What's she like, really? Is she mean?

IRMA. Mean. . . . (*Laughs loudly, meaningfully.*) That depends on you. She can be nice, too, if she wants. Real helluva nice. Ask Greta. . . . (*But the others hush her.*)

(*The silence continues, a little frighteningly.*)

XENIA. (*Suddenly shouts vehemently.*) I am afraid from Mrs. Porsche. She walks always alone—she does not talk like—like women talk—proper women.

FLORA. It's just as if near her it's always cold. (Clumsily.) I can't explain it properly—but it's, well it's as if you start shivering when she comes around. . . . I don't like her.

IRMA. (*Roughly.*) We know what it is. . . .

MAGDA. (*Quietly and firmly.*) We don't know anything. (*Reflectively.*) That's right what you say—she's not the same as us. Doesn't ever gossip or laugh. It's as if she had something on her conscience—I guess she has her troubles too. . . . (*To Ingrid.*) She's next to Frieda, the boss, here. But you don't need to be afraid. In a week's time you'll feel as if you've been working along with us all your life.

XENIA. (*Scornfully.*) Queen Porsche. . . . Looks down on us—all of us except Greta.

FLORA. That's right what Magda said—she keeps herself to herself. . . . But Greta has started to get friendly with her. She's been seen. . . .

MAGDA. (*Firmly.*) She tries to be friendly with other people. I know that, anyway. But then—it's as if she doesn't dare. As if—as if she remembered something that happened and was afraid she'd talk about it by accident. And so then she turns her back—and the other person thinks she's hurt her feelings—without any reason.

(*A solemn, strange silence. The women change their clothes slowly, helping each other. Pause.*)

FLORA. We went and changed our books at the library yesterday.

XENIA. I read last night in bed until half past two. . . . The book told about a hat shop. It was written by someone called Cronin. And I cried—goddam it girls. I thought it was so good. . . .

IRMA. One of the girls in Two said you ought to go to the theater. They say the play at the "New" is good. There's a man with a long nose, ugly as sin, but he can talk so all the women are crazy about him. . . . Sigh-rain-o they call him, and then some French name. Burger-rack or something.

MAGDA. (*Slowly.*) I like that—when you can sit in the theater. But I haven't been there many times. Not enough money—not for a new radio, neither. They're always talking about foreign countries on the radio, but ours hasn't worked for six months—so I can't listen no more. . . . It was a cheap and nice way of enjoying yourself. . . .

IRMA. (*Suddenly shouts loudly.*) Anna, Anna. Grannie. Is Greta at work?

(*There is a brief silence, a silence broken however by whispering.*)

ANNA. Her ma come here yesterday at five o'clock, and asked about her, and I told her the truth, that I hadn't seen her since last Saturday. The old girl cried, too.

XENIA. They say—one of my friends said that Greta was at the Theater Restaurant on Sunday. Pretty drunk, too. Singing at the top of her voice when the orchestra played.

IRMA. There's another one who's going down the primrose path. . . . This brassiere don't fit me at all. I've had it on for a couple of days and already it feels tight.

(*Interest in Greta wanes.*)

FLORA. You can get Italian nylons now for about a dollar. They come in last Tuesday.

ANNA. (*She has gone over to Magda, who has been sitting by herself all the time, and says in a low voice.*) What's the matter? You ill?

(*Xenia notices them and draws closer.*)

XENIA. Something gone wrong, Magda?

MAGDA. I'm *that way* again. My God, it's. . . .

XENIA. Don't they never learn nothing in your home? Jesus, girls. Married for more than twenty years, and making a new baby every second year.

MAGDA. The old man doesn't know how to be careful. Or doesn't care. The doctor told him the last time. But he only starting cursing when we got home. "Do you eat your candies with the paper on them?" he said. . . .

FLORA. Is he working these days?

MAGDA. What a chance. He can make babies all right, but he's not strong enough to go to work.

XENIA. It's—it's beastly. He ought to be castrated.

(*Magda's quiet grief is something that unites them all. They crowd, shrill and loud-voiced, round Magda. Then the factory hall door opens, and Mrs. Martha Porsche enters.*

When the girls standing nearby notice her, they are silent, as if afraid. A charged, unbroken silence reigns.)

Scene 2

(*Mrs. Martha Porsche, the female workers' forewoman, is between thirty and forty. She is the only one of the women who does not wear overalls; her dark dress is covered by a white workcoat. She has, as it were, a mask of self-assurance and strength on her face; they all fear her, and she is aware that the girls sense instinctively her tragic secret. She is a very good-looking woman, finer and more cultured than the others—she represents a type of woman that differs strikingly from the others.*

Around her there is silence, emptiness.)

MARTHA. Good morning.

(*In answer, only muttering is heard.*)

MARTHA. Magda, what's the matter with you? If you're ill, you shouldn't come to work.

XENIA. Magda will again get a little one.

IRMA. That happens sometimes to *women*. Has Mrs. Porsche read about that?

FLORA. (*Goes towards the forewoman, pushing her big belly forward.*) There's a new girl here who's come from the country. Who doesn't know what the city can offer. . . .

(*But she has hardly finished before Irma interrupts violently and threateningly.*)

IRMA. Where's Greta? What have you done with Greta?

(*A whole choir speaks now, in a muffled voice but forcibly: "Yes, we want to know. You better tell us now."*)

MARTHA. Greta? Isn't Greta here?

IRMA. Look, now she's gone pale. "Isn't Greta here?" Greta left here on Saturday at half past two, and now it's Thursday. Nobody knows where she is. Usually she goes to your place. Where is she?

MARTHA. (*Struggling.*) She has not been—at my place. . . . (*Sharply and severely.*) If I were you, Irma, I would choose my words a little more carefully. Your work is not of very high quality.

IRMA. Do you remember Lilian? She's in a hospital now. She stayed at your place and went crazy.

FLORA. It's a disgrace for our room if Greta becomes a whore. It's a dreadful disgrace for the whole factory. And if it's your fault, then we'll see you leave this place. Just as sure as I stand here with my child. If something's happened to Greta, then we'll see you get fired.

MARTHA. You asked me where Greta is. You know yourselves what she's been doing. That started last summer. I've let her stay the night a couple of times, when she didn't dare go home. I didn't let her sleep in the street—is that why you're behaving like lunatics? (*Martha's courage is unwavering—the more threatening the others appear, the more erect and assured she is.*)

IRMA. Listen, we know you. We know what you are. Greta's going all to hell just because of you. And Greta's not the first one. Where is she?

(*The women come nearer to Martha.*)

XENIA. There's a lot of ways to get rid of you. For instance, a little accident

can be arranged. You walk in the hall in your white coat so high and mighty
. . . Queen Porsche.

(*During this conversation, the newcomer has followed events motionless and
scared: she doesn't understand what it's all about. Martha walks through the
crowd, who reluctantly give way, and goes to the girl.*)

MARTHA. You must be Ingrid Larsson. We are glad to have you here, Ingrid. You
can start in the sorting department, along with Irma.

FLORA. Ingrid, look at her. Look at her straight back. Look how beautiful she
is. That's what Old Nick looks like—if what I think's right.

(*But now a loud whistle silences them, calling them in to the hall. They
stand for a few seconds motionless and disconcerted: now it's time to go. Now it's
time to start work, or we'll get fired. . . . Martha looks at them without saying
a word, then the first ones begin to go towards the door. The others follow
unwillingly.*

FLORA. All I say is . . . look out for her.

MARTHA. Get to work, Flora—before you lose your job.

(*Flora follows Xenia and Irma. There is a time for hostilities, and a time for
work. Only Ingrid, Anna, and Mrs. Porsche remain. When the women have
disappeared, Mrs. Porsche loses much of her strength. She stands quite still for
a long time and closes her eyes. We hear the machines in the factory hum into
action, one after the other. Their noise becomes louder whenever the hall door
is opened.*)

MARTHA. (*Severely, without color.*) Anna, is it true? Didn't Greta come to work
today?

ANNA. (*Anna's fear of all her superiors is deep-rooted.*) She's not at work, Mrs.
Porsche. The girl's mother. . . .

(*Martha signals for her to be quiet. She goes stiffly and with an absentminded
expression to a stool and sits. Now we notice her irremediable, appalling aloneness. Round her everything is silent: neither Anna nor the newcomer dare to
disturb her.*)

MARTHA. We cannot—we cannot allow her to live in this way. We must call the
police or the welfare board. (*Then she straightens herself and looks at Ingrid.*)
How old are you?

INGRID. I'm. . . . (*Then in a louder voice.*) They know all right in the office. I
filled out all the forms there. I'm old enough for this work—they said so there.

(*They stare at one another for a moment. Then the newcomer averts her gaze.
What she has experienced in the company of her new workmates has frightened
and mystified her.*)

INGRID. I'm eighteen, Mrs. Porsche.

MARTHA. Don't be frightened. (*Vehemently.*) Don't be frightened of me. Call
me Martha. But—this won't do. We can't stand here chattering like girls in a
school yard. But this matter—it's a case of a good friend who's got into great
difficulties. And these others—you heard them. They think it's my fault. (*And
for a few moments she loses her self-control.*) Idiots. Scandalmongers. They
don't know anything. My God, they don't know anything. . . . (*But she pulls
herself together again.*) Anna—make sure you sweep the floor. The girls have
thrown cigarette ends all over the place again. Ingrid, come here.

INGRID. Anna said—that I was to wait for someone called Frieda.

MARTHA. Frieda? Oh yes—Mr. Lindroos. He's there in the hall. Lindroos is the
foreman. The girls call him Frieda.

(*Martha Porsche and Ingrid go into the factory hall. There is silence—a strong contrast to the women's excited and loud-voiced behavior.*)

(*Anna gets off her stool, wanders around picking up cigarette ends. She tries the cupboard doors, too—one of them has been left open by its owner. Anna looks round carefully, then pulls out a dress and hat, looks at them—glances round again—picks up some pieces of clothing left untidily on the floor, goes to the mirror, and tries them on, sniffs at them. She laughs at her reflection. She takes the clothes off and sniffs them again.*)

ANNA. (*Mutters.*) Smells of cat. They're Xenia's. (*Anna goes on with her work quietly, in the hum of the machines, until she notices a woman approaching from the yard. It is Greta—Margareta.*)

Scene 3

(*Margareta is one of the best-looking women in the factory, but is no longer really young—in her thirties. The previous summer she has had a harsh experience, which has completely changed her life. She is off the rails—to some extent. Everything suggests that she is, as it were, waiting for something. She is consumed by an unceasing restlessness, a restlessness that the pangs of conscience aroused by her recent actions make almost unbearable.*

She enters wearily, like one in a dream. She hasn't slept for two nights, has had a good deal to drink, but is no longer drunk. She is only sick to death of everything, herself included. She is carrying two small parcels.)

GRETA. Hi, Anna.

ANNA. No, no, don't you come here. They're asking about you already. Or if you can manage it, change your clothes quick and go on into the factory. You might get away with it. But Frieda knows and so does the Engineer. You've been away a long time, and your mother come here asking about you, too.

GRETA. I've bought myself some new things—I'll take a shower and change my clothes. I can't go anywhere before I get myself clean.

ANNA. And then you'll go, eh? You can't stay here. Go home to your mother. (*Approaches Greta, bursting with curiosity and hunger for scandal.*) Now you've really been living it up, eh? Did you have—sharp boys?

GRETA. One of them was. He had a big car and a six-room apartment. The other was a Jew—circumcised. The third was just—a man.

ANNA. Were you in the bars every evening?

GRETA. (*Answers as Anna wishes. We're not sure whether she's speaking the truth. She goes farther into the room, listens to the machines, and looks at Xenia's open cupboard. Doesn't know quite what to do.*) What's that? Oh—oh yes. You bet I was. High life, champagne, big money. I've sinned all right. Just like they tell you in books. Now I ought to throw myself on my little bed and burst into a flood of tears. Do I look pretty awful?

ANNA. You're as white as a sheet, and you've got big black rings round your eyes. And you stink. Oh yes, you look as if you've been through it all, all right. They asked Porsche about you. "You seen Greta? It's all your fault." There was nearly a revolution here. No—don't you go laying down there. You can't do that here, Greta. Anyone might come in here; Greta, get up.

GRETA. Got a cigarette? No, I'll go home right away. I'll just take a shower first. I've bought myself new panties and brassiere and blouse. The old ones look terrible—now. I've still got some money, too. Anna, I'm a whore—I let them have it for money.

ANNA. Don't talk about that no more. Don't talk about nothing. Go and wash yourself and go home to your mother and sleep. I don't know whether you'll be able to keep your job. Come on, get up. . . .

GRETA. I ought to cry now. Go away, Anna. I'll get up when I feel like it. Let Frieda and the Engineer come—or anyone else for that matter. They can't do anything to me any more. (*With sudden concern.*) They can't do anything to me any more. . . .

ANNA. (*Scared.*) Don't look like that. Get up from there and come with me. I'll help you. Don't you see—they can call the police and report you. You'll be on their books and be put on probation.

GRETA. Go and bring Martha here. Go and tell Martha I've come.

ANNA. I don't dare. Now, do as you're told.

GRETA. Please. I'll pay you. Go and tell Martha Porsche: Margareta's come and wants to talk to you. She's white as a sheet and she stinks. Ask Mrs. Porsche, can I go and sleep in her little white room. (*But the atmosphere of disaster breaks out in a sudden cry:*) Go away. Don't stand there like an old fool. I don't want you to look at me. You remind me of my mother. . . .

ANNA. Don't shout. Do you want something? Shall I get you a drop of water? And I've got some medicine, too. Have to always have it here—that's the rule.

GRETA. (*Gets up from the bed.*) Don't worry. I'm just going to do what I said I would: have a wash, then get out of here. (*Reflectively.*) In other words: I can't be ashamed any more. I don't have a conscience any more—only a little pain in my heart. (*Stands in the middle of the floor, staggers, and shrugs her shoulders.*) I'll just have a look round the place once more. The girls were—good to me in their way.

ANNA. Flora won't be coming much longer. She's only got a couple of days more here. and Magda's in the family way again, too. (*Goes ahead to open the shower-room door.*) Go and get washed up. I'll give you a new piece of soap. And I'll give you some medicine, too.

GRETA. (*Approaches Anna and the door, but when Anna mechanically offers her a helping hand, shouts:*) Don't touch me!

(*Greta has almost reached the shower-room door, when the hum of the machines suddenly grows louder. Both turn from long usage towards the factory-hall door.*

Mrs. Martha Porsche enters.

Anna shouts in her fright and looks at Martha and Greta for a minute. Then she hurries off surprisingly quickly to her booth. There she bends down over her needlework.)

Scene 4

(*The two women stare at one another, wordless, motionless, for a moment.*

We can perhaps sense that in some way they feel bound to each other. They need affection, protection, understanding—they have never had enough of these.)

GRETA. (*Tries to laugh—manages a dismal imitation.*) Good morning Mrs. Porsche. I have just come from my lover. That is why I am pale and a little sick.

MARTHA. I've been searching for you.

GRETA. I can hide myself well—if I choose.

MARTHA. Why didn't you come to me?

GRETA. I didn't need to. I found people who looked after me all right. Perhaps I didn't want that myself, though.

MARTHA. Your mother knows already—you are ill. You can't go on this way.

GRETA. (*Her mood reaches a climax, and she bursts out—vehemently and hopelessly:*) Mother. We don't even talk the same language any more. Mother can't understand me. I'm an adult. I do as I please. And you—Queen Porsche, I don't want to know anything more about you—not a single thing. (*Quickly.*) I'll go home at four o'clock. I'll go into those pretty little rooms where everything is white and rose pink. I'll warm up some food for myself in the clean little kitchen and drink a cup of coffee while I listen to the radio. I'll wash myself in my shining bathroom and look at myself in the mirror, and see my clean white, smooth body. I'll caress the soft hairs that have always been spotless. I'll go to sleep in my cool, white bed and see clean, cool dreams. (*Hysterically.*) I'll keep myself clean and neat and pray to God that I'll become the supervisor of the seventh machineroom.

MARTHA. Why do you mock me?

GRETA. I don't care for men. No gorilla shall play with my body—do me harm. . . .

MARTHA. You've talked to the girls about Lilian. And now they think it's all my fault—that you're doing what you're doing because of me.

GRETA. I'll never have a child to suck at my breasts. . . . Martha, maybe I am now in a blessed state. One of them made me pregnant. Shall we wait for our little one in your white room?

MARTHA. I thought you were my friend.

GRETA. You helped me. Yes, you really helped me. Last summer. That was a wonderful July, when everything was at its best.

MARTHA. I've talked with the Engineer—you can come back, after you've had a real rest.

GRETA. Yes, you help me. You are complete in every way. You know everything. You are a good friend and have never done me any harm. You have never made improper approaches, never whispered dangerous things into ears bruised with kisses. Perhaps you haven't even caressed me—except as a mother or an older sister. You are white and straight and beautiful. But you aren't strong like a gorilla. You can't do to me what a gorilla can.

MARTHA. (*Painfully.*) You hate me now.

GRETA. (*Excites herself to a kind of unhealthy ecstasy.*) I don't hate you, but I don't want to know any more about you. Go to some other girl in the factory, and leave me in peace. There are more attractive girls than me there.

MARTHA. (*For the first time hurt and unhappy.*) Greta—poor little Greta. (*Almost screams.*) You know it isn't true. You lied to them about Lilian and me.

GRETA. Go home. Go away. Go and hide in your garden where not one wild animal creeps. I hate your beauty. I hate your white skin. I hate your coldness, your calmness. Let me go my own way. That way I'll make it. (*But then her mood changes, she becomes what she at bottom really is: an immature woman—a stubborn, sick child, on the brink of a mental breakdown.*) No. Help me. Sing to me. Protect me. Promise to take me away from here—from this factory and from my mother, from the city and from men. No, not from all men. (*Screams.*) Come. Come to me. Say that you love me. You can kiss me. Don't you dare to come closer. Is Mrs. Porsche afraid?

MARTHA. Greta—poor sick child. . . .

GRETA. (*In the sway of pain and her own unhappiness, her desire to wound and do harm becomes almost unnaturally sadistic.*) Look at her. Look, Anna. Anna, look how restless her hands are. Now she's coming nearer. (*Laughs loudly, hysterically. When Martha stops, Greta advances. When Martha comes nearer, Greta retreats. A horrible, bitter game is being played on the stage.*) Take me. Leave me be. Take me. Leave me be. (*Greta laughs all the time, an unrestrained unhealthy laugh.*)

MARTHA. Greta—Stop it! You're ill. Stop it. *Stop it.*

(*As Martha catches hold of Greta to quieten her, Greta slaps her painfully across the mouth.*)

GRETA. Don't touch me. (*Shocked at what she's done.*) No, no—I shouldn't have done that. I'm sorry. Please forgive me.

MARTHA. (*Retreats from Greta.*) Little fool. Don't you realize, you need help. If I leave you to go your own way, before long you'll be a broken, sick street-girl.

GRETA. (*Again her mood changes. She straightens herself and looks for a long time at the woman before her.*) Did I tell you, Mrs. Porsche? I just came from my lovers. And I can go back to them. (*Turns her back and crosses the stage to the shower room.*)

MARTHA. Greta—you will be alone—so alone (*Reflectively.*) You will be so alone. (*Stands motionless for a moment. Presses her hands together. She has difficulty in regaining her normal composure and hard-won assurance. Shouts.*) Anna. Anna.

ANNA. (*Creeps cautiously out of her booth. Snuffs the air, chews gum, says with slavish humility.*) Was there something you wanted, Mrs. Porsche?

MARTHA. I'm sure you won't say anything about this, Anna. About Greta hitting me. She is ill. She doesn't know what she's doing.

ANNA. Just whatever you say, Mrs. Porsche. I haven't seen or heard anything.

MARTHA. We must help her. We. . . . (*But Martha stops speaking in the face of Anna's stare. She turns her back and stands motionless. Then she goes back into the factory hall.*)

ANNA. (*Curtseys to the door. Curtseys again.*) Just whatever you say, Mrs. Porsche. (*Then she shuffles over to the shower-room door, looks there, looks at the door where Martha has gone out. Then, with indescribable contempt, she snaps.* Cats—goddam—cats.

Darkness gradually envelops the stage.

Scene 5

(In the darkness the factory whistle sounds again—the lunchhour begins. The hum of the machines dies down gradually. As the lighting grows stronger, we notice that Greta is sleeping on the bed by the factory-hall door. She sleeps deeply like a child, her knees drawn up. Anna is bowed over her: she is listening to Greta's breathing. Anna examines Greta's purse and puts it on top of a heap of light clothes—Greta has taken them off. When the doors open and the girls, chattering noisily, come in for their lunchhour, Anna stands in their way—says "Ssh" and shows by gestures that "someone's sleeping here.")

MAGDA. What's up with you? I'll have to get myself a higher stool tomorrow. I'm half-dead already, and only half the day gone. Whatever you waving your arms about for? Girls, look. . . . Look. Greta's sleeping here like a kid, with her knees drawn up. . . .

IRMA. Greta? . . . So it is. Where's she come from? You mean we always ought to lie down straight, on our backs?

ANNA. *(Full of excitement.)* She come here, and looked like—*you know.* Fought with Porsche. I give her some medicine, and she lay down. "I'm finished," she said. "Everything's finished," she said. She hit Porsche. I saw.

(During these remarks and those that follow, women workers are coming in through the door. Some hurry to their cupboards and change their clothes, perhaps to do some shopping during the lunchhour. The others spend their leisure moments each in her own fashion. They take out thermos flasks and lunch packs, group together round the stools and the table—tactfully keeping a little away from Greta—some take out their knitting and so on. There are coffee cups on the table—Anna has made coffee and pours it out.)

ANNA. I didn't dare listen to everything, but when Porsche went near Greta, she hit her. Like this. Then she went for a shower and changed her clothes.

(Ingrid comes into the room also—cautiously, not knowing how to behave. She sits down at a little distance from the others.)

FLORA. If Martha's to blame for the way Greta's been carrying on—well, I'm going to speak to Frieda and the Engineer.

XENIA. You are not afraid no more, no? You lift your belly up, then nobody dare to say or do nothing to you.

FLORA. Do you know what Harry said? "Mother," he said—he calls me Mother now. "If it's a boy, we'll send him to school, to learn." Harry's that sort. He's ambi—er—ambitious.

(Some of the women take off their overalls and sit around in their underclothes. Most of them do something—drink, read novels, mend clothes. Only Magda sits motionless, dumb. What has happened is a greater disaster than anything else.)

IRMA. He's an ambitious old *cock,* is Harry.

XENIA. Harry. Harry. Or John. Or Samuel. Or Prince Philip. When a woman waits her first child, her husband becomes an idol. What Harry has done—he didn't invent that himself. Harry's father knew that trick before him—and your boy, he sure learns it, too.

IRMA. Look at Magda. Hey, you, Magda—ain't you cheering, too? Ain't you going to tell us what your old man said when he heard about it? You don't look as if you're waiting for Santa Claus.

MAGDA. It was so difficult last time. And I can't get anything done, what with the twins. They're at that age when they're up to all kind of tricks. Broke a brewery window and all, and we had to pay for it.

XENIA. Never mind, it'll be all right in the end. We'll have a collection for you, so you can buy something. And you can go on welfare. (*Notices Ingrid.*) And you just sit and listen. You've come to a fine school. This is a general institute of higher learning for married and unmarried women—married and unmarried mothers. Come and have a cup of coffee, and tell us all about yourself. Have you got a boy friend already? . . . Oh, all right, you can sit there in silence if you want.

IRMA. (*She is the most restless of them all, she can't sit still; she is spiteful, too, hurting others because of her own worries. She bows to Flora and taps Flora's stomach.*) Hey, Mr. Director. Are you at home today? (*Jumps out of the way when Flora tried to hit her, staggers over to the bed, and stares at Greta.*) She's all covered in sweat. Forehead's quite wet. How can she sleep through all this row? (*Goes over as if by chance to Xenia. Sits on the floor by Xenia.*) I been waiting for ten days already. But it just don't come.

XENIA. Poor kid. (*Tenderly.*) You poor kid. Have you done anything about it?

IRMA. (*In gloomy defiance.*) Ate mustard and carried rocks. Cleaned the attic and carried things up and down all Sunday, when no one else was at home. Went on carrying so long I just couldn't go on no longer.

XENIA. Have you said anything about it?

IRMA. No—I can't. I can't say anything. The boy's—he's just a kid. We just went dancing. He's learning to play the mandolin. . . .

FLORA. (*Knitting ostentatiously a microscopic blue woolly.*) Could someone hold this wool for me? Anna, bring us a glass of water. Got to take my calcium tablet. It makes the embryo's bones grow, when the expectant mother eats calcium tablets. That's what it says in the book. Then I eats two bananas. Harry says they're good for you.

IRMA. (*Spitefully.*) Oh, why don't you shut your big mouth? Gives me the willies, you always bleating about your Harry. Bananas? What do bananas make grow?

(*But most of the women are respectful of Flora's condition: they let her have the only chair in the room and help her in every way. She is brought a glass of water, and she nods condescendingly.*)

IRMA. (*To Xenia.*) D'you think—have you ever heard that it can come so many days late?

XENIA. I can't tell a lie to you. I have never heard.

IRMA. (*Bounces up, sings loudly, takes a couple of dance steps.*) Taram—tararam, taratam, taratam. Come and dance, Magda. Let's dance a polka, and drive our sorrows away. Now there ain't no boys to mess us about, and there ain't no kids to break their mother's hearts. There's only pretty girls here, white as queens, and fine gentlemen to keep them—I mean keep them company.

FLORA. (*With conscious malice.*) Why should she go on sleeping there? Wake up, girl. We're bursting ourselves with curiosity—we want you to tell us stories about princes and palaces and jazz bands and niggers. (*And Irma dances over to the bed and wakes Greta—shouts.*)

IRMA. Have you been with niggers? The boys say they stink. But that only makes a girl more sexy.

(*Irma's behavior arouses disapproval in most of them. Some try to quieten her.*)

XENIA. Irma, don't you.

FLORA. You don't need to behave like a you-know-what.

(*But it is too late: Greta wakes and rises slowly to a sitting position. She has taken off her dress—Anna has covered her with a blanket. She comes from far away and stares uncomprehending at her workmates, before she realizes where she is. There is silence; all look at Greta.*)

GRETA. (*Draws the blanket round her and says slowly.*) I'm going away. You won't need to look at me any more.

FLORA. No, no—just you lie down there. Just you lie down. We—we're very pleased you came.

GRETA. I've made a pretty bad mess of things.

IRMA. (*Suddenly unhappy and remorseful.*) Greta—I'm sorry. I woke you up. Go to sleep again. D'you want anything. Shall I bring you a cup of coffee?

(*Many of the women hasten to offer gifts to Greta: fruit, some milk, a sandwich.*)

GRETA. (*When Greta sees their kindly attitude, her unhealthily exaggerated desire for sympathy—born of worry and regret—takes practical form. She refuses everything.*) No thank you. Oh, how kind you are. But I must go now. *I don't dare to stay here, in case Martha comes. I'm afraid of Martha.*

FLORA. You don't need to be afraid of anyone while we're here.

XENIA. Anna said—Anna said that you hit her. Did she make the pass at you?

GRETA. (*Wickedly exaggerating, loudly.*) She's a devil. Oh, you know—first Lilian and then me. I can't—I can't tell you what she did. You wouldn't believe it anyway. (*She looks at her workmates for a long time, searchingly, till she has caught everyone's attention.*) I said you'd never believe it. (*Slowly and maliciously.*) I went to her place last Saturday. . . . I was restless, but I didn't want to start drinking. I went to her place at eight o'clock in the evening—I go there now and again—you know that—to borrow books and. . . . And she said. . . . I hadn't had anything to drink. Not much, anyway. I was standing there on the stairs, and I said: "I want to do something bad tonight. I'm afraid of myself. Can I stay here a little while?"

FLORA. And what happened then? What did Martha say? What did she do? (*The moment is unbearably exciting, not one of these simpleminded women thinks for a moment that Greta is acting—that she is offering them only shameful lies.*)

GRETA. She said—I didn't believe my ears when she said. . . . You won't believe it either. She said—beautiful Martha Porsche said: "Yes, you can come in, if you are nice to me." If you are nice to me. You know what she meant. Did you hear, be nice to me.

(*The effect is as Greta intended; her voice is drowned in the general shouts of disgust and horror of the other women.*)

Scene 6

(*The women have risen and gathered round the bed, crouching round Greta They speak with one voice, screaming and shouting spitefully.*)

FLORA. That—that pig.

XENIA. But you didn't go in? Of course not. Anything—but not that. That's crazy.

IRMA. First Lilian and then you. And we just watch with our hands crossed. Porsche can do what she likes—we just shiver and shake when she comes.

MAGDA. (*Raises her voice.*) Greta—is it true, what you've been saying?

IRMA. Look at her. Does she look as if she was lying?

FLORA. What's up with you, Magda? We've heard before that Mrs. Porsche is one of *those*.

MAGDA. Answer me, Greta.

GRETA. Don't stare at me. You know what happened. You know what'll happen to me. I went out and got drunk. I'm—I let the men have what they wanted. . . .

MAGDA. She's not that sort—she's given me money now and then for the children.

IRMA. You don't see things clearly now you're expecting.

FLORA. Irma's right: we just watch, while our mate's treated like that. But it's gone far enough. We'll see that Porsche gets out of here. I'll go and talk to Frieda and the Engineer.

XENIA. We can—drive her away. She gotta leave voluntary. We make her. . . . Put her to stand here in front of us and tell her she is cornered. Greta has proof. Go and bring her here.

GRETA. No—don't do that. I'm afraid.

FLORA. You don't need to be afraid any more. Go and bring her here. Let's drive her away. We'll give her a chance to explain, and then we'll make her get out.

(*And now Flora, fat-bellied Flora, becomes the general of these easily led women. She takes command authoritatively and overwhelmingly.*)

GRETA. (*Shouts, horrified at the effect of her words.*) Let her be. You—you can't do anything to her.

FLORA. Oh, can't we? We're twenty women here, and we know what we want. Don't you be a coward now. We'll help you. Who'll go and get her here? She'll go before the judges now. . . . (*Flora looks at her mates, but they look away. The plan seems rash. Flora notices Ingrid, who has risen and is standing apart from the circle formed by the excited women.*) You—you haven't been with us in anything yet. You don't need to be with us in this, if you don't want. Take your apple and go out in the yard.

INGRID. (*Intends at first to obey, but stops.*) I—I want to be with you. I have to work along with you here, too.

XENIA. Good girl. Here in the Third room we are used to all stick together, though sometimes we quarrel like the cats.

FLORA. You go and bring her here. Otherwise she'll guess there's troubles here. Say that Frieda's waiting at the yard door. He does that sometimes—when he doesn't want to come in 'cause we're running about here half-naked.

MAGDA. (*She is the oldest of them and her life has been more difficult than others'; she now becomes a kind of judge—she is calm and dignified.*) No, no lying. Ingrid, tell her the truth: we want to talk to her abou Greta. She'll come anyway, I know Mrs. Porsche. Has anyone here ever seen her afraid?

(*But their intention—the trial of a perverted sister—puts them into an extremely excited mood. They forget where they are. They are hunters tracking dangerous wild game.*)

IRMA. We won't go to work before that devil's out of here. We'll sit here and won't go in.

XENIA. (*Eagerly, as always.*) Girls—we just sit here on our backsides and the whistle blows: but we don't go in to the work. (*Laughs with unrestrained joy.*) They can call the police or the fire brigade or whatever they like. They can carry us to the machines, but we don't touch them till Queen Porsche is out.

FLORA. (*Like Xenia.*) We'll lock the doors. Ingrid, go and get Porsche.

INGRID. (*Clearly afraid.*) I—I'm not a child any more. I've got a boy friend— back there in the country. We're saving money so we can buy my sister's share of our land. They—they wouldn't fire me, would they?

MAGDA. There's nothing wrong in asking to talk to the forewoman during lunchtime. Go on, you'll be all right.

XENIA. (*Puts her arm round Ingrid.*) You're one of us. You'll be one of us, and we'll collect for a present for your first child. We always do that. It comes dam' expensive, too, when there's thirty women here who do nothing but wrestle in bed with their men.

INGRID. (*Looks at them seriously, proud that she has so quickly been accepted by the crowd.*) I'll do as you want me to. Where is she?

FLORA. Sitting in the last booth in noble solitude. Drinking coffee from a white cup with a gold rim and picking the grease paper from between her sandwiches. You can't mistake her.

(*Ingrid goes.*)

FLORA. (*To the others.*) And we'll stick together, eh? We'll see that Porsche leaves. (*Loud and unanimous agreement.*) And if she won't leave willingly, then we'll sit here so long that Frieda and the Engineer will know all about it. We'll tell them we won't go back to work before she leaves. Do we all agree to that?

MAGDA. We did that once before—remember? Had a sit-down strike. Sat here until Oksa from the machine room was fired. Two days.

FLORA. Sitting don't frighten me. (*Looks round, aware of her strength—a general studying the situation.*) When they come, we'll shut the door after Porsche, otherwise she'll start shouting for help. Leave the key in the door so they can't use the spare key. Anna. . . . Anna. (*Anna, who has been huddled up in her booth, shuffles humbly into the room.*) Have you heard what we been talking about here?

ANNA. Well, you haven't exactly been whispering. How many of you have got a headache and ain't feeling well today?

FLORA. Lock the doors. Close the yard door, leave the key in the lock. Put the iron shutter down, so no one can get in. And make some coffee. Use all the coffee we got here, and give that nerve tonic stuff to anyone who wants it. You afraid of Mrs. Porsche?

ANNA. Yes.

FLORA. If you want, you can go away. Go and have a nice chat with Frieda.

ANNA. I'll take some nerve tonic and cough medicine, then I'll be all right.

FLORA. Don't take too much. Do as I say: lock the doors. And turn the air conditioning on, cause it's going to get hot if we have to sit here for long.

ANNA. (*Peers at them, chewing hard.*) So you believe what that Greta said after all. . . .

GRETA. (*She has risen; she senses trouble ahead.*) What did you say? Are you trying to make out I was lying? (*Bursts out suddenly into noisy weeping.*) Let me out. I don't want to be with you if you don't believe me.

MAGDA. You can't go away. You have to go through with this for everyone's sake. Take some medicine and sit down. Porsche can't threaten you any more.

GRETA. (*Tries to get out: she runs to the door, but Anna has locked it already, Greta swings round, looks at the women. Hopelessly.*) Last summer when—when it all began. . . . She helped me—without asking for anything.

FLORA. (*Tightly.*) Think of Lilian. It was you as told us about that, too. Lilian lived at Porsche's place for two months, and then had to go to the asylum. D'you want to go there too?

GRETA. Let me out, I don't want to be mixed up in this.

MAGDA. You're the witness now. Don't you understand that? Go and sit down and keep quiet. Remember, it was you that started all this.

(*At the same time Mrs. Porsche and Ingrid enter. Ingrid stops by the door, but Mrs. Porsche goes straight towards them. Complete silence.*)

MARTHA. Ingrid said that you wanted to talk to me. What is it?

FLORA. (*Loudly, authoritatively.*) Lock the door, Xenia. (*She does.*) We asked you to come here, because we want to talk to you.

MARTHA. (*When she hears the door close, she starts involuntarily. She retreats from the women—towards the empty wall near the shower-room door.*) Why is the door locked?

XENIA. (*Excitedly, vehemently.*) We will try you, Martha Porsche. We are now the judges. And we can be even the executioners, if we wish.

MARTHA. (*Alarmed at the hostility of the women standing around her.*) What is it? What do you want?

MAGDA. (*She has sat down on a stool near the bed—by the judge's bench, as it were.*) We have evidence against you. Greta has said that you have asked her for something that no proper woman wants from another woman. We are trying you because of Lilian and Greta.

FLORA. (*Threateningly, viciously.*) Now we know what you are—a lover of women.

(There is a brief, intense silence, which Anna interrupts with a sudden out-burst.)
ANNA. Let's have a song, shall we—like in the Salvation Army? Beat the big drum, pom-pom-pom. . . . D'you want a tranquilizer, Martha?

-Curtain-

ACT II

Scene 1

(The play continues from the last lines of the previous act. Anna is standing on a stool.)

ANNA. Pom-pom. . . . "He shall come down. Yea, He shall come down from heaven. . . ."
FLORA. Stop it, Anna. Stop it I say.

(A couple of women quiet Anna down and hustle her back to her booth.)

MAGDA. What have you got to say, Martha Porsche?
MARTHA. *(Stands pressed back against the wall, looks at the women in turn calmly —Anna's interruption has given her time to recover her self-control.)* What are you accusing me of?
MAGDA. Tell her, Greta. Step forward and repeat what you just told us.
FLORA. Don't be afraid. She can't ever do you any more harm.
GRETA. *(Hesitates, comes nearer, shouts.)* I can't. It's so horrible.
MAGDA. You shouldn't just think of yourself now. You must say what we're accusing Martha Porsche of—why we want her to leave this factory.
GRETA. I can't, I can't, I can't.
FLORA. Greta doesn't need to say it again. We're all witnesses to what Greta said. Irma, you heard what Greta said.
IRMA. *(All become a little solemn now, because this matter is strange and rather dangerous. We notice this in Irma. She steps forward, erect and restrained, speaks artificially and with exaggerated care.)* When—when I awoke Greta, she said—she told us that. . . (Quickly.) She looked terrified and said: "I went to Porsche's place on Saturday evening and asked to come in, because I knew that otherwise I would go out drinking somewhere. But Porsche said: "You can come in if you are nice to me. If you do what I ask, you can stay."

(There is a mutter of agreement from the other women.)

MAGDA. Greta didn't say that last sentence, but the first one was right. We all heard it. What have you got to say about that, Martha?

MARTHA. (*Stunned at the lie.*) Did you say that to them, Greta? No, it can't be true.

FLORA. We know it's true. You treated Lilian the same way. Greta told us.

MARTHA. It's an outrageous lie. It's a despicable lie.

MAGDA. Use ordinary people's language, Mrs. Porsche. We haven't been to school for as many years as you have.

XENIA. (*Spitefully.*) What has she got to do with us here? Why a fine lady like her lowers herself to work with ordinary workers?

IRMA. That's easy to understand: this place stinks so much of women that Frieda gets a headache every time he comes here.

MAGDA. Don't talk nonsense. Let's stick to the point. What have you got to say, Martha?

MARTHA. You can't do this to me, Greta, Margareta. I don't know what you did this for, but you know it isn't true. You didn't come to my place on Saturday. You were hiding all these days because you knew I'd make you go home if we met. It's a lie. Margareta, tell these women that you're sick and you lied.

FLORA. Don't yell at her. Speak quieter, 'cause you ain't going to grow much older in this building. We've made up our minds that we won't go to work before you're out. Just so as you know that.

MARTHA. Are you crazy? You can get fired—the whole lot of you. If you start an unauthorized strike, you'll lose your jobs.

MAGDA. That's not true—and you know it. You've been long enough in this place —you know they can't afford to lose twenty women now, when we're soon going to start working two shifts. *You'll* be the one to leave. And we'll make you do it. If you won't leave voluntarily, then we'll report you to Frieda and the Engineer.

MARTHA. You can't prove anything. . . . You just believe Greta's assertions, her word.

MAGDA. Step forward, Margareta Willner. Make your accusation.

GRETA. (*She is in a trancelike state. She speaks like Irma a moment ago, with unconscious solemnity using words that she normally would not.*) I rang the door bell, and she came to open it—she was wearing a black housecoat—and she said. . . . But you heard that already. And she came to the stairs and slipped her hand through my waistband and whispered: "If you are nice to me, you can stay here." (*Screams hysterically.*) She's *one of those.* Last summer she came to my bed. Just ask Lilian. . . .

MARTHA. Why are you lying? You were in bed, crying. You cried all night. Crying like a child about what had happened to you. And Lilian—she was ill. She was what you think I am. . . . Greta, be quiet. You don't know what you're doing any more.

(*But Greta's vehement outburst has set the women off. They threaten in shrill voices.*)

XENIA. Look how she stands there. Look. . . . She can't stand there threatening us. We've heard enough. The—the white cow. (*And half unaware of what she's doing, she takes a partly chewed apple and throws it at Mrs. Porsche.*)

(*The others mechanically follow her example. A whole shower of objects flies through the air. Magda manages to control the situation, she dashes between the women and Martha, spreads her arms, and protects Martha with her body.*)

MAGDA. Stop it! Stop it! She can have you up before the law. Are you gone clean crazy?

(*The powerful figure of their "chairman" brings them back to their senses.*)

FLORA. We're just like a lot of silly kids. Do you think she'd be likely to confess? Let's do what we decided. Magda, you tell her—the decision of the women in Three.

MAGDA. I say clearly and distinctly and in everyday words so that you can understand, Martha Porsche: we want you to leave Room Three and the whole factory. And if you won't leave voluntarily, then we'll go and tell Frieda why we won't go back to work when the next whistle blows. You can have five minutes to think it over. . . . Give her a cigarette and some coffee. . . .

(*During the pause that follows, the whistle summons them back to work.*)

Scene 2

(*The whistle disheartens them for a moment. Silence. A nameless worker laughs, a little shrilly and hysterically.*)

FIRST WORKER. The whistle's blown already. Say, it sure whistled loud today.

MARTHA. (*Approaches them, now sure of herself. Loudly, calmly.*) Go back to your work. (*Pause.*) Did you hear? Go back now. Anna, open the doors. Ingrid, open the doors.

(*But in front of the yard door stands a group of silent women. Ingrid has stopped in front of the factory-hall door. She listens to Martha's words, looks round for help.*)

INGRID. (*Almost giving in.*) I—I suppose I have to do what I'm told, don't I?

(*When Martha goes, straight and calm, towards the door, Flora suddenly steps in front of her. Ingrid stands aside, and Flora stands in front of Martha, pressing herself against the high steel door.*)

FLORA. Use force—against me and my baby. Otherwise you won't get out of here. (*Laughs, seeing Martha hesitate.*) Aren't you going to push me out of the way? Aren't you going to hit me?

(*Flora's boldness is infectious.*)

XENIA. If you touch Flora, you'll be sorry for it.

MAGDA. (*Tired yet firm.*) Make up your mind now, Martha. Go and tell Frieda and the Engineer. You can see we're serious.

MARTHA. (*Her assurance grows again. She goes back from the door and stands in the middle of the stage.*) We haven't come to the end of this yet.

(*We hear indistinctly the machines starting up in the other halls. All stand motionless—all except Anna. She bursts out nervously, but is silenced.*)

ANNA. Soon they'll telephone. The women from Three have gone nuts. . . .
FLORA. (*Shouts hoarsely, shrilly.*) Shut up. Quiet now. (*Puts her ear to the door and listens. She acts as middleman between the outside world and the women's room during the following scene.*) I can hear Frieda's voice. Steps echoing in the room. Now they stopped—started again. Coming to the door. . . . (*Panic stricken.*) What shall I say to him? Have *I* got to speak to him?
MAGDA. Tell him just how things are.

(*The women wait a moment, holding their breath, and then—there is a loud knocking at the door.*)

FLORA. He's trying to open the door.
FIRST WORKER. What's he doing? What's he say?

(*The door is banged harder than before.*)

FLORA. He said. . . . "What the hell?" Now he's shouting. "Hey, girls. The whistle's blown so you must have heard it there, too. Open up. What goddam notion you got in your heads this time?"
IRMA. (*Approaches the door involuntarily—so excited is she—and perhaps for a few moments she forgets that Martha is with them.*) Tell him. Tell Frieda.
FLORA. (*Presses her mouth to the door.*) Stop banging there. You can't get in, anyway. And we're not coming there. We're not coming to work till Mrs. Martha Porsche gets paid off. That's why we're staying here with the door locked. We'll come back when Martha Porsche leaves the factory. . . . Now he's quite quiet. Now he says: "What the hell are you talking about?" He's asking who's speaking. (*Loudly.*) Me here—Flora. (*Listens.*) Yes, that's right, that one: the last one that's expecting. No, we won't open up. Martha's here, and we ain't going to let her go. You gotta promise first.
MAGDA. First she's got to sign a paper. Give notice in writing.
FLORA. (*Through the door.*) Yes, we know that, we know this is an illegal strike. But we don't want Martha here with us. . . . (*Bursts out laughing.*)
XENIA. What did he say? Tell us what he said.
FLORA. He said: "I promise to sleep with you all in turn, if you'll just do as you're told."

(*Scattered laughter: Frieda is a popular man.*)

IRMA. You can just see him saying it. . . . Face red as fire, and scratching his side like this. . . .
FLORA. Don't talk nonsense, otherwise I can't hear what he says. . . . He says he's going to put mice in the air-conditioning vent. (*Shouts triumphantly through the door.*) Do what you like: we're not coming out of here. Not before Martha's

left. Yeah. She's in here now. Alive and kicking. . . . Frieda wants to speak to you, Martha. (*Martha doesn't stir from her place.*) Martha hasn't got anything to say to you. So you can go. You can go and tell the Engineer that the women of Three have all agreed: they won't go back to work before Martha Porsche has left. (*All listen now.*) Now he went away. Heavy his footsteps sound. But that's because the machines ain't running in Three. . . . Well, now it's done, girls. Now Three's on strike. (*Goes towards Martha.*) Now you can see we're serious. We're not working, we're losing wages because of you. Martha Porsche, you gotta leave.

(*The women surround Martha again, threatening and noisy.*)

XENIA. Aren't you afraid? Had we ought to play with you a little? I learned a few tricks before I came here to play on people who can't defend themselves.
MAGDA. (*With authority.*) Leave her alone. Leave her alone. I say. (*To Martha.*) We'll let you out of here; *of course, if you're afraid.* You've heard what we have to say, and you know what you have to do. You're to leave now, before they get men to open those doors.

(*But Martha stands, erect and immovable.*)

GRETA. (*Unrestrainedly.*) Go now. Don't stand there. Say something. Say that you're going.
FLORA. We ought to beat her up. We ought to beat her with wet towels.
MAGDA. Make up your mind now, before it's too late. Otherwise you may have to wait a long time before you see daylight.
MARTHA. (*Goes towards the door, but stops.*) I'm not going anywhere. And I'm not going to give notice. I am innocent of what you accuse me of. What do you think you can do to me? I'm not afraid of you.

(*The phone rings in Anna's booth.*)

FLORA. That's the Engineer there. Frieda's been talking to him already. I—I can't talk to him. I start stuttering soon as I have to talk to the Engineer.
MAGDA. (*Gets up heavily.*) Oh, all right, I'll speak to him. (*The others are silent, as Magda crosses the floor and takes up the receiver.*) Yes—Magda here—Magda Aalto. . . . I'll tell what it's all about: Martha Porsche isn't the kind of woman to be along with proper women. We want her to leave. Till then, we're going to sit here. We're not afraid. You can threaten what you like. But now you know how things are. Goodbye. (*Magda returns; silence continues.*)

Scene 3

MAGDA. (*Goes to the bed, looks at it hesitantly, then lies down.*) Can't do anything except wait and see what they decide to do with us.
IRMA. (*A bit scared.*) What d'you think? Could they block up the air channel?

FLORA. (*Laughs mockingly.*) And murder us all. Silly kid. . . . No, no, they'll make us wait here and won't do anything. They think they'll fix us by just waiting.

The women break up into groups now—preparing to wait. There is silence for a moment. Flora sits in the middle; she looks at her nearest neighbors and talks softly to them. Xenia and Irma sit away from the rest. Magda is stretched out on the bed. The other women are divided into small, quiet groups. At opposite ends of the room, near the walls, Martha and Greta sit alone, silent, uneasy.

MAGDA. Seems queer to be lying on a bed at this time of day, and hear the machines going in the place—queer but nice. (*She laughs, too, now—the women are irresponsible girls being naughty, playing tricks and teasing the mighty adults.*) In the evening they'll bring our old men along. (*Laughs loudly.*) "Ma, we ain't had no soup today. Ma, we got holes in our socks." . . . Ah, let'm wait. Let'm wait now for once in twenty years.

FLORA. Harry'll mo-ber-lize the whole trade union, if I know him. When he hears that we're sitting here, and what we're sitting here for, you can bet he'll make his own department come in on our side. Harry's one of them—one of them—organizators.

IRMA. He's an ole buck-rabbit, I'd say. . . .

XENIA. We sat for three days and nights in a cellar. It was in the war time. I am frightened when it comes dark.

FLORA. We've got the emergency lamps and candles.

FIRST WORKER. It's just like sitting at the bottom of the sea.

IRMA. It's so hot here, too. Sweat dripping down from under your arms. (*Irma is thinking about her own affairs; she is one of the youngest and most restless of them. She can't sit still, she has to get up. She does a few dance steps, hums, notices Ingrid and goes to her.*) What do you think about all this? You're here for the first day and you go on strike straight away. You're a real hundred-percent proletarian. D'you know what a proletarian is? A proletarian is someone who eats real butter every day and can't speak French. . . . What's your boyfriend called? (*Continues her dance, lights a cigarette, and shouts to Anna:*) Anna, you got any coffee? (*Stops near Magda.*) What's it like when you have a baby?

MAGDA. Ask Flora. I've only had seven of 'em—I don't know anything about it. But Flora, Flora's read the books. She knows all about it. Harry reads aloud. . . .

FLORA. (*Magda's mockery hasn't touched her.*) First it's like a pea—safe inside a pertective membrane. The mother has to watch her diet carefully, and mustn't drink or smoke too much.

XENIA. (*Lying lax on the floor like a tired cat.*) In my home country there was one woman that ate coal. She can't help it—so she said. Just took coal from the stove and chewed it. But her baby had a white skin all the same—and weighed ten and three-quarter pounds.

ANNA. (*She has brought coffee again. Fires off her remark so suddenly and loudly that the others start.*) Ought to brush your nipples, or they'll be terrible sore when the kid starts feeding.

(*All laugh at Anna's wisdom—not unkindly, but rather surprised.*)

MAGDA. I didn't know you'd been at this game, too.

ANNA. (*Brusquely.*) Oh, yes—a couple of times. One of 'em's at sea—ain't seen him for thirty years. Yep, I been through it—right from the beginning.

IRMA. Is it true you can't ever forget a child? I mean—there's nothing you love as much as your own kid. Whatever it does, whatever it's like. . . . It's always your own child. . . .

MAGDA. It's a part of you. It's got its food from you, lived in you. Could you say to your own finger, your own breasts: I don't care that much about you. . . ? (*Seriously, beautifully.*) There's nothing in the world like when a child comes, with a tear in his eye, and looks at you and says: Mother—this, that, and the other. I've heard and I've seen seven children like that, and soon there'll be another one, too. But it's worth it. I've had to turn my winter coat three times, and put newspaper in the bottom of my shoes. But it's worth it all the same.

FIRST WORKER. I've never cried like I did then, when it was stillborn. I cried for days, and people said I nearly went crazy. I remember my daughter even now. She was white and lay quite still. You wouldn't believe how white and still that girl was.

IRMA. (*Continues her dance. She's been listening to the others and expressed her solicitude. Now she doesn't want to hear any more. The subject is too near the bone. She stops a little way from Martha and stares at her.*) And what about you then? You call yourself *Mrs.* Porsche. But you can't be a missis— not you. You can't tell us what it feels like to have a baby kicking in your belly. (*The words touch Martha; we see that.*) You can't answer my question. Not you, oh no, oh no. Nor you can't say what it feels like when a man comes to you, and wants. . . .

(*But Irma has gone too far. The others hush her.*)

MAGDA. You got a dirty tongue, girl. You're too young to talk like that.

FLORA. What's the matter with our baby today? Cut it out, can't you? We're too old to want to listen to that kinda stuff.

XENIA. Think what you say. This is the ladies' room.

IRMA. (*Vehemently.*) She just sits there and watches. White and ladylike as a queen. Would you like to see me stripped, eh? Would you like to whisper things in my little ear—run your hands over me?

GRETA. (*Suddenly, loud and shrill.*) Be quiet, Irma. Be quiet. Let her alone.

MAGDA. (*With authority, firmly.*) Stop it, Irma. Go and sit down somewhere or lie down over there in the corner. Stop jumping about like that. *Do as you're told.*

IRMA. Sorry, Magda. I—it's just that—it's hard for me to keep quiet today. I'm used to doing something this time of day—*in there.* (*Points.*)

(*Irma's words make the others restless. There is a pause of several seconds— then the phone rings again. The women look at one another and at Magda.*)

XENIA. That's the Engineer—your friend, Magda.

MAGDA. I'm all right here. Let it ring.

(*None of the women goes to answer the phone. Then Martha gets up, hesitates a moment, and crosses the floor. The women follow her movements intently. Martha goes towards the women who are in front of the booth, and they move*

360

back. She goes to the phone and lifts the receiver. But she replaces it immediately —without saying a word. In silence she returns to her place.)

GRETA. *(She has followed Martha like the others. Now she shouts.)* Why didn't you talk to them? Why didn't you ask for help? Why—why didn't you say you want to give notice?
MARTHA. It's not good for you to sit around with so little on. You might catch cold.
GRETA. Don't you worry about me. Answer. You're going to go away from here. . . .
MARTHA. *(Looks at Greta for a long time—Greta turns away.)* I'm waiting for you to tell them the truth.

(The women oppose this loudly.)

IRMA. Shut your mouth, Martha.
FLORA. You gotta confess.
XENIA. Gag her. Don't listen to her.
GRETA. *(Unrestrainedly.)* I've already told the truth about you.
MAGDA. Be quiet. Try to be quiet now. I was almost asleep. I was in the country, in a boat. We were sitting in the boat, fishing. . . .

(The women quiet down.)

Scene 4

(A long silence follows, then Xenia begins to hum—softly, tenderly.)

IRMA. That's a cradle song, that is—listen. Xenia's singing for our babies.

*(One after another the women join in the song, until the melody fills the room.
Then the lights suddenly go out. In the darkness, shrill cries are heard.)*

XENIA. Don't put the lights out, I'm afraid. Turn the lights on.
FLORA. Anna. Get the emergency lamps and the candles out.

*(But the others sing all the louder in the impenetrable darkness.
A brief pause.)*

Scene 5

(The action continues after some while. The stage is now lit by powerful carbide lamps and many candles in candlesticks. The women are grouped as before.)

XENIA. (*Rises. She is obviously frightened of the closed room. She's still trying to smile, but her smile dies away. She combs her hair, concentrates. Puts on lipsticks, then stops.*) I ought to have a bath. I like that—to be in the shower. I stay there always a long time, real long. Who will come with me? (*Faster and faster and more shrilly.*) The worst was then—then when we were in the camp, when you could never wash yourself. We had fleas. . . . (*Starts undressing with violent movements.*) We were sitting in one of those long barracks, and the doors were always closed. There were only six shallow bowls and more than seventy women. . . . But Porsche must be blindfolded. She mustn't look. (*Screams suddenly.*) I want to get out of here. (*But she rushes towards Martha and catches hold of her.*) There were women like you there, too. We beat one of them up. So the blood ran. *I'm getting out of here now.* (*She suddenly starts to hit Martha, first almost in play, then harder and harder. She says, half laughing, half crying.*) She screamed the whole time—shouted for her mother. . . .

(*The women become restless again. They get up, and some hurry towards Xenia and Martha.*)

GRETA. Let her be. Stop hitting her.
XENIA. So *you* want beating up, eh? All right, you'll get it. . . . (*Goes to Greta and starts hitting her.*)
FLORA. Xenia. What ever are you up to? Don't. . . . That's just crazy, that is.

(*The women get hold of Xenia, but she wrenches herself free, rushes to the yard door and thumps on it hopelessly.*)

XENIA. Let me out. I can't stand it any more. I must have some fresh air to breathe. They are hitting me. They will kill me. I want to get out.
IRMA. (*Runs to Xenia and catches hold of her shoulders—puts her arms round Xenia and consoles her.*) Xenia, don't do that. Don't be afraid. We're your friends, your good friends. . . .
XENIA. (*Still frenzied. Screams out in her fear.*) Can't you hear—they will kill me. Bitte bitte—ich tue was Sie wollen. Bring mir den Himmel, bitte—ach bitte.*

MAGDA. Give her some medicine.

(*Xenia's panic brings Greta suddenly to the center of the stage. She speaks softly at first, hardly audibly, but her voice changes to falsetto, and her words intensify the atmosphere of hysteria. The room is hot, and the women have already been sitting there for hours.*)

GRETA. Let's open the door. Let's go back to the machines. Did you hear what I said? Let's not sit here any longer.
MARTHA. (*Rises and approaches Greta. Greta guesses what is going to happen.*) Not that way, Greta. I don't want it that way.
FLORA. What did you say? Speak so the others can hear.
GRETA. I'm ill. I'm going home now. I can't stay here any longer. I'm going to Frieda to give notice and I'm never coming back.

*Please, please—I'll do whatever you want. Bring me heaven, please—oh, please.

FLORA. You can't leave now. You heard that there's guards at the doors.

MAGDA. (*Coldly.*) What d'you say that for? When you've stood by us for all these hours already.

MARTHA. Greta. (*To the others.*) Let her go. She hasn't slept properly, and you know what she's been doing. Let her go home.

GRETA. (*Almost as hysterically as Xenia a moment ago.*) I want to say one thing. . . . *I want to say to my dear sisters ONE THING.* . . .

MAGDA. Quiet there. What d'you want to tell us?

GRETA. (*Rushes suddenly to Martha and throws herself at the other's feet.*) Forgive me, forgive me. I lied. I've been lying to you. I've never been at Martha's place. She's never done anything to me. And—I lied to you about Lilian, too. . . .

Scene 6

(*Greta's sudden outburst agitates the women. The strained atmosphere reaches its culmination in an unrestrained overflow of their emotions. One old worker begins to laugh convulsively. Anna sings and screams: "Jesus is coming. Jesus is coming today. Are you prepared to meet your Saviour?"*)

IRMA. (*Horrified.*) Look at Greta. She's kissing Martha's feet. She's one of *those,* too. . . . Let's throw them both out.

FLORA. Get up Greta. You're a disgrace to yourself. You're a disgrace to all of us.

MAGDA. Keep away from Greta. We've got to know the truth. We've got to know the truth about both of you.

XENIA. I'm going. Let me out. Oh, why don't you let me out?

MARTHA. (*Lifts Greta to her feet, supports her.*) You poor girl—you poor little sick girl.

GRETA. (*Moved, she turns and looks at the women, then starts to speak—at first with forced restraint, then more and more decisively, as if in a dream, to herself.*) You don't understand. . . . It's beautiful—what's between Martha and me. We're friends. She's the first friend I've ever had. She—we don't *demand* anything of each other. Everything is fresh, quiet. . . .

MAGDA. You lied to us.

GRETA. (*Vehemently.*) I felt safe with her. And what had happened inside of me—I felt safe from that. I felt quiet inside. We just sat and talked quietly. We were friendly to each other. There was nothing nasty any more. No fever, no frenzy.

MAGDA. Do you know what you're done, if you've been lying to us? We're risking our jobs because of this. Jesus Christ, Greta—you've put my child in danger. How can a woman do that?

GRETA. (*Loudly, hysterically.*) I've never done any wrong, I've always been good—d'you hear? I've lived with my mother—just we two. And I've never given her cause for tears. . . . I sewed. I took a course in typing. And then last summer. . . .

FLORA. Last summer. . . . What really happened last summer then? (*To the others.*) If Greta's been lying, then it's all her fault.

MARTHA. (*Appealing.*) You can see she's ill, can't you? She's lying right now. Let her out of here.

FLORA. Greta must tell the truth. We want to know why she did this to us.

(*The women gather round Martha and Greta, who stand against the wall under the white clockface, near the table, the stools and the bed, with the pack surrounding them. All listen—all the nameless workers, as well as Magda, Flora, Irma—and the newcomer. Only Xenia remains slumped on her knees by the door. She sobs—but she can't go on any more. And Anna leans on the same door, unshaken and strangely unreal. She chews unceasingly and repeats Greta's words now and then with indescribable contempt.*)

GRETA. (*Retreats in her fear, gets up on the shabby bed. She is in a reckless and dangerous trance. It is almost as if she were preaching.*) It happened in July, when all the factories are closed down. It's quiet everywhere. I wake up at six in the morning—Mother is sleeping. No—no it wasn't then. It was there before that—it had always been in me. I'm grown up. I am twenty-eight years old, but no man has touched me yet. Laugh at me now. *Why don't you laugh?* Like a young girl, like a dreamy sixteen-year old. Me, a grown-up woman. . . .

ANNA. Take me in your arms, I want to be *yours.*

MARTHA. We never really grow up. We all have our daydreams.

GRETA. Look at me. Look. I stood alone in my room, and it was six o'clock one quiet morning, and I took off my nightgown, and I was naked. I said to my fingers: There's a cheek waiting for you somewhere. I said to my breasts: It's good that you have rested so long. You'll be strong, when the children cry to be fed. And I looked at my body and said: I'm afraid of my man—he who is coming tomorrow. He who will make me an adult. I'll be a faithful wife and a good mother to the children. . . . Why don't you laugh at me? I said the sort of things you can read in true-life stories—things we're ashamed to say—that we all dream about. I am twenty-eight years old—and I have never yet lain with a man.

ANNA. This evening I'll come, under your window. . . .

GRETA. It happened one evening in July. I had nowhere to go. I went to the movies and then for a walk along the shore. I walked through streets that were deserted and hot, and it was eleven o'clock in the evening. A man spoke to me. . . .

ANNA. Lovely evening, honey. Much too nice to be walking alone. . . .

GRETA. He wasn't really young. . . .

ANNA. Grey at the temples. Isn't that distinguished? Goddam distinguished in a man with a good stomach on him.

GRETA. And it—it happened only an hour after I had dreamed of the man who was waiting for me. (*Vehemently.*) I don't know why I did it. My God, girls—he said to me: "Will you come with me to my place? I never felt so lonely as tonight."

ANNA. The wife and kids are in the country, and the maid has her night out. I've got some wine there and some cold food.

GRETA. He walked beside me and caught hold of my wrist. (*She sobs.*) I'm used to that—men talking to me in the street. I'm not ugly. They've swarmed round me like flies, but I've always been proud and never cared for any of them.

ANNA. Oh, geeze, what a bitch. Let's all chase her. Bow-wow, bow-wow.

GRETA. Have mercy on me. I went with a strange man on that quiet July night.

(*Greta speaks in a piteous, helpless tone. She is really suffering deeply. What happened in July was an inevitable catastrophe in her life. . . . Her words arouse surprise. "What's she say? Did she say she went with that man?"*)

MARTHA. (*Loudly, appealing.*) Don't tell, Greta. They won't understand anyhow.
MAGDA. (*With authority, heartlessly.*) So a strange man accosted you, and you went with him. . . . Go on.

(*The silence is deep and heavy.*)

GRETA. (*Screams.*) Just a few seconds before, only a couple of minutes before he came, I was thinking—I imagined I was buying curtains for my house. For my *own* house. The house my husband and me had bought. . . . It was a big house— real big, with a lawn and nice garden furniture. . . . And there was one of those swing seats, with a bright colored canopy. . . . (*Helplessly.*) I felt so heavy when he came near me—as if my legs couldn't hold me up any more—I couldn't think anything, say anything. I just kept repeating one word all the time—all the time. One damned ugly word. . . . *Don't ask why I went with him. I had to—I can't say anything else. Something made me do it—and I had to obey. (More quietly.)* I went with a strange man that July evening—and I loved—his cheap itch. (*shouts.*) So I kept myself pure till my gift wasn't a gift any more. (*Uncontrolled.*) Why didn't I get my love? Answer me. He was just a half-drunk old swine, who was afraid I'd bring lice to his bed. And I loved him. Because at last I had a head for my fingers to caress, hands that did bad things to me. And when he asked, I stayed with him. (*Weeps aloud, rocks herself to and fro on the creaking bed. Then she straightens herself—she is again the Greta we knew before.*) One evening a couple of days later—I went to another strange man and asked: "Have you got a room somewhere—where we wouldn't be disturbed?" . . . This happened, as I said, in July.
INGRID. (*Ingrid interrupts. She runs across the floor in her agitation. She is very upset—she does not understand Greta's confession.*) You're lying. You're lying. I don't want to listen. We're not like that really. It's not like what you say. You can feel yourself getting as hot as an oven, but all the same you only need to just sit hand in hand with your sweetheart—just listen when he says: "We'll get a big mirror to put between the windows." You need to think that one day he'll shout at you: "Is my white shirt ironed?" That's enough for all the other women.
MAGDA. (*Severely.*) You shouldn't have children, Greta, when you're like that. You'd let them run around hungry and half-naked in the streets, while you're washing your hair with some new shampoo. You'd only be an unpaid whore for your husband, never a wife.
IRMA. You were too good for the boys in your own block. I know girls like that. There's some like that in our gang: they take courses and try to speak refined. They sit and sew near the window, so everybody can see how goddam feminine they are. The rest of us are dragged into the bushes in the camping places, and we let it happen if we like the boy, but you scream for help.
ANNA. (*Giggling by the door.*) A maiden's prayer: Help me, kind sir. I don't know what it's really due to, but I feel so weak.
FLORA. (*In an assured tone, aware of her own importance.*) And then you became a sort of half a whore. And one of the worst, 'cause you try to defend

yourself by telling all kinds of fanciful tales. Tell the truth: I was afraid for a long time, but now I'm not satisfied unless I get it all the time.

MARTHA. (*With sudden intensity, but softly.*) They don't understand. They've never had dreams.

MAGDA. Greta, you've said your say. Where does Martha Porsche come into this story?

MARTHA. I met her one evening—she'd been drinking. I'd never taken any notice of her before. She said to me: "Can I come to your place for the night—otherwise I'll do something wrong?"

GRETA. My God, you haven't understood. I did it again—once, many times. I loathe myself. I *hate* myself, when my body doesn't obey—when everything in me forces me to obey that slowly dripping spring. I tried—I wanted. . . .

MARTHA. I thought of telling you about it too: she had taken a deadly dose of medicine—that evening when she slept for the first night in my room.

GRETA. She sat up by my bedside and got a doctor. She saved me. Do you understand what I say—Martha Porsche saved my life.

(*This news astonishes the women, and makes them uneasy.*)

FLORA. Porsche trapped Greta by putting her under an obligation. Greta isn't to blame.

IRMA. We don't want to hear any more. We're young. We're ordinary women, who want *one* man, and we want children that give us trouble and need us. (*And now, at this confusing moment, her self-control breaks down.*) I'm going to have a baby. I've tried to stop it. But I can't do it any more, I'm not married, and we can't get married, 'cause that boy's just a kid, with a motorbike and a mandolin. But I want to have my baby. Listen all of you: I'm going to have a baby and I want to have it.

(*Irma's outburst increases the uneasiness.*)

XENIA. (*She has gathered her strength enough to get up.*) I've got a friend who'll be waiting for me tonight. Tonight I'll be the wife of another woman's husband. And I want to be. I'm in love. I sing to him. I put his head on my arm and whisper to him, like in the movies: Mon amour, mon amour. . . .

FLORA. I'm a married woman, and our baby hasn't come too soon. I'm proud my stomach's so big that none of my dresses won't fit. And I ain't going to dream about dancing no more. I'm going to work myself to death for Harry and my boy—the boy that's kicking inside of me. And I don't intend to go on sitting here just for a whore, and that's a fact.

FIRST WORKER. What have you done, Margareta Willner? Here we are on strike because of you, because you fed us with lies about Martha.

MAGDA. (*Like a judge.*) We haven't heard everything yet. Why did you want to make us believe bad things about Martha Porsche? Why did you lie?

(*Anna ends the scene. She has taken too much medicine, she is now almost drunk: she doesn't care about the dark, the hysteria—even about her own cares. She runs to the center of the stage from her place by the door, staggers and begins to recite.*)

ANNA. O hail, beautiful evening stars of Cyprus. . . . They played that in the Worker's Hall, a hundred years ago. So I said to this man: "Don't you go thinking I'm a virgin. It's a lie. I was a virgin fifty-six years ago—so you'll have to be satisfied with that, sir." Timtiritim, timtiritim.

IRMA. Anna's drunk. She's finished all the nerve tonic.

(The women have a lot of trouble before they can get Anna to settle down.)

ANNA. Who says so? I'm not drunk, not me. I ain't never been as sober as I am now. I wanna talk to Greta. I'll give her a bit of advice. I can give you a couple of phone numbers. . . . No, I don't wanna go to sleep. Let me be.

MAGDA. *(Her voice is heard above all the noise.)* Greta, tell us why you lied to us about Porsche. Or—wasn't it a lie?

(Magda's voice makes them all quiet. The stage is silent.)

-Curtain-

ACT III

Scene 1

(The play continues from the previous scene. When the curtain rises, Anna is still struggling.)

ANNA. I don't want to go to sleep. Open the door for the gentlemen. I've had enough of women. Open the door, I said. *(But gradually her voice becomes softer, and we realize she has dropped off to sleep.)*

MAGDA. We're waiting, Greta.

(The whole crowd of women give their opinion: "They're the same sort. Both of them must leave.")

MARTHA. I'll tell you how things really are. *(Martha stands like Greta, pressed against the wall, near Greta, surrounded by the menacing pack of women.)* She lied to save herself. No, no—not from me. Not from what you think I am. She hates me because she's afraid—afraid of my coldness, my indifference. She's afraid that my disgust will infect her. That one day she'll look at those groping gorillas as fearfully, as nauseated as me. . . . Go on, stare, open your mouth and stare. Why don't you throw that blue coat at me and shout out your contempt for the whole world to hear. *(Her self-control fails: she shouts in pain and shame.)* I don't want to know anything about them. I don't want to know anything about men. I've had enough of them—d'you hear? I was once just the same as all of you, I was a woman like you: I wanted to have a child. I met a man. . . . *(But her self-respect is so strong that she cannot go on. Martha Porsche is not used to unbaring her secrets.)* I—I once met a man. . . .

FLORA. You must tell us now, Martha. Everything's your fault.

IRMA. "I met a man. . . ." What did he say to you? What did he do to you?

GRETA. Don't tell. Let's go away from here. Both of us. And never come back again.

MAGDA. You'd best speak out now. Martha Porsche—for your own good.

MARTHA. I met a man. . . . Is there anything more important you could hear from a woman's mouth? Can you still see in me—what I once was? I had learned to read poetry. I had learned to play father's violin. I had learned to wander through the meadows and pick flowers on Midsummer Eve. I was like Greta. Like Greta in her dreams—I lived in a world where men were quiet and strong, gentle and chivalrous. My mother said:" Do you see that man? He is handsome, Martha. He has been brought up well, Martha. He is in love with you, Martha. You will be his wife, Martha." You'll say that things like that don't happen any more. We know all about love when we're still children. That's not true. We sleep in our white girls rooms—the white curtains flutter softly—and we sleep by our books of poetry. Sweet songs sound in our ears.

IRMA. Like a man lies in bed in his dirty pajamas and bawls: How long are you gonna go on washing yourself? I been lying here for quarter of an hour already.

FLORA. There are kindnesses they don't talk about in them novels: All right, I'll help you to rinse the wash on Sunday morning. . . .

GRETA. Martha, Martha. They'll never understand us.

MARTHA. (As in a dream, under pressure of bad memories.) You hear the organ playing in the church. You see me in my white bridal gown. And everything was like a fairy tale. Everything was good just then. He had never kissed me on the mouth, because I didn't want. . . .

(The women laugh, destroying the atmosphere.)

IRMA. What did I say—did you hear? The man kisses her lily white brow, strokes his moustache and whispers hoarsely: Wait—just wait, till the wedding bells have rung. . . .

XENIA. Martha lay awake all night with a feverish glow in her big eyes and said to herself: What is it? The flowers don't do that. . . .

GRETA. Be quiet. Be quiet.

MARTHA. You are not the first to laugh at me. Everyone laughed—my mother, my sister, my girlfriends.

MAGDA. And that night the white curtains were torn, but you didn't dare to become a wife.

MARTHA. (Painfully.) You are all women like me. Don't you understand, can't you be merciful. . . ? (Uncontrolled.) I'll go away. You have won. Martha Porsche will ask for notice, and you won't need to see her ever again. Can't you —say that it wasn't my fault?

MAGDA. You grew up and were deaf and blind to everything that was dangerous. You didn't want to think that thought to the end—that one day, one night. . . . (Her voice becomes stronger.) Which of us hasn't some morning woken up crying because of the fairy tale that ended? Which of you married ones hasn't had to learn that he wasn't a fairy-tale prince after all? And not even a handsome man any more.

MARTHA. I couldn't give myself. I've never said that aloud before. I'm ashamed that I've told you now. I couldn't. I'm still untouched. I never had children.

But it lives in me as a sorrow and a longing. (*Covers her face with her hands.*) It's all so shameful. Horrible. (*Softly.*) And he—he wasn't a bad man. He suffered for me. And then—I was left alone.

MAGDA. Alone, you said. Every woman is left alone in the end, even though she has a husband and children. The man slips from her hands. He may be at home shouting for food and clothes for himself. But even then he's miles away. And the children grow up and go their own ways. Have you ever met an elderly married woman who hasn't been left alone? Eh? Even though the house may be full of yelling people, eh? (*Magda looks silently round. All she has heard has moved her more than she cares to admit. She points at the two accused persons.*) You dreamed the same thing. You're like sisters. And you had men and didn't have men, and then you went crazy. And you found each other and played like little girls with doll's-house coffee cups and play children that don't need a father. Wake up, I say. Wake up and say: Is it true that only men mean anything? Is life like that? (*In agitation.*) Can you say that? That life—that life for us women first means a man? Or many men? Lie on your back and wait for a man. . . .

FLORA. (*Touché.*) Don't preach, Magda. The nighttime isn't everything. Home's something, too, curtains—and Sunday walks—when you walk with your husband in the city and point at all the things you'll never be able to afford. Nighttime isn't everything, Magda. And there's the children then, too—the coming children.

IRMA. (*Mockingly.*) Flora has only one god—Harry. What Harry's prophet is—that's something you can't say aloud or print in books.

MAGDA. (*In her earlier way.*) We women are crazy creatures. Every single one of us. Flora and her Harry, Irma and what's happened to her, Greta and Martha. It's born in us—to go crazy. And we're crazy once a month, too. (*Loudly, vehemently.*) I knew a girl once. She was the only daughter of our village shopkeeper. Rich and pretty. And she inherited the shop and said thank you to lots of men, but one summer some tramp came begging for food and that tramp stayed in the house. In ten years he drank away the shop and the stock and the money and went away again to roam around the world, and the girl had nothing left except empty pockets and four children. Do you know what that girl said? She said once—I heard it myself: "I'd do it again tomorrow. If I had the chance to choose again, I'd do just the same." That's true. She said that. And cried.

(*The atmosphere changes again. The memories that Magda's words bring back to mind, give rise to new unrest.*)

XENIA. (*Agitated.*) It's true, you all know that. We're blind and deaf. We don't see any faults in a man, we listen to something that is in our own selves. It's true, says Magda, whose man is a good-for-nothing and who has eight children. That's why we're alive. So we would wait for what blesses us. Ask Irma. Ask that pale kid listening there who came this morning. What is life? If that word isn't spelled m-a-n, then I'll eat my scarf.

IRMA. I'll never be like you—never.

MAGDA. But you want to have a child, and don't want the boy to know anything about it. You'll suffer yourself for all three, and love that suffering.

INGRID. I'm in love. I'd do anything for him. And it would be wonderful. I want to do that, all my life.

MAGDA. Did you hear—sounds familiar, don't it? Just as if you'd said it yourself. Ten years ago. Or twenty.

FIRST WORKER. Once he made a table, which never stopped wobbling. And he came in and said, like they always says: "Here's your table. You don't need to buy things when you can make 'em yourself." And I'd been saving up in secret, 'cause I wanted one of them tables with glass on top, but I didn't have the heart to tell him. I just said I'd never seen such a fine table—and went into the kitchen and had a good cry.

SECOND WORKER. He goes to bed with me and it's all over when I'm only half way. But you just have to be thankful, that's all. . . . Thank you very humbly that you gave me a baby.

MAGDA. Do you think I didn't see what was waiting for me? But that boy had a gayer laugh than anyone else in the whole village. And he used to sing, too— then at the beginning. Before he started finding all sorts of little faults for himself. I'd do it again. God help me. I'd live the same way again, if I had the chance.

FIRST WORKER. Here, listen while I tell you: He buys lottery tickets, and I notices it as soon as he gets home. They always think they can lie to us.

SECOND WORKER. Wait a minute while I tell you: I was lying in bed for three weeks with the flu, and he made the food for us. Washed the dishes and fed the kids. Sometimes it felt like I was in church. Compared with being here, I mean.

THIRD WORKER. He hits me. But when he wakes up he cries when he sees the marks. Then he kisses the bruises.

IRMA. The boy gave me a silver cup he'd won—in a quarter-mile race.

INGRID. We've got a sand pit behind the ridge, and we're going to make money out of that. He's going to make a road through the swamp. It'll be more than four miles long—one of these days.

FLORA. You know how it is. Harry can't read too well. He almost has to spell it out. He reads aloud to me every evening nowadays out of this book for expectant mothers. His face was red as a beet the first evening—he was still so shy then. . . .

MAGDA. (*Starts as if awaking from sleep. Goes to the isolated women—Greta and Martha—standing by the wall and looks at them.*) And you two—what are we going to do with you? (*To all.*) What are we going to do now, then?

(*Magda's words bring the women back to reality.*)

Scene 2

GRETA. (*She has followed the last scene closely—listened to Martha's words and the women's outpourings. She has stood silent, staring at Martha. Now that all are quiet she clasps Martha's hand. She has changed again—she is softer, more willing. She asks quietly.*) That's not all, Martha. We both want peace and quiet. Sweet, wordless silence in a room together with good people. That's not all you have to say. . . .

IRMA. What's she trying to be? What's she say? The sermon's over now.

GRETA. (*Loudly, obstinately.*) Tell them, then they'll forgive you.

MAGDA. If you've got something else to say, then say it now.

GRETA. (*Sadly.*) Tell them what happened to you once. Come closer—all of you. We'll tell you something that can't be told in a loud voice. We'll whisper it to you. Then we'll—sing a lamentation for the fate of woman. . . .

XENIA. (*Goes very near to Martha and Greta, looks Martha straight in the eyes.*) I have not noticed before—*in your eye there is fear.*

GRETA. Martha, why do you long to die?

MARTHA. (*Starts speaking again. She speaks stiffly, in a colorless voice—as if she were reciting a lesson learned by heart, as if she were telling of another person, another woman. Her words have a frighteningly powerful effect on all the women.*) We had a country house by a lake. From the jetty where we kept our boat there was a path leading up to the house. You can't see the jetty from the house— there's a thick clump of elms in between. There a little girl grows up. Her father plays the violin. Her mother reads aloud. Round the girl there is quiet. Nobody says bad words. In those rooms there is no place for anything ugly. No one asks: What does *that* word mean? What are the neighbor's dogs doing?

The little girl goes for long walks on her own. She remembers the words from poetry books. She has daydreams. Everywhere only good, quiet dreams.

One evening she goes farther than usual and comes to the highway, where the men and boys of the village loiter. One of them is drunk.

The girl is wrapped up in her own thoughts, and does not notice the men before she is almost in their midst. Then she takes fright and runs away. She runs as fast as she can towards home.

One of the men follows her, catches her. . . .

If only the girl could have shouted. If only she had learned to rage, to hurt, to hit and scratch and scream—she could have escaped perhaps. If only she had been taught to be mean. . . .

MARTHA. She was twelve-years old, a quiet twelve-year-old little girl. Who didn't cry. Who didn't shout. Who didn't fight. She was so afraid. . . . What happened to her was too horrible, unreal—something no one had written poems about. . . .

The man was scared when the girl lay as if she were dead. The man stood there half-naked and looked at the girl. . . .

(*Martha covers her face with her hands and is silent. Then she goes on softly.*) The girl didn't tell her mother about it, didn't complain to her father. Did I tell you—in that house one didn't speak of ugly things. . . .

GRETA. (*All the time she has held Martha's hand. Now she says, quietly and gently as to a little girl:*) That didn't really happen. You've only had a dream— a nightmare. Would you like some milk—or an apple? Then you can go to sleep again. Little Martha, Mother will sit here and hold your hand till you go to sleep again.

(*When Greta has stopped speaking, the women stand still in reluctant silence.*)

IRMA. (*Loudly, hysterically—half screaming.*) The man raped you—is that right? (*But Irma relapses into silence, also.*)

FLORA. (*She, too, goes to Martha and Greta, hesitating, unsure.*) I suppose—I suppose you can't forget something like that.

GRETA. Let us tear our clothes and lament for our sister's sorrow. Let us all weep— all. Our sister is dead. She will not wake to life again. Never again. . . .

INGRID. (*Ingrid, the newcomer, cannot stand this scene. She bursts into tears. She runs to Irma and clings to her.*) Why do they keep talking like that all the time. I don't want to hear any more. It makes me ill. I don't want to be here any more.
MARTHA. This room is not a good place for so many women. It's difficult to breathe. It's not good for expectant women. Nor for the children to come. (*Staggers, seeks support.*)

(*A loud shout from Irma brings them back to their senses. Her young, sure voice cuts the air like an officer shouting "Attention!", and brings them back once more to reality.*)

Scene 3

(*There is a short pause: the women look furtively at Greta and Martha, and talk to each other uneasily.*)

IRMA. (*Shouts.*) She said she'd give notice.
FLORA. What are you going to do, Martha Porsche? We're waiting for an answer.
MARTHA. (*She stands, pale, imprisoned by her own problem, motionless against the wall. She speaks, dejectedly.*) I'm going away from this factory. No—don't think that *you* have scared me. I am innocent of what you accuse me. But I'm leaving, all the same. I've cried out my sorrows for everyone to hear. I've shouted from the housetops and exposed myself to people who don't understand anything. I give up my job. I've done that before. Do you think that you are the first women to drive me away? I don't want to have anything to do with men, and women drive me away. Call the Engineer. Tell Frieda that Queen Porsche wants to give notice.
GRETA. (*Vehemently.*) It's *me* who ought to leave. I lied to you. You know that now. You've got no right to accuse Martha.

(*But now the women's hate returns like a great threatening wave.*)

FLORA. They must both leave. We don't want to see them in our crowd any more.
IRMA. Jesus Christ—listen to me. . . . (*But when she stands in front of Greta and Martha, she can't go on. She stares at them and then turns her back.*) They're—they're like from some foreign country. You can't even talk to them any more.
XENIA. (*She, too, approaches Greta and Martha, but stops.*) You and me—we are not the same sort of creatures. Not even cousins. (*But then her easily moved emotions win: she runs to Greta and kisses her cheek.*) You—you will love some day. And you will be happy—some day. (*Then she is forced to extend her hand to Martha.*) Goodbye, Mrs. Porsche.

(*But the others stand dumb and motionless. They withdraw slowly from Martha and Greta, as if these two no longer belong to their group—as if they were dangerously ill.*)

MAGDA. (*Briefly.*) We can't sit here any longer.
FLORA. Open the doors. The women of Three are going back to work.

Scene 4

(*Now the women feel a new kind of uneasiness—they are stirred by lighter, healthier feelings: work summons them again. They are all in a hurry: they put their things in order, take down their overalls.*)

IRMA. Anyone take a bet? Frieda'll be standing there in the middle of the floor, laughing his head off.
FIRST WORKER. Magda, shall we stay here and do overtime? Shall we make up for these hours?
MAGDA. Someone will have to go and talk to the Engineer (*Looks at Flora.*)
FLORA. (*Nods.*) I'll come with you. We two'll fix things all right.

(*So now it's all over and done with. One of them goes to the yard door and unlocks it.*)

XENIA. Ah, this air. I'm quite crazy about fresh air.
FLORA. Are your cats the same?

(*There is a new atmosphere now—the old, familiar atmosphere of a workday spent together. It seems as if all had forgotten the women standing by the wall.*
They go towards the factory-hall door—Magda and Flora leading.)
SECOND WORKER. (*To Irma.*) Was that really true? What you said about a baby?
IRMA. What's that to you?
XENIA. Well, girls—are you ready? Our gentlemen are waiting in the bedroom.

(*They laugh at Xenia's remark—louder than the joke deserves. Then they go briskly to the waiting machines.*
But before the room empties, there is a brief interlude. The last in the group are Irma and Ingrid. They've already got to the door, when their young cruelty makes them throw out a couple of home truths at Greta and Martha, who remain in the room.)

INGRID. (*To Greta.*) If you happen to be in our part of the country—some time, then don't bother to visit us. My husband and me won't be at home—to you. . . .
IRMA. (*To Martha.*) You heard I'm getting a baby, Martha. And after that I'll have lots of them, 'cause I'm so sexy.

(*Irma and Ingrid put their arms round each others' waists and go out, laughing loudly.*
After a while we hear the machines start up. The hum becomes louder until it is deafening. Suddenly the electric lights come on again in the women's room,

and the stage is brightly lit: the cupboards, the clothes thrown all over the place, and various things the women have left lying about.

Martha and Greta stand side by side as if shackled to one another, against the bare wall.)

Scene 5

(Greta and Martha have been rejected from the group. They are pariahs, and they know it.)

GRETA. Did you hear? They wanted to hurt us.

MARTHA. We're like pariah dogs that can be stoned to death. *(Greta still stands stiffly, but Martha straightens herself. She walks without purpose across the room, stops, mechanically puts some clothes in their place. She stops again.)* They should have—locked their cupboards. Their purses are here. *(Pause.)* I liked them. . . .

GRETA. *(Her self-control fails. She runs to Martha.)* Forgive me, Martha. I don't know why I did it. Do you believe me? I—I didn't know what I was doing. I—I had to. . . .

MARTHA. *(Dully.)* Don't talk about it any more. I'll find a new job all right. I'll leave the town.

GRETA. Can I come with you? *(Vehemently.)* Take me with you. We'll start again from the beginning. I don't want to be left alone.

MARTHA. You betrayed me.

GRETA. I was all to pieces. I had a bad conscience about those days. Don't leave me. Don't go away from me.

MARTHA. I can't go on.

GRETA. Lilian—you let Lilian live at your place.

MARTHA. She was alone and sick. *(Vehemently.)* She was sicker than me. I've told you, Greta—I'm not like Lilian. *I want a friend. I want peace. I want purity.* Lilian was not pure. She wanted to make me unclean, too.

GRETA. Not men—but not women either. Is your life like that?

MARTHA. *(Bursts out.)* Be quiet now. We have talked quite enough today. My God—I'll never forget it: I stood there and told them everything—told everything to those gaping mouths and stupid eyes. Go away, Greta. You've done enough harm already for one day.

GRETA. Please—please can I come with you? I—I won't refuse you anything. . . .

MARTHA. *(Martha hits Greta—a stinging blow across the cheek. Angrily:)* Don't you believe what I say? I have never touched any woman. *(Shocked.)* Why don't you believe me? I swear it's true. I'm a friend. Only—only a friend. . . .

GRETA. *(Retreats from Martha, frightened and upset.)* You're lying, Martha. You don't dare. That is your hell. That's why Lilian got ill. *You walk a borderland that is barren.* A lifeless, voiceless desert.

MARTHA. Go away. Go on, go away.

GRETA. *(Retreats, stops.)* Perhaps, perhaps it's in me, too, already. . . . Sometimes it seems like paradise: your coldness, your white, clean rooms. Two women surrounded by silence. (*Cries out.*) I've never known anything so quiet, so beautiful. What will there be left for me, if you go away? Tell me, Martha Porsche. What will my fate be, if I have to leave this place—alone?

MARTHA. You don't need to leave here. They'll forgive you.

GRETA. I've got men in my blood now, Martha. And that's more dangerous than drinking or taking drugs. (*Approaches Martha again, prays.*) Don't you know what will become of me, if I don't get help?

MARTHA. (*Tears herself away, and goes toward the factory-hall door, away from Greta.*) Go home and get some sleep now—a really good sleep. Then go to the doctor. You ought to go to hospital for a while, to rest.

GRETA. (*Collapses slowly on the floor and bursts into bitter tears.*) The other— it's much easier. No need to do anything except—go out of the gate. . . .

MARTHA. You shouldn't have lied. You shouldn't have forced me to speak.

GRETA. I don't want to become like you—just wait, lonely and cold, for something that never comes. Only *one* coffee cup—only *one* plate, only *one* towel—so long that everything's finished, everything's burned out.

MARTHA. Goodbye, Greta.

GRETA. (*Looks up.*) Goodbye Martha. (*Tenderly.*) I hope—I wish it could happen to you one day—so you could get away from the borderland, Martha. *And come back—or continue your journey. That you—would dare to cry out for someone else.*

(*They look at one another, then Martha leaves the stage. She walks, erect and determined, to the door of the factory hall. She pauses only to arrange her dress and hair.*)

Scene 6

(*Greta sits motionless for a while. It seems as if she were waiting or listening for something.*
During this silence Anna wakes up. The old woman mutters, turns over and sits up—stares round her for a moment uncomprehendingly. Then she guffaws. She notices Greta.)

ANNA. Hell, I been sleeping. Me sleeping, and the machines going. Hey, is it morning or evening? Have I just got here or do I have to leave soon?

(*Greta does not answer. She straightens herself slowly, takes her purse, and opens it. She takes out a mirror, a powder compact, and lipstick and examines her reflection—puts on make-up heavily.*)

ANNA. (*Gets up and comes near Greta. She says nothing, but follows Greta's actions. A pause.*) Did Porsche go away?

GRETA. Yes.

ANNA. And won't come back?

GRETA. She'll never come back again.

ANNA. I slept a bit—didn't hear it all. Was it true what was said about her?
GRETA. *It was true.*
ANNA. I've often wondered about it—if a woman doesn't go with a man, then what the hell does she do. . . . (*Greta stares at her for a moment, and Anna is silent. After a little while she changes the subject.*) Now we're making ourselves beautiful, eh?

(*Pause.*)

GRETA. (*Gets up and goes to the mirror. Stares at her reflection for a long time. Arranges her dress, combs her hair—she has no hat.*)

ANNA. (*Uneasily.*) You look like you was going out to meet some fella. But you gotta go home, Greta. Your ma's waiting.
GRETA. (*Turns towards Anna—vehemently.*) Am I nice looking, Anna?
ANNA. (*Looks critically.*) You are, you are. You're one of the prettiest girls in this department. You knows that yourself.

GRETA. (*Looks in the mirror again. She begins to hum, at first softly, then louder and louder. She turns towards Anna again, does a couple of dance steps—swings her purse, takes a few steps as if she were walking along the street—stops in front of a shop window, looks around—takes out a cigarette and says to a passer-by:* "Excuse me, can you give me a light please? . . . Thank you. . . . Oh, thank you so much. . . .")

   Watching this bit of acting, cynical old Anna starts to laugh. Greta looks at her and laughs, too. Then she suddenly becomes serious. She waits. She listens. She turns to the yard door and appears frightened—then pulls herself together and goes out, erect and bold.)

ANNA. (*Still laughing.*) Bang your heels down hard, so your breasts'll bounce nicely. (*Shouts.*) You're going home now, eh? You're going home now, ain't you Greta?

-Curtain-

Biographies

NOTE: *These biographical sketches were prepared by Philip Binham and Pirkko Kiuru.*

Risto Ahti. Born 1943. Poet and critic. Lives in Oulu, Finland. Collections: *Winter is Heresy* (1967), *Poems* (1968), *Song in Dream* (1972). Has been called a pioneer in poetic methods, and a "mystic who thinks with his skin." He says himself: "What you believe is poetry. In the hierarchy of poetry, Vision is the highest form. . . . Most poetry is closer to science and culture, trade and industry than to life. . . . Words that hit you right in your face, words that force you to hide or that demand you come out, that is poetry, appearing everywhere, perhaps most seldom in books of poetry. . . . I hate skill, I love NEED. I live out of necessities."

Claes Andersson. Born 1937. Poet, psychiatrist, and jazz pianist. One of the leading younger Finnish poets writing in Swedish. His medical background gives his language a modern, matter-of-fact style—he often uses biological terminology. His themes often concern types of today: the speed-mad, office slaves, TV reporters. In his volume of poetry, *The Society We Die in* (1967), his viewpoint is international, his themes death, hunger, and suffering.

Tuomas Anhava. Born 1927. Poet, critic, and translator. Editor for many years of *Parnasso,* a leading literary journal in Finland. Anhava has built up a high reputation as the guide and mentor of younger writers. His "finds" during his work as a publishing executive include Haavikko, Meri, Hyry, Saarikoski, and Salama. He has published six volumes of poetry. They reveal a classical temperament, a search for the absolute. Later poems lean toward an Eastern philosophy; he has shown great interest in the poetry of Japan and China. He is a sharp and controversial polemicist; his views on society are found in his criticism rather than his poetry. His translations into Finnish include Blake's *The Marriage of Heaven and Hell,* a selection of *tanka* poems called *I Listen, Stranger,* and *Anabasis* by St. John Perse.

376

Bo Carpelan. Born 1926. Poet, Ph.D., librarian, and critic. Has also written novels and children's stories. Writes in Swedish. His first poems, published in Sweden, are heavy with symbolism. In later collections, such as *The Cool Day* (1961), the symbolism gives way to a more direct, positive approach. A more recent collection of poems is *The Yard* (1969). His prose poetry in *Minus Seven* (1952) shows a humor also evident in his stories for children, of which *Bow Island* (1968) has been published in English in the United States. His recent novel *Voices in the Late Hours* (1971) has been well received.

Walentin Chorell. Born 1914. Psychologist by training, playwright and novelist. Writes in Swedish. Began writing in the early 1940s; he is the most prolific of modern Finnish playwrights, with a dozen full-length plays for the theater to his name, and fifty or more radio and TV pieces. His plays are dealt with in more detail elsewhere in this anthology. Has also written some fifteen novels. His early novels, such as *Caliban's Day* (1948), reflect the harshness and narrowness of life in Finland at the time. His trilogy *Miriam* (1956–9) is about girls and young women—in his plays the best roles are usually reserved for women. A recent novel is *The Last Game* (1970). Like many Swedish-Finnish writers, his work is well known in Sweden.

Paavo Haavikko. Born 1931. Poet, novelist, and playwright. An executive of the Otava publishing house in Helsinki. His poetry, of which he has published six collections, is dealt with elsewhere in this volume, as are his plays. His novels, mostly written in the sixties, are generally objective, spare accounts of everyday happenings. He takes a wider theme in *Snowless Time,* a short story from the collection *A Glass at the Table of Claudius Civilis* (1964), which is concerned with power and with man's public role and private self.

Lars Huldén. Born 1926. A poet who writes in Swedish. His earlier works are characterized by simplicity and humor; word-play, vital gaiety, together with an everyday tone—an easy union of learning and the common touch. In later works, he is more pessimistic; his themes are those of a suffering world: social problems, overpopulation, the bomb. He has also written cabaret and occasional poetry and has done research on the Swedish folk poet, Bellman. Holds a Ph.D. in Nordic Philology.

Veikko Huovinen. Born 1927. Novelist and short-story writer. Took a degree in forestry and worked for two years in the field before becoming a full-time writer. Lives in Sotkamo in the wilds of northeastern Finland, the setting for many of his stories. In his works, humor and satire are combined with a deep feeling for nature. His best-known character is Konsta Pylkkänen, a highly individual back-woods philosopher based on the author's father. Of his own outlook on life Huovinen says: "It is only an illusion to think man himself can change things much. Man is in a trap, the prisoner of his past and his inheritance. Only death, music, dry vodka, or good humor offer him a small chance of escape." Huovinen shuns all forms of corporate activity. His many novels include *Peace-Pipe* (1956), satirizing war and megalomania, and *The Hamsters* (1957), a charming tale of Oblomov-like men playing a game of Robinson Crusoe hoarding vastly for the Northern winter. A recent work, *The Rascal* (1971), is more serious. It is a life of Hitler based largely on first-hand interviews by the author himself, and it has had considerable success in Finland. Huovinen has also published several collections of short stories or "humoresques" as he calls them. *Before Beirut* in this volume is taken from *Short and Special* (1967).

Antti Hyry. Born 1931. Short-story writer and novelist, Hyry took a degree in engineering but did not practice. In a rare comment on his work Hyry said: "I tend to feel as if the real world only existed before I was twenty." His stories, in fact, often deal with childhood, and reveal a search for a true "feeling of reality." They are bare and objective, like *The Dam* in this volume, which is from his first collection, *He Left the Highway* (1958). This story is also typical in its rejection of technological achievements in favor of simple, traditional activities. Hyry himself was born to a country life. His first novel, *Spring and Autumn* (1958), rejected character, conflict, and plot. In later works, the insecurity of the individual in the city is emphasized.

Helvi Juvonen. 1919–1959. Her six volumes of verse are a bridge between the traditional and "new" Finnish poetry. They are characterized by the use of individual, often mystical images. For herself, she uses the epithets of mole, bear, and rock in her first collection, *Dwarf Tree* (1949). In *From Day to Day* (1954) and *Bed of Rock* (1955) the treatment of religious problems and flashes of intuition are reminiscent of Emily Dickinson, whom she translated. Her *Collected Poems* were published in 1960.

Christer Kihlman. Born 1930. A controversial novelist and playwright who writes in Swedish and has worked as a journalist. His *Se upp Salige!* (*Look Out, Ye Blessed!*, 1960) was perhaps the most successful and provocative Swedish-Finnish novel to appear after the war. *Den blå modern* (*Blue Mother*, 1961) deals with the generation gap. His recent novel is a deliberately frank exposure of his own intimate life (*Människan som skalv*, *The Man Who Tottered*, 1971). Several of his plays, including *12 askelta kuun pinnalla* (*Twelve Steps on the Moon*), have been successfully performed on the Finnish stage lately.

Väinö Kirstinä. Born 1936. Poet, translator, critic, reporter, teacher, and member of the drama staff of the Finnish Broadcasting Corporation. His poetry shows a movement from a detached to a committed position regarding society. His early, quiet lyrics have become more flowing and playful. Though his verse may be fantastic or even irrational, it preserves its lyrical quality even at its most experimental. Kirstinä has a flair for the sharp and amusing phrase: "If you read Saarikoski for 10 minutes/ your breath soon starts to smell of spirits." The title of one of his more recent collections is *Long-term LSD Plan* (1967). Kirstinä's translations include poems by Baudelaire.

Kalevi Lappalainen. Born 1940, Oulu, Finland. Lappalainen graduated from Arizona State University in 1964. "Trippi" ("The Trip"), his first-print poem with illustrations, was privately printed. He has published a collection of his poems, *Outside The Alphabets,* in English translation with *Stolen Paper Review Editions*. His other collections of his poems include *Ihmissyöjän ilmeet* (*The Cannibal's Expressions*), *Automaattia vaanimassa* (*Watching for Automation*), *Puolihevosen hermorata* (*The Half-Horse's Nervetrack*), *Lakana* (*The Sheet*), and a novel, *Keltaisen talon pari* (*The Yellow House Couple*). His translations include *The Europeans* by Henry James and *Reflections in a Golden Eye* by Carson McCullers. His work of object poems has been in numerous poetry exhibitions, including Exposicion Spatialisme, Paris, Oxford Exhibition, and Hors

Langage, Nice, 1973. His work has appeared in such periodicals as *The Nation* and *The Village Voice,* and he will be published in an anthology of writing with Dell Publishing Co., Inc.

Väinö Linna. Born 1920. Finland's foremost living novelist. A self-taught, working-class writer. His fame rests on two works. *The Unknown Soldier* (1954) has sold better in Finland than any other Finnish book, and has been widely translated. Unfortunately the anonymous English translators have failed miserably to do it justice. The novel deals with the Finnish "Continuation War" of 1941–44. When it was first published, it aroused great controversy for its allegedly disrespectful treatment of Finnish officers. Now it is an established classic. The first part of the trilogy *Here under the Northern Star* (1959–62), from which the extract *The Eviction* in this volume is taken, depicts the rural world at the turn of the century and the early days of the Socialist movement in Finland. The second part has done much to change Finnish views on the rights and wrongs of the Finnish Civil War in 1918. The third part of this monumental work brings the story of the working-class struggle up to 1944. Both books have been filmed, serialized for TV, and dramatized for the stage. Since 1962, Linna has published no fiction. His essay collection *Oheisia* (*Appendages,* 1967) includes penetrating judgments on Finnish culture.

Eeva-Liisa Manner. Born 1921. Poet, playwright, novelist, and translator. Manner lived for several years in Spain. Her first collection of poetry appeared in 1944, but her real breakthrough was with *This Journey* (1956). The poetry of this collection is characterized by rich ornament, yet clear verbal precision and skilful treatment of rhythm. In her later works, such as *The Written Rock* (1966), Spanish motifs are to the fore. In *Fahrenheit 121* (1968), the name of which refers to the Spanish heat, she achieves a renewed simplicity, warmth, and intensity. Of these later poems, Manner says that they reflect a loss of former values and certainties; she speaks constantly of "emptiness". Her four plays are dealt with elsewhere in this volume. Her novels include *Girl on the Quay of Heaven* (1951), depicting a child's world where dream and reality merge, and a parody of the detective novel, *Was the Murderer an Angel?* (1963). Her many highly valued translations include works by Shakespeare, Ben Jonson, and Homer's *Iliad* and *Odyssey.*

Juha Mannerkorpi. Born 1915. Novelist and short-story writer, poet, and playwright. Born in Ashtabula Harbor, Ohio, where he spent the first few years of his life. Son of a minister of the Finnish Lutheran Church, he himself studied theology for a while. He spent some time in France: his work is said to reflect the influence of Existentialism (rare among Finnish writers) and more recently of the modern French novel. Stories: In the collection *Circular Saw* (1956), from which *Autumn* in this volume is taken, many stories deal with rather primitive people faced with some overwhelming compulsion. His characters are often lonely; he shows that they have many selves. The rhythmic quality of his prose is striking: "Without rhythm," he says, "there is no language and not much else." Novels: Mannerkorpi uses symbolism abundantly. In *The Rodents* (1958), he treats death and pleasure in destruction symbolically. Of this book he says: "I did not look for meanings, only the scent of significance." He attempted in this and later works, such as *Boat Leaving* (1961), to "make the same things happen in language as in direct experience." His poetry, of which *The Sower Went Forth* to Sow (1954) is an important collection, often deals with the mystery of Christian love. His plays include several monologues, one of which has recently won success at the Helsinki National Theater. His most recent monologue, *Before We Are All Lost,* was given a State Award.

Veijo Meri. Born 1928. His father was a regular soldier, though Meri never served in war himself. His main theme is war and its madness. His style is objective and grotesque. His humor is grim and dry. From Faulkner he learned to believe in the exceptionally great power of the macabre. His war novels include *Manila Rope* (1957, translated into English 1967), *Quits* (1961), and *Defence Post* (1964). They are typically made up of war anecdotes. They contain internal anecdotes that the author feels are of great importance in expanding his meaning. Their passive characters are at the mercy of irrational circumstances. The same lack of order in life is to be found in his "civilian" novels, such as *The Detached Ones* (1959), and *Woman Drawn in a Mirror* (1963). His terse style is admirably suited to the short story. Collections include *Situations* (1962), and *Tales of a Single Night* (1967). *The Killer* (1965), which is included in this volume, can be found from a broader collection of *Stories* (1965). The war theme is continued in his plays, such as *Private Jokinen's Wedding Leave* (1965), which is given more detailed mention elsewhere.

Aila Meriluoto. Born 1924. Married for some years to the writer Lauri Viita. Her *Lasimaalaus (Stained Glass,* 1946), though traditional in form, was a herald of modern Finnish poetry with its aggressive declaration of illusionment. Her debt to Rilke, whom she has translated, is especially apparent in her *Sairas tyttö tanssii (The Sick Girl Dances,* 1952). In later collections like *Portaat (Stairs,* 1961), and *Asumattomiin (Deserted Places,* 1963), she approaches loneliness objectively through cosmic, physiological, and biological images.

Marja-Leena Mikkola. Born 1939. Novelist, short-story writer, writer of filmscripts, cabaret, and social documentary studies. A realistic writer who has lately become increasingly interested in social and political themes, and especially with womens' role in society. Her novels include *Girl Like a Guitar* (1964), dealing with rootless young people, and the less successful *Visitation* (1967), describing the search of two left-wing intellectuals for some kind of social reality. Her story in this anthology, *Boy for a Summer,* is taken from her first published collection of stories, *Women* (1962). A more recent work, *Heavy Cotton* (1971), is a documentary study of women workers in a Tampere textile factory.

Timo K. Mukka. 1944–73. Son of a forest worker, he lived in Lapland. He often describes the primitive aspects of northern Finland. His works contain an element of sexual mysticism; he has been described as "the Lawrence of young Finnish prose." More recently he emerged as a somewhat Rousseau-esque social critic. He was a leading spirit in the annual cultural gatherings called "Arctic Hysteria."

His first novel *The Land is a Sinful Song* (1964) is entitled "a ballad." *From Here to Somewhere* (1965) deals with military training and is strongly pacifist. Mukka describes his Utopia as "a life without arms and war, without state and frontier, without class and exploitation." His *Song of Siberian Children* (1966) is more restrained and objective. He also published poetry, *Reds* (1966), a collection of stories, *Death of a Dog* (1967), and *Snow Fear* (1970), from which *The Wolf*, printed in this anthology, was taken.

Timo Mukka died in Rovaniemi at the age of 29 on 27 March 1973. He did not live to see the film of *The Land Is a Sinful Song*, a harsh picture of postwar Lapland, which was a tremendous success in Finland.

Pertti Nieminen. Born 1929. Poet and translator of Chinese poetry. He views the present through the mirror of Oriental antiquity, seeing the changelessness of change and the endless repetitions of history. His first collection was characteristically called *Stone Age* (1956); this was followed by *Urns* (1958), containing themes from various periods of Chinese history. His *World Landscapes* (1964) is more direct and vital. An exceptionally gifted translator and sinologist, his translations include *Tao-te-king* (1956), an anthology of *Chinese Storytellers* (1958), and a projected six-volume chronological anthology of Chinese poetry, of which *The Great Wind, Jade Wood, Autumn Voice,* (1960–66), have been published.

Pekka Parkkinen. Born 1940. Poet, prose writer, humorist. First novel (*Kuu hehkuu vielä, The Moon Still Glows,* about Paris, 1965) became well known mainly because of its lack of punctuation. Has continued with successful prose experiments: *Shell* (1969), rejects the label of a travelogue (about Portugal), a humorous novel, a lyrical poem in prose—critics agree it is very readable as well as original. *The Little Rider* (1971) records his own childhood with warmth and psychological perception. As a poet he "travels around the skull" with traditional imagery but revolutionary looseness of rhythm and lightness of touch. *If I Loved My Country* (1966) includes significant social comment. *That's Life* (1970) is a playful effort to find "a place without Coca-Cola" and genuine love in modern Hungary.

Henry Parland. 1908–1930. Swedish-Finnish modernist poet. Parland's collected poems, *"Hamlet" Said It Better,* were not published until 1964, so that he is something of a re-discovery. He has been included in this anthology because of his affinities with the poets of the sixties: cool, ironic realism, and international orientation. Parland writes, says Kai Laitinen in his *Finnish Literature 1917–1967,* "with equal impertinence and precocious sharpness of love and bargain sales, influenza, restaurants, and hangovers—and people's boredom and indifference, their fundamental aloneness."

Per-Håkon Påwals. Born 1928. Writes in Swedish. His first volume of poetry appeared in 1956, and heralded a new turn in Swedish-Finnish poetry—after a long period, it was again openly reacting to world events and society. These themes appear strongly in *Memory is a Wing* (1960), and *My Salad Green Lover* (1967). But the private poet's world is still present in his work. According to the Finnish poet and playwright Christer Kihlman, Påwals writes "mobile poetry, intelligent, intellectual, and sensitive poetry, full of life, . . . sometimes ruthlessly grotesque and even surrealistic, and he writes with unrestrained self-irony, imaginative to the point of wilfulness, but still controlled, aware, almost tender, carried by an unusually strong moral and social conscience." He has also written novels and short stories.

Bo Carpelan

Tuomas Anhava

Väinö Linna

Paavo Haavikko

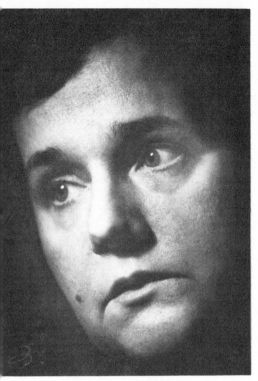

Eeva-Liisa Manner

Veijo Meri

Pentti Saarikoski

Pekka Virtanen

Jyrkki Pellinen. Born 1940. He studied cello and piano at the Sibelius Academy in Helsinki, later deciding to become a writer. His poetry—largely prose poems —is of the senses rather than the intellect. His poetry collections include *As Contrary as Any* (1965), and *It's Hard to Sleep in This Society* (1966). He has also published prose works.

Eila Pennanen. Born 1916. Novelist and short-story writer, critic, and translator. A highly professional writer, her early works, such as *The Barge Leaves at Night* (1945), show the influence of D. H. Lawrence. Later, social trends are dealt with, as in her study of Finnish society, *The Mongols* (1966). Her historical novels, *St. Bridget* (1954), and *Children of Light* (1958)—which deals with the seventeenth century English Quakers—are coolly objective. Her short-story collections include *Patience* (1957) —from which the story in this volume, *Long Ago,* is taken—and *Couples* (1961). Among her many translations are works by E. M. Forster, Iris Murdoch, Nabokov, and Bertrand Russell.

Veikko Polameri. Born 1940. Poet and translator. First studied art and worked as a printer, translating Hemingway at night; gave up art for poetry, and has published three collections, of which he is happiest with the most recent *Dead Leaves of Spring* (1970). He is currently interested in old texts of Finnish folk poetry. He has done much translation of Chinese and Japanese poetry, and was recently awarded a grant for further work on Japanese.

Maila Pylkkönen. Born 1931. Pylkkönen studied psychology before devoting herself to writing. She specializes in verse monologues, in authentic dialect, especially of children and old people, as in *Value* (1959), which has the subtitle "Old Mother Speaks her Poem." Here and in *Air/Echo* (1960), her verse borders between poetry and prose. *Mistakes* (1965) consists of prose fantasies. "The Teacher's Wife" in our anthology is from *Power* (1962).

Niilo Rauhala. Born 1936. Clergyman and teacher in northern Finland; father of six children. His free-flowing verse has been published in three collections: *Summer Ends Here* (1967), *The River Flows Now and Does Not Move* (1969), *I Listen to My Heart* (1971). At his best in small, meditative lyrics about nature and everyday life, at peace. Developing the poem as a pure sermon towards reflecting his own inward landscape, despite the external "whirl and sway": "Because/so many think otherwise/I listen to my heart."

Pentti Saarikoski. Born 1937. One of the liveliest avant-garde writers in postwar Finland. Also known as a brilliant translator. His reputation as a literary *enfant terrible* has made him for many a symbol of unconventionality. A few years ago he caused the Finnish communist party some embarrassment by becoming a highly individualistic member—he stood unsuccessfully for Parliament in 1966. At heart he is a serious writer, often melancholy and despairing. After his first, fantastic, imaginative poems, he turned to committed poetry within the context of society. His theme is the isolated individual who wants to communicate but is crippled by ideologies that have outlived themselves. He sees a world that is fragmented, fragmentary; all he can do is piece together scraps of reality as he sees it. He has published several volumes of poetry, novels, and other prose works. Some of his poetry has appeared in English, translated by Anselm Hollo. Among his recent translations is Homer's *Odyssey*. Other translations include the *Gospel according to St. Matthew,* Joyce's *Ulysses,* Miller's *Tropic of Cancer,* and Salinger's *Catcher in the Rye.*

Hannu Salama. Born 1936. Novelist and short-story writer. Worked as an electrician and a farm worker before becoming a full-time writer in 1961. His earlier works, such as *The Usual Story* (1961), deal with lovelessness, the contrast of old and new, the country and the city. His best-known novel *Midsummer Dances* (1964), in its search for the roots of bitterness and misery, rises to tragic intensity. In this work, one of the characters gives a mock sermon, for which Salama was charged with blasphemy. The case ran for three years in the courts; in the end Salama was sentenced to three months' imprisonment and both he and the publisher were fined heavily. Since 1966, the novel has appeared in a censored form. In *Me, Olli, and Orvokki* (1967), and more recent novels, his use of the first person has been compared with that of Henry Miller. All his writings are characterized by the physical power of his writing. His short-story collections include *Holiday* (1962), and *Summer Widower* (1969), from which *A Girl and a Bottle* printed here is taken. He has also published a collection of poetry, *A Tree at the Ballad's Grave* (1963). With a major novel in 1972, *No Crime without a Witness,* Salama incurred wrath once again—this time from the Finnish Stalinist left wing.

Arvo Turtiainen. Born 1904. A grand old man of Finnish poetry who has been unusually successful in keeping up with the times. A central figure in left-wing literature: one of "The Wedge" group of the thirties. Fought and was wounded in the "Winter War." Imprisoned as a pacifist during the "Continuation War," he says: "I think I would have fought against the Nazis though." Did not publish his first collection of poems, *Change* (1936), until he was thirty-two-years old. He intended them as a manifesto to change the style and attitudes of what he considered the unrealistic, reactionary literary world of the time. He is proud that he was at once accepted by working-class readers, though not by the establishment critics. His collected poems were published in *Poems 1934–1964* (1964). A curiosity of this collection is a glossary of the Helsinki slang that he frequently uses in his verse. His translations include Masters's *Spoon River Anthology* (1947), and Whitman's *Leaves of Grass* (1965).

Lauri Viita. 1916–65. Carpenter from Tampere and one of Finland's major writers. He first appeared as a poet in 1947 with *Betonimyllari (Mixer of Cement).* With its elemental force, its fresh and positive approach, and original expression it aroused great attention. He molded the traditional Finnish poetic style into something new, with the pith and pace of natural speech. His later poetry in *Kukunor* (1949), *Käppyräinen (The Shriveled One,* 1954), and *Suutarikin, suuri viisas (The Cobbler, Too, Is Great and Wise,* 1961) is of equal caliber, and deals with meter and rhyme in new ways. His great novel, *Moreeni (Moraine,* 1950), is a working-class novel partly describing his own family and spiritual growth. The language is electric and mercurial, the message full of energy and confidence. "When you create," he tells us, "create a world." His influence on later realistic writers has been very marked.

Pekka Virtanen. Born 1944. Graduated from school 1965, in New York 1965–66, cultural reporter 1966–68, free-lance journalist 1968–70, in prison 1971, and nowadays an advertising manager. Poetry collections: *Sun in Our Eyes* (1965),

But Now It is Day (1968). Translated Anselm Hollo's *Poems* into Finnish (1967).

Solveig von Schoultz. Born 1907. Her verse and prose, written in Swedish and stemming from the Swedish-Finnish modernists of the twenties, speak of the difficulty and richness of being, and of life's dark undercurrents. Her poetry includes *Nätet* (*The Web,* 1956), and *Sänk ditt ljus* (*Turn Down Your Light,* 1963), from which "Three Sisters" is taken.

Th(omas) Warburton. Born 1918. Writes in Swedish; an influential figure in Swedish-Finnish publishing and literary criticism. The controversial *Fifty Years of Swedish-Finnish Literature* (1951) attacked provincialism and class limitations. His poetry reflects interest in music and in English literature. It is skilfully "polyphonic" and meditative; the themes always convey acute social awareness. Collections: *Thou Man* (1942), *Bread of Clay* (1945), *Divining Rod* (1953), *A Short Guide* (1966), and *Long Live the Revisionisms* (1970). His translations include Joyce, Eliot, Faulkner, and Edgar Lee Masters.

Caj Westerberg. Born 1946. Poet and critic. Perhaps the most independent personality in young Finnish writing. With *Groaning Blissfully* (1967) claimed his place among "poets, who praise each other, blissfully." Original mobility of language and fierce but aesthetic eroticism change into tragic resignation in *Poetry* (1968). *I Am Not the Only Time* (1969) is boldly pathetic but balanced. In *Sunken Venice* (1972) the resplendent imagery reaches mystery and myth, synthesizing nature and tradition, the sea and the city: despair of beauty and the beauty of despair.

Bibliography

There is little primary material in translation from or secondary material on Finnish writing in English. The following list contains much—but certainly not all—of what is currently available. For example, Mika Waltari is readily available in translation but is not included here.

BIBLIOGRAPHIC

Aaltonen, Hilkka. *Books in English on Finland.* Turku: Publications of Turku University Library 8, 1964. (A bibliography of publications concerning Finland until 1960, including Finnish literature in English translation. Appendix has selected books from 1961–63.)

PRIMARY MATERIAL

Anhava, Tuomas. *In the Dark, Move Slowly.* Translated by Anselm Hollo. New York and Sante Fe: Cape Goliard/Grossman, 1969. (First English translation of one of the prime movers of Finnish poetry.)

Haavikko, Paavo. *Selected Poems.* Translated by Anselm Hollo. New York: Grossman, 1968. (Contains *Winter Palace* and fourteen short poems.)

Kivi, Aleksis. *Seven Brothers.* New York: The American-Scandinavian Foundation, 1962.

Linna, Väinö. *The Unknown Soldier.* Helsinki: Werner Söderström, 1970.

Lönnrot, Elias. *The Kalevala.* Translated by Francis P. Magoun, Jr. Cambridge, Mass.: Harvard University Press, 1963. (The best English translation of the Finnish national epic.)

Meri, Veijo. *The Manila Rope*. Translated by John McGahern and Annika Laaski. New York: Alfred Knopf, Inc., 1967.

Saarikoski, Pentti. *Helsinki: Selected Poems of Pentti Saarikoski*. Translated by Anselm Hollo. London: Rapp and Carroll, 1962. (*See* below.)

————. *Helsinki: Selected Poems of Pentti Saarikoski*. Translated by Anselm Hollo. Chicago: Swallow Press, 1967. (This second entry is a revised and later version of the first. These books contain the poems by which Saarikoski first gained his reputation and following.)

Sillanpää, F. E. *People in the Summer Night*. Madison, Milwaukee (Wisconsin), and London: University of Wisconsin Press, 1966.

————. *Meek Heritage*. Helsinki: Otava, 1971.

SECONDARY MATERIAL

Ahokas, Jaakko. "Eeva-Liisa Manner: Dropping from Reality Into Life." *Books Abroad* 47, no. 1 (Winter 1973) : 60–65.

————. "Finnish Drama and Culture." *Michigan Academician* 3, no. 3 (Winter 1971) : 45–53.

Binham, Philip. "Dreams Each Within Each: The Finnish Poet Paavo Haavikko." *Books Abroad* 50, no. 2 (Spring 1976) : 337–41.

Bradley, David. *Lion Among Roses*. New York: Holt, Rinehart, and Winston, 1965. (A very enjoyable account of the author's experiences in Finland; excellent coordination of travel description, personal impressions, and Finnish culture and history.)

Goodrich, Austin. *Study in Sisu*. New York: Ballantine Books, 1960. (A popular history of Finland in World War II; a few errors, such as confusion of the Baltic and White Seas, but in general a good introduction well worth reading.)

Heikkilä, Ritva. "The Finnish National Theater." *American-Scandinavian Review* 49, no. 4 (1966): 365–73.

Hein, Manfred Peter. *Moderne Finnische Lyrik*. Kleine Vandenhoeck Reihe, no. 142, Vandenhoeck and Ruprecht in Göttingen, Göttingen, 1962. (Anthology of fifty-five poems by eleven poets in very sensitive German translations by Hein. Fine introduction. The best book for Finnish poetry, 1920–1960.)

Hyry, Antti. "Description of a Train Journey." Translated by Anselm Hollo. *Odyssey Review* 3, no. 1 (March 1963) : 173–87.

Ivask, Ivar. Review of Kai Laitinen *Suomen kirjallisuus 1917–1967*. *Books Abroad* 42, no. 2 (Spring 1968) : 311–12. (Contains valuable cross-references to more detailed reviews and articles on writers merely named in the review.)

Laitinen, Kai. "How Things Are: Paavo Haavikko and His Poetry." *Books Abroad* 43, no. 1 (Winter 1969) : 41–45.

————. "Väinö Linna and Veijo Meri: Two Aspects of War." *Books Abroad* 36, no. 4 (Autumn 1962) : 365–67.

————. "Finnish Literature 1967." *Books Abroad* 41, no. 4 (1967) : 414–17.

PEN International Bulletin 16, no. 1 (1965) : 34 pp. (This issue on Finland has a number of short but excellent articles, mostly by the writers themselves commenting on their works. The series is available in the United States through Stechert-Hafner, Inc., 31 East 10th Street, New York, New York 10003.)

Rubulis, Aleksis. *Baltic Literature*. Notre Dame, Indiana: University of Notre Dame Press, 1970. (The most recent areal introduction to the literatures of Finland, Estonia, Latvia, and Lithuania. The generality makes it at the same time well worth reading, though limited for any specific writer. Characterized by sweeping generalizations and slanted vocabulary. Weak on postwar Finnish writing (only two pages out of fifty), and discussion of postwar Baltic writing in the homelands is conspicuous by its absence, although much space is given to the various writers in exile. Includes translations.)

Stormblom, N. B. "Väinö Linna and his Tales of Toil and War." *American-Scandinavian Review* 51, no. 3 (September 1963) : 245–50.

————. "Veijo Meri and the New Finnish Novel." *American-Scandinavian Review* 55, no. 3 (1967) : 264–69.

Tarkka, Pekka. "Finnish Literature: The Great Tradition." Translated by Meri Lehtinen. *Odyssey Review* 3, no. 1 (March 1963) : 164–72. (Issue also contains translations of Finnish prose and poetry, i.e., Hyry and Saarikoski, by Anselm Hollo.)

GENERAL NOTES:

The best place to keep abreast of Finnish literature is in *Books Abroad*,* which carries frequent articles and translations, and regular reviews of what is being published in Finland and in foreign translations of Finnish literature. Some of the material in our essays paraphrases our work in *Books Abroad*.

The *American-Scandinavian Review* carries longer translations and articles, when it has them, than *Books Abroad*, but, unfortunately, does not carry them on a regular basis.

For primary material in translation, Germany continues its traditional role in transmitting all kinds of small-nation, small-language writing into a language more accessible to a greater number of readers. Far more literature is available on a continuing basis in German than in any other language but Swedish, which is, of course, the best "tool language" for Finnish in translation.

*Now called *World Literature Today*.